The Danton Case

✣

Thermidor

✣

STANISŁAWA PRZYBYSZEWSKA

The Danton Case

❧

Thermidor

❧

TWO PLAYS

Translated by Bolesław Taborski
With an Introduction by Daniel Gerould

Northwestern University Press   Evanston, Illinois

Northwestern University Press
Evanston, Illinois 60201

The Danton Case translated from the Polish *Sprawa Dantona*. *Thermidor* translated from the German *Thermidor.* Translation © copyright 1989 by Bolesław Taborski. Introduction © copyright 1989 by Daniel Gerould. All rights reserved.

Printed in the United States of America

Composition by Point West Inc., Carol Stream, IL

Przybyszewska, Stanisława, 1901–1935.
   [Sprawa Dantona. English]
   The Danton case ; Thermidor : two plays / Stanisława Przybyszewska ; translated by Bolesław Taborski ; with an introduction by Daniel Gerould.
      p.   cm.
   Translation of: Sprawa Dantona and Thermidor.
   Includes bibliography.
   ISBN 0-8101-0805-4 — ISBN 0-8101-0806-2 (pbk.)
   1. Przybyszewska, Stanisława, 1901–1935—Translations, English.
   I. Przybyszewska, Stanisława, 1901–1935. Thermidor. English.
   1989. II. Title.
   PG7158.P64A28 1989
   891.8′526—dc19   89-2963
                                                              CIP

Contents

Stanisława Przybyszewska and the Mechanism of Revolution: *The Danton Case* and *Thermidor*

The French Revolution was made by the young. In 1789, when the Bastille fell, Danton was thirty, Robespierre was thirty-one, Desmoulins twenty-nine, Saint-Just twenty-two—five years later they all were dead, destroyed by the same mechanism of revolution that they had helped to set in motion. In such perilous times minds and bodies were consumed at a frightful rate. To keep up with the tempo of change was impossible—to fall behind was to be lost. The makers of the revolution had no time to accomplish their goal of beginning the world over again; even before they went to their early deaths, most were exhausted, used up, played out.

Although many attempts have been made to dramatize the French Revolution and give theatrical life to its imposing cast of characters, few of these plays have held the stage for long or entered the permanent repertory. Perhaps the events are too complex, the canvas too vast. Until recently (apart from the special case of Peter Weiss's *Marat/Sade*) there was only one exception to this negative assessment: Georg Büchner's *Danton's Death*, written in 1835, but not performed until the early twentieth century and now recognized as one of the seminal works of modern theatre. With the discovery of the plays about the French Revolution by a Polish author from the interwar years, Stanisława Przybyszewska, I believe that we at last have worthy companion pieces to Büchner's masterpiece, offering a new perspective on the same critical moment in 1794 when the fate of the French republic was being decided.

Büchner's celebrated drama can serve as a natural starting point for my discussion of Przybyszewska's work. Inspired by her reading of *Danton's Death* (eleven times was her final count), the Polish dramatist began a serious study of the French Revolution and decided to try her own hand at the subject. I see several striking similarities in circumstance and sensibility

1

between these two authors whose lives were separated by almost a century. Their plays were the work of very young artists at the start of careers that would be cut short: Büchner wrote *Danton's Death* at twenty-one and was dead at twenty-three; Przybyszewska wrote *Thermidor* at twenty-four and *The Danton Case* at twenty-seven and was dead of malnutrition and tuberculosis at thirty-four.

Both were outsiders, in rebellion against the existing order, passionately committed to revolution after the French model. They knew the fear of the dispossessed and identified with the outcast; both felt the need to tear down old structures, fight injustice, change the world. Their fascination with the Reign of Terror grew out of real dangers encountered in their own lives; they too lived in difficult times and suffered repression. Threatened with arrest for his conspiratorial activities on behalf of "The Society for the Rights of Man," Büchner was forced to go into political exile. "I now stand completely alone," he declared, "but that in itself increases my strength." For her allegedly subversive associations, Przybyszewska was arrested, interrogated by the police, and briefly imprisoned. Retreating ever deeper into internal exile in the cell-like refuge where she remained "holed up" for the last eight years of her life, the Polish author eulogized "this ideal, total *solitude* in which my strength grows invisibly." Despite a theoretical belief in the power of reason to transform man, born of the Enlightenment, both writers grew disillusioned with practical attempts to effect political change, and their works trace the tragic course of the French Revolution as an inevitable paradigm for the future.

While Büchner's withdrawal proved to be a temporary resort, for Przybyszewska solitude was a way of life and, she hoped, the path to creativity, although she had reason to fear the menace of isolation. "One never gets accustomed to loneliness," she declared. In *The Origins of Totalitarianism*, Hannah Arendt distinguishes between these two psychic states in a way that illuminates the Polish writer's dilemma. "In solitude," Arendt writes, "I am 'by myself,' together with my self, and therefore two-in-one, whereas in loneliness I am actually one, deserted by all others. All thinking. . . is done in solitude and is a dialogue between me and myself." Przybyszewska cultivated "the thinking dialogue of solitude," but, as Arendt points out, "The problem of solitude is that this two-in-one needs the others in order to become one again."

Przybyszewska lacked confirmation of her identity through others. "How am I to know whether I am totally dissolving into thin air if no human glance ever fixes me any more?" she asks in one of her anguished letters. "I am bursting with stored-up thinking. I am overflowing with things that ache and burn if they can't find comprehending ears." Her tragedy was never to find the companionship of equals she longed for. What drove this attractive, immensely talented young Polish woman in her mid-twenties to such desperate measures? Was solitude the cruel destiny reserved for her as victim or was it rather the chosen form of her rebellion?

Przybyszewska's life is a study in dispossession, uprootedness, and alienation. Born in 1901 as Stanisława Pająk, she was one of several illegitimate children brought into the world by the Polish modernist playwright and novelist Stanisław Przybyszewski, a former associate of Strindberg and Munch in Berlin's artistic bohemia of the 1890s. Her father's credo, "In the beginning was lust," expressed a *fin-de-siècle* belief in the irresistible power of blind passion that his own promiscuity served to illustrate. The unwanted result of what was for Przybyszewski a brief interlude while on a lecture tour, Stanisława was christened after her father, but she received nothing else that was his, not even his surname, to which, according to the laws of the time, she had no claim.

A natural child, suffering the deprivation of her natural state, Stanisława battled against nature in all its manifestations. The most malevolent of these were, for her, the random and senseless propagation of the species, the biological and physiological necessities of existence, and the base animal side of the human psyche. One had to challenge what she referred to sometimes as that "fiendish little beast Nature," at other times as "executioner Nature." Above all, she was in revolt against the father who had betrayed her—not only by abandoning her and her mother, but also by his failing to be the truly creative person he should have been. Like the youthful leaders of the French Revolution who were her friends and lovers, Stanisława challenged the forms of paternalistic authority that excluded her from sharing in the patrimony.

Conversely, she adored and admired her mother, Aniela, a talented impressionist painter, who, thanks to the patronage of a wealthy Polish family, could afford to give her daughter a loving artistic upbringing, first in Kraków and then in Lvov, in the Austrian section of partitioned Poland known as Galicia. During the first six years of her life, Stanisława's father came to visit twice; he provided no financial support, but occasionally borrowed money from Aniela to cover the expenses of his current love affairs. To escape the censorious whispering of provincial society about her fatherless child, Aniela took Stanisława to Western Europe where the precocious youngster attended local schools, switching effortlessly from language to language, never staying long enough to form ties or make lasting friends.

Upon her mother's sudden death from pneumonia in 1912, the eleven-year-old girl discovered that childhood was over, and that she was totally alone in the world. Already uprooted, she now embarked on the life of a cosmopolitan wanderer and exile, living first in Switzerland with family friends, then in Austria with a maternal aunt, Helena Barlińska, who was to remain a lifelong source of support.

The First World War brought massive displacements and migrations for millions of Poles, who as citizens of three different crumbling empires were scattered across half of Europe and often found themselves on opposing sides in the great conflict. In 1916 Barlińska and her husband left Vienna and settled in Kraków, where Stanisława attended the Teachers Institute and prepared for a career in education. There in 1919, she met for the first time in her adult life the internationally acclaimed Przybyszewski whose name she now became legally authorized to adopt. Passionately in search of heroes, Stanisława grew infatuated with this rakish stranger of extraordinary sex appeal who had unexpectedly entered her life; while the romance lasted, she was ready to worship him as the genius he was reputed to be.

Stanisława acquired both a father and a fatherland at almost the same time. After more than a century's eclipse, Poland had been reborn as a nation in November 1918. But the myth of the father could not survive close scrutiny. Within little more than a year Stanisława discovered how greatly she had overestimated Przybyszewski's talent, and her disdain for what she had recently regarded with almost religious awe was all the more extreme. The rest of her career would be devoted to demonstrating that she could be a better artist than her father by self-discipline and sheer force of will.

During the period of enchantment, serious damage was done to Stanisława's vulnerable psyche. Przybyszewski, who had recently remarried (his first wife, the Norwegian Dagny Juel, had been murdered by a demented admirer) and settled permanently in Poland after twelve years in Munich, was delighted to discover that he had such a bright and attractive daughter, but his possessive wife was so jealous of her middle-aged husband's interest in his previously neglected child that the pair was forced to correspond secretly and meet furtively in hotels like lovers. During one of their meetings, the old reprobate Przybyszewski, a reformed Satanist who had once practiced the black arts and dabbled in devil worship, introduced his daughter to morphine, good, he said, for sharpening one's mental faculties, and to which he had become addicted after bringing his alcoholism under control. This drug proved to be the most deadly bequest from father to daughter, enclosing her forever in an isolated chamber of the mind.

Whether or not the primal scene of seduction was ever enacted (as some of Przybyszewski's letters indicate), the incestuous nature of the father's attentions are obvious enough.

In 1920, at Przybyszewski's insistence, Stanisława moved to Poznań so that she could be near her father, who had just obtained a position with the new Polish Postal and Telegraph Service. There she worked briefly as a post office clerk (developing a hatred for meaningless drudgery), enrolled in music school, and studied philosophy at the university until a nervous breakdown forced her to abandon her courses. It was also in Poznań that, thanks to her father's influence, Stanisława came into contact with the literary and artistic avant-garde. Stanisława's own creative aspirations were as yet undefined; her father's assessment was that, for an illegitimate daughter, she was "too well educated for her own good."

In 1922 Stanisława moved to Warsaw, where she found work as a salesgirl in a Communist bookstore that served as a meeting place for the small, illegal party. After the recent war with the Soviet Union, the Polish authorities had begun a witch-hunt for Bolsheviks and other subversives. During a search for organizers of clandestine activities, Przybyszewska was arrested and sent back to Poznań, interrogated, and imprisoned for a week before being released for lack of evidence. Two years later Stanisława would claim that now she held the social views of which she once had been unjustly accused, but although she did develop a sympathetic attitude toward the Russian Revolution and study Marxist theory, she was much too solitary ever to become a member of the Communist party or grow directly involved in political action.

Upon her return to Warsaw, Stanisława taught in a private school. Linguistically gifted (she was fluent in Polish, German, French, and English), artistically talented in music and drawing, interested in mathematics, medicine, history and philosophy, the twenty-one-year-old Przybyszewska did not yet have a clear direction in life. At this point she was offered—and embraced—her one great chance to escape the isolation for which she seemed destined, given the adverse circumstances of her life and her own pride, perfectionism, and disdain for ordinary humanity. In 1923 Stanisława married Jan Panieński, a young artist she had known in Poznań, and moved with him to the city of Danzig (now Gdańsk), where her husband had obtained a teaching position at the Polish High School. For both husband and wife it was a marriage dictated by reason, not passion, an antidote to the loneliness neither could tolerate. Although she spoke of her marriage as a purely pragmatic venture, Przybyszewska was intellectually attracted to her husband—for her the most profound of feelings—and

grew to love him in her own quiet fashion. She spent her time painting
and doing research on the French Revolution, writing in German several
versions of her first play *Thermidor*. The two years of marriage, from 1923
to 1925, were the most peaceful that Stanisława had known since the
death of her mother.

This short respite from insecurity and loneliness came to an end in November 1925 when her husband died suddenly in Paris from an overdose
of morphine, a drug that Panieński had started taking at the front as a
young soldier in the Prussian army. Her only possibility for close human
contact gone, Stanisława now began her slow descent into isolation and
misery. At first she was able to survive on her small widow's inheritance
supplemented by tutoring. After devoting the following year to her mother's and husband's vocation, painting—a sensuous medium that did not
suit her cerebral disposition—Stanisława discovered that her true calling
was her father's: literature. "I can be a writer, or nothing at all," she declared in the spring of 1927 upon completion of the first draft of her one-
act drama, *93*, with which she hoped to make her reputation. A tense
family drama in the modernist mode, *93* has as its heroine a neurotic
young woman dreaming of greatness who, on the day of Marat's funeral,
almost succeeds in bringing her father to the guillotine. Although the setting is historical, the events and characters are fictional.

So as not to dissipate her creative forces, Przybyszewska gradually gave
up her few pupils, preferring instead to beg from friends and relatives. In
this way she could dedicate all her energy to the task of writing with fanati-
cal singlemindedness. By 1928 she was living in one small room, seven and
a half by fifteen feet, in the wooden barracks belonging to the Polish High
School, which was without electricity or adequate plumbing. There, often
without any coal for the small stove on which her life depended, in the
cold of winter, the damp of spring, the heat of summer, Przybyszewska
followed a grueling schedule of writing and rewriting, a harsh taskmaster, a
pitiless terrorist to herself. Apart from the brilliant trio of plays about the
French Revolution written in the first half of her decade of solitude, none
of her many literary projects for writing novels came to fruition. Despite
heroic determination, she was losing the battle against fate, ravaged by
drug addiction and defeated in her attempt to have the mind triumph over
material wants. By 1931 she had to confront the prospect of starvation; in
1933 she already anticipated "a singularly unpleasant form of death."

In the face of such foreknowledge, Stanisława had the courage to embrace her tragic destiny, even though there were many moments of despair
when she would confess to being "weak and weaponless, afraid and pining

for human warmth." She knew the terror of hunger and cold, of sickness and pain; like a mountain climber or explorer, she pushed herself to new extremes of endurance. Racked by rheumatic pains, she crawled across the floor, like an "animal at bay in the recesses of its hole." But the prospect of losing her wretched dungeon, which she called her "grave," was more frightening than the thought of death. Where could she go? She knew that help from well-meaning friends meant confinement to the asylum or therapeutic hospitalization, which she regarded with the same horror as she did all forms of imprisonment. As the Nazis came to power and made their presence felt in Danzig, she realized that the concentration camps would be the final resting place for people like her.

"I *don't want* to manage the way most people do," Stanisława declared, declining the roles of meek dependence and subservience for which she as a natural child had been cast. Rather than submission, she chose to challenge her father on his own ground—as a writer and thinker, confident of her own superiority. Without social position or means of support, she claimed for herself the status of professional writer, not as an occasional pastime appropriate for literary young ladies, but as an all-consuming occupation. And she further asserted her independence by avoiding the approved specialties of women authors—lyric poetry and domestic fiction—in favor of the most public genre in its most public manifestation, historical drama.

Repeatedly abandoned and dispossessed, Stanisława resolved to define her own circumstances. Of the world, she wrote, "I can survive only if I hide from it." Since there was no secure place for her, she could at least choose to exist nowhere—by retreating into her lair and becoming invisible. She owed no allegiance to any country. Danzig, of divided national character, precariously situated and darkly menaced, suited perfectly her alienated, uprooted psyche. Even when it became clear that the Nazis would prosper, she would not consider moving back to Poland. "I do not have, I do not want to have a fatherland," she asserted. The whole idea of nationality was repugnant to her, provoking what she called her "emotionally inverse patriotism." She disliked Poles as a people, finding them so undisciplined that sometimes she wished to conceal her origins. Even the Polish language struck her as inferior and poverty-stricken. The great authors who constituted her literary heritage were English and French.

These disclaimers of paternity and patrimony—which in effect had been withheld from her—were accompanied by denials of the expected sex roles that men and women have traditionally been assigned. In a paradoxical gender analysis of her creative genealogy, Przybyszewska claimed that her artistic abilities and firm masculine traits of character and logical thought came from her mother's side, whereas her feminine intuitiveness and surrender to inspiration—as well as her dependence on drugs—were derived from her father.

Although there were a number of highly respected women writers in Poland between the wars, such as Zofia Nałkowska, Maria Dąbrowska, and Maria Kuncewicz, Przybyszewska did not identify with other artists of her own sex or aspire to their status. She remained totally outside the Polish literary establishment, and alien to any categorizing by gender. Thought at the level of genius (where she was sure she belonged) transcended individuation. In the highest mental activity, Przybyszewska believed, differences of sex, race, or nationality ceased to matter. Her literary or creative personality, as distinct from her temporal self, was neither male or female, but an androgynous combination of the two. Now that it was growing increasingly possible for humans to live on a plane no longer exclusively material, the position of the two sexes in matters of the spirit should become identical. Przybyszewska argued for the absolute equality of men and women, who—freed from the constraints of the body—would be able to meet on the higher ground of human creativity. Whatever separated male and female, breeding ignorance and fear, was pernicious, whether it be virulent Strindbergian misogyny or militant feminist counterattack.

But in the 1920s and 1930s the revolutionary ideals of freedom and equality were being desecrated. For Przybyszewska, contemporary sexual, political, and social problems were all related aspects of a single crisis. She saw the catastrophic situation in Europe as a manifestation of a universal *mal de siècle*. For her the evil of the times found expression in the image of walls descending everywhere, enclosing minds, creating new forms of imprisonment, both literal and figurative, that caused hatred among the nations, classes, and sexes. "Soon people will stop talking and writing altogether," she mused. In the face of this "concrete wall of silence," there was a need to fight back, to put all one's energies into striking a powerful blow.

Private apprehension and public diagnosis were united in Przybyszewska's cries of alarm, making her a delicate register of the derangements of the interwar years. Starting in the early 1920s, she grew convinced that an evil fate was threatening Europe. The great depression, mass unemployment, and the rise of fascism coincided with her own deteriorating health and fortunes. Stanisława was, by her own admission, predisposed to anxiety, depression, and pessimism, and her predictions of doom could simply be dismissed as the projection of her neuroses on the outside world, were it not for the penetrating accuracy of her analysis. As early as the spring of 1933 Przybyszewska foresaw the fate of the Jews and the horrors to come.

Paradox and contradiction lay at the heart of Przybyszewska's carefully constructed defenses. She extolled the independence of mind from matter as she was slowly freezing and starving in a room seven and a half by fifteen. She inveighed against walls that isolate as the walls of her own cage, covered with mold and frost, seemed to close in about her. Although she strongly identified with individual victims of social justice—Sacco and Vanzetti, the accused in medieval witchcraft trials, the servant girl Rita Gorgon, condemned to death for child murder (for whom she wished to serve as a defense witness)—Przybyszewska considered herself one of the best minds in Europe and had contempt for the mob as a herd of brutish creatures. Her anger at the stupidity and meanness of ordinary human nature was Swiftian in its withering scorn.

Only the heroic aroused Przybyszewska's deepest passions; for her, the fate of exceptional human beings always had a tragic beauty. Przybyszewska's paradigms for tragedy were neoclassical. Like the heroes of Corneille, whom she admired above all, she believed that duty and honor demanded an unswerving commitment to one's calling. She paid tribute to her mother's mathematical, samurai-like steeliness in making no demands on the weak, unfaithful Przybyszewski and thereby remaining forever true to the spirit of their love. From her childhood reading of Schiller's *Don Carlos* and *Wallenstein* came an understanding of noble heroes caught between aspirations for freedom and the fatal crunch of historical necessity.

Encouraged by her complete lack of knowledge of the contemporary world to turn to historical subjects, Przybyszewska found in the French Revolution the one theme that fired her imagination and called forth her best creative talents. Revolution was the most dramatic challenge to nature, setting out to perfect what had been left undone or bungled. The forcible re-creation of man and his institutions in the crucible of violent social change during the spring of 1794 touched on all Stanisława's obsessions.

Unable to find a place in her own age, Przybyszewska sought refuge in another century. She felt more at home in Paris under the Terror than in Danzig under the mandate of the League of Nations, and she chose her companions from among the doomed revolutionary leaders. "Alone with the people who had died so long ago," the playwright began to date her letters according to the revolutionary calendar, which renamed the months and started history anew with the Year One. The ability to live so intensely in the past was one of Przybyszewska's greatest strengths as a historical dramatist, but antiquarian reconstruction of a distant epoch was far from her goal. Rather than taking the spectators back to 1789, the playwright's aim was to bring past events and characters into the present.

In writing *The Danton Case* and *Thermidor*, Przybyszewska wished to reveal a new image of the French Revolution, based on contemporary historiography and seen through the lens of twentieth-century experience. Aware of the current prominence of Büchner's play in the German theatre (Max Reinhardt's first staging had taken place in 1916), the Polish playwright maintained that a thoroughly modern reworking of the famous old theme should be all the more welcome.

By dealing with the same struggle for power between Danton and Robespierre at the end of March and the beginning of April 1794, Przybyszewska made *The Danton Case* a rejoinder to *Danton's Death*. It is an instance of the *Gegenstück*, or counterplay favored by Brecht as a critical response to an earlier work. Whatever were her reservations about its artistry and ideology, no work of dramatic literature—not even Shaw's masterpieces—so completely possessed her as *Danton's Death*. What Przybyszewska most admired in the German play was the powerful atmosphere of the times that Büchner had evoked. What she could not accept was Büchner's romantic vision of revolution and glorification of the nihilistic individualist and sensualist, Danton, although she recognized that such a position was inevitable given the sources available at the time—histories by Thiers and Mignet—and the universal bias against Robespierre, who had been made a scapegoat for all the crimes of the revolution.

The metaphoric style and open form of *Danton's Death*, which lay outside the norms of Przybyszewska's French-based aesthetics, seemed to her barbarically chaotic. Her rejection of Büchner's techniques of juxtaposition and discontinuity indicates just how completely Stanisława had distanced herself from the traditions of Polish drama, since the great nineteenth-century romantic playwrights, Mickiewicz, Słowacki, and Krasiński, used such a loose poetic structure in their works for the stage. Looking to the West for her models, Przybyszewska adopted the sober principles of the *neue Sachlichkeit*, or new objectivity that arose in Germany in the mid-1920s in reaction to the excesses of Expressionism (which Büchner had anticipated and influenced). Documents, facts, clarity, coolness, detachment, reportage were to be most highly esteemed, not outbursts of poetic frenzy.

According to Przybyszewska, *The Danton Case* treats politics in a fashion beyond politics—that is, without taking sides or promoting any ideological position, but also without caricaturing the revolution or portraying its guiding spirit as a bloodthirsty monster. Przybyszewska's special accomplishment was to render human and believable, although not necessarily likable, the most mysterious and misunderstood figure of the revolution, Robespierre. Whereas Büchner had depicted a volcanic but essentially passive Danton, staggering under the burden of mortality while engaged in an unequal battle with an abstract, inhuman Robespierre, Przybyszewska shifted the focus and portrayed the Incorruptible as a brilliant, highly principled statesman confronted by political decisions and their consequences, as he faces the impossible task of governing France on the verge of chaos and preserving the new Republic from the attacks of powerful enemies, within and without. The chief of these enemies is the crafty, unscrupulous Danton, and it is Robespierre's fatal struggle against such a formidable opponent that constitutes the tragedy.

Przybyszewska's principal source was *The French Revolution* (1922–27) by the revisionist historian, Albert Mathiez, who pioneered the twentieth-century rehabilitation of Robespierre. The Polish playwright carries the process of revision one step further, and, departing from her source, makes Robespierre an opponent of the terror who foresees the disastrous course that the revolution will take once Danton and his followers have been eliminated. The turning point in *The Danton Case* comes in Act IV with Robespierre's tragic recognition that to save the Revolution he must destroy it. In an introspective scene after Danton's arrest, the Incorruptible betrays hesitations about his political actions and an awareness of being carried along by a fatal logic.

Przybyszewska lamented that rulers from ancient times, as portrayed by Shakespeare, have no ambitions beyond the personal and seem to lack any conception of social creativity. Her own belief in exceptional individuals capable of sacrificing their private lives for the sake of a higher cause drew inspiration from Bernard Shaw, whose *Caesar and Cleopatra* and *Saint Joan* offered examples of heroic protagonists. Full of enthusiasm for *Back to Methusalah*, Przybyszewska shared Shaw's faith in the accelerated development of superior human minds progressively freed from the weight of matter.

Partly fashioned in her own image, partly conceived according to a Shavian model, Robespierre in *The Danton Case* and *Thermidor* is a transsexual, suprapersonal genius striving to move in realms of pure thought as he grapples with problems of social reality and human nature. His absolute devotion to reason and refusal to compromise cause his alienation from the world around him and lead step by step to his tragic downfall.

When Büchner wrote *Danton's Death* in 1835, it was a "dramatic experiment" dealing with "material from recent history." *The Danton Case* in 1928 looks back at distant events that occurred in the century before last, perceiving them through the prism of recent history. After 1917 the French Revolution no longer occupied the unique position that it had enjoyed for over one hundred years as "the Revolution," but acquired new significance and actuality in the light of what was happening in Russia.

For Przybyszewska, the first important playwright to use this double perspective, a reading of the French Revolution in the light of the Russian Revolution served not as a justification for the terror (as it did for some Marxist historians), but rather as a warning of the course that events in the Soviet Union would certainly take. The analogy between contemporary events in Russia and those that took place in Paris at the end of the eighteenth century revealed "the radical evil of the revolutionary mechanism." It is this mechanism of revolution that Przybyszewska anatomizes in *The Danton Case* and *Thermidor* with great psychological, moral, and intellectual vigor.

The tragedy of all revolutions is that there comes a certain moment when the whole undertaking must be centralized around a single leader. Only by assuming dictatorial powers can the Incorruptible save the Republic, but in so doing he will destroy the freedom he seeks to preserve. "The thought, the will, the energy of a single human brain has to penetrate the entire society and decide its every movement," Przybyszewska explains. Until that moment, the leaders will have to fight one another. The dynamics of *The Danton Case* depend on the contrast between the two protagonists, once allies and now implacable enemies caught in the revolutionary mechanism, whereas *Danton's Death*, in which Robespierre disappears at the end of the second act, has a structure of stasis developing themes of existential dread.

In a "Self-Interview" which Przybyszewska published in 1929, the author explains her understanding of this prototypical pair of revolutionary leaders. Robespierre is the almost perfect genius inhabiting a mental realm foreign to us; we are repelled by his icy, almost inhuman intellectualism. The pure, ascetic Robespierre pursues in revolution higher goals transcending the interests of any group and prevailing over all tactical considerations; he is determined to transform, by force if necessary, natural man into a superior political being. His inevitable opponent is the sensual, cynical, pragmatic compromiser who seeks in revolution opportunities to realize personal benefits for himself and those he represents. Egotistic and propelled by animal passions, Danton is alive to the temptations of power and possessions. By subordinating the creative mind to the natural will, he becomes a renegade to his own calling, but he is intelligible to us and to the highest degree likable. "I *know* human nature," Danton explains. "Instead of senselessly fighting it, I pamper it. . . to make the Revolution accessible."

The argument between Danton and Robespierre has never been resolved in history, nor is it in Przybyszewska's play. Although she confessed to having loved Robespierre longer than any man in her life, the author of *The Danton Case* is so evenhanded in maintaining the balance of sympathies that the audience must make up its own mind. "Sympathy is not determined by admirable traits," Przybyszewska admits, "but rather by strength of personality; the direction it takes does not matter. Therefore Danton is very close to me—with his scoundrelism, his vanity, his tragic destiny—not as lofty, but more agonizing than Robespierre's."

In creating her portraits of the revolutionary leaders, Przybyszewska draws connections between the personal and the political, as does Büchner. But whereas in *Danton's Death* the public self is always shown as inferior to and less authentic than the private self, and the ideology a man embraces is revealed to be little more than an expression of his inner needs, in *The Danton Case* the relationships between essential human nature and revolutionary principles are more intricate and variable. "You are fighting thievery and corruption and they are natural needs without which the state is dying," says Danton, for whom duty stands in conflict with inclination and whose morality is that of a political boss intent on power and profit. Robespierre, on the other hand, has so successfully sublimated his own desires for the sake of the general betterment of mankind that he can assert, "I have no personal life any more." In accord with her psychosexual theory of sublimation, Przybyszewska explores Robespierre's paternalistic homoeroticism with his old friend, Camille Desmoulins, and his inhibitions with Eléonore Duplay, the infatuated daughter of the cabinetmaker in whose house he has a modest room. Rather than reducing public service to ulterior motive, *The Danton Case* unveils the tensions between the personal and the political, leaving open the possibility that superior individuals may commit their lives to ideals.

Przybyszewska saw the structure of *The Danton Case* as musical. To insure the correct tempo, the playwright paid close attention to the rhythm of contrasted scenes, alternating tempestuous public gatherings in the street and at the tribunals with introspective tableaux of private life. The heightened rhetoric of the political platform is opposed to the unguarded conversational tone of men alone with their thoughts. Although, like

Büchner, Przybyszewska indicts the corruption of language by politics, she also celebrates the immense power of the spoken word during the Revolution. Whereas for the author of *Danton's Death*, the rhetoric of Robespierre is rigid, abstract, and ultimately hollow, Przybyszewska acknowledges the poetry and passion of political discourse as well as the terrorism of the word as expressed in insult, invective, and accusation. The excitement of swaying the crowd and unleashing its passions shows that politics, in the hands of orators like Danton, Robespierre, Saint-Just, can be erotic. Possessed of explosive energy, the debates and trials are like sporting events, forms of mass entertainment heightened by danger and watched by the populace with the passionate intensity of gamesters. The offstage trial of Danton is seen from the perspective of the howling mob and scurrying journalists, who use the printed word to mold and manipulate public opinion. Perceiving "revolution as the psychic condition of the twentieth century," Przybyszewska gives her characters a modern sensibility and has them speak a provocative twentieth-century language. Verbal anachronisms and Soviet-style acronyms emphasize continuity between 1789 and 1917.

The Danton Case went through four different versions. The first was elaborately pictorial in the manner of a naturalistic canvas, and the speeches followed Przybyszewska's sources with extreme fidelity. In reworking the text, the playwright reduced the documentary ballasting and concentrated on the universal aspects of the revolution as revealed in the characters. In the final version, the stage directions, although still extensive, are cinematographic rather than painterly, focusing attention on facial expression and play of features. Przybyszewska's use of gestural language (unlike Brecht's social *gestus*) is primarily concerned with presenting one's relationship to oneself. Robespierre's fashion of getting dressed, drinking his broth, brushing his clothes, fixing his cuffs serves to present the Incorruptible as a film scenarist might. Details define the essence of the man: his scrupulosity, precision, and defensive self-enclosure in a world of perfect dreams.

Although she felt sure of its ultimate success, Przybyszewska realized that *The Danton Case*, although "very stageable," would not gain easy acceptance in the theatre because of its extraordinary length—not a fault of her dramaturgy, but a consequence of the theme (which "no woman would dare tackle"). The play called for an ideal stage, actors, and director, who, she acknowledged, would be every bit as important as the author. For this reason, she sent *The Danton Case* to Leon Schiller, Poland's greatest director between the wars, leftist in his political orientation and known for his masterly handling of crowds and of revolutionary themes. Although he liked the play, Schiller had recently lost his job in Warsaw for his daring production of Brecht's *Threepenny Opera* and could not risk anything that might be labeled "red" in an atmosphere of growing political repression. Although *The Danton Case* was staged twice in the author's lifetime—in 1931 and 1933—Przybyszewska lost interest in the fate of her creation in the theatre once it became clear that Schiller could not direct it.

For the sort of production of which its author dreamed, the play would have to wait more than thirty years after Przybyszewska's death. Jerzy Krasowski, the director responsible for the rediscovery of Przybyszewska, staged *The Danton Case* at the Teatr Polski in Wrocław in 1967, launching the work on its triumphal career in the contemporary Polish theatre. But Przybyszewska met her most original interpreter in Andrzej Wajda, whose austere, unadorned staging of *The Danton Case* at the Powszechny Theatre in Warsaw in 1975 made the audience into a dramatic character. Seated in tiered rows on all sides of an extended wooden platform that served as the playing area, the spectators were both observers and participants, entering into events as the jury at the Revolutionary Tribunal and the deputies at the Convention, to whom Robespierre and Saint-Just spoke directly from the podium. The unresolved dilemmas posed by the revolution became immediate, compelling, and deeply moving for those witnessing the performance.

After directing *The Danton Case* once again in Gdańsk in 1980, Wajda was at last able to make his long-projected film version, *Danton*, a joint French-Polish production with Gérard Depardieu as Danton and Wojciech Pszoniak as Robespierre. As the shortened title suggests, Przybyszewska's text was freely rewritten for the film, in favor of Danton, the man of natural appetites and political concession, and at the expense of Robespierre, the ideological maximalist and purist. Wajda admired in Przybyszewska's work the psychologically complex characters, the moral and intellectual truth, and the scope and richness of interpretive possibilities, as well as the forceful evocation of the "pressure of history," to which Poland always seemed vulnerable. Filmed during the period of martial law and released in 1983, *Danton* became an oblique comment on the failed workers' rebellion in Poland and its suppression.

The Danton Case ends on a quiet, brooding note. Robespierre, alone in his monastic room with his acolyte Saint-Just, recognizes that by institutionalizing the Terror he has brought about the end of the Revolution; he predicts his own death and the rise of a dictatorship based on nationalism, money, and aggressive foreign wars. "The future belongs to the late Danton," he observes ironically.

The declining days of the Revolution and the downfall of Robespierre, forecast in the final scene, are the subject of Przybyszewska's earlier play *Thermidor*, to which she returned in 1929, evidently planning a revision that would connect it more closely to *The Danton Case* as a sequel. Written in German, the only version that has survived is in two acts, but lacks an ending. Perhaps the final pages of the manuscript were lost, but it seems more likely that the author never completed the play. She confessed that it was difficult for her to say goodbye to this constant companion of many years. Even in its unfinished form, *Thermidor* is a remarkable study of revolutionary intrigue that offers an original interpretation of Robespierre's seemingly erratic behavior during the last weeks of his life. It was premiered by Krasowski at the Teatr Polski in Wrocław in 1971.

Przybyszewska cast the play in the form of a tense political debate, imposing upon her material the strict unities of French classical tragedy as well as its absence of onstage physical action. *Thermidor* takes place in the late hours of the unbearably hot night of 25 July (7 Thermidor) in the meeting room of the Committee of Public Safety. A long table and a few chairs are the only properties, and the time covered in the two continuous acts is exactly that of the performance itself. The claustrophobic atmosphere in the semidarkness gives rise to the changing moods of an insane asylum, now frantically animated, now morbidly apathetic, as the terror-stricken leaders of the revolution—cut off from the outside world and isolated from the people they once claimed to represent—sink deeper into paralysis and fear.

Thermidor is the final playing out of the revolution in a desperate endgame. In the first act, the playwright takes us behind the scenes of the Terror and with implacable logic shows us the effects of the system on those who have sent so many to the guillotine. Now fearing for their own heads, the members of the Committee of Public Safety conspire against Robespierre, whose unaccountable absence for six weeks has only made more palpable his omnipresent "despotism of virtue." To these politicians of survival, motivated only by self-interest, the Incorruptible has become the worst of tyrants from whom they seek the freedom to indulge their ambition and greed.

The tension of waiting reaches its climax in the second act upon the arrival of the ruthless absolutist, Saint-Just, weary from his recent military victories, and, shortly thereafter, of his sick and disillusioned mentor, Robespierre, whose very presence sends the cringing, petty henchmen scurrying for safety. The remainder of the play is a study in loneliness. Endowed with the mythic dimensions of a blinded Oedipus and martyred Christ, Robespierre has the prophetic powers that accompany extreme suffering. His catastrophic vision of the demise of European civilization signals the end of a dream. The coming century, and our own as well, will be an iron age—of money, imperialistic wars, governments for sale, worship of dictators and the decline of revolutionary ideals. *Realpolitik* and lofty abstractions have forever split apart, leaving Robespierre alone in a nightmarish void. A demented dreamer, a tragic madman, the Incorruptible has a sudden desire to strike out and destroy his own triumphant machine that is bringing victory everywhere to the French army and death to the soul of the country. For a moment he imagines that if he could only recall his generals and endanger the Republic by setting the Revolution back to its precarious early stages, then the people would once again risk their lives for freedom.

The mechanism of revolution is inexorable. The speculative, Enlightenment ideologue Robespierre has lost touch with reality, and must be eliminated as a sacrificial victim so that the nineteenth century— mercenary, corrupt, and bloody—can come into being. No writer has portrayed more incisively and poignantly the tragedy of the Revolution. Drawing upon her own failed life and stubborn dedication to a vocation that foundered, Przybyszewska was able to write with moving insight about Robespierre's defeat. The historiographic prophecies at the end of *The Danton Case* and *Thermidor*, foretelling the rise of the Napoleonic conqueror-gangster, brought Przybyszewska's dramas into her own monstrous age, in which Hitler, Mussolini, Stalin, and other lesser dictators gained power through unleashing the forces of nationalism and militarism.

For success in the theatre, *The Danton Case* and *Thermidor* need all the resources of a professional repertory company with a dozen or more masterful actors capable of establishing character with lightning speed. Whatever the vicissitudes of Przybyszewska's plays in performance—and so far they have done exceedingly well in the state-financed Polish theatre and had qualified successes on subsidized Western stages—*The Danton Case* and *Thermidor* are major contributions to the dramatic literature on the French Revolution. They deserve to be read as well as seen. The intellectual content is demanding, the historical insight penetrating. The dialogue moves easily from racy colloquialism to rhetorical eloquence, while the subtext is psychologically nuanced, rich in dark undercurrents and hidden erotic resonances. The precise, highly visual, and often cinematographic stage directions are addressed as much to the reader as to theatre practitioner.

On the two hundredth anniversary of the French Revolution, called by Tocqueville ''the drama without denouement,'' Przybyszewska's plays are eloquent testimony to the power of its ideas and the importance of its example. In a year when the heritage of the Revolution is under scrutiny and its values a matter of controversy, *The Danton Case* and *Thermidor* are texts that enlarge and enliven the perennial debate between Danton and Robespierre that is still carried on by their present-day partisans.

Daniel Gerould

The Danton Case

CHARACTERS

Maximilien François Marie Isidore
  de Robespierre
Eléonore Duplay
Antoine Louis Saint-Just
Georges Jacques Danton
Louise Danton
François Joseph Westermann
Camille Desmoulins
Pierre Philippeaux
Jean-François De Lacroix
  [Delacroix]
François Louis Bourdon de l'Oise
Jean Marie Collot d'Herbois
Jean Nicolas Billaud-Varenne
Baptiste Robert Lindet
Bertrand Barère de Vieuzac
Lazare Carnot
Secretary of the Committee of
  Public Safety
Jean-Baptiste Amar
Albert Vadier
Lucile Desmoulins
Sénar
Voulland
Jagot

Philippe Lebas
Jacques Louis David
Merlin de Thionville
Edme Bonaventure Courtois
Laurent Lecointre
Etienne Jean Panis
Louis Marie Fréron
Louis Legendre
Jean Lambert Tallien
Marie Jean Hérault de Séchelles
Pierre Gaspard Chaumette
Riouffe
Louis Sebastien Mercier
Le comte d'Estaing Jean Baptiste
Le vicomte d'Estaing
Arthur Dillon
Laflotte
Fabre d'Eglantine
René François Dumas
Armand Herman
Antoine Quentin Fouquier-Tinville
Dobsen
Jean-François Renaudin
Henri Sanson

Spy; Bricklayer; Suzon; Madeleine; Printer; Fair-haired Man; Intellectual; Dandy; Clock-maker; Student; Invalid; Housewife; Lady; Condemned Man; Commissioners I, II, III; Soldiers; Men and Women in the crowd; Barber; Stranger; Janitor at the Committee of Public Safety; Municipal Officer; Policeman; Girondists I, II; Prison Guard; Court Ushers I, II; Journalists I, II; The Dandies; Prison Barbers; People in the Hall of the Revolutionary Tribunal; Deputies in the Hall of the Convention

This list of characters has been prepared by the translator.

ACT I   Scene 1

A street, in front of a baker's. At the corner a gaudy poster. It is dawn, still dark. A BRICKLAYER, *a man over forty, stands by the door; the* SPY, *of nondescript age, is aimlessly walking back and forth in the space before the door.*

SPY [*unnecessary whisper*]. Citizen, have you seen . . . the poster?
BRICKLAYER [*loudly, with reluctance*]. What poster?
SPY. There, at the corner . . . they stuck it up at night again, damn them!
. . .
BRICKLAYER. Let them . . . they've put up so many since the New Year! A poster is nothing new to us.
SPY. But, citizen, it's *them* . . . the Grand Judge!
BRICKLAYER. The Grand Judge!—It's been a week since the Grand Judge went up in smoke. They kissed one another after that.
SPY. Not true at all!—Well, citizen: The Grand Judge is not just anyone! [*still more softly*] To you they blabber that it's Pache . . . the good Pache! the infant Pache!—and I am telling you, let . . .
BRICKLAYER. Will you shut your trap! The Grand Judge, indeed! What is it to me whether it is Pache, or not Pache, who makes a darned fool of you?
SPY. You mustn't be angry so early in the mor . . .
BRICKLAYER [*dawns on him who the man is*]. Go away!

[*The* SPY *gives up. He walks away and hangs round the newcomers:* MADELEINE, *about 30, and* SUZON, *15.*]

SUZON [*stops by the poster*]. Oooh, Madeleine! Come and look! Another poster!
MADELEINE [*stops behind the* BRICKLAYER]. Really, it's an ordinary . . .
SUZON. Not ordinary! Exactly the same as before . . . [*thrilled*] Listen: "Citizens! You have suffered the Convention's rule for two years, and every month you have found it more difficult to get bread. Citizens! Do not let them pull the wool over your eyes! You should know that within the Convention—at its unshaken 'Mountain' traitors are lurking: tigers that devour . . ."

MADELEINE [*vehemently*]. Don't read that nonsense! Come over here, or your place will be taken!

[*Enter: a* FAIR-HAIRED MAN, *an* INTELLECTUAL, *a* PRINTER, *30-40 years. The* FAIR-HAIRED MAN *tries to take* SUZON*'s place, but the* SPY *prevents it.*]

SPY [*in a Napoleonic pose*]. I am sorry. This place has been reserved for the lady.

[*He lets* SUZON *take it, and she absentmindedly nods to thank him. There follow simultaneous speeches.*]

FAIR-HAIRED MAN. What?!. . .

SPY. A true sansculotte doesn't touch places reserved for women.

PRINTER. Oh. . .in that case what's going to happen to the nation's future?. . .

SUZON [*half-whispering*]. Madeleine—Madeleine—, something will come of it, after all!

MADELEINE [*whisper*]. Suzon, will you be quiet?

PRINTER [*indifferently*]. Have you seen that? The Hébertists are bothering us again.

BRICKLAYER. Those coxcombs at the War Office think we still haven't had enough riots and shootings and guillotines!

FAIR-HAIRED MAN. It's all that madman Vincent's fault: the sniveler has an army in order to feed Paris; it pleases him to destroy the Convention with that army! Who knows if he does not fancy the crown. . .

[*Enter: A* YOUNG INVALID, *a* DANDY, *a* STUDENT, *and an* OLD CLOCK-MAKER.]

INTELLECTUAL [*somewhat mysteriously*]. So you think it is Vincent who has been undermining Paris for the last three months? That it is Vincent who has been raising his hand against the government, well—against the Grand Committee itself? Vincent?. . .

DANDY. Then who? Hébert, perhaps? Ha, ha!

[*laughter*]

FAIR-HAIRED MAN. Or Pache?

[*more laughter*]

INTELLECTUAL. Hébert and Pache are puppets, and Vincent is a young little general with the brains of a canary. [*The* INVALID *frowns angrily*] It must be someone of a larger caliber who dares raise his hand against the Committee of Public Safety—today, when that Committee literally bears the country on its shoulders and directs the politics of Europe...My friends: there is only one man in Paris, maybe in the entire world, who would dare to do this.—But it is not Vincent.

SPY. But who?...You have aroused our curiosity, citizen...

[*The* INTELLECTUAL *realizes who the man is—and breaks off terrified.*]

SUZON [*thrilled*]. Who is it? It's he who is supposed to be the Grand Judge, isn't that so? Who is it?...

[*Tense silence. The* INTELLECTUAL *indicates the* SPY *with his eyes.*]

PRINTER [*thoughtful*]. It doesn't matter: this Convention deserves to be thoroughly swept clean—even at the price of riots. Oh, how far have we departed from ninety-two! The government today is a veritable morass of corruption and false...

[*The* INTELLECTUAL *pricks him to warn him. The news about the* SPY *is spread by signs and causes everyone to be silent. In order to draw attention away from himself, the* SPY *approaches* SUZON. *There follow simultaneous speeches.*]

FAIR-HAIRED MAN [*after an unpleasant silence*]. But what's happening with that bread? For the last three weeks things were all right, and now, all of a sudden—one's got to line up again day and night!

[*Enter at intervals: an* OLD LADY, *a* HOUSEWIFE, *five women and six men.*]

INTELLECTUAL [*still pale*]. Well, citizen—it's the war.

PRINTER. It's not the war, it's those damned speculators! The police, the guillotine mean nothing to them; they are impudent like rats.

FAIR-HAIRED MAN. What profits they make! First from their trade, and then His Britannic Lordship Pitt pays them as much again for starving the revolution...

CLOCK-MAKER. Just as he pays those who infect the Convention and destroy our last vestiges of faith...

STUDENT [*softly*]. You know what I think? That sudden food shortage is not natural. It is caused on purpose by those who want to topple the government: they starve us for this reason like beasts destined for the ring!

[*disbelief—indignation—support, still subdued and with a sharp eye on the flirting* SPY]

SPY. Why so sad, little citizeness? Your fiancé has gone to war, eh?

SUZON. Let me be.

SPY. Don't be angry, miss; I want to console you...

SUZON [*shouts*]. Please, go away!
MADELEINE. Away with you!
SPY. I am not talking to you, citizeness. I'm talking to the *young* lady.

[*struggle*]

BRICKLAYER [*nudged by the* SPY, *grabs him by the collar and shoves him*]. You false mongrel, get away from here!

[*immediate understanding among the others*]

INTELLECTUAL [*to the returning* SPY]. Where is your place?
SPY. Everywhere. The street is for everybody.
PRINTER. No loitering outside the line.
SPY [*tries to be brazen*]. So what? Who's going to stop me?
PRINTER. I will!

[*general approbation*]

DANDY. And we can make sure of that!

[*The* SPY *gives up and tries to squeeze in behind* SUZON.]

INTELLECTUAL. Oh no! You should have stood here from the start!
PRINTER [*grabs and pushes him out;* SUZON *is overjoyed at that*]. Go on, to the end of the line!

[*The* SPY *renews the attempt several times, but in vain; he then takes his place as the end of the line, hardly visible. After a while he disappears.*]

FAIR-HAIRED MAN. At last! But still we are too careless!

[*Suddenly a bell begins to toll. Everyone grows still.*]

INTELLECTUAL [*softly*]. What does it mean . . . at this time?
MADELEINE [*suppressed shout*]. It sounds the alarm!!!
FAIR-HAIRED MAN. Good night! We have an insurrection.

[*After their immobility people grow more and more restless.*]

SUZON [*tense*]. I knew something would happen today! . . .
WOMAN A [*shouts*]. Let's go home, quick!

[*Confusion. No one wants to leave the line first—it may be a false alarm, and they will lose their bread. Crescendo accelerando molto:*]

MAN A. And the bread?!

WOMAN B. There's to be another slaughter! Like in September!!
WOMAN A. It's Vincent's gangs now! It will be worse!

[*The shouting turns into chaos. Shouts merge into confusion.*]

SHOUTS. Quick!—Let's go home!—Go back!—Shutters and gates!—Escape!!
Slaughter!!!—What about bread?!—We'll be crushed!—I must have
bread!—I won't go!—Let them slay us: I must—have—bread!!!

[*The bell stops tolling; breathless tension, then a sigh of relief and an outbreak of
nervous jollity.*]

BRICKLAYER [*to the women at the end of the line*]. Idiots!

[*The women call each other names in a cheerful mood*]

SUZON [*with a sigh*]. Pity!
INVALID. It's a new requisition of bells. They try them out for selection.—
This time they are to take them from Notre-Dame too, I am told.
LADY. Requisitions—recruitment—cold—starvation—and our sons who die
in their hundreds every day.—Is this war never going to end?
FAIR-HAIRED MAN. Ask the Committee of Safety* why they don't want to
conclude peace!
INTELLECTUAL. We would really look nice if peace were concluded too early
and dictated by the enemy!
STUDENT [*vehemently*]. Do you think the Committee wages war for its en-
joyment, or something? Or for a piece of land, like the kings do?!
DANDY. All the same, the revolution used to be more jolly. Now it's become
somber and boring.

[PRINTER, STUDENT, *and* CLOCKMAKER *are quietly indignant*]

INVALID. Ah, that's true! How much more jolly it was in ninety-two! On
the tenth of August. . . You know, I would not give that one hour at the
Place de Carouselle, when they injured my paw, for a hundred healthy
arms. A war in the street, it's. . . it's paradise itself.

[*laughter and indignation*]

INTELLECTUAL [*friendly*]. But for whom, and for what, you are fighting is no
concern of yours, is it?
INVALID. Of course, it is! You think it's a joke to fight, under an officer's
whip, about some personal family quarrels of kings—for whom we are

*The Committee of Public Safety.

goods cheaper than honest horses? Oh no, sir! This is not the same as to put the barricades up and down, fighting about the Rights of Man, of our own free will!

CLOCK-MAKER. The Rights of Man!—Four years ago that was the belief for which *everyone*, without any hesitation, gave his life, and even his possessions. Well, four years have passed; we suffer and fight tirelessly; and whatever we gain—is plundered or wasted by our representatives.—The freedom government! The leaders of a free people! A man who has acquired power immediately turns into a swine, always, everywhere; it doesn't matter whether he sits on the throne or at the Conv—

[*Murmur of indignation and fear; half-aroused, it turns into a suppressed shout and breaks off.*]

VOICES [*everyone looks round fearfully for the* SPY]. Has he gone mad?!—Have mercy!—You should be ashamed!—Be reasonable, man! You will pay for it with your head!

CLOCK-MAKER. With my head? That's no misfortune! For a man who has lost his faith death is not so terrible!

INTELLECTUAL. Console yourself, citizen: the revolution has not deviated from its course. But the Rights of Man cannot be secured in six weeks—after thousands of years of slavery.

STUDENT [*to the* CLOCK-MAKER]. Your despair amounts to desertion, do you understand? We have been fighting for only four years; and we shall fight till we die. It is not we who matter, oh no! What matters is the freedom of human progress—maybe only for our grandchildren!

[*The* SPY *appears again.*]

HOUSEWIFE. It's easy for you to talk, master. If you had a family to feed, you would think differently after four such years.

STUDENT [*friendly, indicating the* SPY *with his eyes*]. But I wouldn't think aloud, citizeness.

INTELLECTUAL. And one ought to admire the Convention rather than have petty grudges against it. If among the seven hundred deputies there are a few fools and villains, what of it? What are they compared to one Robespierre, for instance?

[*That name has the effect of a slight electric current.*]

PRINTER. That's a fact: since he has been ill, the revolution slows its pace and begins to totter.

STUDENT [*fervently*]. He's unique. The only intellect capable of embracing the total situation, from every angle; and he is pure.

BRICKLAYER. Exactly. For some who are shrewd—are also thieves...
PRINTER [*whisper*]. Like the "Man of August the Tenth"...

[*The* FAIR-HAIRED MAN *is* indignant.]

BRICKLAYER. ...and often also traitors.—But he alone can be trusted, indeed.
STUDENT. He governs better than the best kings; but will never even think of dictatorship!
FAIR-HAIRED MAN [*menacingly*]. He'd better not try!—But he has served enough already, my friends.
STUDENT. Are you insane?!
INVALID. Yes, it's true! Chaumette also says that he is worn out; and he's quite right!
FAIR-HAIRED MAN. The revolution is completed; now what the Republic needs is peace and liberty; but he draws out war, and terror, exhausts and disheartens the people...
PRINTER. Ah, this one has been schooled by Danton!
INVALID. It's just the opposite, you idiot! Robespierre was all right as long as mild means were sufficient. What we need today is *energy*! We need radical means he's afraid of. Otherwise counterrevolution will infect the entire country, as it has already infected the Convention...
FAIR-HAIRED MAN. Still, I prefer Danton's school to that of Hébert! It's you, traitors, who are starving us! These are your radical means!

[*An impending clash is averted by the entry of the execution squad with a condemned man. The escort has to enter a side street blocked by those waiting, so it must stop. The people give way with difficulty, because those stronger push the weaker ones with every move.*]

FAIR-HAIRED MAN [*softly*]. Oh—or you watch this. Does this make any sense? Every day they escort someone. The very thought of this perpetual public slaughter makes one sick! Why won't that Committee of yours stop it?
DANDY. Hey, who is that?

[*The militia ignores the question.*]

INVALID. Tell us, who is it?
SOLDIER. An emigré. But what business is it of yours?
SPY [*approaches*]. The country's salvation is our business, isn't it?
INTELLECTUAL. What, on foot, for a change?
SOLDIER. Since there's only one, why bother to take him in a cart? He is healthy, so he can walk.

SPY. Sure—one way he can.—But the way back won't be so easy, will it? . . . your lordship? Walk—back? . . .

[*Two or three people give a short laugh, not taken up by the others.*]

MAN B. Why not? Head under his arm and on he walks!

[*The escort moves.*]

SUZON [*trembling voice*]. Oh, my God . . . he's so pretty . . . poor dear!

[*Some friendly laughter—but on the whole the mood is unfavorable. The escort passes.*]

LADY. Oh yes, it really is a sad sight . . .
STUDENT. You should thank God for the Committee's energy and watchfulness! Would you rather the bank notes weren't worth the paper they're printed on? So that anyone could ask a thousand pounds for a bundle of sticks, and rob you of the scraps of food you're at least getting now?!

[*Two armed* SOLDIERS *of the Revolutionary Army knock at the shutter and take their places at either side of the door.*]

VOICES [*murmur of relief, joy*]. At last! Three hours they make us wait! If only we could all get it . . .

[*The* BAKER *opens up. A shout of joy;* BRICKLAYER *goes in.*]

SUZON [*quietly to her companion*]. Who are they?
MADELEINE. I suppose you've never stood in a line?—Revolutionary Army. Vincent's soldiers.
SUZON. What for?
FAIR-HAIRED MAN. To maintain order.—You will see how they do it.

[*The* BRICKLAYER *returns;* MADELEINE *goes in. They stop the* BRICKLAYER, *snatch at him.*]

VOICES. How much is there?—How many loaves?—How much has he got there?—Will there be enough for everyone?—Is there enough?
BRICKLAYER [*shakes them off*]. How do I know? I didn't count!

[*He goes away. Tension in the crowd.*]

WOMAN A [*half-aloud*]. That means—there's not enough! . . .

[*Murmur of anxiety. Tension mounts.*]

MADELEINE [*runs out; whispers to* SUZON]. Hurry—there's only seven loaves left!

[*Exit. The news is overheard and immediately passed on in a whisper which almost instantly turns into shout.*]

VOICES. Seven—seven loaves—what, *again!*—Get in, quick! *I* need them!!—I *must* get them today!!!

[*Before* SUZON *can reach the door, the line disintegrates. The people at the end of the line rush forward, followed by the rest. The* BAKER *bangs the door shut, crushing a woman's hand. A terrible groan of pain. The angry crowd struggle by the door. Shouts, groans, curses. Individual voices begin to emerge from the general confusion.*]

PRINTER [*points to the immovable* SOLDIERS]. We are killing one another. . . and they stand there like monuments, damn them!

[*The crowd eases off a bit and turns against the* SOLDIERS, *not very aggressively at first.*]

VOICES [*angry, but good-natured*]. Well, go on, move—go on! Help us now; what are you here for? Revolutionary Army! They think of nothing but coups! You're just good for stuffing, and your Vincents too! You won't even lift a finger. . . Tell us at least: What are we to do?!
SOLDIER. Go away, go home, quick!

[*Murmur of astonishment, followed by roar of fury. The crowd strikes an aggressive attitude, even pushes at the* SOLDIERS, *but won't dare attack them.*]

SHOUTS. They do it on purpose! They've been bribed not to let us in! Traitors' puppets!

[*The* PRINTER *aims to strike a* SOLDIER, *who fixes his bayonet at the ready. A shrill shout of terror. The crowd leap away from the weapon, like starved dogs from a whip; just one step and no further. There is relatively less noise, because fury and terror stifle voices. A menacing suspense on both sides.*]

SHOUTS. With a bayonet on the people!. . . They've been paid by Pitt! Beasts! Swine! Bandits! To hell with it, I want *bread*! [*a woman:*] Take that spit away from them!

[*No response; the crowd is defenseless, does not know what to do.*]

INVALID [*finds a solution*]. Smash the door!!!

[*The suspense immediately turns into action. The crowd changes direction, to the relief of the* SOLDIERS *who do not defend the crowd's new aim, but even ostentatiously put their weapons down. The shouting grows stronger.*]

SHOUTS. Break the door! There's plenty of bread! He's a profiteer! Smash it! Go on, smash the door!

[*The* SOLDIERS *give way, but the women rush to the door, defend their rights, shouting.*]

WOMEN. Oh no! We want bread *too*! Never! Either everybody gets it, or no one at all! Away! We were here first! Thieves! Robbers!!

[*The crowd grows. Heads appear in the windows. The crowd is delighted, the people whistle, shout, laugh, roar, give sounds of encouragement as at a sporting match. Children throw stones. The men push away the squeaking women and push in at the door.*]

MEN. Go on! Away you wenches!

[*An orgy of storming the door. Suddenly, ex machina, three section* COMMISSIONERS *appear. The crowd grows still at once; only the siege goes on for a few seconds, those storming not being aware of their presence. As soon as they have seen the commissioners, they too grow still. Dead silence.*]

COMMISSIONER I [*in a silence when even breathing can be heard, speaks in an ostentatiously quiet manner*]. What is going on here?

CHORUS OF VOICES [*erupts*]. Bread...no bread...anarchy...for three days ...profiteers...and *again*...on purpose...traitors!...not true... seven loaves...entrance blo...

COMMISSIONER I [*thunders*]. Quiet! Speak like civilized people!

[*Silence. Then articulated voices*]

VOICES. Again only seven loaves! Day after day not enough! He *must* let us in! Has no right! But, look, he slammed the door, the beast! He has a full store, he's a profiteer! [*more vehemently*] Yes, a profiteer! Pitt pays him, and these here too! We must break in the door! We'll see how much he has hidden there! [*approbation*] Break in! We've got to break in!!

COMMISSIONER I [*overcomes the noise*]. Anyone who says "break in" again will be arrested. [*Silence. Faint, sad protest*] If there are seven loaves, those whose turn it is will get them. [*At the end of the original line a shy protest again.*] Who was supposed to get in now?

[*All come forward. Consternation. Laughter.*]

COMMISSIONER II [*to the soldiers*]. And what are you doing here? Standing as a decoration?—How can you allow such scandalous behavior?!

SOLDIER II. What? Is it our fault that he has seven loaves to sell?

PRINTER [*among the chatter of helpless anger*]. Let us share them, friends!

VOICES [*sudden agitation*]. What...is there to divide? Divide, he says... Well! An excellent idea! How many are we? Count! Divide! Divide! Eighteen. How many? Twenty-three—seventeen—*don't move!* Twenty-one. Yes, twenty-one! Straight count! [*protest*] Eh, what can I do with a slice...I *must* take back a loaf! I've been waiting since dawn! I have the right to a whole loaf! No divisions! You should have come earlier! They think everything is theirs by right!

INTELLECTUAL. Then no one will get anything!

COMMISSIONER I. Come on, citizens: stand in threes, quick! Everyone will get one-third of a loaf, and we will inspect the shop.

[*They group themselves relatively calmly, those who are eager forcing the reluctant ones to comply. The* SPY *has approached the* COMMISSIONERS I *and* II, *and whispers to them.*]

COMMISSIONER III [*while the Baker opens up and lets in the* PRINTER, SUZON *and the* FAIR-HAIRED MAN]. I'll go and look. But I doubt if I'll find anything: he's an honest man.

[*He goes in. The* SPY *walks away and watches from around the corner. The* COMMISSIONERS *stand by the door. The* PRINTER *emerges from the shop.*]

COMMISSIONER II [*puts his hand on the* PRINTER*'s shoulder*]. I arrest you in the name of the law.

[*Deadly silence in the street. The* PRINTER *is numb and silent for a while.*]

PRINTER [*regains his voice*]. W-wh-at for?...

COMMISSIONER II [*to the crowd*]. Did he say the Convention should be abolished?

[*General astonishment; gradually the crowd becomes more animated.*]

VOICES. No...Not at all! Well, yes, he did say something...No, not "abolish"! Somebody twisted it! But it was only, well—and that one needn't—that it would be worth—but it was just, well, he didn't think anything— [*with emphasis*] he did not say "abolish"!

COMMISSIONER II. Only what?

DANDY. Swept clean!

[*The crowd bursts into a short laughter which dies out immediately.* SUZON *comes out and stops by the door, terrified.*]

COMMISSIONER II. Never mind. Take the bread and give me your card. In the section committee the matter is bound to clear itself up.

[*He goes away with the prisoner. Simultaneous speeches follow*]

VOICES [*whisper of awe and anger*]. It's that snooper. . . he's been loitering here since dawn. . . He's everywhere, like a louse. . . You see, didn't I tell you? You see how careful one has to be?!

COMMISSIONER I [*to* SUZON, *who takes a step forward*]. You too have to show your card.

SUZON [*numb*]. I?!! . . .

COMMISSIONER I. Yes, you.

SUZON [*out of her mind*]. But I didn't say anything. . . why me. . . [*utters a shout which causes utter silence in the crowd*] Jesus, Mary, they will cut my head off!!!

COMMISSIONER I [*suspicious*]. Hurry up, citizeness. Your card.

[*Takes her bread which makes it difficult for her to look for the card.*]

SUZON. But it's for the family! . . .

COMMISSIONER I. I will only hold it for you. Find the card.

INTELLECTUAL. What has the little one done, commissioner?

COMMISSIONER I. She is alleged to have shown such emotion at the sight of a condemned emigré that one has to assume he was her lover. . .

SUZON [*cocky*]. What?!!

COMMISSIONER I. . . . or relative.

[*The people look at one another, and burst out laughing.*]

VOICES. She said he was pretty, that's all! She was sorry for a handsome boy, she's a silly young thing! To her a boy is a boy!

SUZON. Here's the card. . . And now they will kill me for it!

[*More laughter.* COMMISSIONER III *emerges from the shop and watches.*]

COMMISSIONER I. They will not kill you, now—unless you wanted to become a dictator.—Does anybody know her?

HOUSEWIFE. Of course! She's Suzanne Ferrus, daughter of the barber at number twelve!

VOICES [*amused*]. Let her go! She thinks that now she'll go straight to the
scaffold!

COMMISSIONER I [*looks at the card*]. Yes. . . [*to III*] What do you think: what
are we to do with this bird? Take her to the section for interrogation, or
let her go at once?

COMMISSIONER III. Let her go. We have no time for this nonsense. Only an
idiot could think that an aristocrat would bewail her accomplice in the
street for everyone to hear.

COMMISSIONER I. Well, citizeness—away with you.

[*The crowd expresses approbation.*]

SUZON [*laughter among tears, curtsies*]. Thank you, citizens! [*rushes out*]

COMMISSIONER I. Eh, your bread! Take your bread! [*General laughter.*] [SUZON
*returns and takes the bread; people stop her in a friendly manner. He speaks to his
colleagues*] Well? Have you found anything?

COMMISSIONER III. Nothing at all. I knew he was not a profiteer.

COMMISSIONER I [*coldly*]. Eh, comrade! Beware of over-confidence in people!
Now we must suspect *everybody*! . . .

Scene 2

ROBESPIERRE*'s modest lodgings. The Tribune is sitting patiently, waiting for the
barber to complete work on his hair, and enjoying the early spring day. The* BARBER
*sprinkles the ready coiffure with powder. The patient lifts up a hand mirror—
somewhat suspiciously—and looks at himself in it, then shows in a smile his chalk-
white teeth.*

ROBESPIERRE. Well, this is too much. I look like a gigantic withered cauli-
flower.

BARBER. It's your normal style. Only your face is thinner now and that's
why it may seem. . .

ROBESPIERRE. Maybe.—Do something about it; no one who looks at me will
be able to take me seriously.

BARBER. It's too late today. I will cut your hair again tomorrow.—It's true,
though, that no one among my clients has such bushy hair. A comb just
drowns in it.

ROBESPIERRE [*after a few seconds*]. A propos of clients—you have many sources of information. They say that the Grand Judge tempts people again at night. Have you heard anything?

BARBER [*embarrassed*]. One hears such nonsense...

ROBESPIERRE. So what? Maybe *I* am to be that mysterious being now?

BARBER. Oh, God!—No, it hasn't come to *that* yet...

ROBESPIERRE [*somewhat energetically now*]. Well then?

BARBER. They say th...that...that Danton....

[ROBESPIERRE *sits still. Pervading silence.*]

ROBESPIERRE [*in a natural, but too monotonous a voice*]. Where have you heard this...

BARBER [*more and more ill at ease*]. Forgive me, citizen...I can't...that is I ...I'd rather...not...

ROBESPIERRE [*indifferent*]. Never mind. [*slight knock*] Enter!

[*Enter* ELEONORE DUPLAY, 25. *She stops in the doorway.*]

ROBESPIERRE. Good morning, mademoiselle! Please forgive me for not standing up. Do come in...

ELEONORE [*shakes him by the hand and sits down*]. Aren't you up too early, sir?...

ROBESPIERRE [*grins*]. Too early...after five weeks!—On a day like this even a corpse would get up.

ELEONORE. But the floor still sways somewhat, doesn't it?

ROBESPIERRE. A little—but this adds to its charm.—I can't have enough of the joy of free movement. My muscles are coming back to life...Life is a most agreeable thing, mademoiselle.

[*The* BARBER *retreats by a step and surveys his work.*]

BARBER. Well—I think you are ready, sir.

[*Hands him the mirror, which* ROBESPIERRE *fearfully pushes away.*]

ROBESPIERRE. No...I'd rather not see myself. Thank you. Please come tomorrow at the usual time! [*The* BARBER *bows and goes out.* ROBESPIERRE *turns round in his chair, rest his elbows on its arm and looks with an indefinable smile into the eyes of his equally motionless lover. Suddenly he gets up and gives her his hands.*] Let's greet each other, my lioness. [ELEONORE *rises calmly; they embrace and kiss each other. But this is not enough for her; she slowly falls to her knees, brushing with her face and torso against the shoulder, chest, side, hip, and thigh of her friend. He stands supported by a fairly distant table—in order not to lose his balance, when she has surrounded his knees with her arms—and is tilted*] *back in a delightfully uncomfortable pose. He defends himself—without conviction—with his left hand. When the embrace passes below his hips, he gasps for breath somewhat vehemently and speaks seriously]* Oh, Léo . . . stop it. *[She pretends, of course, not to hear. More softly and more intensely, he says:]* Stop it . . . stop.

[He almost pushes her away. When she gets up, he stretches his entire body anxiously. He tosses his head, as if he wished to throw something off it. With his toes he draws lines on the floor.]

ELEONORE *[sits down. Cheerfully but with suppressed bitterness]*. True, I have transgressed against your principles.

ROBESPIERRE *[surprised, raises his head]*. My principles . . . you?

ELEONORE. You succeeded in ramming at least one of them into my head: "Any manifestation of love in daylight is tactless and in the worst possible taste."

ROBESPIERRE *[sits down]*. Those aggressive principles of a man of action seem so strange to the drowned rat that I am now!

ELEONORE. Thank God. You're beginning to sharpen your claws . . . and trying them out on yourself. *[watches him]* Yes: you are well.—Pity.

ROBESPIERRE. Well, *really* . . .

ELEONORE *[delicately moves her arms]*. Can't be helped, dearest: I was happy thanks to your suffering. You were writhing with pain in the pangs of malaria—but I had you for hours, even whole days and nights. The illness did not even make you ugly: the expression of tragic passivity becomes you. I sat there and learned your features by heart. I did not nurse you: I am not your wife. Anyway, it was better so! In my mother's hands you were safe.

ROBESPIERRE *[looks at her thoughtfully]*. If I could only believe in that metallic egoism of yours, lioness . . .

ELEONORE. My friend: love is not the same as charity.

ROBESPIERRE *[craftily, after a few seconds]*. And children, dearest? . . .

ELEONORE *[astonished]*. Children? *[twists the corners of her mouth]* Man: why do I need a poor caricature, when I have the original?—Let nature install her incubators in other bodies—incapable of happiness.

ROBESPIERRE *[naively surprised]*. Happiness? . . . Ah, it must have been two years ago! *[asymmetrically elongating his mouth]* Yes, indeed . . . our evenings then . . . and nights . . . Our idyllic plans—Great God!—When I thought that one could fulfill one's allotment of revolutionary work in a year or two, and then go back home!—Léo: those days are *gone*!

ELEONORE. Compared to what I have now, I was poor then.

ROBESPIERRE. I loved you then.—Today you are just a sleeping-draught to me.

ELEONORE. I know.

ROBESPIERRE. You are lying, child, even to yourself! Nature in you has grasped at a vain hope—for that lie you are wasting your precious life terribly!—Léo: revolution will last a couple of centuries. I shall *never* be free, do you understand? Never. A succession of twenty-hour days of ever-heavier work until I die. I am now thirty-five...Before I reach forty I shall be a ruin—like a most dissolute fifty-year-old libertine!

ELEONORE. And what of it, dearest? For as long as I can see you, if only in passing, you give my life unutterable joy. When you abandon me, I shall still see you every day from the gallery of the Convention and the club.

ROBESPIERRE. Woman: don't you feel how such slavery *debases* you?! Listen: revolution consumes not only my time—but my whole being. Today I have no personal life any more. I cease to be a man: human sensibility, human feelings, desires—all these gradually wither and fall away in that hellish temperature of concentrated effort. I am becoming an impersonal, monstrously expanding, inflamed brain. Today I can see what is happening to me because I have time...and I feel strange.—Child: I do not love you any more. I am literally *indifferent* to you! Consider: the only chances now of our spending a few minutes together—are the feverish spasms of my lust; spasms which are a vile torment, and result from beastly exhaustion. Do you know, Léo, that it's all the same to me who frees me from that torment?—Do you know that sometimes any random tart takes your place...and that it makes no difference? That if I come to you—it is only because I lack the strength to walk a few blocks and save you at least *that* humiliation?...Léo—woman—this is shameful! Struggle, though it is hard for you—and tear yourself free at last!

ELEONORE [*with a slight sigh*]. Do not exert yourself, *carino*. Is it your fault that fate has destined me for your use? [ROBESPIERRE *frowns. She smiles faintly.*] Why worry? I am here exactly in order to save you wandering about the city when you are tired, and to save you from getting infected. Do I shock you? No, no, chéri: were you to choose even more spiteful words—you would not alter the natural fact that I am your property. Whatever comes from you—is for me the reason for existence, not shame.

ROBESPIERRE [*after a short while*]. I am ashamed for you.

ELEONORE. You're exaggerating.

[*Suddenly she grabs his hand and kisses it. In response* ROBESPIERRE *stoops, takes her head in his hands, and returns her kiss on the mouth, with rapacious intensity.*]

ROBESPIERRE [*with deep sincerity*]. Yes, my friend—I am ashamed for you, that is a fact. But at the same time I am able to feel your excellence. . . today, when after five weeks of rest—the man in me makes a shy attempt at revival. In two weeks. . . you will again mean to me only a female body . . . at hand. Oh, how happy you private people are! . . . And how terribly sorry I am for you, Léo!

ELEONORE. But you will give me those two weeks, Maxime! You've just clearly said so!

ROBESPIERRE [*looks through the window*]. Two weeks. . . of being a free man. Two weeks. . . fourteen days. . . to be one's foolish self, not answerable for anything in the world. . . and at this divine time of year. . . Alas, it's not to be thought of. Four days, though—I guarantee them with my word of honor.

[*He takes out a file and skillfully begins to file his nails.*]

ELEONORE [*almost frightened*]. What? . . . You think you will be well enough in four days?

ROBESPIERRE. I am well already. But—I am maniacally craving *your* life. Pathologically: like a drunk who has been refused alcohol.

[*A knock. He gets up and walks to the door.*]

VOICE [*of a stripling who hands him his correspondence through the door*]. Letters for you, sir. Here's a dispatch from the Committee of Safety.

[*Totally absorbed,* ROBESPIERRE *impatiently goes through the letters standing by the table. Then he opens the dispatch.*]

ELEONORE [*concerned, shyly*]. Maxime, tell. . .

ROBESPIERRE. Hush, *wait*. . .

ELEONORE [*half-whisper*]. You viper! . . .

ROBESPIERRE [*musically whistles the chromatic scale. Reads a few more words; energetically raises his head*]. My holiday is over, Léo.

[ELEONORE *closes her eyes, and quietly turns her face toward the window.*]

ROBESPIERRE [*speaks and reads at the same time*]. In half an hour. . . I must. . . be at the Committee. . . [*turns his eyes from the papers for a while*] And so, I should like to ask you for a cup of coffee. It does not matter if there is no bread.

ELEONORE. At once.

[ROBESPIERRE *lifts his eyes and watches her with a somewhat sad smile, until she disappears behind the door. Then he sits down and is soon lost in thought, looking at the opposite wall. His face hardens. A knock, clearly patterned. On* ROBESPIERRE's *monosyllabic reply,* SAINT-JUST *enters.*]

SAINT-JUST. You are up and about? This is fortunate. [*Without waiting for an invitation, he sits down.* ROBESPIERRE *takes up his file again.*] Did you get Haindel's confession?

ROBESPIERRE [*filing his nails, points to the dispatch with a sideways glance*]. Of course. Just now.

SAINT-JUST. You see, I was right. If you had given me a free hand a week ago, everything would be all right now. As it is, God knows what will happen.

ROBESPIERRE. Nothing's happened and nothing will. It's only the Hébertists.

SAINT-JUST [*Leans back*]. Only! . . .

ROBESPIERRE. Only. Hollow sticks are harmless, even when they want to blow up Paris. We will disband the Revolutionary Army, and put Vincent in prison. Voilà tout.

[*Silence.* SAINT-JUST *watches him critically.*]

SAINT-JUST. Maxime—I have refrained from questions until now—but I am beginning to be concerned about you. Where does this dubious tendency to half- and quarter-measures come from—*in you?*

ROBESPIERRE. My reluctance to shed blood, you want to say? Well, my son, it's because we are standing right on the verge of terror. We are forced to destroy forgers, profiteers, traitors. But unless that terrible instrument is kept under control, unless one can keep in check its tendency to enhance itself—every new step is a step toward disaster.

SAINT-JUST. But if there is no other means of internal defense?

ROBESPIERRE. *If* there isn't—it's another matter. But the schoolboy Vincent, first, is not dangerous—second, is, or was, a revolutionary. That means, for a fraction of the population—he is a *leader.* And to condemn and waste leaders, my friend—is to destroy the revolution at the very core of its existence: in human souls. Because it is then that people *lose faith.* I advise you to ponder over these two words.

SAINT-JUST [*after a while*]. If it were, shall we say, Collot. . . but Vincent! He is followed by a few dozen adventurers at the worst.

ROBESPIERRE. It is enough if a few dozen souls are beset by doubt and despair. Because despair spreads like the plague. Faith—the awakening of a human soul in the working animal—is but a faint flame. If we do not guard it like the Lord's Flesh—we can live to see the day when a dispirited France unanimously asks to return to the bread-giving slavery. And what then, Saint-Just? [*he puts the file away and looks at his friend with an oblique, asymmetrical smile*] Can you imagine the French people compelled to freedom under the pressure of guns aimed by the revolutionary government?. . .

SAINT-JUST [*after a hollow silence*]. These are gross deductions, hanging by a thread. One cannot sacrifice tomorrow for the sake of a future century.

ROBESPIERRE [*suddenly supports his head with both hands, as if it has become a heavy load*]. Platitudes are sometimes. . .blinding. [ELEONORE *comes in, with breakfast. She exchanges friendly greetings with* SAINT-JUST. ROBESPIERRE *gets up and helps her to set the table*] Thank you kindly. . .what, real bread?! Be blessed, beloved of the gods! Antoine, there is no sugar, of course— will you partake of that tar?

SAINT-JUST. I shall be obliged. I did not sleep; I am tired and angry.

[*Exit* ELEONORE]

ROBESPIERRE [*pouring the coffee*]. All the same, Saint-Just. In *this* case the good of the Republic does not require human sacrifices. Don't let's lose our sense of proportion.

SAINT-JUST [*while* ROBESPIERRE *begins to cut the bread, he sips some coffee, lost in thought, then props himself up against the chair*]. Allow me then to complement Haindel's information with two tiny facts: First, there are credible rumors that Desmoulins has produced a new issue—the seventh—in which he openly invokes the public to rebellion against the Committees; second: for the last three days Paris has whispered about the coming coup and about the dictatorship of the Grand Judge as something . . .probable. And you remember, don't you, that the original Grand Judge—who was to be Pache—has been solemnly ridiculed all round the city. Sapienti sat.

ROBESPIERRE [*has abruptly put down the bread and knife after the first revelation. He stands upright with his hands on the table, frowning. More excited*]. Who is it this time?. . .

SAINT-JUST. Nobody speaks the name. That means. . . [*he drinks, takes the slice of bread, but constantly watches his friend*]

ROBESPIERRE [*suddenly tears himself away from the table, walks towards the window. After a short while talks from the heart*]. That damned gang! [*slowly walks back*] Yes. The barber told me the same thing. He even mentioned the name. [*stops*] I did not believe him. . . [*softly, but there is a suppressed shout in it*] Has that boor gone mad?! To save his own skin at the price of disaster for the state... [*falls into his chair. Whispers*] Great God!...

SAINT-JUST. Drink up, or it will get cold.

ROBESPIERRE [*looks carefully at his coffee, but does not touch it. Calmly*]. Since the Hébertists are in Danton's pay, there is no other way out. One has to sacrifice four commanders to disarm him.

[*Attacks his breakfast with determination, but without appetite.*]

SAINT-JUST. Maxime—I am speaking to the old, relentless Robespierre: we shall spare our society much, if we send Danton together with Vincent. At once.

ROBESPIERRE [*turns round stiffly*]. Danton is untouchable, Saint-Just.

SAINT-JUST. The man who caused three weeks of starvation in Paris must perish on the scaffold for that alone, if there exists revolutionary justice.

ROBESPIERRE [*tightens his lips convulsively, raises one eyebrow, speaks very softly, in a tone like sulfuric acid*]. Revolutionary justice!!... [*He looks straight in front of him, stooping, as if there were pressure on the nape of his neck. Suddenly he realizes he is shocking* SAINT-JUST *and controls himself*] Danton is untouchable because Danton is the Man of the Tenth of August. Chance, idiotic as always, adopted *him* as a symbol. Not for a fraction of the population: for the whole of France. To execute him would be to deny the very basis of the Revolution. [*He gets up, restless, almost terrified. Nervously walks round the room.*] But that would not be the end... the execution of Danton would cause an impasse......a succession of logically inevitable disasters...literally the suicide of the Republic!... [*Stops suddenly. Grips his hands; his eyelids twitch*] It is fortunate that Danton is not really dangerous. [*He sits down.*]

SAINT-JUST [*literally does not believe his ears*]. What did you say?...

ROBESPIERRE [*eating and drinking*]. Danton is not dangerous because, as an intellect, he is a nonentity. Action alone, no matter how bloodthirsty, if not animated by an idea—is as menacing as the fist of an angry child, beating against a steel wall. Neither Vincent's coups, nor Danton's cowardly outrages will shake the Republic. It's only the perverse *thought* expressed in alluring words that is dangerous.

SAINT-JUST. My dear friend: that means...Desmoulins?...

ROBESPIERRE [*definitely losing his appetite*]. Yes...Desmoulins. [*pause*] What idea has he been able to provide Danton with...just the sensational and absurd sentiments one needs to blind the masses...That ass, Christ! A talented baby!...

SAINT-JUST [*more sharply*]. The royalists do not hide their admiration for that renegade of the Revolution any more. They give him public ovations . . . [*menacingly now*] Desmoulins will go under the knife, with your approval, or without it.

ROBESPIERRE [*slowly turns his head around. A contest of two wills for a few seconds*]. No. [*again a tense pause*] We will not have a senseless slaughter, when a simpler way exists.

SAINT-JUST [*in a choked voice*]. You know, I should like to get to know this simpler way of yours.

ROBESPIERRE [*gets up, more and more excited. Every few seconds he trembles. With taut hands he embraces his arms at the level of his shoulder muscles wishing to warm them*]. What really matters is to shut Camille's mouth. So we will have his publisher, Desenne, arrested. The seventh issue will not appear, and the fact of the arrest will put a little salutary fear into the avid readers of "Vieux Cordelier." The Hébertists will be put on trial at the same time; if that does not bring Danton to his senses—it will mean he is insane. [*clenches his jaw, trembling*] Let us at least, Antoine, keep our heads, when the hysteria of fear embraces one man after another. And, for God's sake, don't let's turn the Revolution into a slaughter house. That would be a symptom of the government falling prey to panic, my friend!

SAINT-JUST [*on reflection*]. You know, Maxime. . . I advise you to ponder two poems in the new issue, which Camille is said to have dedicated to you: "If you do not know what the times demand, and do not hear the voice of clamoring facts. . . *ineptus esse diceris*."

ROBESPIERRE [*amused*]. He—says that to *me*? He of all people! The impudence of that wonder child knows no bounds. Brrr! Has it really become so cold all of a sudden? Will you be so good as to give me my coat?

SAINT-JUST [*gives it to him*]. What, cold?! [*he is standing so close to him that he feels his abnormally hot body temperature*] That means you have a fever again. You're a fine one. . .

ROBESPIERRE. It's nothing. It will pass.

SAINT-JUST. It will pass, indeed! Oh well. I'll manage by myself. Collot will surely not dare oppose me.

ROBESPIERRE [*puts on his overcoat and gloves*]. No. My return can give us the upper hand. [*faintly supports himself against the doorway*] Four days!! . . .

SAINT-JUST [*glumly*]. Are you delirious?

ROBESPIERRE [*bursts out laughing, which does not necessarily reassure his friend*]. *Not* any more, my dear boy. . . I have just sobered up.

SAINT-JUST [*following him out*]. Well. . . may it be so.

Scene 3

DANTON'*s lodgings. He is asleep on a couch, in the light of an oil lamp. A* STRAN-
GER, *dressed in traveling clothes with a top hat pulled over his eyes, and his face hidden up to the nose in a high collar, enters soundlessly and stands still at* DANTON'*s
feet.*

DANTON [*wakes up, speaks under his breath*]. That you, Westermann? Well
then?. . . [*The* STRANGER *keeps silent.* DANTON *lifts himself up on his elbow,
uneasy*] Who is it?!. . . [*after a few seconds, aloud*] Who's there?!!
STRANGER. Hush, C Three. [DANTON *jumps to his feet. He raises the lamp to his
visitor's hidden face, but the latter holds up* DANTON'*s hand to shield himself*]
You will forgive me for not introducing myself.

[*He sits down.* DANTON *stands dazed for a while; suddenly he starts and checks that
both doors are locked and that there is no light opposite.*]

DANTON [*having drawn the curtain, sits on the edge of the couch*]. Well?
STRANGER [*gives him a flat packet and a piece of paper*]. P Two alias Twelve sends
you this for the decree of 18 nivôse. Will you sign the receipt, please?
DANTON [*glances again at the window; opens the packet by the lamp*]. What. . .
English pounds?! And who will change them for me?
STRANGER. That's your business. You should have prevented Perrégaux's ar-
rest.
DANTON [*being busy, ignores the jibe*]. And a receipt, too! You might be ar-
rested a hundred times on the way back. My writing is known to all
France. I will not give you the receipt.
STRANGER. As you wish. In that case I must give back the ten thousand
pounds to the person who gave them to me. I am somewhat particular
about bookkeeping, you know.
DANTON [*ignoring the outstretched hand, throws the packet at his feet. Gets up
stiffly*]. Good-bye.

[*The* STRANGER *takes up and puts away the packet. He does not move.*]

STRANGER. That is not all. C Three: the Minister knows your present situation. Not wishing to make it worse, he releases you from your commit-
ments. The Central Office will not receive your reports or projects any
more.

[*While the* STRANGER *speaks,* DANTON *slowly leans forward towards him. He controls himself with difficulty. He straightens up and rises to his feet.*]

DANTON [*turns round and starts walking, with his hands behind his back. After a short pause*]. To put it more plainly: Pitt [*the* STRANGER *gives a warning hiss*] thanks me for my services.

STRANGER. I did not put it like that. . .

DANTON [*stops*]. . . . Because Pitt must have heard somewhere that my star is on the wane; so he is afraid that Danton, having rendered him so many services. . . might ask him for one in return! You can reassure Pitt: Danton does not yet intend to beg for anybody's help. Before three days are up, Pitt will shed bitter tears of regret for his credulity. [*he walks away; a pause*] It is not so safe to give notice to Danton. Pitt will learn to see the difference between Danton, and his lackeys and snoopers. Pitt will learn that contracts made with Danton commit *both* parties. [*he sits down, pompous*]

STRANGER. That is exactly the point, C Three, a contract commits both parties. So, when one party takes the money and does not fulfil the conditions. . .

DANTON. I. . . I don't fulfill them!!! Have I not for the last six months been leading the Committee of Safety by the nose, so that they fight windmills, can't take a step, and don't see your maneuvers?! Is it not I who have created, insinuated, disseminated the "Vieux Cordelier"?!

STRANGER. All this has been outside the terms of the contract; the question remains, for whom do you work? Is it really for us? Or for the house of Orléans, our enemy—to whom Danton has promised the crown?. . .

DANTON [*throws himself at him*]. A vile slan. . .

[*The visitor evades him with unusual agility. He now stands in the middle of the room.*]

STRANGER [*comes nearer, speaking loudly*]. Or perhaps for the ally. . .

DANTON [*hisses*]. Quiet, you damned dog!

STRANGER [*stands by the table, separated from* DANTON *by its edge*]. Aha!. . . [*again in half-whisper*] . . . for the mysterious ally in the East, with whom negotiations are conducted through Switzerland for the surrender of Louis' children? [*a short pause*] Or simply for yourself. . . because the Republic is somehow ceasing to serve you? [*he walks away, stops a step farther on*] The principles of loyalty, Danton, must be most closely guarded by those who. . . take up treason—as a profession. [DANTON *responds with a thundering slap in the face. The* STRANGER *is pushed against the table, with a great effort saves himself from falling to the floor. The hat has fallen off his head;* DANTON *eagerly looks into his face with the lamp close to it. The* STRANGER *calmly straightens up.*] Clumsy beast, as always—but for my agility there would have been a crash heard all round the house—the neighbors

would have come... [*he walks away; speaks from the door*] In a word, C
Three: do not count on the Minister's help, when it comes to flying
abroad by night [DANTON's *somewhat artificial laughter*] —for the Central
Office you have now ceased to exist.

[*He opens the door and goes out, quietly closing the door behind him.* DANTON *tries
to control his excitement, breathing heavily. Then he gives a burst of artificial
laughter, shrugs his shoulders, turns on his heel and starts looking for the candelabrum. Failing to find it, he walks to the door on his right.*]

DANTON [*opens the door and calls*]. Louise! Lou-ise!!

[*fast, soft steps*]

LOUISE [*a faint, tiny shape in white*]. What do you want?
DANTON. What have you done with my candlestick? I need light. [LOUISE
*goes to fetch some light; she puts the candles down on the table and wants to go
away.* DANTON *unexpectedly grasps her by both hands and draws her towards
him.*] Louison... I am sorry. [*he puts his arm around her*] You see, my
only one... I have had so many worries in these last days, so much
anxiety—that sometimes I can't control myself, and then I am sorry.
Don't be angry with me. [*he wants to kiss her*]
LOUISE [*tears herself away*]. I am not angry, only leave me in peace.
DANTON. What's that? I apologize for a trifle, as if for God knows what
wrong, and you push me away like someone with the plague?! Enough
of this neverending comedy! [*he holds her tightly against him*]
LOUISE [*looks him in the eyes, from below*]. Why don't you strike me? Isn't that
one of your laws?
DANTON [*yields suddenly; with a sad smile*]. You deserve it, to tell the truth...
[*he embraces her less sharply and more tenderly now*] My reluctant wonder
... [*with some difficulty, unnaturally perfunctorily*] and I know you do not
love me... but I am no disgrace for you, my dear. To be Danton's wife,
child, is no mean thing—wait three days more, and you will know...
how much this monstrous husband of yours is worth... [*he takes her
face in both his hands; softly, intensely*] Louise... I want you to be the mistress of all France.
LOUISE [*starts, terrified; a note of plebeian common sense in her cry*]. Have you
gone mad?!!
DANTON. What, are you afraid? Afraid by my side?! Have the courage to go
mad, yes, you too! [*kisses her passionately*] What—have you forgiven me?
[*She shrugs with resignation.* DANTON *stretches his left hand to reach the chan-*

delier] Well then, come . . . let's put out the light so that you do not have to see me . . .

LOUISE [*goes cold and numb in his hands*]. Georges . . . I am *so* tired . . . I have felt worse and worse for the last few days . . . Georges, please, have . . . [*a spasm in the throat interrupts her speech. She finishes her plea with her head turned away*] have mercy on me! . . .

DANTON [*is holding her very delicately, concerned*]. My only child, why did you not tell me this before? You really look worse . . . Louison, my dearest, what is it? [LOUISE *shrugs her shoulders to signify she does not know.* DANTON'*s face lights up with sudden joy*] Ah . . . maybe you're . . . ?!! . . . [*shakes her with passion*] Louison! Tell me!!

LOUISE [*close to fury*]. Don't pull at me! I don't know!

DANTON [*freezes, very calmly*]. Forgive me, my darling—go, and sleep peacefully.

[*He lets her go, kisses her hair so delicately that she does not feel the touch. She leaves the room. Standing lost in thought by the table, he adjusts his tie, grimacing. Someone's squeaking boots are heard on the stairs.* DANTON *straightens himself up, tense again.*]

WESTERMANN [*enters without knocking, clumsily, as if slightly dazed*]. Good evening. [*falls onto a chair, but lifts himself up at the sight of a carafe on the table*]

DANTON [*waits a while, while his guest pours himself a drink—at last says, irritated*]. Well?

WESTERMANN [*a glass in his hand*]. So you don't know anything yet? [*drinks*] You were asleep again, like on the tenth of August?

DANTON. Will you talk? . . .

WESTERMANN [*pours himself another drink*]. Total washout. [*puts away the glass and sits down*] Ugh, wine fit for women.

DANTON [*having overcome his shock*]. What do you mean?

WESTERMANN. What do I mean? The Committee has sniffed it out, the beasts. Three sections were already alerted; pity. But what can we do? [*he sighs, arranges himself comfortably*]

DANTON [*standing lost in thought*]. Hm . . . well, it would not have worked *now* in any case . . . [*he begins to walk round*] Who knows . . . maybe it's even better so. [*turns to his guest*] What really did happen? Tell me!

WESTERMANN. An hour ago some fifteen people were arrested—Vincent, [DANTON *stops and supports himself on the table*] Ronsin, Hébert—I don't know. The whole crew. [DANTON *sits down and rests his head*] Listen, Grand Judge: don't you have anything better? [DANTON, *without a word, takes another bottle out of the cupboard, puts it on the table, sits down again and*

taps his fingers on the top of the table. WESTERMANN *tastes the drink.*] Ah yes—
this is something. [*drinks with approbation. Wiping his mouth*] Robespierre has come back today. [DANTON *stops tapping*] I saw him in the palace park a little while ago—the Convention is sitting now.
DANTON [*gets up*]. I expect it is. . . [*he paces for a while. Suddenly*] That means
they will disband the Revolutionary Army.
WESTERMANN [*surprised*]. How do you know? [DANTON *laughs harshly*] So it is
said, in fact. . . I don't know anything about that. [*pours himself a drink*]
DANTON [*suddenly stops in front of him*]. You know, West. . . it's a miracle you
are still free. [*pause; half to himself*] A suspect miracle. [*thinks, looking at
the floor. Suddenly he bursts into light laughter*] Ah! It's simple!—They
wouldn't dare!

[*He sits down in cheerful spirits.* WESTERMANN, *hit by some sudden thought,
abruptly puts away the glass.*]

WESTERMANN [*after a while*]. Maybe they just. . . don't know?! [DANTON *indifferently shrugs his shoulders. Another moment passes*] The Convention has
just met in full assembly. . . [*a tense pause. He starts briskly to his feet; supporting himself by putting his elbows on the table he begins to talk across it, softly
and fast*] Man. . . can't you see that Vincent's fiasco is a windfall for us?!
Just consider: all of Paris is prepared for the coup, like a barrel of powder; the Convention has arrested Vincent and is happy that everything
is in order—but meanwhile, I have remained, and I too know how to
light the fuse!. . . You know what we must do? Ring the alarm bells now,
yes, in the dead of night. The insurrection will be like thunder out of
the blue sky—they will not even try to resist. I will not give them time. I
will quickly gather the sleepy Sections—the crew from the sociétés will
let the counterrevolution out of prison into the streets—there will be
total confusion. The enraged mob will, quite by chance, of course,
drown the Convention and put all the bigwigs to sleep forever, starting
with the Committees. On the next day, Danton—Paris will come and
implore you to deign to assume power. You know how it is. . . they will
see in you their only salvation. You will accept; but you will need five
days to overcome chaos—and five days are enough for York to surround
Paris nicely. [*expectant pause;* DANTON *is silent*] We know that Jourdan in
the North will readily let the English through. We, the generals of the
Republic, have also have had enough of that government of lawyers,
who treat us like common soldiers. . . Danton, I *guarantee* you success!
And such a chance comes along only once!
DANTON [*leans backwards against the arm of his chair, puts his hands in his pock-*

ets, looks WESTERMANN *up and down with half-closed eyes*]. To call the English!...To let our inveterate enemy into the very heart of France! To make the City of the Tenth of August a prey to Pitt's paid hirelings! You Judas!!

WESTERMANN [*looks at him with slightly open eyes. Speaks when the first shock is over*]. Dan-ton...not more than a week ago you were considering how York could be brought over after the coup...

DANTON. You fool! A week ago the country's salvation depended on an immediate agreement with its most powerful enemy! Today...the situation is radically changed. Now France can and must relentlessly strive to annihilate utterly that nest of snakes—Not one word more! I have spoken.

[*He gets up, excited, and walks round.* WESTERMANN *sits down again, speechless.*]

WESTERMANN [*shyly*]. You see, Danton...I know very well that I am an utter fool when it comes to politics...and that you are incomparably more clever. Oh, I know that...But...when one already has as much on one's conscience as you, and...

DANTON [*turns round majestically*]. What for instance?...

WESTERMANN [*fast*]. But...of course, nothing wrong...nothing really... but with these crazy revolutionary laws... [*with passion, though softly*] Well, let them find out, for example, that it was you who started that affair with the India Company! But that's nothing compared to...just think how easily it can now come out that it was you who meant to become the Grand Judge!! After all, striving for dictatorship is for them the most horrible of all crimes—high treason is nothing in comparison! If *this* comes out...you're finished.

DANTON [*sits down, in a good mood*]. Oh, yes? And who would finish me?

WESTERMANN. Who? The Committee, of course! Robespierre is back, Danton!...

DANTON [*angry now*]. That ridiculous Committee of theirs would dare to touch *me*?! Or maybe Robespierre would! Let him be back, let him sit on the Committee day and night, let him become the Committee! That anemic weakling does not stand in my way in the least.

WESTERMANN [*lost in thought*]. Well...if you think so...you are cleverer than I am...

DANTON. West, just think: I am backed by big business; I, the man of the Tenth of August, am backed by the people of Paris! And Robespierre? What support has he got? His Jacobins. Full stop. At the Convention everyone must be careful not to pick a quarrel with me, because they know that the Center—a great majority—will always support me in all things! Do you know why you are still free? Because the Committee doesn't dare arrest a friend of mine!

WESTERMANN [*hesitantly*]. Yes, but. . . please don't be angry, Danton. . . you see, Robespierre knows how to intimidate people, like no one else. If he intimidates the Convention. . . nobody will support you. Nobody. Moreover—if you have Paris for you, he has the provinces, and. . .

DANTON [*gets up with a triumphant smile*]. Ha, ha! Just let him try! Let him mobilize society against me! Westermann: I have created a talisman against which Robespierre's mesmeric technique loses all its meaning; it's the "Vieux Cordelier." Thanks to that it is *I* who have assumed control over France's mind. Through it I exert a hundred times stronger influence than that charlatan. Today several million people think as I think and want what I want: because several million people read the "Vieux Cordelier." You know, West, if Robespierre dared to challenge me today, it would mean that he was mad.

[CAMILLE DESMOULINS *rushes in, very excited.*]

CAMILLE [*piercing voice*]. Georges!!. . . [*somewhat calmer*] Oh, you have a visitor. . .

WESTERMANN [*does not move*]. It's only me, Camille—am I in your way?

DANTON. Stay. Well, Camille? Have a drink. Well, what have you done now?

CAMILLE [*avidly drinks a glass of wine, puts the glass down, speaks in a half-whisper*]. Desenne has been arrested, Georges.

DANTON [*after a few seconds*]. . . . what are you blabbing about, boy?. . .

[*suspense*]

WESTERMANN [*gets up to pour another drink*]. And so the "Vieux Cordelier" has gone to the devil. Together with the Grand Judge.

CAMILLE [*hysterically*]. Danton: what am I to do?

DANTON [*still unmoved*]. First of all, be ashamed. You are behaving like a little girl.

CAMILLE. Just think: that damned seventh issue is already with Desenne! And when the Committee reads it—I'm finished. [*falls on the chair, hides his face in his hands*] Oh, Georges, Georges! Why did you make me write such awful things?. . .

DANTON [*glad to be able to take it out on someone*]. Because I didn't know I was dealing with such a stinking coward! By all means, go to Robespierre, fall on your knees, swear that I forced you with a whip to. . .

CAMILLE [*jumps to his feet*]. Georges! How can you insult me in this way?. . .

[*calms down*] You know perfectly well that I am totally devoted to you—
and that I'll never shake Robespierre's hand as long as I live. But give me
some advice!...

WESTERMANN [*rises*]. Danton, I am an ass, agreed—but now even the stupid-
est cretin will understand that one *must* put an end to the Committee.
You see...you didn't know Robespierre, after all. I'll go straight to the
Sections; all right?...

CAMILLE [*curious*]. What?

DANTON. No. Your plan is childish. Not the slightest chance of success. The
Sections would slip through your hands, and they would only pro-
nounce us outlaws and have us executed without trial, as rebels. No.
Thank you.

WESTERMANN. Danton, such an opportu—

DANTON [*out of all patience*]. Shut your trap! So this is your subordination?!
And what has actually happened? Desenne has been arrested! Can't you
idiots see that Robespierre is trying in this way to save what there is of
his prestige?! Tomorrow they will let Desenne go, and that will be the
end of it. And you, Camille, will print the new issue with someone else.

[CAMILLE *makes a gesture of protest, but is interrupted by an energetic knock on the
door. Without waiting for an answer,* DELACROIX *enters.*]

DELACROIX. Your dictatorship has vanished into thin air, my friend... [DAN-
TON *makes a contemptuous gesture*] You know already—so much the better.
And now, by God, let us all be careful: Especially you, poet! I've
brought you an utter fool, Danton. If you can win him over—you will
gain an invaluable weapon against the Convention. For he is passionate
as a madman, and there is no blemish on him. Not the smallest embez-
zlement, corruption, speculation—nothing at all! Bourdon will bring
him in any minute now.

[BOURDON *and* PHILIPPEAUX *enter. The latter greets all present with one silent bow.*]

CAMILLE [*rises and goes up to him*]. Welcome, Philippeaux! You are right to
come to us at last!

PHILIPPEAUX [*coldly*]. I do not belong to you yet, gentlemen.

DELACROIX. I have brought him to you because we have a common cause;
he insists on going his own way...

DANTON [*shakes* PHILIPPEAUX *cordially by the hand*]. And in politics that is a
great risk, and an even greater mistake.—Why should you not join us?

PHILIPPEAUX [*dryly and softly*]. Because I don't know your aims.

DANTON. Why, we are against the unlawful dictatorship of the Committees. . .

CAMILLE. Why, we aim at putting an end to the terror which torments the country. . .

PHILIPPEAUX [*matter-of-fact*]. So you declare publicly. I will join you, if I am convinced about the honesty of your aims.

DANTON. And what are you aiming at?

PHILIPPEAUX [*emphatically*]. I mean to render harmless the Committee of Safety. By arresting Desenne, and abusing the freedom of the press, they have indeed exceeded all reasonable bounds.

CAMILLE [*triumphantly*]. You see, we do have a common cause!

WESTERMANN. And how do you propose to render the Committee harmless?

PHILIPPEAUX. That is a matter requiring great tact and prudence. The Committee has become the heart of the state; so one must not touch it directly. What one has to do—without making any commotion—is to take away from it the resources of power which have outgrown its competence. That power must then be redistributed among the relevant organs, and the Committee must have left to it its original, legal functions.

WESTERMANN [*tense*]. Yes, but *how* do you want to achieve this?

PHILIPPEAUX [*somewhat hesitant*]. In the last resort. . .even with the help of the armed Sections. Because the Committee cannot offer resistance to the general will, expressed directly. But with this purpose in mind, the Sections would have to receive a basic moral preparation, and give guarantees that the prestige of the government would not be impaired.

WESTERMANN [*excited*]. This is the very plan I have put forward to Danton. Word for word. And I happen to have the means at my disposal: Vincent has prepared a few Sections for *his* purposes—all one has to do is to stoop and pick them up!

CAMILLE. What a chance! We must immediately. . .

PHILIPPEAUX [*frowns*]. But general! This would be done without any moral preparation! You would inadvertently carry through. . .a coup d'etat.

DELACROIX. Not at all! The responsibility for the behavior of the forces rests on the leader. So. . .

PHILIPPEAUX [*thoughtful*]. Well. . .yes. . .if the leader can be trusted not to let the situation be abused. . .

DELACROIX. A unique chance! We must have courage!

BOURDON [*softly*]. And it really is high time. . .

CAMILLE. We must act now! Today!

PHILIPPEAUX [*convinced*]. Yes. You are right.

WESTERMANN. You see. But Danton does not want to.

[*general astonishment*]

CAMILLE. For God's sake, Georges! Why not?

DELACROIX. You know...I am flabbergasted.

BOURDON. Well...Danton must have good reasons...

DANTON. I said: no.

[*a moment's pause*]

PHILIPPEAUX. Then you're a coward.

DANTON [*starts to his feet*]. What did you say?...

PHILIPPEAUX. That you're a coward.

[DANTON *rushes toward him.* PHILIPPEAUX *does not move. The others come between them.*]

DANTON [*controls himself*]. Such an insinuation cannot touch me: it is too ridiculous. Philippeaux is a good scholar, but has never encountered the masses. So he does not know that an insurrection *cannot* be controlled by anybody. Sections, once sent to the Tuileries—could suddenly drown the Convention, tear the Committees to shreds—and the leader would watch this powerless.

PHILIPPEAUX. You are slandering the splendid discipline and civic awareness of the Parisian Sections!

DANTON [*calmly*]. No: I know the masses. In a word, comrades: I refuse to approve the coup d'etat, as Philippeaux has rightly called it. We must concentrate our forces on a purely *parliamentary* offensive. We must open the eyes of the general public and the Convention to the Committees' transgressions. We must continue our attack day by day—until we make a hundred thousand breasts utter one shout of indignation, until the people we have roused abolish the new tyrant.

DELACROIX [*warningly*]. Eh, Danton...careful! One false step will be enough to lose the ascendancy over the Center! That is our trump card! If we lose it...then what?

WESTERMANN [*feverishly*]. That's exactly what I've said myself!

[DANTON *pierces them both with a furious look*]

DANTON. Yes! Philippeaux is right: one must not touch the Committee of Public Safety...for the moment. For this reason, my friends, we will not attack it directly, but indirectly—through the Committee of General Security. I have the battle plan ready. Bourdon: tomorrow you will open fire. Demand a close revision of the Security Committee's personnel. You must achieve the arrest of their main agent, Héron. Oh, my friends—it will not be easy for despotism to stifle our voice. The people support us—for they know that in us Freedom has found its last defenders. Courage, comrades!

BOURDON [*murmurs*]. Yes, courage... we are to endanger ourselves, attack the Committees openly... while he, if he occasionally speaks at the Convention... then it's always *for* the Committees.

DANTON [*eyes half-shut*]. What did you say, Bourdon?... I did not quite hear you...

BOURDON [*perplexed*]. No... I didn't...

DANTON. Would you like every child to see through our actions? [*he changes his tone and speaks to everybody*] When the Convention rouses itself and throws off the shameful yoke put on it by a handful of usurpers—the Republic will be saved. Then we shall be able to return to the shadow of our anonymous, modest existence. Peace and quiet among the general happiness will be our only reward, but oh, how sweet.

[*During his peroration he winks meaningfully at* WESTERMANN. *The guests prepare to leave.*]

PHILIPPEAUX [*takes his hat, shakes* DANTON*'s hand*]. Maybe I am wrong. If that's the case—I take back what I have said.

DANTON [*firmly shakes the hand offered to him*]. I respect you and am happy that we have gained such a brave companion.

[*He takes him to the door. Next goes* CAMILLE, *followed by* DELACROIX *and* BOURDON.]

DELACROIX [*softly*]. Somehow I don't seem to like what our Grand Judge is doing...

BOURDON. Let him be. He knows better than we do what is needed.

DELACROIX [*shakes his head*]. But to endanger my position at the Convention!... [*with sudden suspicion*] Ah... unless it's...

[*He goes out throwing a suspicious glance at* DANTON.]

WESTERMANN [*keenly rushes to the returning* DANTON]. Well?... Have you changed your mind?!

DANTON. No. But listen: establish closer contact with the more capable officers of the Revolutionary Army, even though it will be disbanded. From the former soldiers of the Army you will gradually organize a handful of trustworthy people, with some military training. I can pay a few agents. . . And don't lose touch with the popular associations, though they too will surely be disbanded.

WESTERMANN. Aha, so you're not giving up. . .

DANTON. Dictatorship? Yes, I am. I've had enough of this. I'm fed up. [*pause*] But it's good to have a group of armed people handy. . . just in case.

WESTERMANN [*after a while, thoughtfully, slowly*]. Just in. . . case. . .

ACT II   Scene 1

Conference room at the Comité de Salut Public. COLLOT D'HERBOIS *in the chair.*
Present are: BARERE, BILLAUD-VARENNE, CARNOT, LINDET, ROBESPIERRE, SAINT-
JUST, *and a* SECRETARY.

COLLOT [*responding to* BILLAUD*'s request*]. The floor is yours.

BILLAUD [*does not get up, sits relaxed. Speaks in a dispassionate tone, looking at his
hand which plays with a quill on the table*]. Comrades: for three months
now a certain party has systematically aimed at overthrowing the government. Ever more frequent and impudent attacks undermine our authority. You know that at Desenne's the issue of a certain broadsheet
has been found, in which the author virtually calls to arms against us,
the Committee of Public Safety. And yesterday their insolence went so
far as to try to obtain by a trick a decree paralyzing the Committee of
General Security.
   It is time to put a stop to this.

[*Pause. He suddenly stops playing with his quill.*]

   Comrades: I accuse Danton and his faction as the rallying point of
counterrevolutionary elements in France. We must put them out of
action.

[*tense silence*]

ROBESPIERRE [*at once*]. What?! Do you want to deprive the Revolution of its
most important activists?!

[*Silence is over, followed by confusion after a double sensation.*]

LINDET [*against*]. Indeed, this is folly!
COLLOT [*for*]. But Danton is not an act...
BARERE [*undecided*]. Once Billaud starts, he doesn't know where to stop.
CARNOT [*for, with sarcasm*]. It's high time to depri—
BILLAUD. Comrades!!! [*he waits for the ripples to settle*] Robespierre, you
   amaze me. Revolutionary activist? *Danton*?! You must be delirious?

[*murmur of protest by* LINDET, BARERE, COLLOT]

ROBESPIERRE. No, Billaud. Only I remember, and you have forgotten, it seems.

SAINT-JUST. Oh, Robespierre, we remember *too*.

ROBESPIERRE. Try to remember the past activities of the man, whom today you are ready to condemn...

COLLOT. That's right, go on!

LINDET. Go on, Robespierre, tell us!

BILLAUD [*almost frightened*]. Are you mocking us, or what?

BARERE. Well, I am curious...

ROBESPIERRE. Comrades: Danton created a revolutionary center out of the Cordeliers club in ninety and ninety-one, when the Revolution dared not open its mouth under the pressure of monarchist forces. Do you remember how we, Jacobins, let ourselves be outstripped in zeal at that time?

COLLOT [*with a wide gesture*]. Ho-ho!! We remember, we remember the slaughter in the Champs de Mars to which Danton drove all Paris like sheep—and then fled to the country!

BILLAUD [*furiously*]. And we remember the letter found in an iron safe, in which Mirabeau complained about the sums spent on the agent-provocateur Danton... [*sensation, incredulity, quiet indignation*] saying that the Revolution could be reduced to absurdity at half the cost. Better not remind us, Robespierre.

[*murmur*]

LINDET. That's slander!

ROBESPIERRE. What does the testimony of a traitor like Mirabeau matter? Comrades! It was not we who stopped the panicky flight of the government from the capital at the news of the capture of Longwy...

BILLAUD. And we did not expose Paris to the September slaughter, either.

COLLOT. We did not embezzle eight hundred thousand while in office at the cabinet...

CARNOT. Nor did we engage in criminal scheming with the enemy, or deliberately lose the advantage of two victories...

ROBESPIERRE [*butts in*]. It was Dumouriez, not Danton!

SAINT-JUST. It was not he, only his hireling.

BARERE. We did not promise the crown to every interested client in Europe ...

BILLAUD. And it was the incompetent tactics of the first Committee of Safety, not we, who brought the Republic to the verge of bankruptcy...

SAINT-JUST. And it is not we, Robespierre, who now try to break the Revolution in order to avoid punishment afterwards.

[*a moment's silence*]

BILLAUD. Well, Robespierre? Is your attack of fever over?

ROBESPIERRE [*breathes in some air*]. Not one of those monstrous accusations is based on evidence that would stand up in court.

[*protests and approbation*]

BILLAUD. Lawyer's tricks, Robespierre! This is all you have to rely on!

CARNOT. Every one of those charges is an irrefutable fact!

COLLOT [*breaks the argument with an exclamation, as if he has just remembered something*]. Ah!....A propos of evidence. [*rings the bell.* JANITOR *enters*] If you please, ask citizen Amar from the Committee of Security* to come to us. [*turns to his colleague*] I think, though, that you have given up persisting in your...whim, Robespierre? [ROBESPIERRE *is sitting lost in thought; he may not have heard the question*] On the other hand, Billaud ...to make Danton harmless is not such a simple matter. We cannot arrest him outright.

[*approval, particularly* BARERE's]

BILLAUD. Of course not. We'll organize a campaign. First, one must surround him closely and isolate him in the eyes of public opinion....

ROBESPIERRE [*straightens up*]. Comrades: In no circumstances can I agree to have Danton brought before the Tribunal.

BILLAUD [*starts, touched with a horrible suspicion*]. Robespierre...you are afraid!

ROBESPIERRE [*amidst tense silence replies, smiling, in a friendly-mocking way*]. Comrades: Danton is an individual. We are the Revolution. Instead of devouring one another to the joy of our enemies, let us catch him by his paws and compel him to serve us.

COLLOT. Eh, Robespierre! That is a poem of chivalry, not a tactical plan!

ROBESPIERRE. It is easier to cut off heads, I agree. Listen to me: I am convinced that Danton always acted in good faith. [*laughter; indignation; applause*] His wrong ideas prove only that he lacks tactical ability, not that he has criminal intentions. And now he sees to his horror that every one of his mistakes can be given a monstrous meaning. Danton's is a primitive nature, with a weak moral sense. When threatened, he loses his

*The Committee of General Security.

head and is ready to save himself even by committing a crime. Comrades: what is he compared to ourselves? He is drowning! To behead him now—when he is almost defenseless—would be a barbaric nonsense.

BILLAUD [*with hate*]. You have a beautiful soul, comrade.

SAINT-JUST [*sluggishly, as if to himself*]. He is defenseless...that's priceless.

ROBESPIERRE. Yes! His only serious weapon was the "Vieux Cordelier." That was what he captured the minds of the masses with. We have abolished that magazine with a stroke of the pen. Danton *is* defenseless.

COLLOT. Really. Tomorrow Camille will begin to publish the "Young Jacobin." Defenseless!

ROBESPIERRE. It doesn't matter! Danton can neither think nor write by himself; so it is enough...

COLLOT [*softly, his eyes narrowed*]. ...to remove Camille.

[*tension; silence.*]

ROBESPIERRE [*his heart has virtually stopped beating*]. ...to win Camille over, Collot. That baby grasps at every glittering shred of thought. He will become a fanatic for our ideas, if only we are able to dramatize them effectively for him. And Camille as a propagandist is invaluable!—But we are not talking about that calf.

COLLOT. How do you intend to carry these poetic intentions through?

ROBESPIERRE. By arresting, under some trifling pretext—as Hérault has been recently—all the leaders of Dantonist opposition at the Convention: Delacroix, Bourdon, Merlin de Thionville, and the rest. Camille, terrorized by the effects of his mischief, will not speak up again so soon; and Danton will suddenly find himself literally alone. He cannot flee, so—of necessity—he will come to us. We will receive him; and—knowing that the safety of his invaluable person depends on his good behavior—he will exert himself in the service of government till he grows quite thin.

SAINT-JUST. And then he will use his position to sell our secret plans to the English.

ROBESPIERRE. We will guard him...

LINDET [*explodes*]. By lumping the Man of the Tenth of August together with snoopers and counterfeiters, you are degrading Revolution itself!

[*murmur of commotion*]

ROBESPIERRE [*breaks it with a piercing cry*]. O!!...Did you hear this, Antoine?!

JANITOR [*opens the door amidst astonished silence*]. Citizen Amar.

COLLOT. Welcome, Amar.—We are having a heated argument about Danton; Robespierre insists on defending him. Please, repeat to him what you confided to me last night.

AMAR [*sits down. Strikingly pleasant voice; the typical behavior of a high-ranking police officer*]. Well then, comrades—as the person in charge of the investigation into the India Company's blackmail, let me tell you that it was Danton who acted as an intermediary between deputies and bankers, and undertook to spread corruption at the Convention. It is beyond any doubt that if Fabre forged the clearing decree in favor of the blackmailed Company, then no one but Danton instigated the tasty affair. We now have proof.

ROBESPIERRE [*too vehemently*]. I know your proof. Three sentences in the midst of Basire's drivel! Wonderful proof!

AMAR [*unmoved in his calmness*]. Well, those three sentences, Robespierre, have been unexpectedly confirmed.—There was talk, was there not, about the suspicion among the gang, that Danton had had separate dealings with the financiers? [*with a polite look he begs for correction, if wrong*] Thanks to the investigation by our service it became clear that Danton had started visiting Batz towards the end of August. Then he brought over Fabre; eventually small fry were sent among whom the dirty and risky work was distributed: Chabot, Basire, Delaunay etc.

BILLAUD. Towards the end of August!...

AMAR. Yes; Robespierre, that means directly after the violent attack on the Company. When it was already cooked. Helpless. When it virtually begged for gross blackmail. I can produce protocols of the depositions at any time.

[*Long silence.* ROBESPIERRE *supports his jaw on his fist: he does not move.*]

BILLAUD [*quiet, tired, sad—with him those are the signs of triumph*]. Oh, Robespierre! Your once infallible intuition!...

[*Suspense. They all look at* ROBESPIERRE.]

BARERE. What's the matter with you? Are you praying?

ROBESPIERRE [*straightens himself up, then leans on the chair's arm. His hand, lying on the table, catches a sheet of paper and begins to crumple it. He talks to the* SECRETARY, *delicately showing him the door with his head*]. What I am going to say now is off the record.

[*The* SECRETARY *disappears at once. Something in his face and movements attracts* ROBESPIERRE'*s attention even now.—When the door has been closed*]

I am putting my cards on the table, comrades: I do not believe in Danton's integrity either.

[*murmur of aggressive surprise*]

VOICES. Well then?...What do you want?! How could you...
ROBESPIERRE. But even if he is a counterfeiter and a traitor...I do not agree to his execution.

[*He rises. For the first time he talks in the tone and voice of a speaker*]

You are right, Collot: politics is not a poem of chivalry. Justice, gentlemen, is a virtue of almighty God. It is not accessible to us; we must fight. The Revolutionary Tribunal is not just. [*sounds of protest and astonishment on the part of* COLLOT, CARNOT, *and* BARERE] It is not a court of law: it is a weapon. It is there to destroy enemies, not to punish the guilty. One must be aware of this fact, gentlemen—and sacrifice conscience, as we sacrifice life. Fabre, Danton, and Chabot have committed a crime. For that crime we shall put Fabre and associates to death; Danton, whose offense is the greatest, we shall not touch.

[*murmur*]

Danton's execution would push the well-to-do into the ranks of counterrevolution. And until we can impose our laws on Europe, the neutrality of money is a vital matter for us. By executing Danton we would unite the majority of the Convention against us. We would shake the people's faith—unwavering till now—to its very foundations. And above all we would kindle the fire of fear—and condemn ourselves to the rule of terror. Gentlemen: terror is ruled only by *despair*. You know what that means.

[*short pause. Total silence*]

Yes, Billaud: I am afraid. I am afraid of terror; to the extent of being ready for compromise, humiliation, lawlessness—if only to save France from it.
  The good of the country demands baseness from us. The villain and traitor, Danton, must avail himself of the privilege of exceptional amnesty. We must not be just. [*he sits down*]
BARERE [*after a long, empty moment*]. What...Robespierre a follower of Machiavelli? I don't think I have understood you right...

[*weak murmur of surprised arousal*]

ROBESPIERRE [*grins*]. Machiavelli is waiting for you all, fanatics of liberty, comrades—you are all going that way, one after the other.

[*long silence again*]

CARNOT [*weakly at first*]. Yes, but Robespierre...we are opening the campaign on three fronts! This spring we *must* topple the coalition. Think what concentration of effort will be required!And the defeatist Danton will move heaven and earth in order to bring about a speedy peace at any price!

SAINT-JUST. Maxime: a decisive offensive—internal government—creating new institutions in every sector of social life. Doing all that, should we tolerate that mad bulldog at our feet? Where are we to find the time and strength to repulse the everyday attacks?

ROBESPIERRE. Comrades: if Danton is sane, he *must have* realized that the Committee will not be abolished. Danton's surrender is a matter of days.

BILLAUD [*slowly*]. But if...*not*, Robespierre?

ROBESPIERRE [*breathless, after a short pause*]. He will be executed. But then... [*in a voice somewhat changed*] Comrades, it is the last resort which we *must* prevent.

JANITOR [*in haste*]. Citizen Vadier with a very urgent...

COLLOT. Let him come in!

[*Without waiting for an answer,* VADIER *pushes the* JANITOR *away and rushes in. Red with anger, he stops by the table.*]

VADIER. They've started again! This really is too much! An hour ago they attacked the Committee of Security again...

BILLAUD. Where?

VADIER. At the Convention, of course! My friends, this smacks of a coup d'etat! Today they had their way: Héron has been arrested!

[ROBESPIERRE *is motionless, deadly pale. Shouts of indignation and amazement.*]

LINDET. Who is he?

AMAR. Héron?! Why, he is the chief of political police, the only sure agent we've got. Without him we are powerless: we lose control over Paris.

VADIER. It is as if the Convention had dissolved our Committee.

SAINT-JUST. Who started it?

VADIER. Who if not Bourdon de l'Oise?

[*Pause. They look at one another.*]

COLLOT. Your defenseless Danton, Robespierre.

BILLAUD. Surrender, indeed.

ROBESPIERRE [*starts to his feet. Flushed cheeks. Quietly*]. Come, Saint-Just.

COLLOT. Where are you going?

ROBESPIERRE [*with rage*]. To talk to the Convention! I'll tell them to retract every word of that idiotic decree. I will give you your Héron back, Vadier, never fear. [*they rush out*]

VADIER. What? Has he been defending Danton?

BARERE. Ho, ho—and *how!*—I am still hot all over.

AMAR. If he has not gone mad—then he must feel sinful love for that ugly mug.

COLLOT [*thoughtful, with downcast eyes*]. Hm...My friends: the fact is, none of us knows Robespierre. Only God knows what there is behind those ever aggressive eyes...

BARERE. No, gentlemen. You forget that Danton's destruction is the destruction of Camille Desmoulins. You have forgotten how obstinately the Incorruptible compromised his popularity with the Jacobins in defending that little fool. To my mind—there is no mystery.

BILLAUD. Such nonsense you could leave to historians.—And Robespierre is right, gentlemen; it's a bad business. If we topple Danton—we shall then have to rely on terror, it's a fact.

COLLOT. One must be hysterical to be afraid of terror.

BILLAUD [*tired*]. One must be a fool to introduce it rashly. We shall also create a terrible precedent.—But...we have no choice.

BARERE. The fact is, though...whoever forces the decree of impeachment out of the Convention—will take a horrible responsibility on himself.

LINDET. More than a man can bear.

BILLAUD. It's for this that we have been chosen.

COLLOT. Well, gentlemen—let us continue our deliberations. The next point on the agenda is Barthélemy's dispatches from Geneva.—In half an hour two of you will be so good as to go to the chamber. Maybe the delegates will need help.

[*He rings the bell. The* JANITOR *appears*]

Ask one of the secretaries to come in here.

Scene 2

Vestibule of the Convention. There are three entrances: the one on the left leads to the chamber; the one upstage leads to the park; the one on the right leads to the gallery. Downstage on the left is a bench, at the back a group of armchairs round a table. Big windows face the park. DANTON *is seen pacing in a state of excitement.* CAMILLE *rushes out from the chamber.*

DANTON. Well, my boy? Danton's lost, is he? Buried?

CAMILLE [*fervently*]. How could I doubt you, even for a moment! Georges, forgive me that minute of inconceivable blindness.

DANTON [*catches him by the arm*]. Fear, my friend. A most ordinary fear. But today you have gained a new courage, eh? Will you dare to take up your pen again?

CAMILLE. Danton: I will not allow even you to make such jokes.

DANTON [*grips and squeezes him*]. What, you won't allow it?! [*squeezes him stronger*] You still won't?

CAMILLE [*swooning*]. Mm-n-mm . . . oh!

[DANTON *lets him go, but holds him by the arms*]

DANTON [*triumphant half-whisper*]. My boy: do you understand that we have swept away the Committee of Security?! From now on snoopers can't harm us.—From today honest people can breathe . . . and act. [*more softly and passionately*] In a week the Grand Committee will cease to exist. In eight days Paris will have the choice between The Last Judgment on earth—and myself.

CAMILLE [*fascinated*]. Georges: the tormented country calls on you for help! Only you can hear this call. You alone, against thousands of madmen, will save the Fatherland from the hands of her oppressors.—Danton . . . you are great.

DANTON [*pats him cheerfully on the shoulder*]. You cheap flatterer!

CAMILLE [*more softly, clasping his hands nervously*]. Georges: send me to die. I want to die for you.

DANTON [*gives a friendly laugh*]. Better write, instead of dying . . . what use is your corpse to me?

[*from the chamber emerge* DELACROIX, BOURDON, *and* PHILIPPEAUX.]

CAMILLE [*runs up to* BOURDON *and embraces him*]. Bravo, Bourdon! Bravissimo, brother! You've taught them a pretty lesson!!!

DELACROIX [*at* BOURDON'S *other side*]. Vivat Bourdon! Long live the conqueror of Comsur!—Eh, Camille...

[*They come to a quick decision and unexpectedly lift up the victor.* BOURDON, *unprepared, sways and protests.* CAMILLE *faints from laughter.*]

CAMILLE [*staggers*]. Oh!....—Jump, Bourdon—no, I can't—Ugh! [*falls on the chair and fans himself with a handkerchief*]

DANTON [*helps the victor to get down; clasps him by both hands*]. Comrade: through my lips France gives you her thanks. We are indebted to you for the first great victory: you have inflicted on the tyranny of the Committees a wound which will not heal.

[*more loudly*] This victory, comrades, will consolidate the fearful majority behind us. In a few days we will grasp the reins of government and France will awake to *life* after the horrible nightmare of the Terror.

A week from now a hundred and thirty thousand young citizens will return to peaceful work. Our blood will cease to enrich the soil of our frontiers.

A week from now you will embrace those whose groans are heard in the dungeons of new Bastilles because they dared to demand general freedom. Fabre will fall into your ar—

PHILIPPEAUX [*unexpectedly, like a shot*]. What...that forger?!

[*consternation*]

CAMILLE. So you believe that shameless slander, that devilish lie spread by the Committees?! Fabre! That poet with the heart of a dove!...

[DELACROIX *and* BOURDON *exchange a private smile*]

PHILIPPEAUX [*comes in their midst and with his every word lowers the tense atmosphere of the circle*]. Gentlemen: the more I observe your tactics...the less I understand you. I too demand release—of the innocent—but not for such as Fabre! I too wish with all my soul for the return of normal conditions—but not at the price of the state's collapse! You have undermined the Committees, on whom the total burden of government lies today—and you have not up to now created an organ which would be ready to take power from their hands! But in that case, if the Committees suddenly collapse—the state must totter like a blown up fortress! Every child understands this! Are you mocking me?!

CAMILLE. And how do you know, Philippeaux, that we have not found an org... [*he breaks off under* DELACROIX'*s eloquent look*]

DANTON [*radically diverts their attention*]. My dear, if you don't like our action, why did you push yourself among us?

PHILIPPEAUX [*amazed*]. I did?!... It was you people who pulled me in!...

[*A tragic looking face timidly shows itself in the entrance to the right and shouts in a dramatic whisper.*]

VOICE. Danton!... Dan-ton!!...

DANTON [*turns round immediately—gives* DELACROIX *a sign and comes nearer*]. Well?...

[DELACROIX *diverts the attention of the others. Under his attack* PHILIPPEAUX *becomes offended. The Comsal's* SECRETARY *emerges from the darkness, but stays glued to the wall and constantly watches all entrances.*]

SECRETARY. Billaud has accused you of high treason. Everybody except Robespierre wants to execute you.

[*two seconds of clear silence*]

DANTON [*straightens himself. His hands, slightly raised on impulse, fall down calmly*]. Only me?

SECRETARY [*shaking*]. No—these gentlemen too—they know them all...

[*he wants to get away*]

DANTON [*grasps him by the arm*]. Stay!

SECRETARY [*frantically*]. If someone recognizes me, it's the end of me!

DANTON. Is Robespierre's opposition sincere, or false?

SECRETARY [*wriggles*]. How do I know?!—Someone's coming! Coming!!

[*he struggles*]

DANTON. And Saint-Just?

SECRETARY [*shaken by convulsions*]. He's supporting the resol— [*with his head turned to the window*] Christ, it's *him*!!!

[DANTON *frees him and turns away from him at once. The* SECRETARY *gives a momentary look round and disappears into the corridor from which he came.*]

DANTON [*in a loud whisper to those present*]. Eh, you! [*they hear him*] Get lost! [*motions to them*] Get lost! They're coming!!

[DELACROIX *is the first to understand and pushes them all into the passage leading to the chamber.* DANTON *perambulates, cheerfully thoughtful.*]

ROBESPIERRE [*bareheaded, enters first, followed by* SAINT-JUST]. ... here yesterday, and there were only buds. It's very early [*he notices* DANTON, *does not react even with the vibration of his voice*] as it is. Spring is temperamental this year.

DANTON [*from the distance, raises his hand in greeting. Only to* ROBESPIERRE]. Greetings, comrade!

ROBESPIERRE [*with perfect indifference*]. Good day.

[DANTON *exchanges hostile looks with* SAINT-JUST. *They pass each other by. Five seconds later one can hear time itself stop in the Convention, together with hearts.* DANTON *turns to the left and looks after his colleagues with such tension of hatred that his ugly profile, built on the jaw like a stone wall, acquires a certain absurd beauty.*]

BOURDON [*rushes in, terrified*]. Danton... my *decree*!!! They have just...

DANTON. Then hurry and defend it, you oaf! Go on!

BOURDON [*rests against the wall*]. Is it...*I* who am to defend it?!.... [PHILIPPEAUX, *even dryer than usual, slides in imperceptibly; with folded arms he rests his elbows against the table and listens*] Robespierre is furious. The Convention will revoke it on their knees. Comsur will get Héron back... but will not forget!—I shall be thrown out of the Jacobins today!—You come and roar as loud as you can, otherwise the devil will take us!

DANTON. Don't waste time. Left turn!...

BOURDON [*transformed. Leaning forward he moves a step towards* DANTON]. Danton: *I* am not worried by the investigation into Fabre and Vincent's affairs. Danton: it is not for my joy that I attack the Committees day after day.

[PHILIPPEAUX'S *arms drop*]

It is not *I*, Danton, who will be proclaimed dic— [DANTON *throws himself at him. In the struggle, he speaks more loudly*] ...tator on a heap of skulls ... [DANTON *presses on to him, puts his hand on* BOURDON's *mouth.* BOURDON *escapes by ducking under and shouts*] ...of the Committee of Safety. [*It is too late.* DANTON *breathes heavily, shaking with anger.* PHILIPPEAUX's *face turns the color of sculpting clay. Seeing that the attempt to stifle the freedom of speech will not be repeated,* BOURDON *calmly walks to the bench.*] And so *I* will not sacrifice myself for you. [*he sits down*] Go and defend your decree.

[CAMILLE *returns and stands by the door.*]

DANTON [*leans towards* BOURDON *with a satanic smile*]. Go and save your skin,

Bourdon. Were *I* to support you, brother—you would sit in La Force tomorrow.

BOURDON [*starts*]. What... [*calms down*] You can frighten your aunt with such drivel.

[DELACROIX *comes in quietly. He puts some papers into a briefcase, standing next to* PHILIPPEAUX.]

DANTON. Did you see that young man? He's the Comsal's secretary. He's brought me the news that they want to put me on trial. [BOURDON, *galvanized, rises slowly*] Calm down: only me. They don't know anything about you... for the moment. But try... just try to desert me! [*pause*] I am advising you now: put right what you've done wrong! That's my *advice to you*!!—Go on now: it is not healthy to talk to me.

BOURDON [*his hands at this temples, almost out of mind*]. Jesus... merciful... Jesus... [*softly, explosively*] And I knew it would end like this! I knew it!...

[*His hands drop. He looks round dully, goes to the exit.*]

DANTON [*points to the floor in the direction of the chamber; softly*]. Eh, Bourdon!

[BOURDON *turns back. Slowly, almost swaying, he disappears into the passage.* DANTON *accompanies him with a smile; on seeing the terrified* CAMILLE *he senses the presence of more witnesses—he turns round in a flash and stands face to face with* PHILIPPEAUX.]

PHILIPPEAUX [*shaking from head to foot. He can hardly speak*]. Ah... villain... you dirty... villain...

[DANTON *gives him a contemptuous look.*]

CAMILLE. Philippeaux!... have you gone mad?!...

PHILIPPEAUX [*burning like a torch. His physical strength is unequal to the strength of his passion*]. So the state is to fall to pieces... so that Danton can with impunity steal the crown?—So we fight the state of emergency, we attack the Committees—for Danton not to be put on trial between the instigator Vincent and the forger Fabre?!!... [*grasps his head in his hands*] Oh, what a cretin I am, by God... [*again to* DANTON] not to see through you at once! [*spits before him*] Ugh. [*he goes away*]

DANTON [*with a bitter smile*]. A sinking ship, what, you Vendean rat?

PHILIPPEAUX [*stops; over the shoulder, fervently*]. Let it sink as soon as possible!

DANTON. Run to the Committees and inform! They will amply reward you as they did Chabot, who's been in prison for three months now...

PHILIPPEAUX. They know you, what's the use of informing?—For that matter are they any better? [*he breaks down. More and more softly.*] O unhappy ...my unhappy country...

[*He walks out.* DANTON *falls tired on the bench.*]

DELACROIX [*approaches him*]. Things are bad, Danton. They couldn't be worse.

DANTON [*politely lifts his eyes*]. Running away?

DELACROIX. I expect so! Oh, Danton: you've cooked our stew with that decree, well, well!—How many times did I warn you that one must not overdo things? As long as we had the Center under our control, we could hold our ground.—You've had it now: you have provoked Robespierre, and he's deprived you of control over the Center with one stroke! Parliamentary-wise—we are dead and buried.

DANTON [*sleepily*]. Eh, Bourdon can put everything right.

DELACROIX. Put right! Impossible. Robespierre really is angry. You have sent poor Bourdon to certain death.

CAMILLE [*with bitterness turns away from the window*]. And you—are running away!

DELACROIX [*over his shoulder*]. How is it going to help him, if I let myself be buried together with him? [*thoughtful*] To tell the truth, Danton—I don't know how you intend to get away with it now. You let yourself be deprived of influence over the masses by the loss of the "Cordelier"— and today you have irretrievably lost your influence on the Convention. In a word—you have no weapons left.—What are you going to do, if you are indeed accused in the Committee?

DANTON. They have accused me already, brother, you've heard.

DELACROIX [*almost amused*]. So it's *true*?!

DANTON [*sleepily*]. Alas.

DELACROIX [*lost in thought grasps his chin*]. Oh, daammn... [*briskly*] In that case, Danton—we must vanish. Prestissimo. [*having made sure that* CAMILLE *is not listening, he sits down by the sprawling* DANTON *and begins to talk very privately*] —In this respect you are in a particularly advantageous position: approach the Minister about crossing the channel. I shall easily get passes to the coast. We will fly tonight.

DANTON [*with jeering melancholy*]. And take the fatherland on the soles of our boots, eh?

DELACROIX [*puzzled*]. You are not standing on the platform, Danton—what sort of an idea is that? [*after a short pause, more softly*] My friend, take my advice, dig us *both* out, while the way's still clear.

DANTON. The road's closed, brother. I've broken with Pitt.

DELACROIX [*when he has recovered his voice*]. On the Savior's wounds. . . *why*?!!

DANTON. For the good of the state. The enemy of France is my enemy.

DELACROIX [*has guessed it*]. It means Number Twelve is through with you.—
You know, Danton: *it is a pity*. [DANTON *sleepily shrugs his shoulders. His partner decides to rouse him*] Well, listen, my friend: I am not going to let myself be slaughtered for you. I will now fall ill for two days; if in that time you do not get me out of this—I will serve the Committees by providing information, and I'll do it less clumsily than Chabot.—Do you remember our mission in Belgium, eh? . . . A bon entendeur, salut. [*he wants to go away*]

DANTON [*roused now, jumps to his feet and roars, though still controlling the level of his voice*]. You shameless coward! Do you think I would be sitting and yawning here, were I really in danger?! Am I a piece of trash that someone like Robespierre could topple me with one finger? It is one thing to slander Danton behind his back, another—to touch him!

DELACROIX. Two days, Danton.—Goodbye.

DANTON. Eh, Lacroix! How much is precious Flemish lace these days? . . .
[DELACROIX *starts; he turns back somewhat unsure, pale with anger.* DANTON *goes up to him and stands now face to face*] It bound you to me. . . you're entangled with it. . . [*he draws a noose in the air*] Don't try to break those love bonds. . . just don't!

I have reserves you haven't dreamed of. [DELACROIX *impatiently shrugs his shoulders*] But I'll tell you this much: I am now entering the lists *myself*. I'll talk to that Robespierre, who pretends that he would like to challenge me; if I don't twist him round my little finger in half an hour—you can go and denounce me.

DELACROIX [*dryly*]. We'll see. [*turns round and walks out*]

[DANTON *turns to the bench. Through the door he hears the voice of the speaker; curious, he pushes the door ajar and listens with a sad smile, leaning against the doorway.*]

ROBESPIERRE'S VOICE [*strained to the maximum pitch*]. . . . by force to the chamber of secret councils and demanded three heads. He singled out three pillars of our finance administration. You know him. You know his three victims. For that matter, I can see all four of them from where I am standing now. You called them "tolerant." Here is their tolerance. Gentlemen! You destroyed a faction which wanted to smother the Republic in blood, panic, and famine. And now—you are thoughtlessly giving way to another, far more dangerous faction, whose *hidden* leaders have personal gain as their only aim—and know no moral bounds. You are docilely following people who consciously lead the state into the abyss.—Awake, gentlemen—and be vigilant.

[*Fervent applause.* DANTON *half-closes his eyes and laughs bitterly. Suddenly:*]

DANTON. Camille!. . . Come here, listen.

[CAMILLE *approaches.*]

ROBESPIERRE'S VOICE [*overcomes the prolonged applause*]. You have seen your mistake, gentlemen. I do not think that the decree of arrests, forced out of you by subterfuge, is worth wasting any more time on. Strike it out and pass on to more important matters.

[*Thunderous applause.* DANTON *shuts the door. They look at each other.*]

CAMILLE [*after a longish silence*]. I shall stay with you, Danton.

DANTON. Sure. Until such time as Robespierre deigns to beckon you.

[*he sits down heavily*]

CAMILLE [*gently*]. You don't know me yet, Danton.—I said I would like to die for you. As it happens, I shall soon have the opportunity to prove to you whether this was just talk.

DANTON [*gloomily*]. Much good it will do me. . . [*starts to his feet all of a sudden, regaining his vitality*] But what's all this nonsense about dying! I am in no hurry to go under the knife, nor are the Committees in a hurry to confront me! To raise a hand against the Man of the Tenth of August would be an act of madness that even the nutty little student Saint-Just is not capable of! All France would rise against them!

CAMILLE [*shakes his head*]. You know. . . I am beginning to lose faith in the people.

DANTON [*meaningfully and mysteriously*]. The people know their master, my boy. . .

Haha! The noble Robespierre dreams his enchanting dreams of power . . . he is not content to direct the will of the masses: he wants to dominate men to their marrowbones, to transform every individual by force into his paper ideal—every country abounds in such bloody Christ-like maniacs. But I, my child, *know* human nature. Instead of senselessly fighting it, I pamper it. That is the secret of my power. It is enough for me to speak three wisely chosen words, and whole crowds follow me, listen to me, and adore me.—And he—at the price of a horrible effort sometimes forces the people to submission. . . for a short while, after which there is a reaction: ever greater fear and deadly hidden hate.

CAMILLE [*shakes his head*]. Stop it. He has an amazing power over the masses.

DANTON. Haha! Exactly: as long as he watches them. He has no support whatsoever. All his power consists of magnetic juggling tricks known to every fairground swindler. . . that's why he has so smoothly taken the Convention from me; and that's why the Convention will return to me as soon as he leaves the platform. But he is so blind that he has chosen the masses as the foundation of his ambitious ideas, not knowing that they are his inveterate enemy! I don't fawn on the people, as he does; I detest the populace, I prefer good company. But if it really came to a clash—if we both appealed to the masses—all France would rush to my aid. . . against him.

CAMILLE [*roused*]. Then challenge him! Let him fight you!

DANTON. No, what for? I don't feel like straining myself.—On the contrary: I will be reconciled to him. I'll open his eyes to his dreadful mistake; I'll show him its fatal results, now not long in coming; I'll convince him of my superiority—and stretch my hand out to him. If he is in his right mind, he will give way to me. I'll put him on the right road to. . . to the right aim. Together we'll put a stop to this bloody farce.

CAMILLE. Georges: if salvation lies in a compromise with Robespierre, I prefer to die a thousand times.

DANTON [*pats him on the arm*]. You will grow out of it, my boy.

CAMILLE [*with striking intensity*]. Never—as long as I remember.

DANTON [*slightly surprised*]. Oh, really?. . . But you can be consoled: it is not we but he who must agree to a compromise.—And even if it were to turn out that Robespierre was not quite normal—well, I have means of defense at my disposal. And he has none.

CAMILLE [*curious*]. What means?

DANTON [*listens*]. You'll find out. . . Well, they've sung a requiem over our decree. Come on, my boy—let's go. I have a feeling that someone will pass this way soon. And just now I have such abhorrence for mankind that I could be sick at the sight of a colleague's mug. [*looks out of the window*] Well, it's just as I have said. Quick, let's go.

[*In the doorway they pass* BILLAUD *and* VADIER. *Exchange of looks, without greetings. They go out.*]

VADIER [*half-aloud*]. It's time to gut that stuffed brill.

BILLAUD [*emphatically does not answer and waits a while in order to stress it better*]. There's no noise. It means they've followed him. We can wait here.

VADIER [*a veritable mimosa as far as his self-love is concerned*]. You too are sorry for Danton, I see.

BILLAUD. I am sorry for France. To crack jokes about such an awesome dilemma is simply mean.

[VADIER *turns red as a turkey, but the return of the self-styled delegates cuts short the newly erupted quarrel.*]

ROBESPIERRE [*tired, sits down with satisfaction*]. Ugh!—Well, that seems to be settled.—Ah, you've come here too?

VADIER. As reserve.

BILLAUD. Well, did they resist?

ROBESPIERRE. Not a bit. They tried not to faint. Bourdon demonstrated that by decreeing the arrest of their main agent, the Convention paid its deepest respect to the Committees. Ugh!—Well, gentlemen, let's go back. [*rises*]

SAINT-JUST. One moment. Robespierre, don't let's waste time at the Committee: you've realized now that Danton does not intend to put his arms down . . .

BILLAUD. Well? . . .

ROBESPIERRE [*looks at the tip of his right shoe*]. Gentlemen: I'll agree to the fatal necessity, if I *recognize* it. First, I'll try to win Danton and Desmoulins over for the government; I have reasons to suppose that I shall succeed— when Danton understands the situation he is in. When I've carried through my intention, I'll reply to you yes or no.

VADIER. You want to confer with that traitor?!

ROBESPIERRE. Barère, that born go-between, will arrange the meeting.

BILLAUD. You, Robespierre, are to ask Danton for an audience-?!

SAINT-JUST. Beg him to give you his hand! . . .

ROBESPIERRE [*walks to the door, at ease*]. Oh, my dears, what are humiliations, if the state is at stake? [*laughs joyously*] I would fall at his feet, if it were necessary!

Scene 3

Café de Foy, chambre séparée. A table set. DANTON *in evening dress.* DESMOULINS, BOURDON, DELACROIX.

CAMILLE. Georges, what is it? Calm yourself!

DANTON [*ignores him, but agrees, haughtily*]. Are we safe, Lacroix?

DELACROIX [*reveals with one corner of his mouth his unpleasant smile*]. The landlord is watching over there. . . [*points to the main door*] I am watching here myself. [*points to the back door marked in the wallpaper*] And you can't hear through the walls.

DANTON. All right then. [*looks at his watch*] Three minutes to eight. . . [*starts walking again*]

CAMILLE. You know, Georges. . . I have a bone to pick with you. Just think. The Incorruptible has *begged*—humbly begged Danton for an audience! You should have come at half past eight, in a dressing gown, instead of dolling yourself up and waiting. He should at least feel you're doing him a favor!

DELACROIX [*still smiling, with his head delightfully thrown back*]. On the other hand. . . it was high time to grant him that favor, eh, Danton?

DANTON [*looks at his watch again; vehemently*]. Get out of here, all of you! It's eight o'clock.—You go—straight home, Camille!

CAMILLE. Be a sport, Georges, don't spoil my fun. I *must* be here to see him humiliated! Go all the way, Danton! Remember: he wanted to wipe his boots with us! Danton, pay him back! Bend him, you know, like *this*!

DANTON. Idiot. Bourdon, you go home too.

BOURDON [*quietly*]. No. I must hear with my own ears how things stand—so that I know how to tackle the Convention.

DANTON. You will do as I say. No eavesdropping.

BOURDON [*rises*]. Those days are over.

[*They all disappear through the back door.*]

ROBESPIERRE [*comes in* tiré à quatre épingles, *almost rejuvenated. He shakes hands with his enemy, with the false cordiality of a man of the world.*]. Good evening. You have been waiting? I am very sorry. [*sits down*]

DANTON [*sits down with him, distrustful, conscious of his lack of breeding*]. Why didn't you let me invite you to dinner? Are you on a diet?

ROBESPIERRE [*with a cordial, almost youthful smile*]. For God's sake! I hope I'm not due yet for diabetes or ulcers.

DANTON [*puzzled, more and more gloomy*]. In that case you must be afraid of poison.

ROBESPIERRE [*vastly amused*]. So I'm either a diabetic, or a maniac. [*half seriously, somewhat more softly*] No wonder—in *your* eyes. . . I must be a sick man.

DANTON [*feels the sting but cannot quite locate it. In any case, he has had enough. After a short pause*]. Why did you want to see me, Robespierre?

ROBESPIERRE. Ah, that's better. [*leans back, crosses his legs, changes totally his manner, even his voice*] Danton, your maneuvers are paralyzing the government. You were defeated long ago, but you won't surrender.—For certain reasons, Danton, we'd rather keep you than . . . remove you. If you give up your counterrevolutionary opposition and teach your parrot, Desmoulins, some new tune, we guarantee your safety and even—favor in the public eye. I trust you will take advantage of this unexpected boon.

DANTON [*quite confused now*]. You're forgetting yourself, Robespierre. I will continue to resist the Committees to the last drop of my blood. The good of the people is my only law. This is my answer to your insults.

ROBESPIERRE [*his hands entwined round his knee, his head slightly lowered. He raises his eyes, speaks in a somewhat dull voice*]. No catchphrases, please, Danton. I *know* you.

DANTON [*explodes, masking his concern*]. What is that supposed to mean?!

ROBESPIERRE [*looks at his hands, still entwined round his knee*]. It means I have . . . seen through you. A bit late, perhaps, only last autumn. But now I know how you got your fortune, how you treated with the enemy—about the king's life, about the crown, about peace. There's nothing that can make things worse than they are.

DANTON [*firmly supports himself. Leaning over the table, speaks gently*]. Who has told you all this nonsense, Maxime?

ROBESPIERRE [*as if he has not heard him*]. So you see, to speak of the "good of the people" is not in the best of taste, coming from you. But—for certain reasons—I have kept the sad things I know secret until now. And I am ready to go on deceiving public opinion. [*sparks fly from* DANTON'*s eyes*] I am ready to let you go unpunished, if you come to the side of the government. [DANTON'*s face has lost its gloomy expression, and become tense, ironic, sharp*] But this time it won't be a double or triple faced intrigue, my friend!

DANTON [*after a moment's concentration suddenly lifts his head*]. Let's talk like men, Robespierre. Yes, you have the advantage over me. But I warn you, I won't surrender to the government—to all those great Committees, and to the Convention, even if I am defeated. I will not kowtow to those inferior to me.

ROBESPIERRE [*almost pitying him*]. The government's inferior to you, is it?!

DANTON. As every mob is to an outstanding individual. [ROBESPIERRE *rapidly*

raises his head. His face assumes an attentive and hard expression] I will not be
humiliated before that mob. You will accuse me? Very well. I'll destroy
these empty calumnies without any effort at all. . . [*gathers strength to
force an answer*] And. . .you can't have. . .proof. . . [*all in vain. A tense
pause.* DANTON *changes tactics. He opens the bottle, fills both glasses*] All right,
Robespierre, let's skip the catchphrases.—Your health. . .since you're
not afraid of poison. [*They clink glasses and drink.* ROBESPIERRE *does it with
perfect indifference. After a good sip,* DANTON *puts the glass aside. He leans forward, with a tense smile*] I *despise* your government, Maxime. I despise it,
as—you do.

The ring of our despair, my friend, encircles the entire Convention,
both Committees. But we both of us make one exception—for the same
man. [*pause. With narrow smile*] You know well. . .for whom. . .

[*An exhausting pause.* ROBESPIERRE, *behind his immovable mask, tries to conceal
the fact that he is completely mystified.* DANTON *speaks again, more softly and with
a strange warmth.*]

I will not repeat this publicly, or confess it to my so-called friends. That
is why this first confession gives me real delight: I admire—adore. . .
you.

[ROBESPIERRE *is unable to hide his boundless amazement any more.* DANTON *begins
now to drink hard. An involuntary sincerity breaks on occasion through the falsehood of subterfuge, contrasting with it in an elusive, and ever more unpleasant disso-
nance*]

Because you are greater than me. Who was it who managed to make the
government his obedient instrument—who. . .
ROBESPIERRE [*sharply*]. Enough of this.—What are you driving at?
DANTON [*leans towards him with a serious, half-truthful sincerity*]. Reconciliation. You see, Maxime. . .
ROBESPIERRE [*angry*]. I beg your pardon. We are strangers to each other.
DANTON [*with a tinge of noble bitterness*]. Well then, you see, Robespierre;
above the heads of the mob, both within and without the Tuileries—I
am ready to pay homage to *you* as the only man greater than I in this
world. If you agree with me, then I think we can come to an understanding.
ROBESPIERRE [*after a short reflection*]. All right. This is a matter of form.—I've
mentioned my terms.
DANTON [*gently and cautiously now*]. By supporting your action in its present

direction, I would hasten your downfall. For your policy is . . . magnificent lunacy.

ROBESPIERRE. Your accusations leveled at us are childish, Danton.

DANTON. Of course, they are to impress the gallery. Your mistake lies far deeper. [*he leans forward*] You are isolating the Revolution, Robespierre! Your inhuman demands are gradually alienating the most fervent enthusiasts! At your heights one cannot breathe!

Take the terror.—I am not concerned with their stupid heads; heads are two a penny; but you are fighting thievery and corruption, and they are natural needs without which the state is *dying*! It is as if you forbade people to digest! Do you know what you will destroy with your terror? Commerce and industry. You are bringing us to a bankruptcy the country is going to remember for half a century.

ROBESPIERRE. What do you advise me to do then?

DANTON. To bring the Revolution down to the level of human nature. To reduce demands—to the level of what is possible. To reassure financial circles. In a word—to make Revolution accessible. And above all, to free France from the curse of war.

ROBESPIERRE [*half to himself*]. Exactly—when we are on the verge of victory!—You represent five percent of the population, Danton; I represent—seventy percent. You say: make Revolution accessible. I call this: betraying Revolution.—I'd rather see a catastrophe than such a hidden decay.

DANTON [*narrows his eyes*]. But only then would you reach the goal.

ROBESPIERRE. I don't understand a word you say.

DANTON [*a long smile*]. Don't you?

ROBESPIERRE [*angry*]. My aim, Danton, is to bring human existence to seventy percent of the people. So . . .

DANTON. No catchphrases, Robespierre: I *know you*.

ROBESPIERRE [*amazed at first, suddenly casts his eyes away into space, half-smiling*]. I wonder . . . *

DANTON. And you still won't take your mask off, though I see through it to every line on your face?! English blood, no doubt . . . [ROBESPIERRE *reacts with an Irish look, knowing that it is not worth correcting such remarks*] To lean on the mob, Robespierre, that's a terrible risk. How *could* you take this mud as a foundation. They lick your boots . . . for as long as you stand upright like a monument. But if you only shake! At the first sight of danger you will find yourself alone. If you totter, the mob will rush

---

*English words in the original.

to pull you to pieces. They will be red up to their eyes in your blood.—
That's the nature of the mob. The mob *can* be used, but not as your
base! And then, they have to be brought to heel by the whip and by
splendor, not by sermonizing!

ROBESPIERRE [*in a reflecting mood*]. In other words...our program is...ab-
surd?

DANTON [*astonished*]. I should think so! No, Robespierre: I am not playing a
vaudeville for you. I *know* why I don't have to be embarrassed before
you...The Incorruptible one! The people and its soul! You, who play
it like an organ, know it better than I do. That noisy void...How many
men are there? Two or three in a thousand. Less. The rest are trash.
Makes one sick...

Millions, billions of them. Born so that those few have their material
to make their world. *That* material is not worth saving. Every deed costs
hundreds of thousands, but the source is inexhaustible...

Wrongs of the people! Oh, Robespierre, if everlasting sweat in filth
and misery were not the natural element for the mob, they would have
died long ago, instead of multiplying like vermin!—Just try to give them
freedom and they will suffocate like fish on sand.

[*intently, almost awesomely*] Well, Robespierre, now you *know* me.

ROBESPIERRE [*thoughtful*]. Yes...now.

DANTON [*rises, supports himself on his fists*]. Then I will finish what I have to
say and deliver myself into your hands completely.

Oh yes, I did dream of absolute power. What else can tempt us, men
of genius, on this miserable earth? But I have given up. Disgust and the
deadly sadness of loneliness have hampered my drive.

To rule over cattle?—To hold them in contempt...to play with them
...and to keep silent for ever? Life's too short. It's a hundred times better to serve...the man, with whom one can at least be *oneself*.

You know what loneliness is. There was a time when you too were biting your own body under the hellish compulsion of silence. But you
knew how to stifle in yourself that cry of the living soul; I did not. My
trembling human nerves are not made of metal. I can still...cry.

I was looking for a man. I was looking like a hungry animal. Like a
maniac. I still see—like a nightmare memory—those thousands of dead
enamel mirrors where my thirsty face was reflected...until at last your
hostile eyes flashed a live thought to me in reply.

You are stronger than I. You are like a thin blade of steel. Behind the
calm mask there is the abyss of silent contempt...and the will, whose
drive nothing but death will break. It's you whom I adore. I curse you

for it, I should like to spit and tread on you.—It's you, you alone. . . whom I adore in this huge, lousy world, you. . . hero. Oh, I will not let you go. I have let you in on the secret of myself; I will bind you tighter still. I'll force you to take the right road. And I will serve you. . .

I am standing here before you like a man naked. I, who have lied to kings and ministers. . . I will keep faith with you, and with you only. Do you hear me? [*leans intently towards him*] Look into my eyes. . . Incorruptible. . . I have violated your secret. . . there's no need to hide yourself from me any more.

ROBESPIERRE [*raises his eyes*]. Danton; now you make *me* sick.

DANTON [*turns pale, winks, as if shocked, suddenly with quiet passion*]. So you sting, do you, viper? Instead of throwing a net of deceit, as I intended . . . I am literally offering you myself. . . and you'd perhaps like to turn me away. . . eh? All right, try. My life's in your hands; make use of a moment of frenzy. Try, and you will really win the crown, easily and in no time.—The crown that will burn your brains right through. . . before you fall under it. [*more softly*] Maxime. . . do you know what it means— deep down—to be a dictator? It's lethal. . . .

You are still human. You won't be able to bear *that*.

ROBESPIERRE. Are you raving, or am I delirious?. . .

DANTON [*leans to him even more*]. Listen, Maxime. I am appealing not to your human feelings, because you have none, but to your granite will: lean on me—on us, the elite, on the wall of concrete. . . not on a heap of dung! [*turns round involuntarily, speaks even more softly*] I will bring Camille to your side, that's nothing; [*more softly*] I will throw my entire faction at your feet. Just say: yes. One neutral word. I'll make you an emperor, Maxime. . . [*threatening*] Say it. . .

ROBESPIERRE [*rises quietly*]. You will excuse me, monsieur. We were both wrong. It's time to stop this tragicomedy.

DANTON [*leaps at him*]. You. . . weakling!—Just dare. . .

ROBESPIERRE [*grasped by the arm, smaller, at the mercy of a brutal pull*]. Now I understand. You are simply drunk.

DANTON [*hit to the core this time—with a sudden calm of hate*]. Do you know that there are four witnesses to all you have confessed?

ROBESPIERRE. I thought so. And that's why I disappointed them. Good night. [*goes away*]

DANTON [*rushes after him; stifled, indescribable shout*]. Maxime!!. . . [ROBESPIERRE *throws him a look from the door, like a slap in the face, and disappears.* DANTON *staggers and leans on the table. His eyes are wandering, his face gray, stiff, muscles flabby under the fat, his jaw trembling. He breathes loudly.* DELA-

CROIX *enters softly, with a deadly smile.* DANTON *controls himself at once and speaks briskly*] Well, you heard, I suppose?

DELACROIX [*poses himself by the door like a caryatid, as is his custom*]. Of course, my friend!

DANTON. A cautious beast, eh? Now he will at least have respect for me. I hold him in the palm of my hand.—Where's Camille?

DELACROIX. He's just run away, cursing like anything.

DANTON. So much the better. [*shakes his hand*] God, that kid!...

DELACROIX. Danton, the Girondists are still hiding in the forests. Let's go south. We'll squeeze through the Pyrenees. It's a chance...our last.

DANTON [*vehemently*]. You damned fool! Haven't you just heard they will not touch me! [*short pause*] A propos...you've reminded me of something. Westermann told me a couple of days ago that we could count on two thirds of the ex-Revolutionary Army...if it came to anything. Drop by to see him and find out the details about equipment, weapons, organization and so on. I had no time to ask him then—and I may forget.

DELACROIX. Very well. [*with a peculiar gleam in his eyes*] I'll pass on tomorrow any information I get, all right?

DANTON. Tomorrow...You know, I'd rather have it tonight. I'll be too busy tomorrow.—Come in an hour to the Enfants-Rouges. I have nothing to do now, so I'll entertain myself by visiting a few sections. Show myself, chat...It's worth reminding the people about one. One must not lose touch...

DELACROIX [*in the doorway, with slight stress*]. So in an hour...we shall talk again.

Scene 4

A wide passage between the chambre séparé and the main room. Light coming from the wings. SAINT-JUST *is sitting by one of three small round tables.* ROBESPIERRE *emerges from stage left. He does not see his friend in the semi-darkness.*

SAINT-JUST [*softly*]. Maxime! [ROBESPIERRE *shivers.* SAINT-JUST *rises, takes him by the elbow and leads him to a settee by the wall.*] Sit down! Let's talk. [ROBESPIERRE *arranges himself comfortably across the settee, leaning against its arm. He straightens his legs and crosses his feet, folds his hands on his chest, leans his head back to have support. Knowing him,* SAINT-JUST *can guess the result of the meeting*] Well then—all in vain?

ROBESPIERRE [*echoes indifferently*]. In vain.

SAINT-JUST. You've realized at last...

ROBESPIERRE [*sleepily*]. Mmm...

[*pause*]

SAINT-JUST [*more softly*]. Maxime: how *could* you make light of such an enemy?

ROBESPIERRE. I did not know him...

SAINT-JUST. Well, really!...

ROBESPIERRE. ...just as none of you know him. [*suddenly leans forward*] Alas, Antoine: he is not a vulgar, harmless epicurean pig.—He has a strong, fertile, and poisoned mind. It's just such a mind, equipped with perfect creative faculties—with impeccable logic—with dazzling imagination— and based on the absurd and giving birth to lies—that Satan himself must possess. Oh yes: I've made a fatal mistake. Danton is a source of the plague.

SAINT-JUST. Eh, you're using exaggerated words.

ROBESPIERRE. I shudder sometimes when I hear youthful foolishness speak through you, Antoine.—Words! What, if not words, shook France out of her foundations in eighty-nine? What keeps up faith in men today, what gives revolution its purpose and direction? In what else does man's spiritual life express itself?—Words!

SAINT-JUST. Let them. What does the influence of Danton's thoughts, and his words, mean—against the power of yours?

ROBESPIERRE. Is that what you think?!—My dear: the truth is always modest and not easily accessible, while a lie glistens from afar. It pervades the mind like oxygen in the blood.—My thought is powerless against Danton's poetic ravings, because his cheap lies take root much, much more easily.

Oh, if you could only hear him! The splendid scope of his premises— that encompassing gesture of synthesis—the monumental perspectives of a fictitious world...all this simplified to a convenient absolute!— Certainly, a man with a trained mind will smile sadly;—but the minds of the masses are *not* trained.

And *how* persuasive he is! How his gaudy stage effects produce results! Those generalities...childish and hellish!

No wonder Camille was lost at the very sight of such splendor. And we thought that it was he who fed Danton with ideas! Antoine: if Danton had more courage, he could bring the monarchy back in a month. If we give him time...he may do it. [*short pause*]

It can't be helped. He must be killed, as soon as possible. [*rises*]
Good-bye. I'll call a plenary session of the Committees for tomorrow
. . .afternoon.

SAINT-JUST [*also rises*]. Where to, Maxime?

ROBESPIERRE [*with indifference—but turns his eyes away*]. To Camille.

SAINT-JUST [*bars his way*]. Maxime. . .don't go to him.

ROBESPIERRE. Why ever not?!. . .

SAINT-JUST. Maxime—do not go to him! You have defended him—not only
for political reasons—to the point of causing a scandal. You will not save
him, and only. . .

ROBESPIERRE. What's this to you, Saint-Just?. . .

SAINT-JUST. Shall I tell you?—I am afraid about our cause, Maxime: your
manly blindness is worse than my youthful foolishness. Don't you
know him?! He's a cocotte, not a boy, that Desmoulins! Do you think
he will listen to what you are saying to him? He will begin to play with
you, utter empty phrases, assume noble airs. And you will watch helplessly how that pup with relentless consistency runs under wheels.
While tortured thus, you will confess everything, in order to make him
see the light at last. . .you will disclose your plan and forewarn the
whole gang. [ROBESPIERRE *shrugs his shoulders*]
    Maxime—Maxime—let your six months of flirting with. . .high. . .
treason be enough!. . .

ROBESPIERRE [*calmly*]. Who do you take me for, Saint-Just. . .a woman?
That I should betray a government secret. . .out of affection?! You
know, I should like to feel indignant for your indiscretion, but it really is
too absurd to get angry about.—Good-bye, friend.

SAINT-JUST. Hush! So you want to call us tomorrow afternoon? Why not in
the morning? Why not tonight?

ROBESPIERRE [*looks him up and down, slowly, systematically, head to toe, then says*].
Car tel est mon bon plaisir.

[*He goes out, followed by his friend's sad smile.*]

Scene 5

DESMOULINS'S *lodgings.* LUCILE, *22, is sewing, seated by the lamp;* CAMILLE *rushes
in, ill-tempered, throws off his cloak and hat, falls on the sofa and assumes a depressed pose.*

LUCILE. Well...? [*when her husband makes a demonstrative gesture*] Oh, my spouse! We've done something foolish *again?!*

CAMILLE [*assumes his typical position: elbows resting on knees, jaw on fists*]. Eh, you know, Lucile... [*she rises and acts an imploring mime*] You should really stop clowning when I... [*straightens up*] And yet, damn it all, I should be glad!... [*looks at her*] I have heard both the tigers talking confidentially.

LUCILE [*becomes serious and sits down near him, interested*]. Ah?...Well.

CAMILLE [*rises*]. Declaration of war! [*begins to walk round the room, somewhat nervously*]

LUCILE [*starts, terrified*]. What?!...

CAMILLE [*excited, pays no attention*]. Yes, and a very good thing too! Robespierre ought to be taught a bitter lesson: he will get it at last! Yes: I am glad. I am glad!

LUCILE [*stands by the table, en détresse*]. And how did this...?!

CAMILLE. He knows perfectly well he can't stand up to Danton. Otherwise he would not have asked him—ah yes, Robespierre...asked for an audience! The fact is, though, that Danton did not know how to humiliate him properly. That was what made me mad.—Sweet Jesus, if he had only...asked *me!!*...

LUCILE [*leans over the table, desperately*]. But listen, Ca—

CAMILLE [*turns round and stops*]. Lucile: do you remember how he used to make me a laughingstock at the club? Do you remember? They trembled before me, and he made a clown of me! And you have no idea how he humiliated me in private. It passes human imagination.—I'll get my own back now.

LUCILE [*almost shouting*]. Camille! How did it happen? You clearly said that Danton himself wanted a reconciliation?!

CAMILLE [*suddenly comes to his senses—sits down*]. Well, you know, I...didn't understand it really. I couldn't hear very well...In a word: I can't make out this muddle any more.—No, I am not a good politician.—But what of it! I am a great poet; and that means more...doesn't it, Loulou?

LUCILE [*pale with anxiety*]. Yes, of course, but...

CAMILLE [*straightens himself up suddenly*]. Oh, Danton's flatteries could have been a kind of sarcasm!...Of course!—O what an ass I've been! Well, *now* I understand all: Danton let him feel his inferiority so acutely that the enraged braggart rejected a reconciliation—even though by doing so he rejected the last chance of saving his neck! [*he jumps to his feet and starts perambulating again, rubbing his hands*]

LUCILE. Are you *sure* of this?—So you did hear?...

CAMILLE. Not everything, but it's all quite clear.—Well, so much the better. We will repay him the debt of humiliation, with a usurer's interest! I have been longing for that moment for three months now!

LUCILE [*supports herself by the table, stunned*]. And I have been trembling for three months. My most terrible forebodings have come true.

CAMILLE [*stops*]. Lucile, don't say such things, or I shall come to hate you as well! I am going to change; is Horace asleep?

LUCILE [*rouses herself*]. Yes. . .you must not wake him!

[*the bell rings*]

CAMILLE [*going away from the entrance*]. Great God! Who can that be?! Loulou: I am not at home.

[*He disappears. A knock on the door.* LUCILE *answers.*]

ROBESPIERRE [*enters bowing*]. Is your husband in?

[LUCILE *is numb with joyous surprise*]

LUCILE [*stands still, responds very late*]. . . . Yes. He'll be back in a moment. Won't you be so good as to wait?

ROBESPIERRE [*takes off and puts aside his hat, walking stick, gloves*]. With pleasure.

LUCILE [*approaches him silently from behind. When he straightens himself and turns round, she grasps him by both hands. She is standing just in front of him, in the middle of the room*]. Maxime. . .How *fortunate* that you should come today!. . .

ROBESPIERRE [*astonished, embarrassed*]. To what do I owe this hon. . .

LUCILE [*looking at him intently with all the might of her soul*]. God himself must have sent you. . .Surely not to mock me?!. . .Oh how awfully you've changed. I hardly dare to call you in a familiar way by name. . .

ROBESPIERRE. Yes. I have aged considerably.

[*They stand without moving.*]

LUCILE. Oh no! Only. . . [*having found the right description she erupts with nervous laughter*] Robespierre has grown far above the towers of Notre-Dame; but Maxime—has ceased to exist.

ROBESPIERRE [*thoughtful, looks ahead*]. Not—yet.

LUCILE. Maxime. . .is it true t-that. . .things are going to get worse? [ROBESPIERRE *confirms emphatically, having quickly stifled his surprise*] So the only hope is in you. [*still grasping his hands she pulls him over to the sofa*] I am helpless, Maxime. I'm in despair. Camille is an irresponsible child who has to be watched over and led by the hand. But I don't know anything about the world myself!—I've undertaken a task I'm not equal to. I am too weak and too stupid.—Why did you move away from him, Maxime? Why did you...leave him?...

ROBESPIERRE. As God is my witness, it was the other way round. And I did all I could to keep him by me.

LUCILE [*distrustful*]. Yes?...I must have been wrong... [*looks into his eyes again*] Be a man once more, Maxime! You are noble. I know you. Forgive him...just once more!—And take him under your protection!

ROBESPIERRE. That is why I have come. Moreover, I have nothing to forgive him for *personally*.

LUCILE. Does that mean...oh, Maxime!—Can I really be at peace?! Can I entrust him to you?!...

ROBESPIERRE [*thoughtful*]. I wonder which of us two is...more anxious for him, Lucile. [*short pause*] But we don't know if *he* will trust me. [*with sudden, suppressed passion*] Lucile, your influence is greater than mine. Help me!

LUCILE [*impressed, but dubious*]. You think so?—What am I to do then?

ROBESPIERRE. You must break Camille's association with Danton and his group, *at any price*.

LUCILE [*terrified*]. I?!...But Maxime: I'm a woman, I cannot meddle in these things!—It would be tactless and so...repulsive that our relationship would never recover!

ROBESPIERRE. No. The opposite rather.—But even if it were true: might it not be better to sacrifice your dignity and love than...his life...?

LUCILE [*moves back, her hands drop*]. ...his...his...

ROBESPIERRE. If he remains with Danton, Camille will hit the bottom, Lucile! —Do you know what that means? It's a state of the soul in which a man becomes capable of blackmail, deceit, and selling government secrets! You must make a sacrifice of your exquisite tact, Lucile, and help me with *all the means* possible!

[CAMILLE *rushes in and stops, numbed, to his horror feeling a pang of joy. He suppresses it with an outburst of rage*]

CAMILLE. I thought I distinctly said I was not in!

[ROBESPIERRE *is careful not to irritate him, and so does not smile*]

LUCILE [*rises*]. You should be ashamed, Camille.—I'll leave you two alone. I'll see you before you go, Maxime!

[ROBESPIERRE *gets up and bows.* LUCILE *goes out.*]

CAMILLE [*stands in front of him, his hands behind his back*]. How did you dare
to come here?
ROBESPIERRE. I must talk to you about *important* things, Camille. But first
you must sit, or stand aside; I find it uncomfortable to talk looking up.

[CAMILLE *sits down, bent in a pose typical for him.*]

CAMILLE. Talk.—I know you. You have come here to torment me. [*he
straightens up*] You know what: our talk can't lead anywhere. Better not
to try.
ROBESPIERRE. You are in danger. I want to warn you.
CAMILLE [*shaken for a second*]. I, in dang—
ROBESPIERRE [*taking his chance*]. From *tomorrow*, Camille, a state of war will
begin between Danton and us. You don't know this yet. I have come to
. . .ask you: don't choose sides rashly. You don't know the danger
threatening you. Danton's friendship is not a disinterested one. . .
CAMILLE. First, Robespierre, Danton's friendship does not concern you.
Second: I am an adult and capable of looking after myself.—And, being
a fighter for liberty, I do not fear death.
ROBESPIERRE. Death is a trifle. But there are also such things as. . .deporta-
tion to Cayenne. Or an escape at night, in disguise, starving, to enemy
country.—These are things. . .worth thinking about.
CAMILLE. You will not wake a coward in me; and our friendship is stronger
than your envy. You will not break it up.
ROBESPIERRE. Those are barricades of dead rhetoric.—Why don't you dare
be yourself, Camille? Do you think yourself inferior to others?

[CAMILLE *is momentarily bewildered*]

Manly friendship is, perhaps, the noblest manifestation of human relations. But your association with Danton is not, my boy. The first condition of friendship is—mutual independence. But you have sold yourself
into a degrading, sentimental slavery, and Danton unscrupulously exploits your talent for his own dark purposes. This is an ambiguous part-
nership, not friendship.
CAMILLE [*badly shaken*]. You will never understand me, Robespierre.
ROBESPIERRE. Camille, I suppose you know that as a politician you're nothing.
CAMILLE. Maybe.
ROBESPIERRE. Not "maybe." It is so, my dear.—And as far as I am concerned, you know that, first of all, I am utterly honest; secondly, I

make relatively fewer mistakes than any of us. [*silence*] Camille, you know that, don't you?

CAMILLE [*overwhelmed*]. Well, yes, I do. Yes.

ROBESPIERRE. So, when you accused me in "Vieux Cordelier" of hidden ambitions and errors—you acted against your own better judgment. [CAMILLE *raises his head and gives a brief terrified look*] This is what you have been brought to. Danton does not like to expose himself to any danger . . . and he is engaged in three clandestine intrigues at the same time. So he finds himself a youth, whose virgin innocence is familiar only with the official shape of politics, but who cannot get the hang even of that. Then he implants ideas in him—oh, they sound lofty enough in their general sentiments, but in their application they act. . . in a way other than the naive speaker had imagined.

Calling for mercy and tolerance you thought you were saving the country. But in fact you saved counterrevolution from collapse. Such was Danton's intention. Camille, throw off at once the contaminated rag of that "friendship."

[*silence*]

CAMILLE. Even if these monstrosities are true—and I have no reason to believe you—*I* will keep my loyalty to Danton. If he betrays me—it is his affair. Why should *I* renounce my honor?

ROBESPIERRE. An excellent way of taking care of your honor. . . through high treason.—Because your attacks on the government, supported by all the factions of reaction, are just *that*!

CAMILLE [*definitely losing ground. He rises*]. Then I will throw down my pen—and defend Danton against blows with my bare breast. Having lost a sword in me—he will find a shield.

ROBESPIERRE. You find this heroic posture becoming, no doubt? And pleasant?—But do you know what? I pity you.

CAMILLE [*stiffens*]. You want me to slap you?

ROBESPIERRE. Well, at last! To get a sign of genuine life out of you—one has to scratch your vanity. The one point where you still react. . . you poor fool!

CAMILLE [*twists in his chair, covers his eyes with his fists*]. Oh, you. . . you. . . beast!!!

ROBESPIERRE. You see how defenseless you are, Camille? Just as much against accusations as against flattery. One can knock you over with one finger! Up to now you have risked only prison; but during a crisis one has to pay for every *word*—with one's life. For Danton you are just a pawn in

the game. To start with he lets you compromise yourself absolutely, because he knows your...vacillation; then he will entrust to you every
dangerous task. You will not realize the criminal nature of your own ti-
rades; and before you know it, the lid will close on you.

[CAMILLE *gets up and walks up and down*]

In a cause for which one lives and acts it is worth dying, or even being
sent to Cayenne.—But a moment of ecstasy with the rhythm of words
one can't understand?...

CAMILLE [*after a longish silence*]. Well, Robespierre; you've achieved your
purpose. You have shattered my illusions forever. You have destroyed
everything in my soul that was there to be destroyed. You can now rejoice.

ROBESPIERRE. I am rejoicing—because that "everything" was a tangle of
lies.—If only they would not grow again, Camille!

CAMILLE. Max...Robespierre: your presence gives me physical pain. Go
away.

ROBESPIERRE. I must first have your assurance that you will break with Danton and remain strictly neutral.

CAMILLE [*suddenly alive*]. Never now, dearest! Never! *Such* shame can only
be washed away with blood. Now I will simply force my way to the guillotine.

ROBESPIERRE. Well, just try. Try to compensate for the loss of two years of
your life—with the perfect nonsense of your death. I only wish that
while riding in the tumbril you don't come to see how monstrously
comical such a way out is. That would really be...the end.

[CAMILLE *slowly slumps in his chair and hides his face in his hands*]

Checkmate, Desmoulins.

CAMILLE [*suddenly rises heavily and stands in front of him*]. Get out. [ROBES-
PIERRE *shakes his head, slowly, seriously.* CAMILLE *begins to shake all over*] Get
out...get out...or I'll...strike you! [ROBESPIERRE *suddenly rises from his
chair and puts his hands on* CAMILLE'*s shoulders.* CAMILLE *twists himself at
first*] Ugh!...No!! Don't touch!!! [*He calms down and relaxes. His face
unexpectedly assumes an expression of adoration. He lifts his hands up to* ROBES-
PIERRE'*s chest, then lowers them.* ROBESPIERRE *slowly lets him down into his
chair.*]

ROBESPIERRE. ...that means one can begin a new game.

[*He sits down.* CAMILLE *continues to sit lost in thought, in a posture typical for
him.*]

CAMILLE [*after a while lowers his clasped hands to his knees. Speaks to the floor*]. You mean you would take me back, Maxime?...

ROBESPIERRE. My friend, *I* don't greet my guests with the words: "how did you dare."

CAMILLE. After all the insults I hurled against you... [ROBESPIERRE *shrugs his shoulders*] My God...how you must despise me!

ROBESPIERRE. He simply *must* have his melodrama!

CAMILLE [*strangely changed—raises his brow*]. You are great, Robespierre—but in your breast there is a burnt-out brick instead of a heart. [*rises suddenly and supports himself against the arm of his chair*] Do you know that I pity you?

ROBESPIERRE [*lifts his head high, but does not see* CAMILLE]. Because of my anatomical defect?

CAMILLE. Yes.—I am the happier by far... [*speaks with a growing tenderness, but clenches his teeth*] ...if only because I can suffer...like a damned creature... [*speaks ever more softly, with passion*] you green-eyed monster ...because of *you*.

ROBESPIERRE [*claps his hands, but hides his embarrassment*]. Camille, don't be a bore.

CAMILLE [*with growing passion*]. I am not boring you. I am making you hellishly embarrassed, making you lose your poise.—Would you refuse me that innocent satisfaction—for certain words...for certain looks...after which I still have scarlet stains on my face?...

ROBESPIERRE. I need comrades, my boy. I have no need for friends modeled on Shakespeare's sonnets. And slaves I treat as such.

CAMILLE. I shall be a comrade to you. I shall be anything you like. I'll change my nature from top to bottom as you wish...as proof of the "mutual independence" you require. [*he returns to his seat*] What am I to do now?

ROBESPIERRE. Free yourself from Danton *at once*. Then you will side with the government, or remain neutral; as you like.

CAMILLE. You've said it. I'll write to Danton right away. [*smiling*] He will make certain everybody else knows it...I can hear him now.

ROBESPIERRE [*cautiously*]. This...will not be enough, Camille.—Because your association was not a purely private matter.

CAMILLE [*slightly disturbed*]. Well?...

ROBESPIERRE [*after a few seconds' reflection*]. Voici: tomorrow morning you will appear in the Convention, revoking—but without your typical reservations!—your attacks on the Committees. Then you will write, as the eighth issue of the "Cordelier," a similar revocation concerning the content of the earlier issues. [CAMILLE *goes numb, his eyes widen*] Then you must publicly order all the copies of the seventh issue, including the original manuscript, to be destroyed.—That is all.

[*a long, terrible silence*]

CAMILLE [*at last leans backwards, with a long, broken sigh*]. Ah.... *Yes*!!! [*he bursts out in a hysterical laugh and slumps*] Ooo, Maxime, Maxime, Maxime!...

[*His head falls on the table, his body shaken with sobbing.*]

ROBESPIERRE [*rises soundlessly and snatches him by the shoulders with quiet brutality*]. You hysterical maniac, what is it now?!!

CAMILLE [*releases himself with a wild jerk; looks into his eyes, from below, furious*]. I have come to understand you at last......dearest. [*he gets up, assumes the arrogant, curved posture of a youth—puts his hand into his pocket, takes a chainlet out and begins to toss it up on his hand, talks with a slightly bent head*] It turns out that...after all, *after all*, I have some value, I, a flunky, a fool, a nonentity? I am worth enough for the Incorruptible one to sacrifice...his human dignity, in order to win me over?...

[*A misunderstanding:* ROBESPIERRE *thinks that* CAMILLE *has seen through his most intimate feelings. He turns pale and gray with anger and fear.* CAMILLE *notices this—and attributes quite different reasons to it.*]

You are afraid...you are afraid of us, you, unyielding, Invincible one! You *are* afraid!! That is why you have degraded yourself like the lowest whore!—In vain did you fawn at Danton's feet: he sent you packing! So you wanted to delude me, at least! After all, I am so stupid! Am I not?— But my printed words kindle spiritual fires from the Channel to the Pyrenees; such a weapon is not to be despised...when one is trembling with deadly fear for one's own skin?—You thought it was enough to lift your finger, didn't you?...Isn't that what you thought?! Who could resist your eyes?—They are beautiful, that's true; but I won't commit treason for them.

[*He turns away and walks to the window.*]

ROBESPIERRE [*follows him, trembling with fatigue*]. What is it, my boy? How can you attribute such motives to me? Don't you know me...?

CAMILLE [*turns away, timidly*]. I don't know you. I never knew you. I don't understand your damned politics.—I saw a giant in you...You miserable villain...I adored you...

[*He supports his arm against the windowpane, lowers his head on it.*]

ROBESPIERRE [*takes him into his arms, almost leans on him*]. Camille...Camille, my child...Camille—have pity...on me...

[CAMILLE *shakes him off brutally.* ROBESPIERRE *leans on the windowframe.*]

CAMILLE [*in a harsh, dry, almost brittle voice*]. Enough, Robespierre. Don't degrade yourself to no purpose. You have lost. [*turns his head, looks at him*] You coward...vile—lying—coward... [*he utters a shout, suppresses it by pressing his face into the hollow of his elbow*] Aaaaoou!!!

[*He bursts out sobbing again. Pause.*]

ROBESPIERRE [*in a strange voice, as if in a trance*]. I have come—at the last—moment.—If...you don't do what I ask, you are lost. [*His heart begins to beat so violently that he sways slightly and cannot catch his breath.* CAMILLE *turns round amazed at the uncanny change in his voice. He begins to sense the truth and is silent.* ROBESPIERRE *continues as if hypnotized.*] I have spoken... [*awakened by* CAMILLE'*s piercing look, he draws back with a great effort which causes his voice to falter*] not one word too much.

[*He leans hard against the windowframe, blinking his eyes as if in a daze.*]

CAMILLE [*calm now, turns away again. With contempt*]. Yes, I see.

ROBESPIERRE [*recovers, speaks softly*]. Camille, I swear to you I have spoken the truth.

CAMILLE [*suppresses without effort the last pang of premonition*]. I am not keeping you, Robespierre. [ROBESPIERRE *tears himself away from the window, walks upstage to collect his things.*] The gate may be locked; I'll send you the key right away. [*bows stiffly*] I bid you farewell.

ROBESPIERRE [*loudly*]. Goodbye. [CAMILLE *goes out;* ROBESPIERRE *sinks onto the sofa and rests, looking dully in front of him. He gets up when* LUCILE *enters*] Will you be so good as to give me the key. I'll leave it with the caretaker.

LUCILE. Maxime...Robespierre...In God's name, what happened?!...I trusted you so absolutely!...

ROBESPIERRE. I did not guarantee I would succeed.

LUCILE. *Why* did you come to see us...today of all days?...But you won't tell me. I am stupid to ask.—For God's sake, have pity and *tell* me the truth!!—I implore you: tell me the *truth*!!!

ROBESPIERRE. I did tell you the truth.—But if you don't believe me any more ...what use is there of more words?—Please let me have the key.

LUCILE. Well, now I don't understand anything at all...Oh, how could you!!—No. I am sorry. [*She gives him the key.* ROBESPIERRE *kisses her hand*] Please, don't be angry with me!...

ROBESPIERRE. There is nothing to be angry for—but what difference does it make now?

[*exit*]

ACT III   Scene 1

Comité de Salut Public. LINDET *in the chair; present are* BILLAUD, COLLOT, CARNOT.

BILLAUD [*taps his fingers impatiently on the tabletop; looks at his watch*]. What time did he call us for? For two, if I am not mistaken?

LINDET [*taking out his watch*]. It's only ten to two, so what do you want?

COLLOT. Why are you so sour, Lindet? Aren't you awake yet?

CARNOT. Robespierre *could* have waited till tomorrow, though. He's so relentless!...

COLLOT. What are you saying? I do marvel at you all: for the last few days Robespierre has been bossing us here like a king, while you...

LINDET. You've found something to talk about again?!

CARNOT. It's a fact. He decides everything himself, thinks our time is at his disposal...

COLLOT. Without a word to us he abolished the taking of minutes...

BILLAUD. He's right there! A secretary is a potential spy. But really, this is no time to bother about etiquette! My friends, Robespierre saw Danton today: if he has called us at night, it means he has an important argument to his advantage.

CARNOT. So you think he's as stubborn as ever?

BILLAUD. Robespierre is not a waverer. But we *must* remove Danton, gentlemen: Robespierre *must* agree. You two, instead of opposing me, should stand behind me: let's form a united front. And we must not leave here until he backs down.

CARNOT. Quite right. We must hurry. Because of Danton we can't move forward one step.

BILLAUD. We will even plan our campaign today, if possible. It's not an easy task, my friends. Above all, Danton must be isolated in the Convention and deprived of the support of public opinion.

CARNOT. I am afraid that this preliminary action will take us at least a month, gentlemen. [BILLAUD *motions his disapproval*] Can't be helped, Billaud: we *must* be assured of public support. To act prematurely would be disastrous.

COLLOT. Of course. The bourgeoisie would set the country against us. We

91

would draw new disturbances, uprising, civil wars on our heads—and above all, a split in the government. Really, it is better to devote a little time to this matter. . .

BILLAUD [*thoughtful*]. No doubt about it, I know that myself. . .but a *month*!. . .

COLLOT. The fact is, though, that Robespierre's relentless resistance is. . . suspect.

BILLAUD. Sure, if you can't calculate the simplest effects of your actions. . . you, politicians!

COLLOT. It may be so, Billaud, it may be so; but that quivering concern for Danton signifies something more than the shrewdness of a statesmen. Believe him, if you will, that he fears the terror like the plague; I know the terror, and I know that when used in moderation. . .

LINDET [*blinks his eyes*]. In moderation. . .two hundred and seventy-three victims a day, unforgettable shootings in Lyons. Thoughtless destruction of factories, store houses, whole districts. All done more thoroughly than by an enraged enemy. In moderation!!!.

COLLOT [*starts to his feet*]. Who asked you to interfere, you. . .underling?!

LINDET. Thank you for that honorable title, hangdog.

[COLLOT *throws himself at* LINDET, *restrained by those near him.*]

BILLAUD. No brawls here.

CARNOT. Don't pay any attention—say what you began to say.—Well?

COLLOT [*gives* LINDET *a hostile look*]. Well then, by all the devils in hell, Robespierre lies! [*deep silence*] My friends, isn't he a leader of genius?. . .

BILLAUD. He is. So what?

COLLOT. So what?!—Just think. . .what has every leader of genius in history become, without exception, as if compelled by a law of nature?. . .

CARNOT [*quietly*]. A dictator. . . [*silence again*]

BILLAUD [*breathless*]. They were not revolutionaries!. . .

COLLOT [*with a smile of superiority*]. My friend! It's a human pattern: he who begins as a genuine democrat, ends as an absolutist, honestly convinced that he is saving the country.

CARNOT [*thoughtful*]. Listen, Collot. . .even if that were true, what is the relevance of all this?. . .

COLLOT. What relevance?! My friends! Robespierre has the talent and the will, but he does not know how to go about securing the throne. Danton, on the other hand, has *ample* experience in this field.—Robespierre knows a lot about Danton. What would be simpler for him than to make use of that knowledge and secure Danton's services?. . .

LINDET. Great God!...

COLLOT. Why this meeting in private?—Gentlemen: if those two did not come to an agreement long ago, then they did so today.

BILLAUD [*slowly*]. Robespierre...a blackmailer!...No, Collot. It's not possible...even though he may have set out on the road to high treason.

COLLOT. So you admit that that's possible?...

[BILLAUD *remains gloomily silent*]

BARERE [*rushes in*]. Greetings!...Ugh—I am late. But Robespierre is going too far... [*sits down*] Why are you all so solemn?

COLLOT. You don't even seem to know why you were told to get up at midnight?

BARERE. To tell you the truth— I don't.

BILLAUD. So, it wasn't you who mediated—like a lackey—between our colleague and Danton? It wasn't thanks to you that those two giants came together for a chat?

BARERE. What's bitten you?...Of course, it happened thanks to me—but ...Ah, I see.—You are in a hurry!

SAINT-JUST [*rushes in*]. Good evening...He's not here yet? Thank God.

CARNOT [*looking at his watch*]. *He* is not here, but you are ten minutes late, Saint-Just.

SAINT-JUST [*charmingly*]. Oh, how you remind me of my school days!—But, the fact is I am surprised at this call. Only a couple of hours ago he clearly said he would call us tomorrow...

[*Those present exchange anxious glances.*]

ROBESPIERRE [*enters hastily, his clothes unchanged. Silence as if in a church*]. Good evening, gentlemen. Forgive me for having made you wait. [*unfriendly but quiet murmur*]

COLLOT [*blinks his eyes*]. You speak like a king to his ministers.

ROBESPIERRE [*sits down distractedly*]. And how should I have spoken?

[CARNOT *and* COLLOT *indignant;* BARERE *and* SAINT-JUST *burst out laughing.* ROBESPIERRE *does not seem to hear.*]

BILLAUD. Robespierre: we should like to have a definite answer about the Danton case.

ROBESPIERRE. I demand that Danton be put before the Revolutionary Tribunal within the next ten days.

[*deadly silence*]

BILLAUD [*with a sigh, after a long suspense*]. Well—thank God we have reached agreement so smoothly.

[*Murmur rises again and intensifies:*]

BARERE. What?...In ten days?...
COLLOT. What a rush all of a sudden!...
CARNOT. This is impossible.
BARERE. Please, may I speak?—Robespierre: your motion terrifies me. It's not possible for us to deal with Danton within ten days. First we must prepare public opinion, gain support, encircle him. We can't begin our attack earlier than a month from now.

[SAINT-JUST *laughs*]

BILLAUD. Have you finished?—Let me speak, Lindet! A month is absurd. With intensive propaganda we shall prepare the ground in ten days. Then we can act.

[*Murmur of confusion.* COLLOT *applauds.* BARERE *and* CARNOT *signify their doubts.*]

SAINT-JUST. Yes...ten days for us mean also ten days for Danton...
ROBESPIERRE. Comrade chairman!...Saint-Just is right. My conversation with Danton was quite...final. If, therefore, Danton is not fired with a passion for martyrdom—he will, not in ten days but *tonight,* either escape...
LINDET. I wonder where to? Who will receive a destroyer of monarchy?
ROBESPIERRE. Rather, who will receive its secret agent?...As I was saying, he will either escape or organize a desperate coup. We must not imperil the general safety any longer.
BARERE & BILLAUD. Well then, what??
ROBESPIERRE [*takes out his watch which causes a moment's silence*]. In an hour from now—at half past three—Danton must be in custody.

[*pandemonium*]

BARERE. What...*tonight?*!!
CARNOT. Have you gone mad?!

[LINDET *rings his bell*]

BILLAUD. Im-poss-ible, comrade.
SAINT-JUST. Good! You're your old self at last!
COLLOT. What a crazy idea!

[*after the outburst a moment's respite*]

SAINT-JUST [*avails himself of the calm, looks Robespierre in the eye*]. Danton . . . and his *associates*.

COLLOT. You are proposing the Committee's suicide, Robespierre.

CARNOT. We must not expose ourselves to certain defeat.

BILLAUD. Let me speak! Robespierre: Danton has the capitalists behind him. You said so yourself. If we act prematurely, we shall draw on ourselves a lavishly financed uprising in the suburbs and a panic rebellion in the Convention. We shall achieve the government's destruction and Danton's apotheosis.

[*excited applause*]

COLLOT. True! Quite true!

CARNOT. This is indisputable.

[LINDET *rings his bell briefly*]

BARERE. No one will agree, Maxime.

ROBESPIERRE [*shouts*]. I wish to speak!

[*uproar grows,* LINDET *rings the bell*]

OPPONENTS. The discussion is closed!—Motion is rejected! No more!

LINDET [*ringing the bell*]. *Quiet,* damn it!

BILLAUD. Will you be quiet at last!

[*the uproar dies out reluctantly*]

ROBESPIERRE [*strains his voice*]. But it is because Danton has powerful backing that we must act like lightning!—Give him not ten but three days, and the gold of the financiers will create him an army, hundreds of leaflets will drop on Paris, French blood will boil at the sound of his call, while in the Convention the dead and huge weight of the Plain will shift to the right in one night; and it takes only a few hours to fill the gallery with one's men—when one has the means. Gentlemen: Danton right now is a beast at bay. Look out!*

[*stifled murmur*]

CARNOT. And yet . . .

COLLOT. Damned nuisance . . .

*English words in the original.

BARERE. By God, we must find a way. . .

BILLAUD [*loud*]. If so, we must take a risk. One of us must attack Danton to-morrow morning at the Convention. If he is present, let him defend himself; if he isn't. . .

SAINT-JUST [*interrupts*]. . . . it means he has run away; and the Coalition will have gained a source of valuable information.

ROBESPIERRE. But if he is there, he will triumph.—Danton is not Hébert, gentlemen. This is exactly what he expects; he is busy preparing for the Convention—and tomorrow he will rush to the rostrum and roar. Those he has not convinced during the night with his gold, he will con-quer in the daytime with the might of his voice.—And what shall we do then, gentlemen? When the Convention, with the galleries, yells in spasms of rapture? Which of us will go drown out that miracle-making thunderous bass? My drawing-room contralto, perhaps? Or Saint-Just's low-pitched tenor?—We must act at once, comrades.

VOICES [*subdued*]. He's exaggerating—we can't succeed—well, who knows? . . .—One way or the other—defeat is certain.

BILLAUD [*loud*]. Unfortunately, Robespierre—you are right.

[BARERE *utters a shout of protest*]

ROBESPIERRE. The Committee of Security has the right of preventive deten-tion, as far as deputies are concerned. We must call it into session to sanction the warrant of arrest.

[*the last sharp outburst of protest, but its tone shows that the opponents know they have lost*]

COLLOT. The Convention will tear us to shreds, Robespierre!

[LINDET *vehemently rings the bell*]

BARERE. Why did you stir him up, Maxime! This is all your fault!

ROBESPIERRE. We shall deal with Danton in the same way as with every crim-inal in the Convention up to now. Even so, his arrest will be a surprise, because the masses unthinkingly expect special treatment for Danton. The city will learn about it at about eight-thirty. That's when the Con-vention begins its sitting. I shall be there to inform the Convention my-self. If there is panic—I shall deal with it, because it will be a *natural* panic.—Well, do you trust me to be up to it? [*assent: decisive from* BIL-LAUD, SAINT-JUST, *and* BARERE; *qualified from the rest*] Well then: I will straighten out the moral stand of the lawmakers, and after me one of us

will make a report on the Danton case, with the motion for the decree
of arrest and impeachment.

BARERE [*among slight commotion*]. But who feels he can draw up this report
by nine? Because I . . .

SAINT-JUST [*almost without contempt*]. Calm yourself, Barère: we won't put
that load on *your* shoulders. I will submit the report. I've got it ready.
[*he takes out the script*]

BILLAUD. Read it!

ROBESPIERRE. Allow me to have a look at these notes first. It will save time.

[COLLOT *and* CARNOT *remain silent.*]

BILLAUD. All right. [SAINT-JUST *hands the manuscript to* ROBESPIERRE, *who begins
to read it.*] Well then, we are agreed with Robespierre's plan, aren't we?

CARNOT. If we have to choose between two evils . . .

COLLOT. Can't be helped, we have to stake everything on this move . . .

BARERE. What else can we do? Nothing . . .

ROBESPIERRE [*lifts his eyes from the manuscript*]. Well, gentlemen—what are we
waiting for? Let the chairman call the Committee of Security . . .

LINDET [*rings the bell; to the* USHER]. Will you send messengers to at least six
members of the Committee of General Security. It's urgent.

USHER. Those gentlemen are about to end their meeting . . .

BILLAUD. So much the better. Let them come here. [*exit* USHER] Now we
have to consider the associates that must be arrested with Danton. [*general attention;* ROBESPIERRE *raises his head*] Here is my list: Delacroix [*silence*], Philippeaux . . .

LINDET. Completely innocent.

SAINT-JUST. In his intentions—maybe; however, we are judging the effects.

COLLOT. He led the attack on the Committees together with Danton.—
Who else?

BILLAUD. Legendre and Bourdon de l'Oise . . .

ROBESPIERRE. No! They are harmless tools. Don't let's make a slaughter,
gentlemen! Careful with the terror!!

LINDET. The first human word this night . . .

BILLAUD. Very well. Let them live.—Desmoulins.

[*total silence*]

ROBESPIERRE [*bites his lip, somewhat pale*]. As a friend of Desmoulins, I shall
abide by your decision . . . Don't you think, though, that one could . . .
give him a day . . . one day, to enable him to come to his senses? . . .

BILLAUD [*shakes his head resolutely*]. No.

SAINT-JUST. What a weapon in the hands of the Dantonists, even if only for a day!—Impossible, Maxime.

ROBESPIERRE. No?. . . [*unanimous assent*] All right. Then these three will go with Danton.

[*He goes on reading, but somewhat absentmindedly.*]

BILLAUD [*raps his knuckles on the table*]. Lindet, ring the bell once more. . . ah, they're coming.

USHER. The gentlemen from the Committee of Security.

[*He brings the chairs that were standing by the wall. Members of Comsal rise. Enter:* VADIER, AMAR, SENAR, VOULLAND, LEBAS, *and* DAVID—*the last two are* ROBESPIERRE's *followers.*]

AMAR. We'd better warn you first. You must be wondering why we too had to meet at night. Well, we have just ordered the arrest of General Westermann.

[*Members of Comsal exchange glances.*]

COLLOT. A fortunate coincidence. Why did you do it?

AMAR. As a pretext we used Westermann's part in the Hébertist coup, proved long ago. . .

VADIER [*after a moment's silence*]. But in fact we did it because Westermann clearly aimed to gather a band of guerillas from among the disbanded Revolutionary Army. And when Westerman is said to be gathering something for *himself*. . .

BILLAUD. If so, you will be glad at our news: we have decided to arrest Danton with three associates.

[*sensation*]

DAVID [*avidly*]. When?!

COLLOT [*triumphantly*]. Now, gentlemen!!

[*exclamations of astonishment, fear, approbation*]

VOULLAND. Ho-ho!!

VADIER [*with a long whistle*]. Well, well. . .We don't lack courage, it seems! . . .

AMAR. It's a crazy idea, gentlemen. . .how come. . .

SENAR. A mortal leap from one extreme to another. . .

JAGOT. From one absurd step to another.

SAINT-JUST. If you refuse your cooperation, we will appropriate your right to order the preventive detention of deputies . . .

ROBESPIERRE. And you know that the Convention sanctions such usurpations for good, if they have proved successful . . .

[*indignant noises by Comsur members*]

VADIER [*red in the face, shouts loudest*]. What impudence!! *Such* cynicism must . . .

AMAR. Hush, Vadier. They are right. If it has to be done, it is better to do it now.—Agreed, gentlemen.

VOULLAND. But the responsibility!! We can't carry it.

BILLAUD. We will take it on *ourselves*. The war is being waged between Danton and the Committee of Public Safety. If we don't succeed, it is *we* who shall fall. You will not be touched; after all, you are the political police . . .

SAINT-JUST. . . . not usurpers of monarchic power.

COMSUR VOICES. All right, agreed.—Better to do it now.—All right, we will issue the warrant. It's up to you to save things afterwards.

VADIER. Very well, get yourselves run over. I'm not stopping you.

BILLAUD. Go on then, issue the warrant.

SAINT-JUST [*looks round*]. Where are the forms?

COLLOT. Never mind the forms, a sheet of paper will do!

[*They get up, look for paper.*]

SAINT-JUST. Nothing doing without the secretary . . . [*attacks the cabinet, breaks fingernails*] Locked—of course.

ROBESPIERRE [*tears away half a sheet from* SAINT-JUST'*s notes, gives it to them*]. Here is some paper.

BILLAUD [*takes it and sits down.* SAINT-JUST *brings him the ink and pen from the* SECRETARY'*s desk*]. You from Security, dictate.

AMAR. The Committees of General Security and Public Safety hereby order that Danton—who else?

BILLAUD [*writing*]. Delacroix—from the department of Eure-et-Moire, Camille Desmoulins and Philippeaux—I am listening . . .

AMAR. . . . all members of the National Convention be arrested and taken to the prison at the Palais du Luxembourg, where they are to be placed in solitary confinement. The mayor of the city of Paris is to execute this order forthwith—Representatives of the people . . . and signatures.

[*The warrant is circulated round the table.*]

ROBESPIERRE [*privately to* SAINT-JUST]. Antoine: three facts are tendentiously twisted. But the act of indictment must be impeccable! Every inaccuracy opens the way for defense. And the bare truth about Danton is more than sufficient.

SAINT-JUST. Comrades! I must make some alterations in the report. I'll read it to you before the session, at seven-thirty.

BARERE [*pulls a face*]. Two sittings in one night! No, thank you...

BILLAUD. I don't think it's worth going home. Those who are free can sleep here. [SENAR *signs after* ROBESPIERRE *and hands the warrant to* LINDET, *who affixes the seal and folds it, then rings the bell*] Hallo, Lindet! You have not signed!

LINDET. I have been elected to care for the revolutionaries, not to murder them. [*to the* USHER] Take this to the town hall. Most urgent! [*he rises*] The meeting is closed.

[*Members go out in groups.*]

AMAR [*to* VADIER]. Well, I wonder if tomorrow at this time the Committee of Safety will still exist...

BARERE [*to* CARNOT]. By God, what is going to happen tomorrow at the Convention! I shudder at the thought...

Scene 2

DANTON'*s apartment. A candelabrum on the table. Windows wide open: a warm spring night.* DANTON *and* DELACROIX *enter in soaked overcoats and hats, which they keep on.* DANTON *stops in the middle of the room; he looks round distractedly.* DELACROIX *has the familiar Satanic expression of a fellow conspirator. They stand ill at ease, as if in a strange house; long silence.*

DELACROIX [*slightly ironical*]. How refreshing this sudden, fragrant shower! Tonight is the first true night of spring...quiet but intense. I feel such an influx of life-blood that I want to embrace the whole world.

[*pause*]

DANTON [*looks at him as if he has just awakened. After a while*]. Why did you come here?

DELACROIX. For the pleasure of your company... [*a somewhat ominous silence*] Well, have you decided yet?

DANTON. What?

DELACROIX. To escape! [DANTON *turns away and shrugs his shoulders*] What's the matter with you, Danton? [*goes round to look him in the face*] Can't you see the position you're in?

DANTON [*looking down gloomily*]. I've never had any illusions as far as the populace is concerned.

DELACROIX. Indeed. I remember. [*blinks his eyes*] And I suppose you know also that Westermann has been arrested?

DANTON [*looks at him sluggishly; sits down heavily*]. When?

DELACROIX. An hour ago. [*silence again. Impatient now*] Well?

DANTON [*inertly shakes his drooping head*]. No.

[*Rises. Walks to the window, stands there, his hands in the pockets of his overcoat.*]

DELACROIX. All right. So long, brother.—I've lost the best part of the night because of you . . . and every minute counts. Now I must wait till five A.M., or else I would be noticed at the gates. [*goes to the door*] Goodbye, Georges. [*Goes out.*]

DANTON [*does not seem to hear him. After a while sinks into the chair again, seems to disintegrate. Throws his hat on the floor. Notices his state and gets up with difficulty*]. Pull yourself together, Danton, my friend! [*Takes his overcoat off and throws it on the arm chair. Tired with this effort, he sits on the edge of the sofa. He rubs his forehead; walks to the cupboard, opens it, pours himself a large drink and downs some of it avidly, as if he had a fever.*—DESMOULINS *rushes in without knocking, agitated, no hat, overcoat unbuttoned.* DANTON *looks round, glass in hand*] Well? What do you want?

CAMILLE. I must talk to you, you bloody beast!

DANTON [*drinks up, pushes away the glass*]. Oh! Temper, temper. I can enjoy a little distraction. [*sits down*] All right, you can perform now. [CAMILLE *leans against the table and looks at him without uttering a word*] Well? . . . You've forgotten your lines?

CAMILLE [*slowly*]. And to think that I . . . I believed in you?! . . . But you are just hideous, Danton . . .

DANTON [*with a slightly bitter smile*]. How perceptive of you!—Is that what you wanted to tell me?

[*for a while they silently look at each other*]

CAMILLE [*suddenly*]. Danton, I once told you that you were a great man and that I would like to die for you. I want now emphatically to withdraw every word.

DANTON. *Your* words! As if I ever regarded you seriously, suckling?

CAMILLE. My eyes have been opened. Somewhat abruptly... but I've just about survived the operation.—I was blind—blind as a bat... I thought you were heroes, but you are just miserable villains! I've seen through you at last. You have destroyed me, you coldblooded beast. You poisoned my mind, sapped my strength. For you my talent has been wasted in the journalistic gutter.—Know at least that, used, destroyed, filthy as I am, I can still spit in your face. [*straightens up, ready to go*]

DANTON [*interested*]. So, Robespierre has deigned to lift his finger at last?

CAMILLE [*shakes*]. Don't dare mention him! [*leans toward him across the table*] I've spent my life on my knees before the two of you. I've worn myself out in your service. And you both knew slyly how to exploit my blindness. From now on I am a *free* man. I don't care what happens to me... but I've broken with both of you, rotten idols, forever. [*turns away*]

DANTON [*sits calmly*]. Camille!

CAMILLE [*over his shoulder*]. What do you want?

DANTON. Come back. [CAMILLE *stops*] What are you blabbing about? What do all those metaphors mean?

CAMILLE. What's that to do with you?

DANTON. And what does "both of you" mean? Have you offended Robespierre again?!...

CAMILLE. Offended him... I've seen through that monster.—He nearly caught me in his snares again.

DANTON. What's this? You've been to see him?

CAMILLE. I to see him? It was he who had the effrontery to come to me and he fawned on me shamelessly all through the evening!—But I put a stop to that. He won't dare approach me again.

DANTON. Have you... have you gone mad, you miserable fool?!!—How's that?—You found out that we were lost and... just then you rejected the only, improbable, wonderful chance to save your skin?!...

CAMILLE [*blinks his eyes, tries to hide his fear*]. What? Are we lost?

DANTON. Didn't you hear our conversation through the door?

CAMILLE. But you defeated him...

DANTON [*leans back*]. I defeated him?... Camille, your stupidity makes me furious.—Try to understand: I approached that maniac, that devilishly sly madman, *like a man*. Like an idiot, I blabbed all my heresies to him. I gave him irrefutable proofs against myself. I condemned myself to death!

[*silence, only breathing heard*]

CAMILLE [*rouses himself*]. You will defend yourself all right! The people are behind you!—He knows he can't face us: why else would he be flattering us?

DANTON [*impatient*]. Defend myself!—The people!—I have just come back from a few section headquarters.—Camille, the mob has already forgotten I ever existed—and now they look at me with such "love" that I have lost any wish to speak. We are isolated like lepers. Tomorrow, or the day after, the entire Convention will fall on us and pull us to bits.

CAMILLE [*motionless*]. So he was telling. . .the truth. . . [*pause. Suddenly*] But in that case why. . .*why did he*. . .?

DANTON [*in his demoniac vein*]. . . .want to save you? [*fascinated*] It seems inconceivable.—But to me this is as clear as daylight; you, my boy, are the only person in the world whom that monster has ever loved. . . [CAMILLE's *hoarse sigh*] with a desperate, painfully true love.

[*long silence*]

CAMILLE [*shaking, suddenly erupts in a cry of nervous joy*]. O my God!!! [*controls himself a little*] For. . .this news, Danton. . .I forgive you everything. [*turns to run away*]

DANTON [*slightly lifting himself in the chair*]. Camille! Where are you going?

CAMILLE [*with near hysterical laughter, in the doorway*]. *Where*?!!!

DANTON [*points to a chair*]. Wait—just a second.—Sit down. [CAMILLE *turns back reluctantly, but remains standing, resting his hands on the arm chair*] You see. . .I know Robespierre better than you do. . .

CAMILLE. Unfortunately—it's the truth.—O God, how *could* I doubt him! . . .

DANTON. . . .and that's why I am afraid of a certain. . .misunderstanding. [CAMILLE *raises his head, somewhat frightened*] You said something about having offended him. . .but surely, you haven't called him a villain, or anything like that, eh, Camille?

CAMILLE [*numb*]. I'm afraid. . .I did. . .

DANTON [*worried*]. Hmm. . .that's bad, my child. . .You see, in those people made of wood, or stone, such a sentiment, once frustrated, turns into inexorable hate.—Robespierre will *never* forgive you. If you try to see him, you'll only expose yourself to much unpleasantness.

CAMILLE [*breathes deeply*]. It doesn't matter. Let him get his revenge. He would be right. I've deserved the heaviest punishments.—But I must kneel before him, no matter what is to happen to me.

DANTON [*quietly*]. Nothing will help you now, Camille. . .

CAMILLE. It doesn't matter about me, but he must know that now I understand. . .and. . .that [*he chokes*] that I. . .am. . .awfully. . .sorry.

[*he wipes his eyes and nose*]

DANTON [*with a quiet smile*]. So you think he will believe you now? Even if—by some fluke—you managed to get to him, what would he think about your sudden contrition? He would think that you'd realized at last the danger you're in and are afraid of him.

And *how* he can finish off those he has defeated—you have had the opportunity to observe more than once. He is as revengeful as the devil.—You remember how he has already made a laughing stock of you once, mocked you at the Jacobin club?

CAMILLE [*leans heavily against the table*]. I remember . . . he saved me from expulsion by doing it. [*more quietly, leaning more towards the table top*] And I, fool that I am . . . understand this only now . . .

DANTON. Hoho! He could have saved you at less expense. You touched his morbid sensitivity—but that was only a joke, Camille! . . . You'll see, he will make you commit suicide for shame.

CAMILLE [*straightens up, helpless*]. My whole life would be poisoned. . . . I must at least write to him! . . .

DANTON. He will publish your letter . . . With his comments. [CAMILLE *throws himself onto the chair. Long silence.* DANTON *speaks considerately*] Well, will you risk it? . . .

CAMILLE [*gets up, shaking his head helplessly. Can hardly speak*]. No.

[*He goes away as if slightly drunk.* DANTON *watches him go. Suddenly he bursts into restless, soundless laughter. He bares his teeth in a grimace, but his eyes remain downcast and sad. He gets up to have another drink. But the bottle is empty; he throws it away, but without any impetus. He seems vacant. Suddenly rouses himself, kicks the bottle under the bed, closes the cupboard and knocks at the door on the right.*]

LOUISE [*from within, anxiously*]. Is it you, Georges? . . . Wait . . .

DANTON. Don't be afraid, darling. I must talk to you. Open up.

LOUISE. No . . . you mustn't come in. I'll come to you. [DANTON *waits with his head bowed.* LOUISE *enters dressed in a white peignoir.* DANTON *kisses her hands passionately and pulls her to the table.*] Let me be. What is it you want?

DANTON [*sits motionlessly, looking at her*]. I had to . . . see you. My little bitter treasure, you . . .

LOUISE. And that's why you had to wake me up?!

DANTON. You know my selfishness . . .

LOUISE. Yes, indeed I do. [*she gets up*] Good night.

DANTON [*restrains her*]. You must listen to me, Louison. Sit down, please. [LOUISE *sits down, impatient*] Your parents are still living in Fontenay, aren't they? [*she nods, surprised*] How do they manage?

LOUISE. All right. My father should be grateful to me. At the price of having sold my person he has improved his business. He is even a bigwig in his commune. He must have been begging again, I suppose?

DANTON. No.—But you will have to go back home, my treasure.

LOUISE [*leaps to her feet, in mad hope*]. What? . . . Are you going away?!! . . .

DANTON [*passes his hand across his head, gloomily looking at the tabletop*]. Yes . . . I am going away.—For a long time.

LOUISE [*trembling for joy, almost in a whisper*]. Is that true? [DANTON *looks at her, feels a terrible pain, his face darkens and twists into grimace, like the ugly face of a newborn baby. He starts to his feet, goes to the fireplace and faces it, shivering.* LOUISE *comes nearer to him, watching him from a distance of two steps. With revulsion, fear, and indignation*] Georges! What's the matter with you? Have you gone mad?

DANTON [*turns his head away from her, mumbles*]. Mmm . . . go away . . . it's nothing . . . get away from here! [*Frightened, she withdraws behind his chaise longue. He controls himself, walks back to the table*] Ah . . . I was choking. It's all right now. Come and sit down, Louison.

LOUISE [*suspiciously stands by the table, watching him pitilessly*]. Have you been drinking?

DANTON. Alas, no. . . . So you'll be glad to return home? . . . [*his voice falters*] Eh, Louise?

LOUISE [*unmoved*]. *Very* glad.

DANTON [*swallows with difficulty. After a couple of seconds*]. Listen: you will find a considerable sum in my desk. Not in government vouchers, of course. I will not entrust it to Monsieur Gély for you; knowing him, I am sure you will guard it better yourself. But, my child, you must be very careful and not let anyone know you have large sums of money. The glorious Republic would confiscate everything. You have to wait until . . . until *normal* conditions return. You understand?

LOUISE [*slowly*]. It means you are escaping . . . probably for ever?

DANTON [*bursts out laughing, for no reason*]. Yes, probably! [*he leans sideways towards her, kneels, embraces her thighs*] Oooh, my own . . . my only . . . only one!

LOUISE [*feels the first pang of pity. Brushes her hand across his head*]. Georges, what's the matter with you tonight?

DANTON [*his eyes closed in ecstasy, but speaks matter-of-factly*]. Nothing, except that I love you very much . . . love you . . . my little [*whisper of consuming passion*] . . . woman . . .

LOUISE [*anxious, tries to evade him nervously*]. Let me go...please! Let me go, Georges!...

DANTON [*starts to his feet suddenly; grasps her above the elbows*]. You will give me this last night, do you hear? You won't fool me with your migraine tonight!

LOUISE [*stiffens in his arms like a statue*]. Georges, I am pregnant.

DANTON [*lets her go and rests his hip against the table. Out of breath, menacingly*]. Don't lie to me!

LOUISE [*shrugs her shoulders haughtily*]. I know you want to have a child, so you *must* be careful with me. Remember I am not yet grown up! God knows how this will end...

DANTON [*dazed, rubs his forehead*]. Pregnant...now... [*falls on the chair*] Bloody hell!!!

LOUISE [*brusque*]. If you want to talk to me, behave like a human being.

DANTON [*looks at her as if he has forgotten about her presence. Not offended, he kisses her fingers*]. Don't be angry with me, my darling. [LOUISE *sits down*] You will be free now, child. Think about it and tell me: do you really... hate me?

LOUISE. I don't know. Until now, yes. [*intensely*] Tonight, Georges, for the first time in my life I have looked upon you as a human being... [*smiling unpleasantly*] Think of that!

DANTON [*startled*]. My God, Louison...why? I have never done you any wrong...

LOUISE [*repulsive smile*]. No wrong!! You bought me like a dog, you raped an innocent and terrified girl! My fright, the torments I suffered obviously gave you special pleasure!

DANTON [*aghast*]. My child...I swear I didn't know...I was certain that if you once tasted pleasure...

LOUISE [*with a murderous smile*]. Man, have you ever looked at yourself in the mirror? [DANTON *blushes like a boy brutally put to shame by an adult;* LOUISE *softens somewhat*] You know, Georges...if you were a bit more subtle, more understanding...who knows if...But it's too late to talk about it now. Please forget me and do not look for me when you come back. [*she gets up*] I wish you better luck over there, Georges.

DANTON [*gets up somewhat solemnly, takes her by the hands*]. My little Louise ... [*kisses her right hand*] I am going to my death. [*kisses her left hand*]

LOUISE [*stands still, blinks her eyes*]. How is that?

DANTON [*shrugs his shoulders*]. Yes, Robespierre's insatiable envy has achieved its aim. I was bored to nausea with all this messing about with the rabble's concerns. I relied on my enormous merits. And it's happened. He has stolen my popularity.—And faced with those who are defenseless even Robespierre takes courage. In a day or two he will give the sign and his trusted Convention, well schooled by him, will throw me to the Tribunal to be devoured.

LOUISE. You know about it and yet you walk straight into the fire...Go away, man!

DANTON. No, darling. Life in the world as it is now is not worth lifting a finger for. Let that paltry lawyer have his satisfaction for once. Let him think he was able to bring Danton down!—He will soon pay dearly for his little ambitions... [*grins thinking about the future*]

LOUISE [*thoughtful*]. That's funny...from the very beginning I thought Robespierre would sooner or later defeat you.

DANTON [*transformed completely*]. Oh, did you? You thought so? Why, may I ask?

LOUISE [*caught at first, recovers her composure and maliciously exploits the situation*]. Why?...Because you have been behaving just as my father did. [DANTON *grows pale with anger*] When he was threatened with bankruptcy because of the competition from another shopkeeper, Duval,... [DANTON *assumes a menacing posture;* LOUISE *sits down and continues*] ...there was talk about Duval from morning to night: how incompetent, stupid, jealous and vile he was. And the worse things became, the more father praised his own talents and despised Duval. So when I listened to what you were saying about Robespierre and yourself, I came to the conclusion...

DANTON [*keeps a grip on himself, but is out of breath*]. Enough, you told me once already. [*Walks round the room. Every time he returns to the table, he takes up the interrupted monologue. Quietly*] Aha...she knew...she has known for a long time, the silly girl! [*His face darkens. He approaches her.* LOUISE *hides her fright with difficulty, but she is still challenging him with a fixed smile*] Ugh! Of course. Robespierre is my enemy, therefore he must be the object of your ardent sympathy... [*across the table*] I suppose you would gladly give yourself to him, eh? [LOUISE *starts to her feet in anger, makes a step forward—he, intense, with electrified hands, frightens her with a sudden roar*] Stand still, or I'll harm you!! [LOUISE *withdraws a little, leans back against the table. He walks around her, voraciously*] Oh...how happy she is now...how her eyes smile at the prospect of my death! [*pointing to her*] This...this is supposed to be a wife, damn her!!! [*shakes for a while, panting; speaks bowed to the floor, softly*] I am really alone. [*Walks to the window; stands there for a while—his back to her—until he has calmed down. Then he returns and stands by the table, facing her.* LOUISE *has withdrawn be-*

hind the chair, but is bravely facing him] It's your own fault. I would have let them butcher me without a word, but your incredible female stupidity has made me angry. [*works himself up again*] To compare me . . . me to that fat pig, old Gély. Me! My utter contempt for the cowardly intrigues of that Committee weakling. . . [*more and more excitedly*] To compare my contempt, so complete that I would not even deign to break his bones . . . to the fidgetings of a shopkeeper! [*clenches his fists in the ecstasy of anger*] And when I think that the rabble—just as stupid as a woman—are willing to lick that monkey's shoes for letting myself be murdered by him! . . .

[*a pause. He breathes heavily*]

Oh yes . . . if this is so . . . I'd rather make the effort and crush that horrid reptile, those obnoxious intrigues I have ignored for too long. . . [*he straightens himself in a sudden renewal of energy*] Just you wait. I'll show you what your Robespierre is worth . . . I'll show him. He has been setting the Convention on me like dogs, for months, but I will turn them back on him in one night! Me defenseless?! Oh no! [*looks through his pockets, hastily changes their contents, grasps his hat*] I must organize a band . . . immediately go to work on the Center group. Put my people in the galleries . . . d'Espagnac will find enough money to buy all the Parisian mob. That mad dog, Robespierre, will fall into his own trap, until . . . [*he stiffens, turning to the door, hears noise at the gate;* LOUISE, *excited in her feeling of vengefulness, approaches the table with catlike steps*] What? Already? Imposs . . . [*Steps on the stairs climbing to their top floor.* DANTON'*s eyes are roving for a while. Suddenly he claps himself on the forehead, with a—not quite successful—smile*] Of course. He wouldn't dare . . . attack me, a free man. He must first bind my hands and feet! [*Steps in the corridor. Raises his voice*] But as long as I have the mouth and lungs of a Danton—your tricks are in vain!

LOUISE [*with a faint smile, quietly*]. You poor boaster.

DANTON [*grasps her so quickly that she cannot evade him. While the police knock loudly, he embraces her—does not even know himself whether out of love or rage*]. You . . . ah, you! [*he kisses her by force, hastily*] Only death will free you from me now. In a couple of days I shall return triumphant! [*he rushes to let in the municipal* OFFICER *with four* POLICEMEN]

OFFICER. Citizen Danton, I arrest you in the name of the law. [*takes out a sheet*] Here is the warrant.

DANTON. Very well. [*seeing the warrant*] I know, I know. I've got my hat and

I don't suppose I shall need my overcoat on such a lovely night. . . It's not raining any more, is it?

OFFICER [*embarassed by this unofficial question*]. No. . .

LOUISE. Where am I to send my husband's things?

[DANTON *turns away from her.*]

OFFICER [*politely, but surprised at her calm*]. To the Luxembourg palace, citizeness.

DANTON. Come on! Marchons!

[*They go out.* LOUISE *shuts the door; breathes fully, uttering a sigh of liberation; pushes the hair off her face, then calmly picks up the candelabrum and goes to her room.*]

Scene 3

Hall of the Convention. Upstage: a rostrum with the chairman's dais, table for the secretaries, and two rows of seats at the foot of the dais. Stage left and stage right: two ends of the horseshoe made up of amphitheatrically rising benches. The group of delegates on the left are marked in the following by 1, 2, etc. The other group, in the middle, at the foot of the dais are marked I, II, etc.

2 [*stopped by 1, while 5 approaches them*]. Yes—I too noticed something when I was on my way. . .

5 [*quietly, to them*]. Gentlemen, why. . . [*the rest cannot be heard*]

I [MERLIN DE THIONVILLE [*to* III *and* IV]]. Yes, it's certain! This morning at half past three!

3 [*runs towards the center. Shouts*]. Eh, do you know anything?

2 [*shifts from 1 and 5 to the end of the bench; 4 moves away; 6 remains alone*]. What's happened?

III [*angry*]. You're spreading old wives' tales!

1 [PANIS]. Ah, but *everybody* has heard something. . .

5. In the street, everywhere. . .

II [LECOINTRE] [*gets up from his seat on the side, approaches*]. My concierge says he saw. . .

I. Exactly! He *saw* them being taken. . .

[*The group come close together.*]

1,2,3,5. Whom? Whom? Who was taken? What has happened exactly?

III. I shall never believe this.

VI. Nor I. No!

VII. They wouldn't dare, the devil they would.

[*The first group moves toward them.*]

1 & 5. But what's happened? Tell us at last!. . .

A [COURTOIS] [*rushes in, shouts*]. Comrades: Desmoulins has been arrested!!!

⌐ I & II. Oh! You see?! Didn't I tell you?!

  4 & IV. Desmoulins?. . .No!—Not he! Philippeaux!!

L 3,5,VI & VII. Arrest. . .What, Camille?! When?! How do you know?. . .

B [*rushes in*]. Gentlemen—what's happening in town?. . .

⌐ VOICES [*astonished*]. What's that? Who then?. . .

  VOICES [*skeptical*]. Not true! Contradictory rumors! Someone wants to cre-
L ate chaos, that's all!

A. Comrades! I've seen it myself!

2 & IV. Whom? Camille?!

A. Yes, Camille! Under escort, at half past three!

VOICES [*anxious whisper*]. Camille. . .Half past three. . .that's right!. . .So
it's true?. . .

I. That means *more* of us have been arrested!

⌐ 1. *Better* and better! Congratulations!

  VOICES [*shouts of concern*]. More?. . .how's that?!—Without a word having
  been said?. . .We don't know who! We don't know what for! What does
L it all mean?. . .What's happening?! Impossible!

C [*rushes in breathless followed by others; shouts on the steps of the dais*]. Friends!
At half past three this morning they arrested Delacroix, Philippeaux,
Camille Desmoulins. . .and. . .

D [FRERON] [*in a melodious bass steals the thunder*]. And Danton!!!

[*Delegates start to their feet.*]

VOICES [*whispers of awe*]. What?! Whom?! Danton!. . .It's not possible!
What, really?! Danton. . .Danton—arrest. . .When?! When?! Also this
morning? Danton himself! What's he done? Who dared?

I. It's the work of the Committee of Safety!

VOICES [*shouts*]. Impossible! That would be lawlessness! No, the Committee would never. . .—Where are his followers?—Legendre! Le-gendre!!
Delacroix—Bourdon—Lacroix—not here! All have been taken! Their entire party!!

I. Oh, gentlemen! This is just the beginning! The Committee is growing!
VOICES [*whispers of indignation*]. To arrest innocent people...Behind our
backs! The Committee had no right! This is really too much!

[LEGENDRE *and* BOURDON *rush in*]

VOICES [*expressions of joy*]. They're here! They've come! Thank God! Look,
here they are! Of course, it wasn't true! Nonsense! Listen! Is it true?!
That Danton...What? Has Danton?...Where are the others?...
Bourdon! Where are the others?...
BOURDON [*out of his senses*]. I may be arrested any minute!...
LEGENDRE. Friends, we are lost!
A [*on the steps of the dais*]. Gentlemen! Terror has been imposed on the gov-
ernment of France!!
VOICES [*shouts*]. Lawbreakers! Lawlessness! The Committee is threatening
the Convention! Terror!! *Terror*!!!
6 & VIII [*opposition*]. Bravo Committee! Long live the Committee, away with
the traitor Danton!

[*shouts of growing anger surround these two*]

VOICES. Long live Danton! Long live the Man of August the Tenth! The defender of Liberty!
I. Comrades! We must defend ourselves. Our lives and the honor of the
government are at stake!
3 & 5. No more obedience! Down with tyranny!
I. Listen...We demand that Danton be heard from the floor...
6 & VII. What?!!! *Never*...By what right?!
VOICES [*applause*]. Very good!—Yes, from the floor! They *must* hear Danton
...They must agree! [*they pass it on to others*] Remember: from the
floor!—They must hear him!—We all demand this!—Unanimously!!
I. Once Danton speaks—he wins!
II. What could they charge him with?!
I. Then the Committee will have to revoke that vile abuse...
VOICES [*approval*]. This morning!—Now!—Let them give up their power!—
Take it away from them!
VOICES [*frantic shouts*]. The Committee men have betrayed us!—They are
traitors!—They want to butcher us so that they have all the power!—
Tyranny!—Down with secret dictatorship!—Down with the Commit-
tee's terror!—Down with the Committee of traitors!—Take the power
from them!!

A [*jumps one step higher than* MERLIN]. And when they revoke this, we'll dissolve them immediately!

[*thunderous applause*]

6 & VIII. Traitors!!—This is a coup against the government!!

[*commotion grows*]

VOICES. Dissolve them! Dissolve the Committee!!!—Down with the tyrants!—Away with them!!

D. The Committee will stand before the tribunal!!

VOICES [*thunderous applause*]. Bravo!—Indict them!—All nine of them!—The Committee before the tribunal—before—the *tribunal*. . .—To the guillotine!!

[USHERS *enter. Knock of halberds. The deputies hurriedly take their seats.*]

[*Majority begin to sing.—Down stage left*]

A. Bourdon, you must act at once. . .

VOICES. Yes! Yes! Bourdon, to the rostrum! Courage, Bourdon! We are all with you! Go on! Long live Danton!

BOURDON [*trembling*]. Gentlemen—I. . .I—can't. . .I don't know how. . .I . . .

VOICES [*mocking him*]. Ugh, coward! He's trembling all over! Look at how green he's become!

II. Then you must do it, Legendre.

VOICES [*demanding*]. Legendre!—On the rostrum!—You must speak! Go on!

[*The Chairman enters. He is* TALLIEN, *a Dantonist.*]

LEGENDRE. Very well. I am speaking on behalf of you all! [*walks toward the* SECRETARIES]

I, A & D. Yes, we are all with you! The country is behind you! All France is with us!

[*A deadly, tense silence follows this exclamation.* TALLIEN *walks to his chair but does not sit at once. The* SECRETARIES *take their places at the table; the chief* SECRETARY *writes down* LEGENDRE'*s name. Behind the Chairman are a few more deputies, among them* ROBESPIERRE *and* SAINT-JUST, *who sit upstage on the right, close to the dais.*]

TALLIEN [*ceremoniously takes off his hat*]. Representatives; the meeting is now open.

LEGENDRE [*to the* CHAIRMAN]. I wish to speak.

TALLIEN. Speak.

LEGENDRE [*gathers his strength*]. Representatives of the people!—I have just learned—with surprise—that last night four members of the Convention were arrested. [*Watching one another cautiously,* ROBESPIERRE, MERLIN *[I],* LECOINTRE *[II],* COURTOIS *[A], and* PANIS *[1] rise and approach the* SECRETARIES. *They quietly ask for the right to speak; having received it, though we do not know in what order—they approach the dais, to occupy strategic positions.* SAINT-JUST *watches them*] I hear that one of the four is Danton. I do not know who the others are. But what do names matter?—As for Danton, comrades—I am ready to vouch for his integrity with my life . . . [*subdued applause; whisper of approval, glances, secret signs*] and I move the motion that—whoever the others might be—they should answer their charges from the floor. Since they are charged, they must have the chance to explain themselves . . . [*clearer, nervous whisper of approval; the speaker motions them to be silent and continues, encouraged*] . . . *then* you will judge whether, by any chance, personal conflicts—I will not say, envy—influenced the warrant for their arrest, which so astonishes us.

[*He descends amid loud, fervent applause. Five candidates to speak approach the steps;* ROBESPIERRE'*s shrewdness assures him victory. The others try to stop him, but he has blocked the access with his person and refuses to be removed.* SAINT-JUST *tries to position himself between* ROBESPIERRE *and his rivals.* ROBESPIERRE *interrupts the applause with a shrill shout; tense, unnatural silence returns.*]

ROBESPIERRE. I request—the right—to speak!

[*In spite of the* CHAIRMAN'*s assent, the other four have no wish to give up.* PANIS *tries to climb the dais from the outside.*]

MERLIN, COURTOIS, LECOINTRE. I was here first! It's not your turn!—We are first! Get away from here!—It's not your turn to speak!

TALLIEN [*rings the bell delicately*]. Gentlemen! . . .

ROBESPIERRE [*turns his head back*]. Citoyen Legrand: whose turn is it now?

SECRETARY. Yours, Robespierre.

FOUR DANTONISTS [*let him go and rush to verify this*]. Not true!—Deceit!—It can't be!

[*The Convention waits breathless.* ROBESPIERRE *too waits, until they are satisfied. The four bend over the list, murmur something, walk away, shrugging their shoulders, and take their places at the foot of the dais. Only now does* ROBESPIERRE *walk briskly to the platform, and* SAINT-JUST *leaves his position.*]

ROBESPIERRE [*in a full voice, but somewhat subdued because of a strange hush in the hall*]. Citizens...

[*Pandemonium breaks out.*]

VOICES. Let Danton come forward!—Let Danton speak first!—Let Danton take the floor!—No! Let Danton ascend the rostrum! It's Danton's turn!—Danton!!—We want Dan-to-on!!!—You're out of turn!—You will not speak!—Come down!—Down from the rostrum!—Down! Down with the Committee—Down with the tyrants!—Down with dictatorship!

COURTOIS [*rises, turns; with a fully outstretched arm points at* ROBESPIERRE *from below. Roars like a bison*]. Down—with the dic-ta-to-or!!!

[*All this time* TALLIEN *rings the bell laboriously, a little tired, like a blasé altar boy. But* COURTOIS'*s exclamation frightens the Convention. A pause signifying astonishment follows, and since* ROBESPIERRE *waits patiently and it is obvious he is ready to go on waiting until they grow tired, after the pause there is only a murmur, full of resentment, which soon ceases. The silence that follows signifies gloom.*]

ROBESPIERRE [*sighs*]. It's a long time, gentlemen, since we began our sitting with such an outburst of temper. The excitement of those present, unusual even within these walls, proves that an *important* matter is about to be decided. Today we shall see what we value more: the Republic—or a few individuals.

Today, gentlemen, we shall prove whether we deserve to rule the country.

FRERON. Today we shall see whether *you* deserve to rule, tyrants!

ROBESPIERRE [*transfixes him with his eyes*]. I will raise this point too...in a moment.

Legendre demands that the Convention listen to the accused from the floor.

VOICES. We all demand this!—All of us!—The entire country!!!

ROBESPIERRE [*waits until total silence is restored*]. But when the representatives Chabot, Basire, Delaunay, Fabre, Klotz and Hérault were arrested— nobody thought of asking similar privileges for them. You now wish to accord to these four what you have refused to so many others? On what grounds?

[*the opposition, cornered, reacts with a helpless murmur*]

Legendre says he has heard the name of Danton only. The entire Convention knows the remaining three. Why does Legendre deny this

knowledge?—Because he knows that among those three are such as Delacroix, for instance; and to defend Delacroix one needs to be shameless.

[*again a helpless, more irritated murmur*]

But he has mentioned Danton. Because Legendre thinks that this is the
name of a privileged person. Many think as he does.—We will correct
their mistake, gentlemen: we do not grant privileges to anyone.
6 & VIII [*joyfully*]. Bravo! Exactly!

[*fierce hiss of the opposition*]

FRERON. The Man of August the Tenth does merit some respect!

[*loud murmur of strong approbation*]

ROBESPIERRE [*louder*]. That's it—the Tenth of August. Gentlemen, above all,
the Tenth of August, the giant change from one system to another, was
the work of twenty-five million people straining to the utmost of their
strength; the work of a united will of the entire people, at a cost of their
genius, effort, and sacrifice that thought cannot encompass. [*At this
stage a few people show signs of approval. The opposition is, of course, silent*] Who
would dare to assume, by himself, the title of Man of the Tenth of August? Who would dare to focus on his miserable person the glory for a
million sacrifices, a million deeds, a million creative thoughts?! Besides:
Danton's participation in the process of that upheaval was not even particularly marked.
VOICES [*shouts of fear, indignation, outrage*]. What?! Danton's participation
. . .not mark. . .August the Tenth! What will he say next?! What calumny! How dare you! Vile envy!
ROBESPIERRE [*does not wait for the noise to subside, but speaks more loudly*]. But
when the victory was achieved, he was there to gather for himself all the
laurels. Thus legends grow round those who are unworthy. I am the
first to admit that Danton has his merits—but what of it?

Comrades: every one of you has achieved great things. But each of
you knows that the most excellent "merit" is only a link in the chain of
tasks for which we live and die: it is just a simple duty. To fulfill one's
duty, gentlemen, is something self-evident and gives no one the right to
claim gratitude or distinction, or a prize! We all know that none of us
can claim a privileged position for anything.

To claim a privilege for Danton would, therefore, be just. . .naive, if
that man *were* an unblemished hero. But since we all know—all, that is,

with the exception of a few misguided people—that Danton's career has been a succession of social crimes...

VOICES [*murmur of awe*]. Aaah!...Danton...Danton!...How's that?! Crimes!...A succession of cri...what does it mean?!...

ROBESPIERRE [*maximum volume*]. ...so this demand becomes also—a proof of shamelessness. [*dead silence*] That varnished idol, glittering on the outside and rotten within for a long time now, deceives society and spreads moral infection. We shall see whether the Convention has enough strength to topple that idol, and wake the idolaters from the trance of their adoration—or whether it will allow that clay colossus to drag it down with himself—and falling, deprive France of her government.—We shall see.

VOICES [*much more significant applause*]. He talks well! Down with the idol! We will topple it! We are strong enough, Robespierre!

VOICES [*the opposition now roused to action*]. Don't let yourselves be deceived! It's a lie! It's a horrible calumny! Danton is our great leader!

LECOINTRE. Robespierre! To hear the accused from the floor is not a privilege, it's simple justice!

[*vehement applause, but numerically lessened*]

ROBESPIERRE [*addresses himself to the opposition*]. What?! Justice?! So you have no trust in the Revolutionary Tribunal?

[*silence, as if after thunder*]

VOICES [*shy protests*]. No...no...never...no one will ever...The Tribunal is beyond reproach—the court has our full confidence...

ROBESPIERRE. In that case do not enter within the scope of its functions, for it is an insult!

VOICES [*thunderous applause*]. Very good! Well said! Bravo, Maxime! Go on, speak, Robespierre! Open their eyes at last!

VOICES [*the opposition, near to despair*]. Sophistry! He wants to fuddle you with empty phrases! Don't let him turn your heads! *We* are the government!

MERLIN [*desperately*]. Let us defend ourselves, by Jove!!

[*The* CHAIRMAN *rings the bell, in an ordinary way*]

ROBESPIERRE [*has meanwhile caught his breath*]. But this is not all.—I see that some of you, gentlemen, question even the warrant of the arrest. If so
. . .

[*The entire Convention leap to their feet.*]

VOICES [*applause, though considerably stronger, is drowned among the shouts of protest*]. No! Never! You've done well! We confirm it! Bravoooo!!!!
VOICES [*the opposition in a paroxysm of rage*]. Yes! We won't allow this! All France objects! [*laughter and hisses from* ROBESPIERRE'*s followers. Threats*] This is brute, cynical force! Abuse of power! Tyranny! Shame! You will be put to trial!!

[*Hisses and stamping of feet get louder. One deputy is hit on the head with a notebook, another with a paper ball, and—jumping over the bench—goes to retaliate. Fistfights begin. The* USHERS *separate the fighters. The* CHAIRMAN *rises and puts on his hat; gradually the commotion stops.*]

ROBESPIERRE [*having waited through it all*]. . . . if so—if you think that Danton must be judged according to a different code from the unknown Basire—pass a vote of no confidence in the Committee, dissolve it, and put us, members, on trial. [*murmur of indignation among his followers; the opposition is gloomily silent, helpless at this move*] How you justify this later on to the people, whose will is your law, is another matter.

[*a tired and somewhat sheepish silence*]

VOICES. We have nothing to reproach the Committee with. We have unbounded confidence in you. [*they warm up*] Up with the Committee! Long live the Committee! Bravo! Bravoooo!!!

[*glum murmur of resignation*]

ROBESPIERRE. And so, comrades, you see that a decree based on Legendre's motion would put you to shame, would be a proof of cowardice. The government of a society so threatened as ours—may not endanger its dignity. What happens to France when trust in us is lost?
VOICES. Quite right! Well said! Don't let's put the Convention to shame! Let us defend the honor of the government! We confirm! [*many voices in unison*] We con-firm! Legendre's motion is rejected!

[*applause*]

COURTOIS. Have you gone mad? If Danton fails, we are finished!!

[*hisses, whistles, shouts*]

MERLIN [*in despair*]. Fools, you expose yourselves to slaughter!!!

[*the noise dies down, cut off by with fear after such a strong expression*]

ROBESPIERRE [*in the midst of the silence*]. These two gentlemen have confessed their guilt.

MERLIN [*starts to his feet*]. What did you say?. . .

ROBESPIERRE. The Assembly has accorded full confidence to the Committees and the Tribunal. [*shouts of approbation*] And only criminals tremble before organs of social protection.

[*Strong applause.* COURTOIS *and* MERLIN *solemnly rise from their seats and cross the hall.*]

COURTOIS [*from the door, on the opposite side*]. You will accomplish your work of envy, Robespierre. But woe to you when Danton falls! The weight of that crime will crush you to pieces!

[*They go out.*]

ROBESPIERRE. That is the most common argument of all.

Well; and even if, by some mystic law, the destruction of a criminal were to become my ruin—would that be a social setback? Which of us cares about private danger?

There are among us many people of high moral standards—the Convention's work and deeds testify to that. I am sure that these people admit I am right.

VOICES [*ardently*]. All of us! All, Robespierre! The whole country!

[*vehement outburst of laughter, quickly stifled*]

ROBESPIERRE. I put the motion that our order of arrest be confirmed. [*Applause begins. He raises his hand*] And that Legendre's motion be rejected.

[*Thunder of applause.* ROBESPIERRE *descends.*]

LECOINTRE & FRERON [*through the applause*]. Never! Better to perish!

TALLIEN [*tired*]. Gentlemen, who votes for the motions of the last speaker? [*nearly everyone rises*] Who is against? [LECOINTRE *and* FRERON *rise*] Both motions are decreed on a majority vote.

[SAINT-JUST *arranges formalities, wishing to speak*]

LEGENDRE [*pale, rises*]. Robespierre! I did not intend to put Danton above the common good!

ROBESPIERRE [*sits down, tired*]. I don't impute this to you at all.

SAINT-JUST [*amidst solemn silence*]. I come here to accuse the last partisans of the monarchy. Before I put forward my detailed report, I will summarize the case for you in a few words. The Revolution is an outstanding deed of the nation which has proved that the human spirit is capable of breaking the omnipotence of nature by virtue of a higher law. You know *this* history of the revolution. But there also exists another, which is *not* the work of the whole nation. The other history consists of a long tangle of treason, deceit, venal intrigues, dirty conspiracies and provocative coups.

The Committees have ordered the arrest of the main hero of this *other* epic.

Danton's aim was not even power: that is a temptation reserved for purer natures. He was drawn to money. Danton held on consistently to kings and magnates, because they are the most copious sources of gold. Through his boss, Mirabeau, he served the Court as an agent-provocateur... [*exclamations of surprise*] Have you forgotten the slaughter at the Champ-de-Mars? Danton provoked the petition of twenty thousand, because the Court was looking for a pretext to introduce repressive measures! Do you remember how Robespierre warned the club? [*murmur of assent*] The Court was shaking, so Danton served at the same time the House of Orleans, enemy to the King. Danton imposed Philip Égalité and his son on us: he prepared those members of the Highest aristocracy a safe little nest in the very center of revolution!

From the Tenth of August, Danton has striven to seize power in the state—to sell it to the enemy who offers the most. From the Prince von Braunschweig to the Duke of York, there has never been a lack of candidates! And he has aimed to gain his end by *all possible means*. There are such means, gentlemen, as artificially contrived shortages of food. That was the way that the Hébertists were preparing their coup. And when one considers that their Grand Judge was to be—Danton!...

[*strong, though quiet commotion*]

And then there is something one would rather pass over, simply for shame: Danton, he, the Man of August the Tenth, was the prime mover of the India Company's blackmail. He was even indirectly involved in the falsification of the decree that resulted from it.

[*astonishment passes into anger*]

Every one of these charges is supported by evidence. Listen to the report, and then judge.

[*growing murmur erupts into shouting*]

VOICES. Not necessary! Long live the Committees! [*tremendous applause*] Now we know Danton! Down with the traitor! A conspirator! A blackmailer! Agent-provocateur! Let's have the decree! [*general demand:*] Decree of indictment!!!

BOURDON [*somewhat uneasily enters the dais and raises his hand*]. Gentlemen! I was myself for quite some time a victim of Danton's perfidy. I have realized my great mistake. I think, Comrades, that we must give the Committees a firm proof of our trust; for this reason I propose to issue the decree of indictment [*applause begins*] against these four villains—without waiting for Saint-Just's report.

[*General applause. An outburst of uncontrollable laughter is heard.*]

TALLIEN [*amidst threatening murmur growing through the applause*]. Why do you laugh?

PANIS [*rises, red in the face, roving eyes*]. I apologize to the Assembly. . .it is a nervous manifestation with me. . . [*he bites his lips*] at particularly. . . [*he chokes*] . . .solemn. . .mom. . .ents. . .

[*He stifles his laughter with a handkerchief and hides amidst an unfriendly murmur.*]

TALLIEN [*depressed*]. Who votes *against* Bourdon's motion? [*Nobody moves. In a glum voice*] The decree of indictment has been passed by acclamation.

[ROBESPIERRE *exchanges a fleeting, imperceptible glance with* SAINT-JUST, *who remains on the dais to read his report.*]

ACT IV   Scene 1

Luxembourg. A room in the palace, rearranged to serve as a prison cell without the tendency to cause maximum discomfort and degradation characteristic of our modern prisons. It is possible to open the big window despite the iron bars across it. On the right, by the table, PHILIPPEAUX *is reading, but he occasionally takes his eyes off the book to look outside; on the left* CAMILLE *is standing by the window, crying.*

PHILIPPEAUX [*impatient*]. Calm yourself, Desmoulins, please. Aren't you ashamed to blubber so in front of strangers?

CAMILLE. Do you realize it's the eleventh of Germinal today?! Do you know what it's like when one looks at *such* a day...through bars?!

PHILIPPEAUX. I do, because I am doing it myself. If you go on like this, I'll ask for a separate cell.

CAMILLE [*raving*]. No!!...I beg you, Philippeaux...don't leave me! I think I'd go mad, if I were left alone...do not turn away from me... you of all people! [*a new outburst of crying*] He rejected me...and went away. Crossed me out.—And he won't even know that every nerve in my body is calling to him! Jesus!! [PHILIPPEAUX *reaches for the bell.* CAMILLE *grasps his hand*] Forgive me...I don't know what is happening to me any more... [*he chokes*] I've lost him...now—forever.—Have pity... and help me, or I shall perish!!! [*throws himself on the bed*]

PHILIPPEAUX. You will die in five days, Desmoulins. [CAMILLE *goes numb. His crying stops like a switched-off radio.*] I advise you to accept this and not entertain any hope. When death is something absolutely certain, one ceases to suffer.

CAMILLE [*starts to his feet*]. It's a lie! We can win the trial!

PHILIPPEAUX. A fatal illusion. This is a political trial, and politics is governed by immutable laws of mechanics, not by your ethical sentiments. We have clashed with the Committee. The Committee is stronger, and *we* shall perish.

CAMILLE [*an instinctive reflex to stifle thought*]. But I don't want to perish! I have the *right* to live, damn it!...

PHILIPPEAUX. A living creature has rights only as long as it is able to preserve them. And then—would you really prefer to live and see how the work of humanity's liberation is being carried on—by madmen and thieves?
...

121

[*Enter:* HERAULT, CHAUMETTE, MERCIER, GIRONDIST I *and* II, RIOUFFE, *two* ROYAL-ISTS.]

HERAULT. Greetings, brother bankrupts. . .
MERCIER. In the name of our common Holy Widow Guillotine!

[*laughter, nervous excitement*]

HERAULT. Oh, Camille! My dear boy, how are you?
PHILIPPEAUX [*comes forward*]. Gentlemen, there must be a mistake: we are imprisoned in solitary confinement.

[*Sensation. Tremendous laughter*]

VOICES. That's good! What an eccentric! Who is he? Ssh. . .it's Philippeaux! Which one?. . .Ah, that one?. . .
CHAUMETTE. It's Philippeaux all right: he sees to it himself that orders issued against him are not violated.

[*They shake hands.*]

RIOUFFE [*has whispered to the group of royalists and Girondists*]. Listen. . .they should know!. . .

[*Shouts. General tension*]

HERAULT [*among excited murmur*]. There is a persistent rumor here that. . . Danton has been arrested.

[*nods, expectation*]

PHILIPPEAUX. Last night, I think; but I really don't know anything.
CAMILLE [*terrified*]. What, him too? But that's impossible!
MERCIER. I knew all the time it was just gossip.

[*nods*]

RIOUFFE [*with the group of Girondists approaches* CAMILLE; *they surround him*]. But we have the honor to see here the famous author of the "Street Lamp Prosecutor."
GIRONDIST I. Brissot occupied this room!
GIRONDIST II. But he did not cry—even over your wicked lampoon!
RIOUFFE. Twenty-two corpses. . .it's no mean burden—for *such* shoulders!
ROYALIST I [*they both approach*]. Let him be! The "Vieux Cordelier" has paid dearly for the "Prosecutor's" mistakes!

[*embraces* CAMIILE]

ROYALIST II [*stretches out his hand*]. Camille, no irony is intended: we thank you in the name of France.

[CAMILLE, *consoled, returns the embrace and smiles.*]

PHILIPPEAUX. Camille—that's the Comte and Vicomte d'Estaing.

[CAMILLE *withdraws horrified.*]

CAMILLE [*quickly regains his composure*]. But above all—companions in misfortune. Brothers: thank you for those consoling words. [*they shake hands*]

[*Enter:* DANTON, DELACROIX, WESTERMANN, FABRE D'EGLANTINE—*who is very ill*—CHABOT, DILLON, LAFLOTTE. *Everybody gets up. Shock of astonishment.*]

GIRONDIST. What. . .it's really Danton!. . .
MERCIER. So it's true, after all!
CHAUMETTE. How is it possible?!

[*All except the* ROYALISTS *rush toward him, speaking simultaneously:*]

HERAULT. I would never have believed it, Georges. . . [*shakes both his hands*] I shouldn't say I'm glad to see you here. . .
RIOUFFE. If they succeed in murdering you—the Republic will die with you.
FABRE. If Danton could be imprisoned, it means the Republic has already died.
DILLON. The achievement of August the Tenth—a plaything in the paws of nine greedy simpletons!
CAMILLE [*ignoring* DANTON]. Oh, Dillon!—Greetings, my dear!

[*They embrace.*]

ROYALIST I. Listen, let's be civil. . .after all, he did what he could. . .
ROYALIST II. For himself. . .and who knows if not for the rebels. For that matter, do you shake hands with your hirelings?
DANTON [*frees himself of the group and approaches* PHILIPPEAUX, *who is reading; he bows to* PHILIPPEAUX]. Do we by any chance disturb the honorable gentleman?
PHILIPPEAUX [*lifts his eyes*]. Not a bit. You and your gang do not exist for me.
RIOUFFE. We have been watching your struggles, gentlemen—but we did not expect the big crash before the end of May.
WESTERMANN. The end of. . .May?—when is that?
FABRE. True! You all are from the same geological era. . .
CHABOT. How about you?

FABRE. I've been here since January the thirteenth. Since the prehistoric times when there were still Januaries and Mays.

ROYALIST II [*to the floor*]. When the affair of the India Company was the newest sensation. . .

CHAUMETTE [*has worked it out by now*]. The end of May, Westermann, is the beginning of the month of Prairial.

DELACROIX [*leaning against the door:—bursts out laughing*]. Hohoho! By then the quicklime will have dissolved our skeletons!

[*sudden, embarrassed silence—as if he has said something tactless*]

FABRE [*with a sigh*]. Is there a bit of a chair somewhere, gentlemen?
[*simultaneously:*]
CAMILLE [*starts to his feet*]. Fabre!. . . Come over here, sit by us on the bed
. . .

[*He places* FABRE *on the right, with* DILLON *on his left. He freezes halfway through a cordial greeting.*]

FABRE. Oh, thank you. . . [*surprised*] What. . . have I changed so much?. . .

CAMILLE. No. . . it is I who have changed. My eyes have been opened. . . by force.

[*A mutual coolness develops which they try in vain to disperse.*]

DANTON [*has made himself comfortable with* HERAULT *on* PHILIPPEAUX's *bed*]. Eh! Try to organize some chairs!

DELACROIX. At your service, esteemed sir. Who's going to give me a hand?

[*He goes out with* CHAUMETTE *and* DILLON.]

WESTERMANN. Danton is unique. Already the entire prison staff takes orders from him.

FABRE. You were to be isolated. But he's had a word with the overseer, and . . . [*points to the room*] this is your isolation.

DANTON [*meaningfully*]. Yes, my friends: I know how to appeal to the soul of the people.

HERAULT. Oh, if you only knew what was happening here this morning! Where the news came from—no one knows, but suddenly the whole palace began to hum. Nobody would believe it; nobody could prove it; some thought, with every new noise, it was the signal for a fresh slaughter—in a word, outcry, crush and panic—we looked almost like the Convention.

[*The three prisoners bring in some chairs. All those present sit round* DANTON *in a semi-circle.*]

DANTON. And now, gentlemen—let us talk seriously.

[*protest*]

DELACROIX. Eh, stop it! All in good time, Danton. *Now* we can give up all that.

WESTERMANN. You should have taken the trouble two weeks ago!

HERAULT. Oh well, death is certain now . . . why should we rack our brains about it all?

DANTON. Just a minute, gentlemen. Committees too are only men.

FABRE. But it is they who have power, not we!

DELACROIX. You have found that out too late!

MERCIER. Nonsense. Better tell us some fresh gossip . . .

ROYALIST II [*sees* PHILIPPEAUX *opening the window*]. Let us go into the hall. It's suffocating here.

FABRE. The hall is crowded with snoopers.

DANTON. This is the only big cell. We have to stay here.

DILLON. Let's come to business at last.

[*again the protest of those who are reluctant*]

DANTON [*stifles the protest*]. Well, my friends, I have just had a message from Merlin. [*tension rises at once*] Would you believe it: Robespierre and Saint-Just have enforced the decree of indictment against us . . . It was carried by acclamation, at eight in the morning!

[*indignation and suppressed fear*]

WESTERMANN. I know what I would do with that Convention! A pack of stinking cowards!

FABRE. It's not even cowardice any more; it's a clear suicide mania.

DANTON. That means tomorrow we shall be taken to the Conciergerie . . .

[*a sudden, terrified silence*]

CAMILLE [*shouts in the silence*]. Christ! . . .

DANTON. . . . because in three days or so they will begin our trial. [*breathless suspense. He suddenly explodes*] Brothers, wake up! Your hands are tied, but what of it? You still have your teeth and your voice to defend yourselves! Our lives are not dirty rags, we will not give them up for nothing! If we are to perish—let us at least leave our murderers a souvenir that will choke them!

WESTERMANN & DILLON [*excited*]. Well said! But how are we going to do it, Danton?!...

DANTON. And then, it's not true that we have to perish! Who is that government, those judges?—Yesterday's scum, dressed in judges' robes today!

[*Those present become animated and divide into skeptics and enthusiasts.*]

DELACROIX. Stop that humbug, Danton! After all, they've managed to get you, haven't they?

GIRONDIST I. But on the other hand...now that we've got Danton?...

DILLON. Oh, Danton is an enemy the Committees will have to take into account!

DANTON. Just get rid of your apathy—and we shall all be saved!

CAMILLE [*excited*]. You're a rogue, Georges...but you don't lack nerve!

PHILIPPEAUX [*outside the circle—calmly, over his book*]. Desmoulins, don't let yourself be deluded! We haven't got a chance!

[*general indignation*]

VOICES. What sort of croaking is that?! A prophet of misfortune! We know his kind! Careful...maybe he's a spy! [*from whispers to shouting*] Throw him out! Go away, you! Go on! Out!

CAMILLE [*faintly*]. No, don't...

LAFLOTTE [*approaches*]. We don't need snoopers here. Out with you!

[PHILIPPEAUX *closes his book with a finger still in it, gets up and goes out. From the door:*]

PHILIPPEAUX. I can't go into the hall as it would give you away—are the cells near here free?

VOICES. Go to the devil! How thoughtful of him! Get out, quick!

[PHILIPPEAUX *calmly walks out.*]

ROYALIST [*points discreetly to* LAFLOTTE, *speaks quietly*]. Yes...but who is *he*?

VOICES [*suppressed*]. Does anyone know him?...I don't...Who knows who he is? So many idiots around...better throw him out. Then he will go and denounce us...

DILLON [*gets up and puts his hand on* LAFLOTTE's *shoulder*]. Don't insult my friend. I vouch for him.

LAFLOTTE [*bows*]. Laflotte, ex-envoy of the government in Venice.

CAMILLE. Stop all this stalling, will you!

FABRE. Your self-confidence, Danton, makes me wonder how they are going to group us together. That Delauney, Chabot, and myself will be linked with you is certain at any rate . . .

[*a whisper of embarrassment, mockery, surprise;* DELACROIX *utters a "hm"*]

CAMILLE. How's that? Why?

[*The* ROYALISTS *hem and haw, and exchange smiles*]

HERAULT. And how about me? Or Westermann?

CHAUMETTE. Impossible. You two are remnants of the Hébertists . . .

DELACROIX [*demoniacally*]. Exactly! . . .

[*Again a current of mutual understanding.* DANTON *wishes him a sudden and unexpected death.*]

DANTON. Yes, my friends: that is quite possible. I advise you all to get ready! [*a murmur of disbelief and protest*] Oh, friends, diplomats of the good old regime! Robespierre's Committee will show you what true perfidy means! They will throw on my head all the crimes of the world. But I have strong shoulders.

FABRE. Yes, but . . . really. Ideological crimes and . . . well . . . political and financial ones are quite different things. If you allow yourselves to be implicated in the affair . . . of the liquidation decree—you will be very coldly received by public opinion.

CAMILLE. You can't allow such calumny, Danton!

[*Smiles, delicate nudges.* CHABOT *gradually turns red and clenches his fists.*]

DANTON [*lost in thought*]. Yes. [*he sees* FABRE*'s smile*] You, Fabre, belong with us, of course—it is well known that you have not even been touched by that forg . . . that matter. But [*he turns to Chabot*] I am very sorry, you, those two Jews and those others are total strangers, as far as we are concerned . . .

[*tension*]

CHABOT [*rises slowly, shaking with rage*]. Strangers!!!! And who was it that brought us to Batz? Who was the first to think of blackmail? Who persuaded us to take part in the forgery?!! Who?! And now you people want to disown us!!!!

[*Those present watch the clash intently, with obvious amusement.*]

DANTON [*haughtily*]. You must be mad!

[CHABOT *looks as if he is about to get an attack of apoplexy*]

VOICES [*impatient*]. This is no time for arguments! Never mind! Get on with it!

DANTON. I alone—do you hear?—*I alone* can save us all. So you'd better not interrupt, or else you will drown with me!

[*he changes his tone*]

Friends, a political trial is not a trial, but a duel. And *this is* how we must treat this case from the start. The government accuses us? Very well, we must accuse the government. There is only one power which has the right to judge both parties: the people.

So, we shall counter every accusation—with an accusation, in the form of an allusion. But with these half-revelations we shall terrorize the Committee to such an extent that they will be compelled to stop the trial at any price...

DELACROIX. ...exclude us from the court and execute us without trial. A fabulous plan!

FABRE [*among general commotion*]. Indeed, Danton. This is the shortest way to the guillotine.

CHAUMETTE. Exclude?! Impossible. The tribunal and the committees would be lynched if they did such a thing.

DILLON. Exactly! You forget the effect Danton's voice has on the masses!

DANTON. That's right. My voice is our infallible talisman. It will immediately electrify the mob...I mean the public in the gallery, and then the government will not be able to risk lawlessness.

HERAULT. Danton always has gigantic ideas. But that's the right scale these days.

DELACROIX. But my friends, it is not enough to talk big. You will immediately bring *part* of the gallery to hysterics with your roar, Danton—but not *all* of them! And from time to time one will have to answer a...justified charge?...

WESTERMANN. Then one has to refuse to answer!!

[*laughter*]

FABRE. Quiet. That's not such a bad idea. Do you know what you should do? Answer only in the presence of the prosecutors, that is to say the Committees. This is a sure way, because once Danton sets the tone of the masses—the Committees will not dare to cross swords with him in public.

[*murmur of interest*]

MERCIER. Yes—but it's risky. The masses are so unpredictable. . .

DANTON. I know. Just in case of difficulties we shall add another condition: they must bring on the defense witnesses first [*approbation*]. We shall choose them from among the deputies: Courtois, Legendre, both Merlins and so on. And to that we have to cling with our claws, because: either the Convention will not want to produce them, and by so doing releases us from answering the charges—or it will produce them and thus give us a terrible weapon against itself. Moreover, such a substantial concession is tantamount to surrender and the first symptom of somebody's ascendancy exerts a miraculous influence on the crowd.

[*applause*]

RIOUFFE. Yes. . .you can indeed succeed in this.

CAMILLE. We must succeed!

FABRE. Well, well, my friends—after all, we are in real trouble.

DANTON. In any case—I shall either perish, or get you all released!

[*excitement grows*]

ROYALIST I. Danton! Do you realize that you have revived hope even in us . . .after two years of total despair?

[*excitement grows into a commotion*]

MERCIER. Your trial, Danton, is the outbreak of a holy war against the tyrants!

[*accelerando*]

CHAUMETTE [*leaps to his feet*]. In which all of us must take part!

GIRONDIST I. There are so many political prisoners now that, united, they can have a great influence. . .

[*Apart from* DANTON *and* FABRE *no one has remained seated.*]

DILLON [*a tone of discovery*]. That's it. . .united!. . .

MERCIER. We must organize prisoners of all parties. . .

ROYALISTS. Of course! We have a common cause!

RIOUFFE. And in all prisons!. . .

ROYALIST II. Then to join forces with a crowd of suspect, threatened malcontents still at large. . .

MERCIER. It's enough for us to organize—to become a power equal to the government!

DANTON [*rises*]. Listen! [*silence*] Our relatives must establish an external league. We must invent a system for correspondence. Let Dillon write at once to Camille's wife...

CAMILLE. For God's sake! Don't involve Lucile in this!!

DANTON. Don't be an egoist, boy! She can move all of Paris!...Let her begin propaganda for the league. I'll make up the list of potential members...

LAFLOTTE. And I'll get the letters out. I know a guard who's devoted to me, he'll fix it!

HERAULT. We mustn't count on victory...but if...

WESTERMANN. If—then that will be the end of the Convention, of the Committees, of all that shameful tyranny of lawyers!

CHAUMETTE. It will be a new August the Tenth!...

GIRONDIST I. And the dawn of Freedom at last!...

DELACROIX. Gentlemen, gentlemen. Don't excite yourselves.

[*An uneasy* GUARD *comes in softly.*]

GUARD [*in a trembling whisper, to* CAMILLE]. Citizen...a visitor is waiting for you...

CAMILLE [*wants to run*]. Who?...My wife?! Where?...

GUARD [*holding him back*]. No...no...oh, please listen!...You *mustn't* tell, please...I said that, by mistake, you are in another cell...

CAMILLE. What mustn't I tell? What is it?

[*The others crowd round them.*]

VOICES. What's the matter? Who is it? What's happened? Why does he beat about the bush?...

GUARD. Gentlemen...quiet, please by God!...

[*Impatience turns into anxiety.*]

PHILIPPEAUX [*comes in*]. Desmoulins, Robespierre is waiting for you in cell thirty-five. [*Those present rush away in various directions and go numb.*] It's down the corridor to the right. [CAMILLE, *deathly pale, gives* DANTON *a long look, expressing thoughts for which there are no words.* PHILIPPEAUX *returns to his place.*] Go on, man. Quick.

CAMILLE [*amid deadly silence—half moans, half howls*]. O-ooo...Dan-ton!...

DANTON. What are you waiting for, Camille? Go and save yourself!

FABRE. Nobody is stopping you, Camille...

CAMILLE [*wrings his hands, whispers*]. What am I to do?....

PHILIPPEAUX. Go at once, Desmoulins!

DANTON. Last night you wanted to beg him for mercy, and there was no time—go now!

[CAMILLE *turns to him, petrified*]

WESTERMANN. We shall all die—why should you die with us?

DELACROIX. Surely, you'd rather go home in a week than...to the Square of the Revolution?

DANTON [*politely makes way*]. Please go, Camille...

CAMILLE [*straightens up*]. Please tell the gentleman that I do not wish to see him.

GUARD. But, sir...I can't say that...

PHILIPPEAUX. Desmoulins, it's moral blackmail, and you give way to it!

CAMILLE [*close to fury*]. Tell him what you will! I shall not go to see him and that's final!

FABRE. Tell him that Camille is not at home!

[*Laughter. They turn the* GUARD *out.*]

GUARD [*in despair*]. Gentlemen!!...

ALL [*with the exception of* PHILIPPEAUX]. Go on, out! Tell him what you will, it's your business!

[*They push him through the door.*]

DANTON. Well, Camille, for once you have behaved like a man. Let's go!

[*They all go out, except for* DESMOULINS *and* PHILIPPEAUX.]

CAMILLE [*stands dejected*]. After all...honor required it...

PHILIPPEAUX [*lifts his eyes*]. You lack the strength not only for love, but even for the simple thirst for life.

[*A gloomy dusk falls.*]

CAMILLE [*throws himself on the bed*]. Ah, I wish I were already dead...

Scene 2

DANTON'*s home.* LOUISE *opens the door after the bell has been rung by* LUCILE, *who stands in the doorway heated, haggard, hoarse.*

LUCILE. Is Madame Danton in?

LOUISE [*indifferent*]. Please come in. I am she.

LUCILE [*looking at her with a frightened expression*]. *You* are Louise Danton?... The deputy's *wife*?...

LOUISE [*as before*]. Yes, indeed. With whom do I have the pleasure?

LUCILE [*in despair*]. How old are you?!

LOUISE. Sixteen. Who are you?

LUCILE [*soundlessly*]. Lucile Desmoulins...What do I need this teenager for! [*she turns back*] I am sorry. [*she stops and returns*] No matter. You *must* help me.

LOUISE [*ushers her in*]. Please sit down.

LUCILE [*sits down*]. How do you intend to help save your husband?

LOUISE. All steps on my part would be pointless.

LUCILE [*after a moment of dumbfounded silence*]. Do you realize how serious the situation is?

LOUISE. Naturally.

LUCILE. One must act at once. I am free. I can do anything within human power...but I don't know what!! And no one will tell me, no one, absolutely no one!!! Oh, how despicable people are...I've lost a whole day. And Camille writes...from prison...I read the first letter. I don't even open the others. For I mustn't—I *must not* go mad!!!!

LOUISE. Have you tried to do anything?

LUCILE. What a question!...Of course, first I tried to bribe the more important judges. Some of them will take part in this trial at any event... But it didn't work. Why don't they want to take the money?! I've been thrown out, like a dog, eighteen times!

LOUISE. Of course. That was pointless.

LUCILE. I've knocked on the doors of all the judges, the prosecutor, the president of the tribunal. I was not received anywhere. Money, entreaties, obstinacy, nothing helped. It's like a wall.

LOUISE. Exactly.

LUCILE. My last hope is Robespierre. That's why I am here. You will be let in to see him, because nobody knows you; I'll slip in behind you. We will stand barring the door and not budge until he gives way to us. If he tries to throw us out or leave—I'll stab myself right there in front of him. Camille loved him more than me...Please, get ready at once. Don't put any powder on!

LOUISE [*calmly*]. Before an enemy of Danton I will not humble myself at any price.

LUCILE. Child! What does humiliation mean when the life of one's dearest is at stake?!

LOUISE. This is absolutely pointless, madame Lucile. [LUCILE *utters an angry and desperate cry*] But please listen, maybe I can help you. [LUCILE *forces herself to pay attention*] You will *write* to Robespierre and tell him that your husband was planning to return to the government's side; and because it is too late now, he would like at least not to be mentioned by Robespierre as an enemy. You should on *no account* ask him for mercy! The letter must be handed to him directly, in the street. [*she gets up and collects some writing utensils from a sideboard*] Please write it here.

LUCILE [*sits down, depressed*]. Well, I'll try...But it's such a poor half-measure...

LOUISE. I am offering you the *only* way.

[LUCILE *dips the pen in ink, hesitates*]

LUCILE. Thank you... [*she writes a few words; stops; collapses*] Oh, my God, how powerless we are!...

[*The bell rings loudly.*]

LOUISE [*rises*]. Excuse me. [*she goes to open the door;* LUCILE *tries to write.* LOUISE *returns, followed by* LEGENDRE] ...Yes. She's just come.

[LUCILE *turns round and leaps to her feet.*]

LEGENDRE [*to her*]. Citizeness...

LUCILE. A man at last! Listen, monsieur: if Danton falls, the Convention will be at the mercy of the Committees, and the Committees at the mercy of Robespierre, who has forced this trial. Isn't that so?

LEGENDRE. Yes. And so...

LUCILE. And so one must stop this!

LEGENDRE. Precisely. Lis...

LUCILE. You listen to *me* first! Legendre, you know how to kill... [LEGENDRE *nearly jumps, given such a start*], as a butcher, of course. Ambush Robespierre tonight and kill him! [LEGENDRE *draws back, dumbfounded, then he smiles.* LOUISE *shakes her head slowly, looking at the table*] He usually walks back home in the mornings—the streets are empty—nobody will know that it was you—and all France will breathe! But you must not delay: tonight! Legendre, you will save the country!!

LEGENDRE [*pats her on the shoulder*]. We've gone a little crazy, haven't we... well, there's nothing strange in that. [*he prevents her outburst with a gesture*] And now please listen.

[LEGENDRE *sits down.* LOUISE *calms* LUCILE *by touching her hand; she prevails on her to sit down too*]

LEGENDRE. Ladies, between ourselves, the Convention have made fools of themselves. Robespierre turned our heads this morning, we let ourselves be carried away by him, as usual—and now we're beginning to realize what we have decreed and bitterly regret it. Well, it's always the same. But the prisoners are wiser. They have invented a most ingenious plan. . . Citizeness, do you remember General Dillon? [LUCILE *nods*] He places his hopes in you. Here is a letter from him.

[LUCILE *snatches the letter without a word and goes towards the window. From her movements it is clear she has revived already.*]

LOUISE. What plan is that?

LEGENDRE. Danton intends to move public opinion in his favor from the dock. If he succeeds—the Tribunal will not dare to touch them. And the Committee will be powerless because the Convention will not be so obliging next time. . . What matters now is to give Danton support on all sides: the political prisoners will organize themselves everywhere, and all the oppositionists who are free ought to unite in an external league with the chief committee.

LOUISE. If it's just a matter of having the prisoners released—why this organization? Or that league. . . Oh, Legendre: this smacks of a bankrupt Hébertist plan.

LEGENDRE [*frightened*]. Citizeness, have some sense! Who would think of such a thing! [*more quietly*] But even if. . . just compare the circumstances. Then Paris was sleepy, today it shakes with excitement. Then no one had serious reproaches for the Committees; today, my dear lady, the Committee's despotism has alienated half the people, and above all the Convention itself! [*still more quietly*] Believe me: if somebody had the courage *today*. . . but hush! Let's not waste words.

LUCILE [*folds the letter and approaches*]. I will not fail them. By tonight the league will exist and act. Have you got the list of addresses?

LEGENDRE [*gives it*]. Here you are. On the first page are Danton's friends.

LUCILE [*looks through it carefully*]. . . . that is to say, capitalists. Very important: we must gather quite a few people from the suburbs. Agitators must be paid, galleries filled—at both the Club and at the Convention—and we will even have to surround the Tribunal.

LEGENDRE. For God's sake! Not so loud.

LUCILE. The rich relatives of the accused must devote half of their movable possessions. . . .

LEGENDRE [*leans back*]. Hohoho! Just try to tell them so!

LUCILE [*folds and puts away the list*]. I will tell them, Legendre. And I'll explain to the stingy ones that the fall of Danton means a dictatorship of relentless terror and immense fiscal burdens. In order to prevent *that,* they will all open their purses. [*she turns to go away; speaks over her shoulder*] Legendre, I'll be grateful to you till the day I die.

LEGENDRE. Eh, citizeness! [LUCILE *stops by the door*] You are known. If you begin to run about the city, spies will stick to your tail. Let Madame Danton take half the addresses. [LOUISE *calmly shakes her head*] What's that?!

LUCILE. It's a waste of time. That woman has no heart.

LEGENDRE. Wait, wait. And why don't you want to help? It's your husband we are talking about!

LOUISE. I know. But, first of all, your plan is absurd...

LEGENDRE [*angry*]. And why is that, madame?

LOUISE. Why? Because the Committee is too clever to let itself be duped in such a childish way, and too powerful for gangs of bribed ragamuffins to harm it. Secondly, the conspiracy [*an angry gesture from* LEGENDRE] is bound to be discovered very soon and will hasten the death of all the accused...

LUCILE. Christ! How *can* she say something like that!!

LOUISE. Lucile, you'd better follow *my* advice. Don't let yourself be involved in this madness.

LUCILE [*wavering for a moment*]. No. This is no time for half-measures. And if we lose, well...at least we shall all perish together.

LOUISE. Ah, in that case, it's another story. As far as I am concerned, life is smiling at me again right now, so I will not throw it out of the window for fear of what my neighbors think. I will not take part in your plotting nor spend a single sou on it.

LUCILE [*calmly, her hand on the door handle*]. That is called baseness, madame.

LOUISE. Yes, indeed.

[LUCILE *goes out.*]

LEGENDRE [*comes closer to her in a familiar attitude*]. Oh, what a clever little head you have! So, you have already found someone to console you after your dear husband? A bit early...but not surprising with such a pretty face...

[*He wants to embrace her.* LOUISE *calmly rises and takes away the writing utensils. She destroys the letter, hardly begun.*]

LOUISE. I don't think you are raging with the flame of devotion, either.

LEGENDRE [*sits calmly, smiling*]. Well...no, no. I wish the brave Madame Lucile success with all my heart—and I shall be awfully glad, and so will the whole Convention, if they succeed. For the moment, however, I prefer not to enter the Committees' greedy mouth.

LOUISE [*closes the sideboard*]. Exactly. And now please leave me.

LEGENDRE [*gets up, suddenly frightened*]. So that you can run straight to Comsur and denounce me, is that it? Just dare do that and you'll see, you little . . .

LOUISE. Informers' business does not pay, Legendre! Chabot's fate does not encourage one to imitate him!

LEGENDRE. That's why I advise you to sit still! Listen, little one. If you squeak just one word—I'll say you have invented this plan. And then good night, pretty eyes! . . .

LOUISE. Ah, so it's *you* who want to betray them? I am not stopping you. There is the door.

[LEGENDRE *leaves, suspicious and in a rage.*]

Scene 3

The Vestibule of the Revolutionary Tribunal. A barrier across the center separates the court's entrance on the left, from the entrance to the gallery. USHER I *upstage left,* USHER II *downstage right. In the wall on the left a third door leads to the jury room. The crowd is gaily excited with this mass entertainment.* FOUQUIER-TINVILLE *is reading the act of indictment behind closed doors. Silence.*

JOURNALIST I [*enters briskly on the left, shows two pieces of paper*]. Editor of the "Freedom Lantern" from Versailles. Here is my pass.

USHER I. What, *another* one! [*checks the document*] You must have rushed here from all over France?!

JOURNALIST I. I daresay! Get on with it!

USHER I [*returns the papers*]. But it's standing room only. All the seats have been taken since midnight.

[*from within:*]

FOUQUIER'S VOICE [*as the* JOURNALIST *enters*]. . . . that in collusion with the enemy . . .

[*A hardly audible murmur of indignation.* DANTON'*s stifled shout. On the right* PARTY I, *consisting of two persons, rushes in.*]

CITIZEN I [*to* USHER II, *who controls the passes*]. Is the Act of Indictment over?
USHER II. The prosecutor is just coming to the end.

[*Within:* DANTON*'s voice heard amidst silence.*]

CITIZEN II. Oh!—Can you hear him?!...
CITIZEN I [*snatches the passes from the* USHER]. If only we can find a place!...

[*They get in, with difficulty. Through the open door* DANTON*'s voice is heard:*]

DANTON'S VOICE. ...Vile Saint-Just, you will answer before posterity for this sacrilege!...

[*With the door now closed,* HERMAN, *the president of the tribunal, admonishes him calmly, then turns to* FABRE. DANTON*'s words are followed by the first, very slight murmur of interest; it stops while* FABRE *is being interrogated. Order. On the left:*]

JOURNALIST II [*in traveling clothes, rushes in. Stopped by* USHER I, *he hands him his card*]. The editor of the ''Banner'' from Reims! Let me in!!
USHER I. Where's your pass?
JOURNALIST II. What is that now?!...
USHER I. The Assembly has issued a decree: the proceedings cannot be recorded without a license from the Committee of Security. [JOURNALIST *without a word turns to the right.*] Those who write in the gallery are arrested! And there is no room, anyway.
JOURNALIST II [*stage center*]. Has that Committee gone ma...

[BILLAUD *and* VADIER *enter.* JOURNALIST *speedily disappears, while they give him an unfriendly look.*]

VADIER [*to* USHER I]. Stand by the entrance: many more will come. They could smash the door.

[USHER I *walks to the corridor on the left.*]

DUMAS [*rushes in and bumps into him*]. Is the prosecutor still speaking?
USHER I. He has just finished, citizen vice-president.

[*He disappears.* DUMAS *greets the deputies with a hasty nod.*]

VADIER. Let Fouquier come out to us as soon as he can.

[DUMAS *nods and enters the chamber.*]

[*From within:*]

FABRE'S VOICE. . . . And Delaunay are utter strangers to me. With Chabot I have never exchanged a word. . .

[*On the left:*]

VADIER. All seems to be in order. There was no need to panic!
BILLAUD [*ominously*]. Patience, friend.

[*From within:*]

[HERMAN *turns to* DANTON. *An expectant stir. Then a more distinct, slowly growing murmur of interest.* DANTON *begins loudly but very calmly. He warms up gradually.*]

[*On the right:*]

[PARTY II *of five people rushes in.* USHER II *has to intercept them energetically.*]

USHER II. Hullo there! Your passes? . . .

[*Simultaneously, on the right:*]

CITIZEN I. Quick! Be quick about it!!
CITIZEN II. Now it's beginning! What a show . . .

[*On the left:*]

DUMAS [*rushes from within; at first he holds the door half-open*]. Fouquier begs to be excused: he can't come just now, not even for a second . . . [*they talk inaudibly*]

[*From within:*]

DANTON'S VOICE [*more and more vehemently*]. . . . I have something to do with that scoundrel? Who *dared* to place that thief Chabot next to *me*?! Have you no shame at all?! We, the vanguard of Revolution—the purest . . .

[DUMAS *shuts the door, remaining in the Vestibule.*]

[*On the right:*]

CITIZEN I. What nerve!
CITIZEN III. He's right! To put him together with those worms!
CITIZEN IV. Come, come . . . The Committee knows what it's doing.

[*On the left:*]

[DUMAS *returns to the chamber.*]

CITIZEN V. Danton is no angel, Poireau!

[*From within:*]

HERMAN'S VOICE [*very calm*]. . . . will prove whether the grouping of the accused is justif. . .

[DANTON *has established contact with the crowd. From now on tension can be felt. Murmur grows. Partisan protests take root, but the court is still in control of the crowd.*]

[*On the right:*]

CITIZEN I [*inspection over*]. At last!!!

[*They grab their cards and rush in.*]

CITIZEN IV. Oh . . . we shan't get in! . . .

[*They struggle in the open door among hisses asking for quiet.* CITIZENS II *and* IV *manage to get in, the others push in vain.*]

[*From within:*]

DANTON'S VOICE. . . . behind my back. Let them dare to stand and face me here and repeat their shameful slander.

[*A murmur of tense but growing approval.*]

Let them dare, and I will crush them to a pulp before the people, with facts from their own careers!

[*The murmur now signifies delight, largely because of the fun, but partly in moral approval.* BILLAUD *sends* VADIER *a sarcastic smile.*]

I will reveal such bottomless shame in their lives that they will not dare to look the world in the face again!

[*The crowd is puzzled; involuntary questioning exclamations, not addressed to anyone in particular.*]

They've crawled out of nothingness to throw mud on me. But I will push them back into nothingness with *one word of truth*!

[*The first inarticulate shouts. General commotion. The bell is rung for the first time; the noise abates at once, but the murmur of excitement does not cease. By the entrance a stubborn, though quiet argument goes on.*]

DUMAS' VOICE. The barrier will break! Lock that door!

[*This is followed by a relatively calm dialogue:* DANTON–FOUQUIER–HERMAN. *The three people refused admission do not resist.*]

[*Simultaneously, on the right:*]

CITIZEN I. Let's go to the window!
CITIZEN III. There's a crowd by each one of them.
CITIZEN IV. They've been sitting on each other's shoulders since morning . . .
CITIZEN I [*by the door*]. Hush! . . . You can hear everything that's going on.

[*They glue their heads to the door.*]

[*On the left:*]

BILLAUD. Well, everything going all right? . . .
VADIER. That Fouquier is a bungler . . .
BILLAUD. They are both too weak. And it will be worse. This is only a prelude.
VADIER. Well, Robespierre must always have his way . . .

[*On the right:*]

PARTY III [*of seven, rushes in and brushes aside the* USHER]. There'll be a battle, you'll see! What a voice, what a voice!

[*At the door, a conflict with* PARTY II]

PARTY II & USHER. There isn't any more room. It's locked!

[*They try to open the door, but do not dare bang it. They follow the three who have been excluded by putting their ears to the door. An argument ensues because there is no room for them all.*]

PARTY III. Really! Locked! Damn! Make some room, devil take you!

[*Two find a place, and won't budge.*]

A NEWCOMER [*has discovered a door on the left*]. Let's go . . . here!

[PARTY III *follows him.*]

PARTY II & USHER. Eh, you! Hush! Not there! It isn't allowed! It's the Court's entrance!

[*On the left:*]

BILLAUD [*quietly*]. Citizens, there is no more room: go away.

[*The bold newcomers stop in their tracks; one, who has already crossed the barrier, turns back.*]

[*On the right:*]

PARTY III [*stops*]. Court's entrance. . .—what, not allowed? Why? Leave it. Hard luck. Let's go.

[*They go away, with the exception of two who remain by the door.*]

[*Within:*]

[DANTON*'s voice, very serious and emphatic. Murmuring in the chamber has given way to a profound and attentive silence.*]

[*On the right:*]

CITIZEN III [*with satisfaction*]. By the evening that Fouquier fellow will turn grey like B. . .

CITIZEN I [*all of a sudden intensely attentive*]. Quiet!! List. . .

[*Concentration and tension shared by everyone. An unusual, motionless silence everywhere. They listen*]

[*On the left:*]

VADIER [*has approached the door; in an excited whisper*]. Eh, Billaud! Come and listen. . .

[*They listen in concentration. A moment of total suspense.*]

[*On the right:*]

CITIZEN IV [*half whisper*]. Hullo!. . .What does this mean

CITIZEN I [*whispers, with passion*]. Shut your trap!. . .

[*Again total silence*]

[*Within:*]

[DANTON *has finished. A fuller and more vehement murmuring erupts: the crowd has now established contact with one another. There are nervous conferences, speculations, questions, answers, denials. Excitement mounts: the bell is used more and more frequently, its effects ever more shortlived. The accused have also grown excited and talk to one another; their voices cannot, of course, be recognized.* HERMAN*'s embarrassed answer is drowned in the nervous though still stifled commotion. The crowd begins to take sides: most support the accused. But the essentially gay tone does not change.*]

[*On the left:*]

BILLAUD [*vehemently*]. That's what I expected! I *knew* he would think of that!

[*On the right:*]

CITIZEN IV [*insists*]. What is he on about? What witnesses?
NEWCOMER II. For the defense...
CITIZEN III. His colleagues from the Convention...you know, it's a *great* idea!
CITIZEN I. Will you be quiet?!...

[*Within:*]

[*The first clear and sharp approving voice emerges from the crowd's murmuring. It provokes a tongue-in-cheek protest, a high-pitched female cry, and much stronger approval from other voices, confirming, demanding. The bell hardly helps at all now.* HERMAN *for the first time raises his voice energetically, which results—gradually—in relative calm and silence.* HERMAN *and* FOUQUIER *turn to* HERAULT. *A calmer dialogue follows, but* HERAULT, *with his good humor, makes people laugh. The laughter in the gallery, stifled at first, is always silenced by the sound of the bell.*]

[*Noise erupts at the end of the long corridor.*]

[*On the right:*]

CITIZEN IV [*attention now relaxed, since* DANTON *has finished*]. Well, if things go on like this!...
CITIZEN III. Oh no! Things have not even begun!

[*On the left:*]

[FOUQUIER *enters, red, sweating, angry.*]

[*From within:*]

DANTON'S VOICE [*interrupts someone else's interrogation. From now on he interrupts more and more frequently*]. ...we categorically refuse, until they bring our ...

[*Vocal support from the crowd ensues. As if it were a game, the excited crowd falls into hysterical unruliness. There are short, provoking shouts, such as: "That's it! Hear hear! He's right! Go on! Don't let them stop you! Bravo! This is their right!" Of course, one cannot hear the words through the closed doors, but in spite of its vehemence, the support does not acquire aggressive character: it lacks serious political*]

*orientation, or passionate indignation, that magic lever of all mass movements. A
short clash between* DANTON—*supported by* HERAULT, DESMOULINS, *and*
WESTERMANN—*and the distinct but still calm voice of* HERMAN.]

[*On the left:*]

FOUQUIER [*to those who have not been admitted*]. You are not permitted to
stand in the corridors. Please leave.

[*On the right:*]

CITIZEN I [*still unsure of himself*]. But if there is no room inside . . .
CITIZEN III [*more audaciously*]. Can't be helped! We must stay here!
NEWCOMER II. We have the right even to stand on the roof!

[*On the left:*]

FOUQUIER. Please—leave—immediately!

[USHER II *approaches, reluctantly.*]

[*On the right:*]

THOSE NOT ADMITTED. Why? Is this a new decree, or what? Or maybe the
Convention has abolished open hearings? Yes, why not!

[*On the left:*]

FOUQUIER. Away with you, or I'll have you thrown out!!

[*On the right:*]

THOSE NOT ADMITTED [*much less vocal now, and withdrawing slowly, pushed by the*
USHER. *They retaliate by mocking* FOUQUIER *in half-whispers.*]. Ah, he takes it
out on us. Here he plays the lord. Out here he's stuck up. But in there
he crawled under the table! He's just staggered out, look how red he is!

[*They leave.*]

[*On the left:*]

BILLAUD. Citizen Fouquier . . .
FOUQUIER [*in despair, staggers against the barrier*]. Wait!!! . . . By God, let me
catch my breath, or I'll burst!

[*He wipes his face with a handkerchief.*]

VADIER. So soon.

[*Outside, on the right, the noise increases*]

[*On the left:*]

VADIER. What's happening *there* now?!

[*Two* USHERS *run from the chamber in the direction of the noise.*]

[*Within:*]

HERMAN'S VOICE [*irritated, but still controlled*]. . . . that it's *not your turn,* Danton?!—And as for you, citizens, I warn you again . . .

[*There follows* DANTON'S *reply: he is familiar and mocking, finally he addresses the crowd directly; part of those in the gallery fall in with the jeering tone;* DANTON *incites them, but they are still somewhat subdued.*]

[*On the left:*]

FOUQUIER [*to the* USHERS]. Where are you off to?

USHER III. The president ordered us to guard that entrance, they are trying to storm it.

[*The* USHERS *rush off to the right, having jumped over the barrier.*]

[*Within:*]

[DESMOULINS *is being interrogated among the now abated murmurings. His tone, gaily provocative at first, gradually turns into hysterical exasperation, expressed in high-pitched cries. The crowd shows, ever more freely, partly sympathy, partly— particularly later—scorn. Women show compassion but also laugh at him in shrill voices. It means that though the Court has lost its authority, it is likely that* DES- MOULINS *will provoke deadly French laughter deriding both him and his party. For this reason* DANTON *interrupts more and more often, addressing the crowd. He provokes each time a more vehement reaction.* HERAULT, WESTERMANN, *and* DELA- CROIX *follow his example.* HERMAN'S *sharp bell is now effective no more than thirty seconds at a time.*]

[*Outside, on the right:*]

[*The noise abates for a while.*]

[*On the left:*]

FOUQUIER [*rises*]. Gentlemen: report to the Committees that, at the request of the accused, the Convention must send as witnesses without delay the deputies—Cour . . .

BILLAUD. We know. And the Committees report to you, prosecutor, that it
is high time to display some energy.

FOUQUIER [*indignant*]. Some—energy!!...So what am I supposed to do?!
Am I to make a spectacle of myself, as he does?!

VADIER. Exactly! You let him shout so that the whole city can hear!

[*Within:*]

[*Just at this point* DESMOULINS *begins to shout. The dialogue between him and
judge* DOBSEN, *supported by* HERMAN, *threatens to degenerate into a quarrel. On
hearing the crowd's laughter,* DANTON, *with the support of his colleagues, throws in
sarcastic remarks, most often at the gallery, to turn this laughter back onto the
heads of the Court. The galleries react approvingly, taking up and repeating the
jokes. This contact is ominous for the Court, which nonetheless ignores it for the
time being.*]

[*On the left:*]

FOUQUIER. And how am I to shut him up?! Have you gone mad?! For that
matter: why are you interfering with my work here? You are not
present, but still express opinions?! By what right?!

BILLAUD. The Committees keep an eye on you, Fouquier. We know every
word.

FOUQUIER [*his voice stifled with anger*]. You dared to send snoopers on me, the
public prosecutor?!!...

VADIER. How else, Fouquier! Your vacillation does not inspire confidence!

[*Outside, on the right:*]

[*The noise is louder again.* USHER II *goes there to deal with it.*]

[*On the left:*]

BILLAUD. You should know that I have demanded your arrest.

FOUQUIER [*choking, almost staggers*]. My...my a...

[*Speechless pause*]

[*Within:*]

[*For the first time* DANTON *roars with laughter. The galleries join in, quite openly
now.* HERMAN *reacts with his first outburst, betraying resources of energy which
make the crowd think. Some grow respectful, others are overawed. In spite of* DELA-
CROIX' *sarcastic reply and* DESMOULINS' *provocative laughter, the galleries sober up.
An angry murmuring now.*]

[*On the left:*]

BILLAUD. But for Robespierre you would already be behind bars. . .
VADIER. He did it in order not to delay this trial. . . apparently.

[*Outside, on the right:*]

[*The noise gathers strength.* USHER I *runs across from the other corridor.*]

[*Within:*]

[*Among renewed murmuring, which then abates,* HERMAN *begins to interrogate* DELACROIX. *When he sees that the tension has fallen, he hands the interrogation over to* DUMAS *as his deputy and goes out.*]

[*On the left:*]

FOUQUIER [*erupts. His voice, quiet at first, gradually gets louder*]. By all the devils in hell, conduct your damned trial yourselves! Do what you will with that beast that roars and bellows like an elephant being slaughtered! I tell you: bring him those witnesses, and soon, or else the devil knows what will happen!

[*He wants to run away.* BILLAUD *stops him.*]

BILLAUD [*having motioned* FOUQUIER *to stay*]. Our reply is: either you bring the trial to a *certain* conclusion, or else—the next trial will be *yours*.

[*Shouts by the entrance.*]

BILLAUD. The means are your affair.
You will refuse him witnesses. [FOUQUIER *starts.*] One does not send reinforcement to the enemy. That is all.

[*He turns to depart.*]

FOUQUIER [*shaking with fury*]. You *must* send the witn. . .

[*Outside, on the right:*]

[*By the entrance a noisy struggle.*]

[*On the left:*]

[HERMAN *rushes in and stops, followed by four* USHERS *who have come to help their colleagues.*]

[*From within:*]

DELACROIX'S VOICE. . . . Miączyński lied! I did not say anything about war
booty! For that matter Danton was always. . .

[*Tension grows again, and the absence of* HERMAN'S *energy and capability makes itself felt.* DANTON *interrupts forcefully;* DUMAS *falls into a rage and, by so doing, loses the remainder of his authority and control over the crowd. He engages in an ever more vehement quarrel with* DELACROIX. *They beat the table with their fists.* DANTON *from time to time throws in a brief shout, as if spurring on the horses, and this is taken up by his colleagues and by the gallery. The crowd, delighted, roar with laughter and shout, but curiosity restrains them from indiscriminate shouting or yelling. An angry murmur—a dangerous symptom of serious commitment—once awakened, does not now cease. Soon* DELACROIX *and* DUMAS *try to outshout one another.*]

[*On the left:*]

HERMAN [*out of breath—hands* BILLAUD *a piece of paper, which the latter refuses to take*]. Gentlemen, here is the list of the defense witnesses. Please, *do*
hurry; you can hear what is happening.
VADIER. You should not have allowed this to happen!

[FOUQUIER *turns back and approaches them.*]

[*Outside, on the right: negotiations; a truce, but not peace*]

[*On the left:*]

HERMAN [*amazed, dignified*]. You don't know what you are saying. They do
not want to answer until we call. . .
BILLAUD. Even if they were to break the walls down—you will refuse!
FOUQUIER. But we have no *right*!!!
HERMAN [*steps one pace back*]. What!! Impossible. They have right on their
side. The crowd now supports them unanimously. We *cannot* refuse.

[*Within:*]

[DUMAS *has won. His uncontrolled shout has stimulated all of a sudden a passionate,* serious *protest from another element in the crowd: those who have taken part in each of the* grandes journées *of the last few years not just for the orgy but—unconsciously—for the salvation of their souls. This element is characterized by the utmost vital tension; thus, in accordance with a law of nature, everyone follows the lead given by these people. The protest is so loud that one can almost hear the words:* "Let him speak! Do not interrupt the accused! Freedom of speech in court!" *A short lull, during which* DELACROIX *ends the sentence, previously interrupted by the vice-president.*]

[*On the left:*]

HERMAN. Please, judge for yourselves.

[BILLAUD, *visibly shaken, is wavering.*]

FOUQUIER. And they keep threatening to make revelations against all of you!

VADIER. Billaud, we shall have to send those witnesses.

BILLAUD [*without contradicting them*]. We will have to surround the building with troops.

[*Gestures of fright.*]

FOUQUIER. This is madness! The people. . .

[*Within:*]

[DANTON *falls like a bomb into the suspended chorus, which immediately erupts in a previously unattained fullness. The aroused fanatic element does not now reappear openly, but tangibly, disturbingly accompanies the element of merriment. An orgy ensues:* DANTON'*s roar floats in triumph on the foaming waves of shouting, laughter, the hysterical squeals of women, whistles and subterranean hubbub. Throughout the bell is rung frantically.*]

[*Outside, on the right:*]

[*All that is happening revives the struggle, which in a moment spills into the corridor.*]

[*On the left:*]

HERMAN. Gentlemen, I shall be compelled to suspend the proceedings!

[*Outside, on the right:*]

[*They are now in the corridor. The rumble goes across the whole building. A concerted noise.*]

[*On the left:*]

FOUQUIER [*jumps at the salutary thought that has occurred to him. He shouts as if to be heard in a typhoon.*]. Listen!! [*He drags the others out front*] Let the Convention itself decide the question of witnesses, since they are its members!

[*General relief, though* VADIER *is still uneasy*]

BILLAUD [*after a second, with relief*]. Very well. Fouquier. Go and tell them, Fouquier. [VADIER *drags him to the exit on the left.*] But you must send the letter to the Committee of Safety!

[*Both stop for a while, in spite of their haste, and give him a sharp look, which he ignores.* FOUQUIER *goes inside.*]

[*From within:*]

DANTON'S VOICE [*jeering amidst the noise*]. . . . French people? How the judges twist the law? [*sarcastic and indignant approval*] The witnesses for the defense. . .

[*As a result of* FOUQUIER'S *bell and—doubtless—the signs he makes, the noise gradually quiets down, then definitely subsides.*]

[*Outside, on the right and on the left:*]

[*In the corridor on the right the attackers have won; one can hear, too, that on the left, at the end of the longer corridor, people are forcing the entrance. From the right the victorious* PARTY IV *of nine people rushes in. Every few seconds new people come, in groups of four, two, five.*]

[*On the left:*]

[BILLAUD *from the front on the left,* HERMAN *from the door at the back, both turn to the center.* VADIER *wants to escape to the left, but withdraws, on hearing that the siege goes on there too. He tries to hide, somewhat shaken.*]

[*On the right:*]

PARTY IV [*in very good humor*]. You can hear him right across the bridge. . . The walls are shaking, just look! He may still win, I tell you! Well, which way now?

[*On the left:*]

HERMAN. You there! What do you want?

[VADIER *remains behind his colleagues.*]

[*On the right:*]

PARTY IV [*storming the door on the right*]. Get in! We want to get in and listen! [*They bang at the door*] Eh, open up! Open up! We'll break down the door!!

[*On the left:*]

HERMAN. There is—no more—room! Please leave!

[BILLAUD *hastily bars the door on the left with his person.* VADIER *crouches in the corner on his right, because. . .*]

[PARTY IV *has discovered this door and rushes to it with a shout of triumph.*]

[*On the left:*]

HERMAN. This entrance is off-limits! Show respect for the court!

[*They push him aside good-humoredly.*]

PARTY IV. That makes no difference! We can go in anywhere! We want to go in! [*jeering*] Respect, eh? Deal with Danton first! Bunglers! They've run away from the prisoners! Cowards! [*to* BILLAUD] Out of our way!

BILLAUD [*in an unexpectedly powerful voice*]. I am a representative of the people!

[*This makes an impression. The impetus is lost, they do not dare to touch him. The masses stop, calm down—grumble and jeer at first, but soon listen attentively, in silence.*]

[*Within:*]

[*Amid a cooler—sober—silence* FOUQUIER *announces the intention to turn to the Convention. This is followed by businesslike discussion and agreement.*]

[*Outside, on the left:*]

[*The masses have forced the lock and are noisily coming down the corridor.*]

[*On the left:*]

BILLAUD. Citizens! Whoever disturbs public peace, does the enemy a good turn—even more so today than ever before!

[PARTY V, *a whole crowd, rushes in from the left, but on seeing the solemn behavior of their predecessors, stops and grows silent too. Only the first few of* BILLAUD'S *words that follow are drowned by the noise.*]

Go back! Or else the Convention will surround the Tribunal with troops and no one will get as far as the windows!

INVADERS [*indignant, but half-hearted murmur*]. Troops. . . he says troops. . . What, they want to surround the court?! [*individual voices*] How is that?

The trials are public! We have the *right* to listen! You're ready to shoot too! Just as in the tyrant's days!. . .

BILLAUD. But you have no right to insult the court! Citizens, in the tyrant's days you were a rabble. . . [*a lion-like growl, but attention deepens*] Today you are free citizens. *You* are the masters of the city now [*a few shouts of approval*] and that's why you are responsible for keeping its peace. Your government is there to serve you, not the other way round. Support it, instead of obstructing! [*a more intelligent expression of approbation from several people*] Go then and watch over the peace yourselves.

[*Within:*]

[*The accused express agreement. Excitement, but order.*]

[*In the center:*]

INVADERS [*a murmur of childish obstinacy*]. Some talk! What sort of masters are we, if we're not allowed to do anything! To hell with it! I want to listen to what goes on, and that's it! [*energetic support from the others*] Quiet, you, he's right! Yes, yes! He's right! Well said! Come on, let's go back!

[*They withdraw, partly of their own free will, partly dragged by others who are stronger.*]

VOICE [*taken up by all. Hats raised.*]. Long live the Convention!

[*They separate and go out right and left.*]

[*On the left:*]

HERMAN. Billaud—the Tribunal thanks you.

[*BILLAUD receives his handshake coldly, with a scornful shrug for his own merits.*]

FOUQUIER [*comes back*]. Ugh! They've agreed. . .

[*Within:*]

[*A muffled murmur of excitement; the accused chatter, full of hope.*]

DESMOULINS' VOICE [*very excited, but intimately*]. . . .it's certain, because the Convention will send them to us at once. [*outburst of nervous joy*] Oh, friends. . .!!

[*On the left:*]

FOUQUIER [*shuts the door behind him*]. We have gained perhaps a quarter of an hour's peace. I'm going to write the letter; [*to* HERMAN] you can sign it in the chamber.

[*He opens the door in the center of the wall which leads not only to the jury room, but also to a kind of foyer.*]

BILLAUD [*over his shoulder*]. To be handed to our Committee, remember!

[*A second's hesitation, full of piercing looks*]

VADIER [*stops, asks in a tone sharp as a needle*]. Why?

[BILLAUD *ignores him.*]

FOUQUIER [*from his door*]. But let them hurry with their reply, for God's sake!

HERMAN [*from the door leading to the chamber, with a smile involuntarily heroic*]. For this is like a voyage on a burning ship, gentlemen!

[*All go out.*]

Scene 4

398 Rue St. Honoré. ROBESPIERRE, *without vest or tie, is asleep, his head resting on his folded hands on the edge of the dressing table. Awakened by a knock, he raises his head, twisting it slightly, but does not reply.*

ELEONORE [*enters, stops—speaks very softly*]. Oh. . . sorry. I didn't realize you had come back.

ROBESPIERRE [*without even glancing at her*]. Quarter of an hour ago.

ELEONORE. Will you be going out again?

ROBESPIERRE. In ten minutes. What do you want?

ELEONORE. What can I get you?

ROBESPIERRE. Nothing. Leave me in peace.

ELEONORE [*protests*]. But!. . .

ROBESPIERRE [*with ominous calm*]. Have pity; stop it. [*He presses his fingers to his forehead with a grimace of pain and impatience. He emits a soft snarling groan, without opening his mouth*] Mmmmmm-mmm. . .

[*Meanwhile* ELEONORE, *not at all put out, competently and quietly restores order among the chaos of clothes, towels, papers, and pulled out drawers in the room. In a word, she removes the unambiguous traces in the room of a short visit by a man who has rushed home for twenty minutes, irritable, only half-conscious due to migraine and insomnia—in order to change his clothes and prepare himself for a further seven hours of parliamentary wrangling.*

While doing all this ELEONORE *glances at him with a constrained half-smile, slightly mocking. He must by chance have noticed it or felt it. Anyway, he turns his head a fraction in her direction. He does not see her clearly because focusing his eyes causes him too much effort.*]

ROBESPIERRE [*usual voice*]. Léo.

ELEONORE [*turns to him, relaxed*]. Yes?

ROBESPIERRE [*extends one hand to her; he leaves the other on his forehead*]. I am sorry. I'm going insane.

ELEONORE [*clasps his hand with a gay smile*]. Oh, Maxime. In your place I would be the very devil. But listen to me: are you starving yourself on purpose? [*She asks this question in a matter-of-fact way, without irony*]

ROBESPIERRE [*knits his brows, painfully trying to remember*]. Am . . . I starving myself? . . .

ELEONORE [*half-smiling*]. Only since yesterday noon.

ROBESPIERRE [*astounded, drops his hands*]. By all the saints!! [*gets up*] And I've been wondering what is the matter with me! . . .

ELEONORE [*runs to the door*]. You'll have some broth right away.

[*Out of the room she calls downstairs. Meanwhile* ROBESPIERRE, *standing close to the dressing-table, wipes his forehead helplessly and slowly with the back of his hand, then, just as aimlessly, presses both hands against it, wry-faced, near tears, like a man too long tormented. On the entry of his friend, he controls himself less than sufficiently, which she ignores with a somewhat merciless tact*]

ELEONORE. While you drink this they will prepare you something more to eat. Why are you standing? Sit down.

ROBESPIERRE [*with inert movements puts on his vest*]. Thank you. I don't want anything else. [*he must have some rest*]

ELEONORE. Very well. I'll tell her.

[*She is standing at the edge of a table in the middle of the room, while* ROBESPIERRE, *enraged by his weakness, washes his face with eau de cologne, then turns round and arranges his hair in front of the mirror.* ELEONORE *at last decides to speak*]

Maxime . . . is the Danton case taking a bad turn?

[*He turns slowly towards her, frightening in his immobility.* ELEONORE *looks down at the floor in order not to let herself be overawed. Almost in a whisper*]

Tell me, Maxime.

ROBESPIERRE [*gives her a vacant look*]. Why do you think so? The newspapers
. . .

ELEONORE [*shrugs her shouldlers heavily*]. The newspapers! How can one trust the newspapers!

[*Short pause. He is waiting like a statue; she raises her eyes at last*]

Maxime, during no other danger—the worst of crises—*never* did you look as you do now.

ROBESPIERRE [*turns back to the mirror, with an evil, dry smile*]. Well, if you judge a political situation by my looks!

ELEONORE [*as if to herself*]. But it is the surest way.

ROBESPIERRE [*turns suddenly and quickly. He is pale, his face twitches slightly. Speaks in a subdued voice*]. Léo. . . I am not very patient today. Please don't tease me.

ELEONORE [*suddenly approaches him. Disguises her anxiety with a bright, mocking smile*]. And you have pity on me. You know yourself what it is to be concerned. . . [*grabs him by the shoulders*] What is it, man?!

ROBESPIERRE [*looks down at the floor*]. This trial is a risky duel, but I am almost certain of victory. As long as the Convention does not lose its head—and I have power over the club, I have no reason to worry.

ELEONORE [*her hands drop, she looks at the wall*]. What a consolation. . . [*A knock. She runs to the door, takes the tray*] This will do. You've told me all.

ROBESPIERRE [*walks to the main table, but does not sit*]. Thank you.

[*They eye each other, both calm.*]

ELEONORE [*an outburst in a half-whisper*]. In that case *why* this expression of . . . despair?

ROBESPIERRE [*starts. Knits his brows, controls himself*]. I have my cares, dear child.

[*He takes the bowl in both hands, but does not lift it, as it is too hot.*]

ELEONORE [*with a bitter smile on only the lower part of her face*]. Really?! Have you had one hour free from your cares, ever since I've known you?! [*more excitedly and softly*] A year ago you were for a whole long week just one step away from the guillotine, but you did not look at the world so oh . . . [*still softer*] like . . . someone besieged.

ROBESPIERRE [*with an almost gay laugh*]. Oh God! The guillotine!

[*He lifts the bowl and blows on the surface of the soup.*]

ELEONORE [*now calmly*]. Maxime—strike me, if you wish. But I will not budge from here until you tell me.

ROBESPIERRE [*sighs with pretended patience; supports himself against the table on widely spaced hands*]. Woman, *I* am in no danger. Not at all. Only . . .

[*He drops his head. In this state of weakness and depression he cannot resist the temptation to share with someone else the Chinese torture of a certain thought. Monotonously*]

The Danton case is a dilemma. If we lose—the whole Revolution is as good as lost. And if we win . . . the same is probably true. [*a short pause*] Five—years—of struggle, suffering, innumerable victims . . . all for—nothing . . .

[*Stooping over the table with an outstretched neck, he looks for a while at the infinity before him. He breathes slowly; his calm face has assumed an expression of concentration, tension, and fascinated horror—the expression which strikes us on looking at his last profile portrait. At last he calmly shuts his eyes and straightens up*]

I must not say that.

[*He lifts the bowl and drinks. His eyelids and nostrils quiver. With an almost devout expression*]

I am returning to life.

ELEONORE [*looks at him attentively*]. Such thoughts are a typical sign of exhaustion, Maxime.

[ROBESPIERRE *gives a deep sigh and goes on drinking*]

ROBESPIERRE [*wipes his mouth. With the voice of one resurrected*]. Let's hope you are right . . . although . . . At any rate, as long as that devil does not interfere with my work, it's not a great misfortune. [*looks at his watch and whistles*] I must hurry. Thank you kindly; I feel much better.

[*He takes a tie prepared for him, neatly attaches it round his neck.*]

ELEONORE [*inspects the state of his cuffs which are laid out*]. To the club?
ROBESPIERRE [*fastens the tie*]. That's right. [*Puts on his coat*]
ELEONORE [*curious*]. Listen—is it true that Legendre is presiding at the moment?
ROBESPIERRE [*buttons up his jabot in front of the mirror*]. Mmm . . .

[*Having finished, fixes the cuffs.*]

ELEONORE. But I hope they don't make things difficult for you?
ROBESPIERRE [*busy with his right cuff*]. For the last three days nobody has made things difficult for me—as long as I am looking at him. [*A knock. Without raising his eyes*] Come in.
ELEONORE. See you tomorrow, Maxime.

[*They nod goodbye to each other. In the doorway* ELEONORE *passes* FOUQUIER *and* BARERE.]

BARERE & FOQUIER. Good day.
ROBESPIERRE [*fixes the last button. Without raising his eyes*]. Welcome. Well, what news? [*takes his eyes away from his sleeve at last and looks at his guests. They shake hands*] Oh, it's you, monsieur Fouquier. We are meeting in private for the first time, if I am not mistaken. [FOUQUIER *nods in affirmation*] Do sit down. [*They sit. He stands before them, examining his stockings and shoes. He discovers a spot just above the knee, so he takes a brush and cleans it, while he speaks*] Barère, I am glad to see you. Please suggest to the Committee of Security that particular attention should be paid to the prisons. Danton's arrest must have acted like an alarm-bell on the others. I am sure they are organizing themselves and plotting. And all we need now is a rising of political prisoners in the capital.
BARERE [*shyly*]. You think so? . . .
ROBESPIERRE [*straightens up*]. Yes, I think so, and very much so.

[BARERE *opens his eyes wide, more surprised than offended by such a tone.* ROBESPIERRE *sits down impatiently, his head positioned straight, but supported by his hand*]

Why have you come?
FOUQUIER. Robespierre, this trial has taken a dangerous turn. Danton drives the galleries into a frenzy. Instead of answering accusations, he utters slogan after slogan and attacks the government. And it *works*, Robespierre! He is now so sure of his public that today he dared to challenge his accusers to a trial before public opinion. Today's session had such a . . . disturbing course that if it is to go on . . .
ROBESPIERRE [*motionless*]. If it is to go on, my friend—then tomorrow France, surrounded by armies on all sides, will wake up without a government, her capital occupied by the enemy.
FOUQUIER [*emphatically*]. And so, Robespierre?!
ROBESPIERRE [*supports himself against the table, leaning over the top. He speaks calmly as if about something obvious*]. And so, Fouquier: three days have passed; tomorrow Danton must perish.

FOUQUIER [*leans back in his chair, knits his brows angrily*]. What sort of an answer is that?

ROBESPIERRE [*as above*]. Tomorrow the death penalty must be passed, Fouquier. It is up to you to substantiate and pass it. *We* will take care of what follows from that.

FOUQUIER [*unable to comprehend*]. But you must understand: Danton's influence on the masses is greater than ours. We are bound by law and conscience, he—by nothing at all; and *everybody* is on his side. When he begins again tomorrow . . .

ROBESPIERRE [*comfortably*]. You will deprive him of the right to speak.

FOUQUIER [*starts forward*]. The accused?! The people would tear us to pieces—and rightly so!

ROBESPIERRE. The people would . . . will have more respect for you. And it is indeed about time, prosecutor! Danton challenges us to a trial before public opinion? Very well! What possible harm can his revelations do us?

[*He retreats from the mirror and examines his attire from all sides.*]

FOUQUIER. One more thing . . . [*cautiously, uncertainly*] Yesterday we sent the Convention a letter, containing the demand of the accused. We sent it to the hands of the Committee of Safety . . .

[*He looks at his companion.*]

BARERE [*very embarrassed*]. Why . . . then . . . what has . . .

ROBESPIERRE [*slowly returns and sits on the table*]. What has happened to it? I have embezzled it. It's in my pocket.

[*He slaps his hip.*]

BARERE [*astonished, innocently*]. But why . . . ?!!

ROBESPIERRE [*very calmly, but with somewhat stronger emphasis*]. Because it is not my wish that the Convention should decide such an important question without my supervision.

FOUQUIER [*motionless, scarlet, a vein on his forehead bulging like a rope*]. Robespierre: this is the cynicism of a despot.

ROBESPIERRE [*still calm*]. I took upon myself the responsibility for bringing Danton before the court. Whoever gives the responsibility, also gives the full power to act.

The Convention will reply to your letter when it learns what I think about it. I will read it—if I read it—when the right moment comes.

BARERE. But now every minute . . . !

ROBESPIERRE. The Convention's reply, if it is given, will be negative.

FOUQUIER. This is so shameful a transgression of the law that even those who are indifferent will be revolted.

ROBESPIERRE. If we withdraw an inch, we are lost. [*somewhat less sharply*] I understand you, Fouquier. But the law of universal good neutralizes all other laws. If you consider the destruction of Danton in these circumstances to be a violation of the law, then you must violate the law.

FOUQUIER [*rises with genuine dignity*]. Robespierre: I am a judge, not an executioner in your service.

ROBESPIERRE [*still sitting on the table, but tense*]. Not in my service—but in the service of society this is exactly what you *are*—an executioner. [FOUQUIER *steps back a little, stunned*] We deliver into your hands the enemies of the Republic who must then be, not judged, but removed.

[FOUQUIER *sits down, lost in thought.*]

BARERE [*trembling with nerves*]. By God, just consider! For three days Danton has been inciting Paris against us; how can we provoke the already enraged masses still further?!

FOUQUIER [*roused from his thoughts*]. Exactly. I repeat: you have not seen what is happening. We must make some sort of concession to keep our . . .

ROBESPIERRE [*slides from the table like a snake*]. If you dare to utter one more doubting word, I'll send you to prison straight from the courtroom. Warn your colleagues: that goes for all of you. The Committee of Security is watching. Vadier will have a warrant ready for each one of you. [*more softly*] One gesture or look will be enough.

[FOUQUIER *looks him in the eyes, with contracted jaws.*]

BARBERE [*indignant*]. But Robespierre, the court cannot fulfill its functions under the duress of terror!

ROBESPIERRE [*throws his head back, flashing his teeth in a smile*]. We'll see if it cannot! Terror, gentlemen, is the universal law! [*to* BARERE] You are now beginning to understand my long resistance, are you not? [*He looks at his watch. The guests get up*] I shall be late. Damn it! [*he grabs his hat and gloves*] Have I explained the situation to you sufficiently?

FOUQUIER [*ironically*]. Oh, perfectly. I have understood you. [*seriously*] You can count on absolute subordination.

ROBESPIERRE [*shakes his hand while rushing to the door*]. That's the style.*

*English words in the original.

[BARERE, *who is at some distance from him, gives a parting nod.*]

FOUQUIER. I hope that for the time being no dagger is aimed at your heart . . . but *only* for the sake of the state.

[ROBESPIERRE *breaks into sonorous, pleasant laughter and disappears.*]

BARERE [*on his way to the door, lost in thought, whispers*]. But I have stopped cherishing that hope.

[FOUQUIER *looks at him sharply, without surprise.*]

ACT V   Scene 1

The Conciergerie—a medieval-type prison. A cell, connected with another through a grating in place of a door. Four beds: two upstage and one by each wall. DELACROIX *is sitting on a bed;* DESMOULINS *is standing on the table, at which* PHILIPPEAUX *is reading; he looks westward through a skylight.*

WESTERMANN'S VOICE [*from the adjoining cell*]. For three days I've been racking my brains. . .hey, are you asleep?

DELACROIX [*rushing to the grating*]. Asleep? Tonight? I envy those that can!

WESTERMANN'S VOICE. . . .I've been racking my brains as to whether they *can* prove that I took part. . .

HERAULT'S VOICE [*sound of his jumping off the bed. Vehemently*]. They can't prove anything against anybody! Absolutely nothing! That's why they must fake their proof!

DELACROIX. Fouquier would have shut Danton's mouth long ago, if he'd had proof. . .although. . .

[*He stops, lost in thought, scratching his neck.*]

HERAULT'S VOICE. For God's sake, don't do that!. . .

[DESMOULINS *leaps off the table and approaches.*]

DELACROIX [*puzzled, drops his hand*]. What?

HERAULT'S VOICE. Nothing. . .nothing. It's all right. [*with a nervous smile*] I'm so nervous that I'm liable to hysterics.

CAMILLE. Me too. I'm dropping from fatigue, and yet I cannot stay still in one place.

HERAULT'S VOICE. Three days in a row, a good eight hours each day, in that roaring hell—who can stand it!

FABRE'S VOICE. Brothers, fatigue is nothing: we are tortured by *hope*.

[*The vehemence of their protests is exaggerated, convulsive.*]

WESTERMANN'S VOICE. Silly talk!
CAMILLE. What an idea!

[*Because it is getting dark,* PHILIPPEAUX *closes his book and sits down sideways on his bed—the one closest to the door—leaning back on his elbows.*]

DELACROIX. You know, Fabre, you've spoken the truth. As long as I thought we were finished, I slept like a log. But since I've been watching Danton's success, I can't sleep a wink. All night I weigh our chances. It's enough to drive one mad!

HERAULT'S VOICE. Oh yes. Danton has at last shown what he can do. To be in the dock and yet, within an hour, literally to hypnotize the audience and use it as a weapon, this, gentlemen, takes genius.

CAMILLE. That's why the Tribunal is surrendering *already*! It has agreed to call our witnesses, and, of course, this. . .

FABRE'S VOICE. No, no; not *agreed,* but it has left the decision in the Convention's hands.

DELACROIX. Two—days—ago! And no reply as yet!. . .

DESMOULINS. So what?! The Convention cannot refuse, so it comes to the same thing!

WESTERMANN'S VOICE. My friends. . .do you realize that the third day has just passed?. . .

[*a significant lack of response*]

DELACROIX [*after a somber pause*]. Why do you remind us?! I'm sure that since this morning each of us has tried in vain to forget about it. . .

[*silence again*]

HERAULT'S VOICE [*after a long delay*]. Courage, friends! Public opinion supports us; the Tribunal barely holds its ground; they cannot. . .

FABRE'S VOICE. Do you know what I am afraid of? The Tribunal may not dare to condemn us because of the people, but neither will they dare to release us because of the Committee. Before the scales tip one way or the other, we could hang suspended in mid-air for weeks.

[*muted exclamations of fear and terrified protest*]

PHILIPPEAUX [*motionless, unexpectedly*]. Have no fear. Three days have passed: tomorrow they will condemn us to death. [*All turn to him, speechless. Dead silence*] Even if the Tribunal loses its voice, it will still pass sentence.

[*The others recover their speech, but their voices tremble somewhat.*]

WESTERMANN'S VOICE. What's all this? Why should that happen?!

CAMILLE. You should be ashamed of yourself! Aren't things hard enough for us as it is?!

HERAULT'S VOICE. Would you kindly stop getting us down?!

PHILIPPEAUX. Danton's provocations are discrediting the government. Robespierre would not be Robespierre, if he were to put up with it.

FABRE'S VOICE [*after a while*]. Oh, how I envy you your certainty!...

DELACROIX [*lost in thought*]. You are right, Philippeaux. What sense is there in getting drunk on illusions? Public opinion, you say? And what can we, cut off from the world in the Tribunal's dungeons, know about opinions circulating beyond these walls?! What is happening in the city?—What does Robespierre intend to do? How...

WESTERMANN'S VOICE. Robespierre! Always and everywhere that Robespierre! Devil take him...

[DANTON *rushes in. They instinctively gather round him.*]

CAMILLE. Georges! Any news?...

HERAULT'S VOICE. What's happening downtown, Danton?

DANTON. I've got news all right! Just you wait! Confound it, haven't you got a candle in here? Ah, yes.

[*He has found one and lights it.*]

HERAULT'S VOICE [*he can be seen by the grating, though not very clearly*]. Ugh, what a dog-hole! How can they dump people here who are... still alive! ...

DANTON. Take heart: tomorrow we're going home.

DELACROIX [*turns round*]. Oh, stop it, will you.

HERAULT'S VOICE. Oh, give us hope, Danton! We're sinking without you!

DANTON [*with a satisfied smile*]. Well, hasn't Danton recovered, eh?! [*softer*] Listen: the league of those threatened is growing all the time...

WESTERMANN'S VOICE. Come closer, Danton!

[*They move to the grating.* PHILIPPEAUX *remains motionless until they have all gone to sleep.*]

DANTON [*in forceful half-whisper*]. Your wife, Camille, is canvassing and has collected four thousand two hundred livres already...

CAMILLE [*joyously surprised*]. Lucile!... [*suddenly frightened*] Oh, but *why* have you...

DANTON. She will take care of herself, my boy. Boyd and a few other bankers are offering the governing committee twelve thousand. Boys from the suburbs will surround the Tribunal tomorrow with a secret cordon. Pâris has won over three sections—that means nine cannon, brothers. Political prisoners are organizing everywhere. . .

FABRE'S VOICE. And the organization is led by lambs. We know them well enough.

DANTON. Even if we do, what of it! The lambs know only too well *whom* they must now serve. But all thi. . .

PHILIPPEAUX [*in a whisper like the lash of a whip*]. Gentlemen!!. . .

[*They disperse in a flash. A* GUARD *brings in water and then leaves.*]

HERAULT'S VOICE [*among frightened murmurs*]. Maybe he was standing by the door?!

PHILIPPEAUX [*loudly*]. No. I heard his footsteps approaching.

[*Relieved, they gather together again.*]

WESTERMANN'S VOICE. Well then? You said. . .

DANTON. Tomorrow at noon general Savigny will come to our aid with five thousand men!

[*whispered cries of astonishment and joy*]

HERAULT'S VOICE. O. . .the same kind of rumors, word for word, circulated before the king's execution, and then neither. . .

DANTON [*vehemently*]. Don't you know the difference between a rumor and *news*?!

DELACROIX [*suddenly*]. Danton: any child would see through such preposterous drivel. Why are you deluding us, man?. . .

DANTON [*restraining his anger with difficulty*]. You ass, if you had a tiny bit of brains you would see right away that it *has to* happen! To save my. . .our heads is a matter of life and death for the entire state! And you are surprised that France is prepared to defend us?!

FABRE'S VOICE. Exaggeration spoils the best arguments, Danton. Besides, you forget that three days ago France ceased to be the mistress of her own will. By issuing the decree of impeachment the Convention de facto put absolute power into the hands of Robespierre. Do you think that will make him more conciliatory?

DANTON. Ah, that is exactly the point! Ha, ha! Maxime has done me a very good turn by having systematically concentrated power in his own hands for years: all I need to do now is to take from him. . .a ready-made dictatorship!

[*Sensation. Silence*]

CAMILLE [*horrified*]. Then you really...!
FABRE'S VOICE. But how?!

DANTON [*becoming excited*]. Tomorrow, brothers, the grand finale will take place! At noon they will carry us from the courtroom on their shoulders. And in the evening Robespierre, Saint-Just, and Billaud, outlawed, will go to their sleep in quicklime. And France will commemorate that day as her second civic holiday.

CAMILLE. No, Georges. You will spare Robespierre's life. You must *prove* that you are greater than he!

DANTON [*in a sudden, cold concentration*]. He...should be *hanged*. The guillotine is too good for him. No. You are right, boy, yes: I will spare his life—may it be a long one—on condition that he will spend it in...Cayenne.

[CAMILLE'S *protest*]

FABRE'S VOICE. Georges! Are you at least *sure* that tomorrow will be the end?
DANTON [*taking off his boots*]. I am just as sure of it as that I shall win!

[*They lie down to sleep.*]

HERAULT'S VOICE. Well...let's try to get some sleep anyway. We can't influence the future one way or another.

[*a moment's silence*]

CAMILLE [*after a moment's reflection, passionately*]. No, Georges, I have not been mistaken in you. Maxime doesn't know you...

DANTON. I should think not! Do you suppose he would attack me, even from behind, if he really knew me? It does not matter, I am grateful to him. His wickedness roused me from apathy.

CAMILLE [*carried away by a dream*]. You *are* great, Georges! You are a power; and a genius. You are right: in *your* hands—dictatorship will become the salvation of France.

DANTON [*also giving in to a dream*]. I'll smash the revolution with an iron fist . . .

CAMILLE. So that the republic may flourish at last!

DANTON [*softly*]. On all five continents...my name...precedes the names of great crowned geniuses! Splendor...the divine splendor of the royal Louises revived...around my little, clever Louise... [*suddenly bursts into laughter; more loudly*] And I thought that the world had become odious to me! I thought I had had enough of struggle, pleasure and power! I—Georges Danton—weary of life! Great God!!

DELACROIX [*sleepy*]. How this hymn for two voices lulls one to sleep like a fairy tale...

DANTON [*disguises offense with laughter*]. Well—we must gather our strength for tomorrow. Good night!

[*Sleepily muttered answers.* DANTON *stretches out his hand toward the candle.*]

CAMILLE [*nervously*]. No!!! Georges, please don't put it out!...

DANTON [*with outstretched hand*]. But why?

CAMILLE. It's so horrible here...please leave it, I implore you!

[DANTON *shrugs his shoulders and turns away to face the wall.*]

CAMILLE [*after a while, shyly*]. Georges...

DANTON [*from the wall, his voice completely changed, brusque*]. What?

CAMILLE. Georges, tell me the *truth:* do you really believe that...that we'll win?...

DANTON [*composed again*]. Silly boy! I don't just believe, I *know*! It is not a matter of belief, it's common sense!

[*Silence; the measured breathing of four men who are trying to fall asleep. After a while* DANTON *turns round cautiously, as quietly as possible, and leans on his elbow, watching the candle. Then he begins to observe his hand; makes some movements with his hand and forearm. Having examined his knee, he pulls his legs up sharply and then straightens them out again. Suddenly he lies down flat, stiffly on his back, and immediately gets up, as if in panic, and sits at the edge of the bed. He looks round closely observing his colleagues. He thinks that they are asleep, not having noticed when* DELACROIX *quietly raised his head, watched him with his usual smile and turned back to face the wall.*]

DANTON [*whispers, very slowly*]. You should be slapped in the mug, brother Danton, as long as that mug is well set in place.

[*Involuntarily he strokes his throat, religiously in love with that smooth, compact, unbroken surface...realizes this and tears his fingers away. He supports his head on his fist, the elbow on his knee*]

DANTON. The idiots. It has turned red! Of course! The skin *must* turn red from the blow...why should it only *feel* the blow...idiots! [*stops and softens his attitude for a while*] The skin...of a woman...

[*Pause. Suddenly he begins to tickle the nape of his neck. Stops; clasps his hands on his knee*]

The sensation of pleasant coolness. That's what he said. The doctor, damn him.

[*he feels his head with his fingers, embraces his jaws, blinks his eyes ecstatically*]

Pleasant. . . coolness!!. . .

[*Breaks into laughter and sobbing, wrings his hands, presses his forehead against the inner curvature of his elbows, heavily leaning onto the pillow. In a voice hoarse from laughing and the fury of suffering*]

Devil take him!!!

PHILIPPEAUX [*lying on his back, head resting on his folded hands—suddenly in a half-whisper*]. Danton.

DANTON [*freezes. After some seconds with suspended breath, with hatred*]. What do you want?

PHILIPPEAUX. Come over here. I don't want to shout.

DANTON [*eager for company, he approaches*]. Sir, by talking to me you will soil your mouth. [*but he is already seated at the edge of* PHILIPPEAUX*'s bed*]

PHILIPPEAUX. We are in the grave's waiting room, my friend. Here. . .

DANTON. Damn it, what's the matter with you?! Well, maybe I did exaggerate a bit just now; but we really do have a serious chance. . .

PHILIPPEAUX. Maybe. In any case, here personal life ceases. All feelings run cold. I am filled already by a great indifference from beyond time. Let us forget our quarrel, Danton.

DANTON. What, you want to hold out your hand to me, a vile scoundrel?!

PHILIPPEAUX. Those are worldly notions. Without question you are one of the causes of the colossal disaster which will shortly befall our country. But from here. . . I see in it only a negative phase, biologically necessary in the lives of societies. But in you. . . and in myself. . . [*his smile undermines* DANTON*'s pride*] Don't let's be ridiculous, my friend.

[*He holds out his hand.*]

DANTON [*gives him his hand*]. Let it be so. . . with the proviso, of course, that our possible. . . return to the world of the living will annul this peace treaty.

PHILIPPEAUX. So much the better, since you are aware of it.

DANTON [*rises, but would prefer to stay*]. Is that all?

PHILIPPEAUX. No. Danton, do you know that if you had not provoked the court—quite pointlessly as it happens—you would have made it possible for nine people to be saved? More than half of your comrades?

DANTON. I like that! Nine mediocre fools! One hour of my life is worth more than the sum total of their nine empty existences! And for them *I* should have...

CAMILLE [*shouts in his sleep*]. Wait!...Not that key—wait! Don't go away!! Oooh, wait!!!

[*The candle goes out.*]

DANTON [*leans towards* PHILIPPEAUX. *Suddenly in a startlingly true tone—softly, excitedly*]. Nine people...You know: I would turn France inside out—I would sacrifice my sons—even my wife—to poison Robespierre's life. Let me perish: very well. But he—the murderer—must pay for it. Pointlessly, you say?! Sir, my voice in the Tribunal marks the future of that red Irish monkey. I can see in the eyes of the rabble, whose thoughts I am dictating, how my revenge is growing. [*breaks into a soft laugh*] Ah, the beast has snatched the power at last, yes! But I will see to it that he has it sweet and jolly!

CAMILLE [*wails*]. Yes...for everything...for everything, only *forgive* me!!

DANTON [*furiously*]. If I...I, Danton...were to let myself be murdered with *impunity*, like a random stupid country conscript...If I were to allow the fruits of that crime to be reaped in peace...all for those nine fools?! Were I to do that...I would really be worth as much as they are.

PHILIPPEAUX. But what did you have against saving that boy—whom, without any reason, you have driven to suicide?...

DANTON [*gives* CAMILLE *a contemptuous look*]. Should I have gratified Robespierre, do you think? For that matter, it will be better for Desmoulins himself to die than to prostitute himself again.

PHILIPPEAUX [*simply does not understand at first; suddenly begins to laugh with sadness*]. Ooh, Danton, Danton!!

DANTON [*greatly hurt, returns to his bed*]. Good night.

Scene 2

Comité de Salut Public, the morning of 16 Germinal [*5 April*] . BARERE, CARNOT, COLLOT, ROBESPIERRE, SAINT-JUST.

CARNOT. Robespierre, this is illegal.

COLLOT. The Court addressed the Convention, not you!

CARNOT. The usurping of power always begins like this!

COLLOT. We demand that you give us that letter. It's high time to pass it on.

[*Supported by* CARNOT *he holds out his hand.*]

BARERE. Robespierre, there is not a moment to lose! They will tear the Tribunal to pieces!

CARNOT. On what grounds should we refuse them witnesses?!

COLLOT. Hurry up!!

ROBESPIERRE [*stands up, very pale. In a muted voice*]. I will not hand this letter over, even if you use force. Especially today, when the government is beginning to lose its head!

COLLOT [*loses all patience*]. Man!...You...

[*interrupted by* BILLAUD, *who rushes in, throws off his cloak and sits down*]

BILLAUD. Robespierre, is it true...

ROBESPIERRE. That I've intercepted your letter? Yes.

BILLAUD. Thank God. It must be destroyed.

[*The others start up in indignation.*]

CARNOT. What does this mean?!

COLLOT. Why?! What's happened?

BARERE. Well, really!!

BILLAUD. I've just been to the Convention. Don't show yourself there, Robespierre: the galleries will lynch you. Danton's star is ascending every minute. It's worse than I thought. Let us prepare ourselves to be arrested; it could happen any moment now.

BARERE. We? Arrested?! What for?...

SAINT-JUST [*gets up from his chair; to* ROBESPIERRE]. Shall I go now?

ROBESPIERRE. Wait. So the Convention is on Danton's side already? That is not natural. Someone is behind this in a big way.

BILLAUD. That I don't know. At any rate, the galleries have gone mad, and that's what is decisive at the Convention nowadays. Fouquier writes that he is not sure whether he can hold his ground. The public demand the immediate release of the prisoners. There is no question of the death penalty. At best the trial and this dangerous suspense will be prolonged for goodness knows how long.

[*General commotion.* ROBESPIERRE *turns his chair aside and starts walking restlessly.*]

BARERE. Listen, Billaud! Will they really...

COLLOT. But they can't arrest us!

CARNOT. And again we're saddled with anarchy!

BILLAUD. Robespierre, quick, tell us what we are to do?

ROBESPIERRE [*stops, looks down at the floor*]. We should obtain a decree by which the president could exclude Danton from the proceedings.

[*The unrest is growing.*]

CARNOT. Exclude! The court would bring disgrace on itself!

BARERE. What an idea! From him whose fault it all is!

COLLOT [*gesture*]. Please—go and get the decree. You're welcome.

BILLAUD [*irritated*]. We should! Oh, my friend, it is easy to give an order; but tell me, how can it be executed?

ROBESPIERRE [*lifts his head, helplessly*]. I don't know, gentlemen. [*awful din ensues*] For the moment I can't see any way out myself. We must secure for ourselves the support of the Jacobins, maybe even the sections—and wait. I only know that we cannot back out.

COLLOT [*throws down the pen with which he was fiddling*]. No! This is too much!

BARERE [*frantically*]. Robespierre, will you understand at last that we are threatened with the guillotine!!

COLLOT [*grimly*]. And I have no intention of provoking it!

[ROBESPIERRE's *look, devoid of expression, persistent, overawes him a little; the following speeches are uttered in rapid succession, almost chanted:*]

CARNOT. We are defeated, Robespierre. We must give in.

BARERE. Why should the court not release Danton, as it has so many others?

CARNOT. You said yourself: what do humiliations mean, if what matters is the government?

BARERE. We will withdraw in an impeccably honorable way!

COLLOT. If we give way, the Convention will not harm the Commi . . .

ROBESPIERRE [*has approached and bangs his fist on the table.*]. Enough of this!! [*Unfriendly silence. He goes on in a trembling, subdued voice*] Cowards! The Revolution has chosen you as its *leaders*!! Withdraw? With honor, in the Danton case! What is a disgraced government worth, even though they spare its life? What will a servile Committee be worth for France?! The guillotine! A misfortune indeed! Oh yes, my friends, of course, we shall put our heads on the block if we lose! Of course, we shall suffer the consequences! As though it mattered to anyone what happens to *us*, if Danton's gang seizes power!

Saint-Just, write to the Jacobins and the sections. I am going to obtain the decree. In half an hour you will know whom the guillotine is waiting for this time.

COLLOT [*bangs the table with his hand*]. No. I don't agree.
BARERE. Dispose of your own life, not ours!
CARNOT. Now I really don't know what to think...
BILLAUD [*rises, touches* ROBESPIERRE *on the shoulder*]. Have some sense, man! It is *you* whom they curse aloud! They will not let you utter a word. You can only make the situation worse.
ROBESPIERRE. Eh, it can't be as bad as all that.
CARNOT. Or let us go together.

[*They rise;* BARERE *last.*]

COLLOT. It doesn't make sense—but if it's...

[VADIER *rushes in, shaken, aged.*]

VADIER. Wait! Listen first!

[*They stop, remain standing.*]

COLLOT. Has something else happened?
BARERE. Has the Tribunal has collapsed already?

[*All, except* ROBESPIERRE *and* SAINT-JUST, *go back to their seats.*]

VADIER [*broken. In an old man's voice*]. We are surrounded by a plot which embraces all of Paris.

[*motionless suspense*]

ROBESPIERRE [*under his breath*]. I sensed something of the sort...
SAINT-JUST. Alarmists' bluff! Beware!
VADIER [*indignant*]. Bluff! For three days the agents in all prisons...
ROBESPIERRE [*grimly*]. Ah, the prisons!...

[*He briskly walks round the table and sits down*]

VADIER [*moans*]. But we didn't find out, for who could have supposed...
BILLAUD [*sharply*]. To the point!
VADIER [*sits down heavily*]. Police commissioner Wichterich brought us this morning a prisoner from the Luxembourg, called Laflotte. He was the Republic's envoy in Venice. Laflotte supplemented the agents' reports. Gentlemen, the element of counterrevolution is far more powerful than we had thought. Danton's arrest has pushed them to this coup. All the prisons are organized, while Desmoulins' wife and relatives of the Dantonists have widened the league in the city. Funds have been given by

three bankers and many private individuals. They bribe and incite the people on a huge scale. The plot is said to include hundreds, maybe thousands...

BILLAUD [*in a low voice*]. Well, well, well!

VADIER. I repeat what I have heard: in the galleries of the Convention, in the court room, at the Jacobin club, everywhere among the public there are swarms of paid instigators. The Tribunal is said to be surrounded by a cordon. The public are to force the release of the accused. If this cannot succeed, they are to be kidnapped. In the chaos that will follow others are to open the prisons, arm the political prisoners and send them to the Tuileries.

BILLAUD [*after a while, among silence*]. Vincent redivivus.

SAINT-JUST. Raised to the second power.

[*Depressed silence again.* ROBESPIERRE *slowly places his elbows on the table, and his forehead on his joined hands.*]

COLLOT. Well, Robespierre. You can't win this time.

CARNOT. You will have the collapse of the state on your conscience!

BARERE. And our lives.

[*silence again*]

BILLAUD. Well then, Robespierre? What *now*??

ROBESPIERRE [*slowly uncovers his vaguely roving eyes*]. What...what is it you want?...

[COLLOT, VADIER, *and* BARERE *give a hateful, derisive laugh.*]

BARERE. What is it we want!

COLLOT [*grabs* ROBESPIERRE'*s wrist forcefully*]. You have forced this idiotic trial on us, you have! You have brought disaster on us! Save us now, you and your damned ambition!

VADIER [*with an old man's sarcasm*]. Well? What now, dictator, what!...

ROBESPIERRE [*in a sudden fury which reminds one of a bristling cat. Hooks his fingers together*]. What now? You are saved, you idiots, be happy! You've escaped the *guillotine*! We have won the Danton case, by God!!

[*He starts up from his seat, walks to the window and, standing there, takes out his handkerchief and pulls it about with his fingers, fighting tears.*]

SAINT-JUST [*speaks to divert attention from* ROBESPIERRE]. Of course, friends, now that the Convention is threatened, it must obey us. All their resistance will cease as soon as they learn how things are, I promise you. And the common front of the Convention and the Jacobins, led by the Committees, will easily crush this rebellion.

[*relief at this breakthrough*]

BARERE [*jumps to his feet with joy*]. But of course! Oh, thank heaven for this conspiracy!
VADIER [*straightens up*]. I can breathe at last.
CARNOT. Yes. The government has been saved. Oh!...
COLLOT [*rises*]. Hurry, let us go and tell them!

[*They move to the door.*]

BILLAUD [*stops them*]. Hm...Saint-Just, if those people have an ounce of brains, they must have secured themselves above all the support of a majority in the Convention.

[*They look anxiously at one another.*]

ROBESPIERRE [*turns round*]. This is not a plot, man; it's a childish impulse born out of fear! You heard: Camille's wife! Old men, and women!

[*The others approach him.*]

BILLAUD. In that case, Robespierre, what's on your mind?
BARERE. You say yourself that this plot is our salvation, but...
VADIER [*slyly*]. Are you so sorry for Camille?
ROBESPIERRE [*contemptuously to him*]. For Camille! Friends, don't you see what this conspiracy means? Even if it has saved us for the moment, what of that?
BILLAUD [*casts his eyes down. Somewhat grimly*]. Yes...I understand.
BARERE [*gives him a look*]. Well, I envy you.
ROBESPIERRE. You still haven't grasped it, Barère? We have entered on the path of terror. It's our *first* step! Just the beginning...and what results already!...

Hundreds of people, you say...hun-dreds—of people... [*he erupts in a muted cry*] No! This I didn't know...this I had not foreseen...My God!!! No...No!!...
VADIER. But who was it who has pushed us onto that road, eh? Whose fault is it?...
ROBESPIERRE. Death and damnation!!!* Five years of the whole nation's

*English words in the original.

bloody work goes to the devil, and he's wondering whose fault it is! It's *nobody's* fault, you blubbering idiot,* we *had to* execute Danton, and now we *must* go on, even though from now on every step will move us farther away from our target!

SAINT-JUST [*anxiously*]. Maxime. . . mind what you are saying!

ROBESPIERRE. You too should know what is now awaiting you! We must massacre the few dozen fools who have concocted this farcical conspiracy. That slaughter will cause the fury of thousands. There will be plots. We will have to kill, kill, kill, all day long. We shall become executioners. The nation will curse us. Revolution will become a torture. . .*for the people*!!

The world will regress because of us. All the plagues of the past will return. *We* shall bring them back, we and no one else! Power will have to be concentrated and concentrated all the way to. . .

BILLAUD [*who has been listening with rapt attention; after the last few words, he leaps to his feet soundlessly*]. . . . all the way to where?. . .

COLLOT [*craftily*]. All the way to dictatorship.

[ROBESPIERRE *remains silent, twisting his hands.*]

BILLAUD [*amidst the dead silence—his words thrown across the table to* ROBESPIERRE *ring out like a shot*]. You are lying!!! [SAINT-JUST *rises, giving him a threatening glance*] You want to kill off faith in us, you cursed Judas. . .

SAINT-JUST [*like a whip*]. Be quiet!

BILLAUD. . . . so that we won't stop you from reaching for the crown! What is Danton beside you, you vile poisoner?!

CARNOT [*calmly*]. If you have given way to despair, shoot yourself, please, for you are more dangerous than a mad dog.

SAINT-JUST [*shaking*]. You cheap playactors! Try to understand first of all what is said to you! Every swine delights in being shocked, every blockhead explodes, when he doesn't underst. . .

ROBESPIERRE [*painfully knits his eyebrows*]. Hush, Antoine! You are right. It is a crime to say such things. It is a crime to think such things. . . [*suddenly*] Listen. Appoint a commission. Maybe—maybe I am to blame, and in that case it would be possible to turn back! Judge me! Go through my activities—my speeches—find that point where my error began! Billaud, Saint-Just, Carnot—you are just as capable as myself. Judge me! Redress the harm that I have done! It can be done, for sure, only you must. . .

---

*English words in the original.

BILLAUD [*lifts his hand to interrupt*]. You are in too great a hurry for the guillotine, my dear fellow. Come to your senses. If you have committed a cardinal error—it is now in any event too late. And we haven't won the battle yet. . .

VADIER [*gets up like someone awakened*]. But we have lost a great deal of time. Robespierre, go to the Convention, tell them about the conspiracy.

ROBESPIERRE [*falls onto his chair*]. I can't. I am deadly tired all of a sudden. I have no voice left.

SAINT-JUST. It doesn't matter, stay here. I will tell them—and demand that decree at once.

VADIER. What decree?

BILLAUD. That the Tribunal has the right to exclude the accused from the proceedings. [*rises*] Let's go together.

VADIER [*rises to follow them*]. Mmm. . .it's a brilliant idea.—I'll come with you. I will take the decree to the court myself.

ROBESPIERRE [*lifts his head, which was resting on his hand*]. And it is not even worth mentioning that the Dantonists are demanding witnesses. . .

[*The others exchange meaningful glances.*]

Scene 3   *Part 1*

The Revolutionary Tribunal. Members of the court are seated upstage on a rostrum. In front of them are the accused in two rows on two opposite benches. In the first row: DANTON, DESMOULINS, PHILIPPEAUX, DELACROIX, FABRE, HERAULT, WESTERMANN. FABRE *is seated in an armchair as the principal accused, to stress the ''conspiration de l'étranger,'' faked by him, which was related in an abstruse manner to the East India Company blackmail, and is the only point linking all the sixteen accused men. In the second row there are nine accused, among them* CHABOT. *Members of the jury are seated on a bench along the walls. Below, in a space several meters wide by the walls, there are galleries separated from the rest of the hall, packed with members of the public. There are a dozen or so chairs in the space between the barriers, but most of the members of the public here are also standing.*

The crowd is composed of a genuine audience and the agents of the league. The latter are armed—a fact carefully disguised. Scattered among the public, they make signs to one another, later even to DANTON. *The public form a motley crowd. The women belong to two distinct classes, the rich and the poor, and, though fiery in their temperament, are in the minority. The proletariat form the majority, today in a sinister and at first expectant mood. These people enthusiastically fall under the spell of* DANTON*'s hypnosis, for he plays on the human passion for rebelliousness. The exceptions are* ROBESPIERRE*'s followers, among whom there are more women than in the other party. In moments of crisis these people are jeered at, ridiculed, totally over-awed by the others. The young people fall prey to passion noisily and with total irra-tionality: they are the first to mimic the prosecutor and to throw missiles at the court. There are some members of the middle class, who support the accused with a certain dignity; and a few dandies of both sexes, who incite others and excite them-selves for their own enjoyment. There are also some serious—intelligent—people of all classes, who manage to resist suggestion and warn others about it.*

The basic mood is that of expectant tension. They all know that it is the fourth day, and sense the crisis approaching. At first it is the dandies and the young people who have the upper hand, with their maliciously joyful behavior against the back-ground of tense silence.

DOBSEN [*to* PHILIPPEAUX]. Have you been a personal friend of Danton?

PHILIPPEAUX. No. I joined him only recently for a couple of days.

FOUQUIER [*terribly hoarse. In the galleries a barely audible, almost doubtful, echo of mimicking*]. But a decisive couple of days!

PHILIPPEAUX. I'm not denying it. Soon, however, I realized that there was a considerable difference in our views and aims, so I broke off the passing acquaintance.

FOUQUIER. Evidence points to the fact that your attacks in connection with the Vendée case were a part in their plot; a part aided and abetted by a foreign power.

PHILIPPEAUX. Oh no, gentlemen. My life is at your disposal, but not my honor!

[*He sits down. A vague murmur of approbation.*]

DANTON. You're very much mistaken, Phili. . .

[*The crowd, though still silent, pulsates—tense.*]

FOUQUIER. You have no right to speak, Danton!

[*The first, muffled but unmistakable sounds of mocking and giggling. Also hisses asking for quiet.*]

DANTON. No right to speak?! So take it away from me, go on! Have the guts to admit publicly that you've got an advance on our heads!

[*The crowd slowly livens up. Voices, hardly more than whispers: "He's warming up." "Quiet! Listen!" Every sally of the accused is accompanied by more and more widespread, though still muffled giggles and signs of approbation.*]

DANTON. Don't let yourself be cheated, Fouquier: the head of the Man of the Tenth of August is worth more than thirty francs, at any rate.

THE DANDIES [*half-aloud, the same general mood*]. Yes, that's it—wonderful! Go on, go on!

FOUQUIER. You call yourself the Man of the Tenth of August... [*He is mocked more boldly and by more people. But there are also irritated hisses demanding quiet*] ...but when the Court asked you why you stayed in the country throughout the whole period of preparations, and at home through nearly all the night of the upheaval, you had literally nothing to say in your defen...

[*louder, delighted, excited murmurs*]

VOICES IN THE GALLERY. Oh, now there's going to be something...It's starting! Listen! Look...just look at him!...

DANTON. You miserable scribe from the Châtelet; do you dare to abuse *me*?! Do you think that I am, like you, so bereft of all dignity that I should stoop to soil my mouth by answering your filthy slanders?!

[*Approbation expressing itself in murmurs; the dandies and the young are amused, but the proletarians keep a deadly silence. Two whispered cries: Bravo Danton! Go on, show them what you can do!*]

FOUQUIER. Catchphrases, instead of facts. Always the same.

DANTON. Catchphrases...eh? Listen, Fouquier. Thank God on your knees that I have not yet crushed your idiotic calumnies with only one of the many *facts* I do know. Who invented the story that I stayed at home? Robespierre! The same Robespierre [HERMAN *rings the bell from now on till the end*] who on the 10th of August spent twenty-four hours trembling in his cellar, buried in the coal.

VOICES IN THE GALLERY [*still half-whispered protests and laughs*]. Now he's letting them have it! That was good that was! Not true! What a vile invention!

HERAULT. No wonder he envies Danton his fame—he who envied Marat his funeral!

[*Laughs and protests erupt in a sharper tone.*]

FOUQUIER [*bangs the table with a file because DANTON is opening his mouth again*]. We have lost three days through your empty shouts, Danton! [*murmur of approbation in the second row*] If you do not want to answer, then at least keep silent!

[*The agents exchange glances; a stifling expectant silence returns.*]

TWO VOICES. Eh, eh! He has the right to speak! Don't interrupt the defendants!

[*An impatient hiss demanding quiet overawes the protestors.*]

FOUQUIER. Does any of the accused wish to add to his defense?

[*A sudden commotion among the accused, expressions of fear and consternation. A whispered murmur grows to a stifled shout.*]

THE ACCUSED. What do you mean *add*?!... But I haven't even begun! They didn't even let me speak! What is that supposed to mean?... Add already?! But all the time has been taken up by Danton's roaring! Three questions and... What sort of a trial is this?!...

HERMAN. Your defense has been interrupted, Philippeaux.

PHILIPPEAUX [*to the indignation of the others*]. I've said all that I had to say.

FOUQUIER. No one else then?

[*The protest—not muted any more—is vehement, desperate, chaotic.*]

DANTON [*to his followers, quietly*]. Be quiet... let them exceed the bounds! ...

[*He manages partly to calm his row, though there is still a hum in the silence.*]

HERMAN [*rises*]. The hearing of the defendants is over; the prescribed time expired yesterday. I now ask you citizens of the jury: are you sufficiently informed?

[*Members of the jury look anxiously at the galleries; they talk among themselves, obviously in doubt. A change of attitude among the audience: from now on there is a distinct ascendancy of the proletarians and agents. A serious, hard aggressiveness, for the moment in the shape of a tense readiness. The dandies are somewhat abashed and apprehensive.*]

VOICES [*the first—nervous, in a whisper*]. Ah, it's happened... Well, we'll soon see... Oh, now, look!... [*the second—surprised*] What, already?! ... How is that possible? Why, they've only just begun!...

THE ACCUSED ROW 1 [*whisper*]. Well, the moment's come... You're trembling, don't pretend that you're not! It's the tension. We'll succeed. I am quite confident. Well...

RENAUDIN [*foreman of the jury, in spite of doubts on the part of some members*]. Yes.

[*During the* JURY*'s consultation, and now, the first barely perceptible signs of communication between the agents and* DANTON]

DANTON [*as if* RENAUDIN*'s reply was a cue—leaps up*]. The hearing will be over when *I* have finished!

[*Murmuring in the second row. A new commotion in the crowd, excited and serious.*]

[HERMAN, *with an indifferent gesture, gives him the floor, at the same time giving a sign to members of the jury who happily sit down again*]

HERMAN. We have just been asking. Why didn't you express the wish to speak at once?

DANTON. France! You have lived to see the day when the stoutest pillars of Liberty have been lumped together with this German-Jewish riffraff and thrown into the pit of shame!

[*Whisper of agitation, even admiration. A few people smile or shake their heads*]

CHABOT [*among an unfriendly murmuring of people in his row, half-whispers*]. I wish he would just shut up! He has sung his own praises for three days, and it's still not enough for him!

DANTON. Countrymen! My entire life lies open before you. I have been your comrade and leader for five years. [*excitement grows, expressed in agitated murmurs*] My name shines like a seal on every holy page of your history. In me, the Man of the Tenth of August, the Revolution has found its living symbol; on my forehead the sign of Liberty is shining! [*The murmuring, though muted, becomes more intense. The pulse has obviously quickened. The first applause, but discreet, so as not to drown the speaker*] With you I threw the rotten throne down from its pedestal. [*the applause—though still muffled by rapt attention—is growing*] and from the heap of rubble created new power in a month!

[*a dozen loud cheers*]

SHOUTS [*still few*]. The people haven't forgotten, Danton! We remember, comrade!
A VOICE [*from an unknown direction*]. . . .With the help of eight hundred thousand, which disappeared without one receipt!

[*menacing murmur of indignation—a few shy giggles*]

DANTON [*with a smile*]. This is the sort of lie with which they want to obscure the glory of my merits! Citizens, I demand an answer of you! [*quiet now, they are all ears*] Are we entitled by law to call witnesses in our defense?

GALLERIES. Yes! Yes! You are!

FOUQUIER. Danton! You are not allowed to address the gallery!

[*Three or four people mock him now, though still timidly. They stop because of the awesome silence of* DANTON*'s serious followers.*]

SHOUTS [*short, demanding*]. Quiet! Don't interrupt! Let him speak!

DANTON [*over his shoulder*]. Show me the paragraph! You forget that it was I who founded this Tribunal! You'd like to teach me, eh? [*drowning* HERMAN*'s bell*] Has the Court sent the Convention our list of witnesses?

GALLERIES. Yes. Has it?

DANTON. Where are they? We will answer most of the questions only when the witnesses arrive! By what right does Herman want to close these proceedings?

GALLERY [*more numerous shouts*]. Right! Where are the witnesses? The defendants must not be denied! It's their sacred right! Bring the witnesses! The witnesses!!

FOUQUIER. The Convention will reply at the time and in the manner it deems fit.

[*People are disoriented somewhat and quiet down; the Convention is still sacred.*]

HERMAN [*diplomatically*]. Since the Convention initiated the charges, how could the accusers testify for the defense?

[*The galleries quiet down even more; they recognize the legitimacy of this argument.*]

DANTON. Did you hear that miserable evasion?

[*a weak, uncertain murmur of affirmation*]

People of France! I, Danton, appeal from this parody of a court to you!

[*Bell. Shock. New tension. The silence of concentration.*]

No one else but you has the right to try me, a giant of the Revolution!

[*muffled approbation*]

If the Convention delays with sending witnesses, I demand that my accusers—both Committees—be called here, before the tribunal of public opinion.

[*Breathless tension. Inarticulate expressions of emotion, admiration, approbation—still muted, though*]

DANTON. And then, [*with emphasis*] when *both sides* have had their say, you the people will decide which of us—I, or the Almighty Committee of Safety—is *guilty*.

[*Open applause. Great excitement.*]

CAMILLE. And who is the last defender of Liberty!

FOUQUIER. You have no right to provoke the public!

[*His voice falters and is drowned. The bell is rung frantically. In a few seconds the applause changes into a storm. Shouts are not controlled any more; opposing sides clash; the neutrals are astonished, anxious, frightened, disoriented.*]

FOLLOWERS. Don't *you* talk about the law! We demand the Committees' presence! Let the Committees stand here! Let the Committees come! It is easy to accuse one behind one's back! Let the Committee face Danton! The Committees! The Com-mit-tees!!!

NEUTRALS. What do they want?...But they are right. This smacks of a planned coup. Let's be on our guard! But this looks like a riot! Let's leave here while there's still time! By God, what's going on here?! Have they gone mad?!...

OPPONENTS [*few*]. Come to your senses! People! Have respect for the Court! It's a provocation to riot!! It's the enemy's doing! Beware! You're defending plotters and traitors!!

[*The others throw themselves on them, shut their mouths, even beat them. Those who are curious, like* PARIS, *climb on chairs.*]

HERMAN [*puts his hands to his mouth*]. The hearing is closed!!

[*Movement in the densely packed mass of people. The agents communicate among themselves and push their way to the back of the first row of the gallery; those who were in the center make their way gradually to the front.*]

ACCUSED. This is an outrage! Villainy! We haven't been able to speak and now we're being gagged! This isn't a trial, it's a massacre!

DANTON [*has noticed* PARIS]. Pâris! Run to the Convention! Say we are calling the Committees! And that our right to speak is being unlawfully taken away!

[PARIS *makes his way through the crowd.*]

FOUQUIER. Members of the jury will go for their deliberations!

[*Half of them get up, the rest refuse, because they do not dare.* RENAUDIN, *determined, fearless, in vain tries to convince them.*]

DANTON. My countrymen! This trial is mass murder in broad daylight!
FOLLOWERS [*while neutrals and opponents quiet down, partly drowned*]. Do you
hear?! It's not a trial, it's a massacre! It's murder! Shame!!!

[*Four* GENDARMES *take up positions at the edge of the rostrum. Under the menacing pressure from* HERMAN, FOUQUIER, *and* RENAUDIN, *members of the jury fearfully rise and follow their leader to the door on the left. The crowd rushes in their direction. There is almost a pandemonium.*]

THE CROWD. Stop! Not a step further! Don't move! We won't allow it! We
won't! There was no hearing! We won't let you repeat the massacre of
September the 2nd!!
VOICES [*continue quite clearly*]. We demand immediate acquittal! Acquittal
without deliberations!
CHORUS. Free them! Free them! Free them at once! Free Danton! Free
them all! Yes! Free them! Long live Danton!
HERMAN. I will. . .call. . .the soldiers!!

[*Shouts, uproar, the shrieks of women—howling and hisses. Members of the league reach for their weapons, though still hiding them.*]

SHOUTS. The soldiers! All right, call them! Go on, just you try! Just you
dare touch us! Just wait, you bandits! Go on, call them! Afraid of prisoners under guard, they are! Cowards! Cowards! Murderers!!!
THE ACCUSED. Bandits! Hangdogs! Paid executioners of the government!
Traitors! Murderers! Pitt's lackeys!

[*They begin to throw balls of paper at the court. The people follow suit, throwing all kinds of objects. The league members reveal themselves openly. Amidst the frenzy a majority of the crowd join them, grouping themselves around those armed.*]

CAMILLE. People of France! We're being murdered! Defend your defenders!
DANTON. Courage, brothers! Force against force!

[*The* GENDARMES *are ready for action.* HERMAN *will not let them use their weapons. He gives a sign to the* USHER, *who rushes out.*]

GALLERIES [*frantically*]. Long live Danton! Hurrah for Danton! Down with
the Tribunal! Down with the Committee! Away, away with them!

Down with the Committee!! To the lampposts! The court to the lamp-
posts! The Committee to the guillotine!! To the guil-lo-tine!!!
WESTERMANN [*jumping onto the bench*]. We stormed the Bastille together!
Let's attack together now! Ça ira!

[*At these words, the league members push the people forward. They break down and
jump through the barrier, and push to the dock. The accused were waiting for this
moment in order to mix with the crowd. But they notice the* GENDARMES *pointing
their rifles at them and pause for a fraction of a second, remaining in the dock. At
this point the soldiers quietly and very quickly come in and cut off the dock from the
public. The crowd withdraws and freezes in suspense.*

In the escape attempt only PHILIPPEAUX *did not take part. He remained alone on
the bench with crossed legs, as if in a drawing room.*

*The essential unity of the crowd has been broken. From now on there is a mutual
distrust, and partly a definite sobering up, which prevents any new union or action.*

*The accused in the first row have been thrown back on the bench, and are now
guarded.*]

DELACROIX. Well, we've had it.
FABRE. For a moment I had hope . . .
HERAULT [*laughs through tears*]. Oh . . . I feel tired.
CAMILLE [*in a vibrant half-outburst*]. It's not true! The people will not desert
us!
WESTERMANN [*aloud*]. Don't let them frighten you! We too are armed!

[*meaningful glances among the judges*]

DANTON. The traitors on the Committee have taken off their masks! They
want to compel you to silence with volleys!
GALLERIES [*1: amazement, indignation*]. What . . . bayonets?! So you want to
shoot at us! At defenseless people! . . . It's worse than in the tyrant's
days! [*2: energetic approbation*] You see? Now they will throw us out. Of
course, what else could they do? If the public doesn't know how to behave . . . [*3: sober ones*] People, have some sense! Danton is Pitt's agent!
It's a coup against the government, and you fools are helping in it!

[*The impetus is broken. The crowd inwardly collapses in no time.*]

HERMAN. Citizens, do not lose your heads! The enemy takes advantage of
your emotions!

[*Suddenly members of the league have lost their trust and are isolated; in vain they
try to hide. A silence denoting disorientation.*]

FOUQUIER [*clearly, amid silence*]. Citizen members of the jury, please.

[*Exit* JURY.]

GALLERIES [*a weak, vague protest*]. But...you didn't hear them...Where are the witnesses? How can you...

[*Ominous silence; the overawed protests melt in it.*]

THE ACCUSED [*2nd Row*]. We are lost! That's the end! It's Danton's fault! Danton is to blame!

DANTON. People of France! The tyrants are butchering your truest friends— and you just stand there watching?!

[GALLERIES: *a convulsive, but very weak commotion.*]

HERMAN. Danton! Will you stop inciting them, or I shall order you to be taken away!

[*On his order two* GENDARMES *approach* DANTON.]

GALLERIES [*murmur of horror*]. What...remove the defendant?! Yes, he has only himself to thank for it! But this is illegal! Hush! Be quiet, you! My head's spinning!...

DANTON. You've gone too far, Herman! I was silent before. Now—I shall speak—the truth.

[*An expectant silence ensues. There is an argument about the exclusion of* DANTON *among* HERMAN, *who is against it,* FOUQUIER, *who insists, and the* CHIEF OF THE DEPARTMENT, *who hesitates. After the last two words of the following speech, a short, dead pause.*]

Do you know, why they have been paid to do away with me? Because I am the only barrier...between Robespierre...and the crown.

GALLERIES [*Whisper—*1: *tension caused by this sensation*]. What...what... what did he say?!...Did you hear?! Robespierre!...The crown... Quiet, listen! But Robespierre!!... [2: *indignation—more loudly*] What a shameless calumny! It was he, Danton, who wanted to climb the throne!

[*The conspirators, now forgotten, take courage. They make cautious signs, exchange glances.*]

FOUQUIER. With this slander you've sealed your fate, Danton!

[*He resumes the argument, which is broken off several times to listen to what is being said; the argument becomes more and more heated*]

GALLERIES [*shouts of excited curiosity*]. Don't interrupt! Let him speak! We want to know! Speak, Danton, go on!
DANTON. Robespierre has been creeping toward the throne for five years now! Like a miser for gold, he has been greedy for power! I alone was barring his way, but the traitor has vilely tricked me!

[*He stops for a few seconds to observe the effect.*]

GALLERIES [*more excited whisper*]. You know, this could be the truth...Go on! What childish lies! How could Robespierre... Hm, who knows?
. . .
DANTON. People of Paris! Conquerors of the Bastille! Freedom is being murdered and you are asleep! The cowardly government has capitulated: until now they used to say: "the Committee wishes it so," three days ago they started saying openly: "Robespierre wishes it so!" People of Paris, choose! Today is the last chance! The cause of the Republic is in your hands! Let them murder us, follow in the footsteps of the Convention, and you will sell yourselves, to your everlasting shame, into a captivity such as France has not yet known!

THE ACCUSED [*Row 2, whisper excitedly*]. Look! Look! They're moving, it's a fact! They will save us still, you'll see! But careful now! We mustn't even blink until. . .

[*similar excitement in the first row*]

HERAULT. Courage! We are not finished yet!
CAMILLE. You see, didn't I tell you?! The people will not let us. . .
DELACROIX. Don't let yourselves be fooled again!
GALLERIES [*excited whisper*]. You know, I have suspected it for a long time. . . I knew there must be something in it! Already in ninety-two Robespierre. . . You. . . stop it. He knows what he's talking about. Did you know that Robespierre intends to capture the Dauphin? It's a fact!. . .
SHOUTS [*frantic youthful voices—they drown in a void of silence*]. Robespierre is murdering Liberty! He's reaching for the crown! We must stop him, brothers! Don't give way to the tyrant's henchmen! Let's save Liberty! Let's save Danton!

[*They cease speaking because of the deadly lack of response, and gradually sober up.*]

VOICES [*murmur of scorn*]. Be quiet, you ass! Careful, he's a snooper. Well,

it's just idle talk now...Never mind, they'll stop soon. Shame on you,
idiots! You know, *such* nonsense!...Leave him be; they believe him,
the idiots. You're right, he's got hired people here. Well, no need to fear
now.

Scene 3   *Part 2*

USHER [*bangs his halberd*]. All stand for the representatives of the people!

[VADIER *and* BILLAUD *enter. The Court rises. The soldiers salute. The crowd is now
completely silent.*]

VADIER. Citizen president. Here is the new decree issued by the Convention.

[*an excited commotion among the accused: frantic tension—sparks of hope. Muted
murmuring*]

BILLAUD. Citizens! We have discovered an extensive plot [*the accused freeze.
A few sighs of dismay*] to free the defendants and overthrow the government of the Republic.

[*an electric tremor round the entire hall*]

Desmoulins' wife [*sharp cry by* CAMILLE] has spent large sums to bribe the
suburban population. Citizens, beware! There are *swarms* of enemy
agents among you!

CAMILLE. Bandits! They want to murder my Lucile!

DANTON. Don't let yourselves be fooled...

[*The conspirators panic and try to hide. They are made obvious through their isolation; all eyes turn to them.*]

THE ACCUSED [*Row 2: furious outburst*]. Shut up! Enough now! Be quiet at
last, you damned swine! Shut your trap! We're all threatened because of
you!

HERMAN [*reading*]. The National Convention decrees: that the Revolutionary Tribunal shall bring proceedings in the matter of the plot by Danton
and others to a close, without any further adjournments. It is also decreed that the president shall use all legal means to confirm the authority of himself and the Tribunal, in the event that an assault on the part
of the defendants were to be repeated.
    It is further decreed that any of the defendants who resist or behave in

a derogatory manner towards the national Judiciary, should without delay be excluded from further participation in the proceedings.

[*a murmur of respect, awe, astonishment, and admiration*]

DANTON [*leaps to his feet*]. Citizens, I take you for witnesses: did we resist the national Judiciary, or behave in a derogatory manner?
A VOICE [*passionate, youthful, amid icy silence*]. No! Never!

[*threatening murmurs; more numerous are the jeers*]

A VOICE [*ironically*]. Oh, only from time to time!. . .

[*Laughter erupts, somewhat muted out of respect for the deputies, but irrepressible.*]

DELACROIX [*half-whisper*]. Congratulations, Danton.
FABRE. Thank God it's the end. I'm barely alive anyway.

[*Dismay and depression dominate among the accused.* WESTERMANN *clenches his fists and whispers curses, red from anger;* CAMILLE'S *eyes have a mad expression.* PHILIPPEAUX *looks at him thoughtfully. A few seconds' suspense.* DANTON, *foaming at first, looks round the faces. On seeing them he suddenly becomes calm.*]

DANTON [*so calm as to be almost gentle*]. Vile, cowardly mob: no one will change you. You're a lion when it comes to destroying the helpless, but the sight of a puppet in uniform throws you into a fit of panic. I know you, rabble. I know how much your zeal and your oaths are worth. I know you will stand and gape, oh yes, like a herd of cattle, when they bind and take me to the scaffold.
  But to laugh like a bunch of morons at this shameful moment, instead of blushing for your baseness. . . is something more than villainy. It's your unfathomable, filthy, irrepressible *stupidity*, you inane flock of sheep.
VOICES [*angry*]. Stop raving! Shut your trap at last! What insolence! [*astounded*] What?. . .What is he talking about? What does he want? For whom is this meant?. . .What does it mean?
DANTON [*softly*]. My contempt is such that I forgive your baseness, you rabble—you eternal Judas. He who knows how to play on your reflexes has you in the palm of his hand, can use you for whatever he wants. But your stupidity, rabble, is elemental; sprawling, spreading over the entire earth, filling its every square inch, world-shaking. Neither God nor Satan can move it from its place. [*short pause*] So for this one thing—for your utter stupidity—I curse you, rabble, you human litter.

[*the mystified public stand motionless, open-mouthed*]

And so I leave you to be the prey of a tiger, who will revive for you the times of Tiberius. Free Nation! You will bathe in your own blood up to your eyes, before you fulfill the destiny I have endowed you with. But you will fulfill it! Robespierre's corpse will soon rot beside my own!

[*a sudden short murmur of indignation*]

FOUQUIER. Will you finally be quiet!

DANTON [*turns round in a flash*]. And as for you, honorable Tribunal, you cesspool of thieves, blackmailers, and pimps, I'll tell you just this, Robespierre's hangdogs: you're not worth spitting at.

FOUQUIER [*exchanging signs with the president*]. You are excluded from the proceedings. Take him away!

[DANTON *gets up laughing and is escorted away by the gendarmes. Among the accused a murmur of indignation and despair.*]

CAMILLE [*jumps to his feet, tears up the notebook containing his defense, throws the bits at the prosecutor*]. You hideous ape of a prosecutor, take that, and that, and that! Officially hired murderers.

[*Spits. At a sign from* HERMAN, *gendarmes grab him. He is furious.*]

No! Don't you dare touch me!

[*The crowd regains its ease and begins to express scorn. Jeering and mocking.*]

Let me go! Let me go, damn you!! I will not let myself be butchered behind my back!!!

[*The galleries laugh heartily.*]

You have to hear me, judges! Let me defend myself! I am utterly innocent!! Judges!!!

[*The gendarmes tear him away and drag him. The crowd laughs, overjoyed.*]

HERAULT [*tugs at his sleeve*]. Be quiet, you fool! You're making yourself ridiculous!!

CAMILLE [*almost carried in the air*]. Ah. . .you swine! Cattle, not people!!

FABRE [*rises, stretches himself, yawning*]. The honorable Tribunal will allow me to exclude myself!

[*The crowd, silent now, pays attention, amused, gaily applauding each prisoner in turn.*]

HERAULT. And me. . . You should have started with this instead of boring us for sixteen hours a day.

[PHILIPPEAUX *goes away without a word.*]

DELACROIX [*goes with them, ignoring the court*]. No, Hérault. They do not have to listen to the accused, but when they enumerate his crimes, they feel obliged to look at him.

WESTERMANN [*to all*]. Kiss me goodbye all of you, rabble, you know where.

[*Admiration, even applause. The first row leave all together.*]

[*Simultaneously:*]

THE ACCUSED [*Row 2: a whisper of dull despair*]. It's the end. We'll all go. It's better to know in advance. And all because of that roaring swine! Would that raving madman!. . .

GALLERIES [*Whisper*—1: *excited*]. Well, that's over. . . Ugh, I've got an earache with all that shouting. Wasn't it worth it, though. . . Well, they did lose their heads for a while [2: *mysterious, thrilled*] D'you know, they wanted to kidnap them. Most assuredly, I saw a pistol!. . . Didn't I tell you?! Now they're in hiding, hard to look for them! Yesterday one of them was talking in the street about it, I heard him. . . [*The crowd disperses quickly, chatting*]   [3: *uneasy, whisper*] What was he blabbing about Robespierre?. . . Well, who knows?. . . For some time now I myself have thought. . . It's a fact that Robespierre is more powerful every day. . . [4: *indignant*] Not true! Robespierre never. . . You know, he lives like a worker! What a scoundrel that. . . Riffraff! And you even wanted to help, fools! [5: *relaxed, carelessly*] Are you waiting for the jury? What for? No question, they'll all go. After *such* a scandal! They're playing cards in there, there's no need for any consultation. The show is over, let's go. *I* am not waiting any longer. . . [6: *thoughtful, serious*] We must be very careful now. . . and hold our tongues. This conspiracy is a bad omen, you know. We're in for a bad time. Such a judicial slaughter means that the government is in a poor way. Quiet, for God's sake!. . .

[HERMAN *hands some water to the exhausted* FOUQUIER]

HERMAN. Well, God be praised. . . but devil knows what the outcome will be. The people will not forget. . .

FOUQUIER. Oh, thank you. I've got a headache. That swine has not done so much harm in five years as he did today!

HERMAN [*sudden fear*]. If only the jury doesn't. . .no, they won't. He antagonized everyone. It's a clear-cut case anyway.

FOUQUIER. But we're going to have a hard time with Robespierre, that's for
sure. [*imitates him*] You will deprive him of his right to speak! [*laughs nervously*] Haha! Deprive thunderclouds of their voice, once they start roll-
ing. Or a pack of hounds, once they start howling! Deprive, indeed!

HERMAN [*softly, sulking*]. This is only the beginning, Fouquier. . .soon we
shall see worse things.

FOUQUIER. What a bloody job!. . .

Scene 4

*The vestibule of the office at the Conciergerie; a vaulted basement chamber, very
somber. Upstage a narrow staircase leading up to ground level. The office entrance is
on the left. Skylights just below the ceiling. The general appearance more or less corresponds to the well-known painting by Muller at the Louvre, "Appel des dernières
victimes de la Terreur." Soldiers are posted by the walls. There is also* SANSON, *the
executioner: an elegant, modest, serious person, with four assistants, and four barbers. They are all suspended in mid-movement, listening to* DANTON's *last display
offstage.*

CLERK'S VOICE. . . .and accomplices, guilty of both conspiracies agains. . .

DANTON'S VOICE. Get stuffed with your sentence! Gang of ruffians! They
didn't even dare to sentence me to my face!. . .

CLERK'S VOICE. . . .against the safety of the Republic. . .

DANTON'S VOICE. Republic, indeed! A pack of cowardly villains, who can't
even take a risk in committing their crimes!

CLERK'S VOICE. . . .to death by having his head cut off.

DANTON'S VOICE. Stupid rabble! Only posterity will dare to judge. . .

[*He rushes in, sees those present. A few moments of inner suspense. Looking round,
he ends somewhat abstractedly, soberly—an amazing contrast*]

. . .me.

[*The* BARBER *shows him a chair.*]

Ah yes.

[He sits down, tears off his collar, gives a sign over his shoulder]

Go on.

[WESTERMANN, DELACROIX, PHILIPPEAUX *are brought in.* WESTERMANN *is sulking and fuming.* DELACROIX *is very uneasy. Pause. The* BARBERS *cut the hair covering the napes of their necks.*]

DANTON *[begins quietly, amidst silence]*. I depart. And I leave behind a terrible chaos. No one among them has any idea of how to govern. Robespierre! His Committee!...Gods, indeed!! Without me everything will fall apart in three days. They will sink into terror up to their ears, it's the only method of fools. Hoho! First they will cut off heads by the dozen, then—by the hundred. The entire Convention will go.

BARBER *[uneasy]*. Citizen...please be still or I may injure you.

DANTON. You will begin the work *[he points over his shoulder to* SANSON, *who lowers his eyes]* of that gentleman, eh? Haha! Not bad! The ungrateful people will soon find out what they have lost in me. But despair and re-pentance will come too late. The Revolution today disgraced itself for ever and ever. I, the murdered, am blushing in shame for the murder-ers. They call it a Tribunal!!

WESTERMANN. You helped to set it up, Danton.

DANTON *[looses all patience]*. I helped?! Did I *help* anyone, or rather, did any-one help me to carry on these two shoulders, at the steep edge of a prec-ipice, France—raging in the spasms of transformation?! Everything that the Revolution won, everything it has created—is *my* work.

But a treacherous thief took advantage of the path that I had opened. He stole my achievements one after another, and turned them into a scourge of humanity. It's because of him that...

PHILIPPEAUX. It's no good, Danton. You will not outshout the fear within you.

DANTON *[startled to the point of dismay]*. Fear?!...

PHILIPPEAUX. Yes, fear. You can hardly croak, it's painful to listen to you. But still you dare not be silent, even for a moment. Oh, how you're trembling...your hands are cold and wet, hmm?—and your face as if it were made of clay...

DANTON *[out of breath]*. You dare to...

PHILIPPEAUX. Oh, if it's any consolation, I am no better. I thought I had overcome that animal in me which wants to *live* at any price. But no. My bowels are twisting inside me. It can't be done. One *cannot* look death in the eyes with equanimity. It is better not to pretend.

DANTON [*haughtily*]. I can imagine that such a state must be unpleasant. But you are wrong when you think that *I* share it. Do I tremble? . . . Yes! I am trembling from pain, from anger at thinking about the fate of our country, given over as a prey to that outlandish beast. . .
You did not know him well. You have no inkling what sort of a character he is. . . For instance, do you know that he displayed a most tender, caring friendship toward Camille? Even an hour before he gave the order for his arrest. He is an authentic, perverse Nero.

[*he grins with intense satisfaction*]

He's got what he wanted, the fool. They tremble before him. He is the ruler. And he thinks he can now do without me!! Oh, he will get to know the bliss of power! I give him three months: that's how I've fixed public opinion. Before the shameful death I have in store for him, I want him to go mad; or hang himself.

DELACROIX [*with a crafty sigh*]. You know, I am sorry for you.

[DANTON *is speechless.* WESTERMANN, *then* DELACROIX *get up and have their hands tied behind their backs.*]

PHILIPPEAUX [*gently, after a few seconds' silence*]. Do you really not yet see that today you are nothing, that you are a wreck?

[DANTON *gives him a frightened glance and lowers his head*]

You were a splinter from a social mass in the last phase of its life. As a person you are a mediocre provincial lawyer. Your importance was functionally dependent on a given situation, just as the importance of zero depends on its position among the integers. Your phase ended on the tenth of July. Since that day you have just been an echo: naggingly troublesome, but—no matter how hard you tried—harmless.

[PHILIPPEAUX *gets up; an executioner's assistant cuts his collar off.* FABRE, HERAULT, CAMILLE *are brought in. The latter is in a daze and sways on his feet, but later regains full lucidity.*]

FABRE [*looks round*]. What now? [*They sit*] Ugh, I am so tired. . . it will be something to be able to stretch oneself. . .

HERAULT [*whispers*]. Fabre. . . have pity on my nerves.

PHILIPPEAUX [*continues relentlessly*]. Oh yes, Robespierre will fall. And in a terrible manner. Because at a certain point of the present, critical phase—he must fall, by virtue of the mechanical law of equilibrium.

[DANTON, *crushed, gets up heavily. The remainder of his collar is cut off.*]

CAMILLE [*feels the scissors against his neck and jumps like a trout, with a piercing shout*]. Aaaaah!!!

FABRE. Quiet, Camille! That doesn't hurt!

DANTON [*startled, turns round and roars*]. Be quiet, you ass!!

[DANTON *turns pale, supports himself with his hip and hand against the table.* CAMILLE *sinks onto the chair. A steely gentleness on the part of the barbers and executioners' assistants.*]

PHILIPPEAUX. . . . and your lies, your totally indifferent death—will not weigh that much [*he picks a wisp of cutoff hair from his shoulder and blows it away*] on his fate.

[PHILIPPEAUX *puts his hands behind his back to be tied.* DANTON *breaks down. He lowers his head, supporting it on both hands.*]

DELACROIX [*rubbing the base of his head against the nape of his neck*]. Ugh. . . ! I already have the "feeling of pleasant coolness" that old Guillotin promised us. . .

[*One of the executioner's assistants approaches* DANTON *with a rope.*]

DANTON [*turns round, his vision blurred; speaks in a weak voice*]. I. . . I can't. In a moment. [*falls onto the chair*] I feel sick.

[*He slowly lowers his head down to his shoulder, at the edge of the table.*]

WESTERMANN [*cruelly*]. A-ha!. . .

[*They all cluster round* DANTON.]

FABRE [*tries to mitigate appearances*]. There's nothing strange in this: he has been straining his voice continuously for four days. . .

HERAULT. He's barked for four days on one note! The fiercest dog would not have done it.

DELACROIX. With that record, brother, you will pass into history!

DANTON [*raises his head from his hand*]. Go on, you flunkeys! Set the dogs on the master when he's down! Scorn him, jeer at him, get even for all the years of your humble service!

DELACROIX. More respect for your lord! Don't you know that one hour of his life is worth more than the sum total of our empty existence?

[*jeering excitement, some ask for an explanation*]

HERAULT. I've heard that too! We have a gracious master, indeed, fellow morons. Nine of us would have remained as orphans in this unkind world, but for his care and concern for our welfare.

[*a sharper note of hatred*]

PHILIPPEAUX [*stands supported by the wall*]. Leave him be. Each of us tries to defend himself from the knowledge that, like millions before him, he has botched his job and been cancelled out.

[*A dead silence ensues.*]

HERAULT [*sudden outburst of bitter laugh*]. But one can't defend oneself for long!...

WESTERMANN [*sullen*]. Yes, you're right. I know, for I've bungled it too. I did it just once: at the time of Vincent's coup. I let a civilian confuse me. And that should have been the great moment of my life. I threw it away.

HERAULT. Eh, Westermann. You don't know what it means to throw one's life away. But I! I, who was born to adorn elegant salons, let myself be pushed into the role of a fanatic! I, who through no fault of my own, have lost honor and life, and pointlessly made myself ridiculous for the sake of a cause which meant nothing to me. Ugh, what nonsense— nonsense—*nonsense* in such a defeat!

[*All three stand up.*]

DELACROIX. You are not the only one whom the current has carried into the absurd, Hérault. I am—to put it mildly—a bandit by nature, and yet I did not dare to be either a carefree soldier-plunderer, like Westermann [*the latter does not enjoy the compliment, judging by his expression*] , or a stock-exchange shark, like Batz and Boyd. No, I duly proclaimed the country's salvation, like everyone else. Only sometimes in my odd spare moment did I manage to pinch something—and I let myself be caught!

PHILIPPEAUX [*with a kind of admiration, says to no one in particular*]. And to think that even so...states develop by means of *such people*.

FABRE [*thoughtful*]. After me will remain the names of the months and a handful of comedies. It's not much but still it's *something*.

CAMILLE [*while his hands are being tied*]. And after me—after my talent, the greatest in France today—what will remain?—a gutter rag! [*to* DANTON, *standing over him, in a truer tone than usual*] You stole my talent, you stole my life, but you didn't even know how to use the stolen treasure!— because of you I lost my honor; because of you I am dying so young; because of you Lucile is perishing; because of you, you empty idol, I have been rejected by Maxime! And what advantage have you derived out of so much ruin? Nothing! Zero! Destruction, and that's all! You've bungled even your villainy!

DELACROIX. Well, he's managed to make quite a pile. And that's something . . . although he doesn't feel all that well either. [*he slowly bends over the motionless* DANTON] It weighs heavily on your stomach—the wasted hypocritical life, the life rotten to the core, eh Danton? O, if only one could vomit up *oneself!*

DANTON [*suddenly recovers under all that jeering*]. Whine, you blunderers! Drown yourselves in tears! I have no regrets! I knew how to make good money, and how to spend it—which is even more difficult. I knew how to fondle girls, and how to drink, like few others did. Now I am full, but I know that it was good. [*he offers his hands to the executioner's assistants*] Robespierre's account will be sadder, when he comes to stand here in a few weeks' time!

HERAULT. Bravo, Danton! Hold out! Don't admit to anything, even though you're sick, though your soul is howling, like a dog over a dead man! Lie, lie and lie to the last breath!

FABRE. That's right, careful with the truth, friends. Do you know how one must think in our situation? That the sacrifice offered to an illusion, a useless sacrifice, is the most beautiful. That it is a good thing to wear a jewel, or to give it to a public charity, but that it is *beautiful* to throw it into the sea.

Any truth can be tolerated in a tragic guise; and tragedy is not very hard to come by.

DELACROIX. I would take my hat off to you, Fabre—if I still possessed a hat, and had the use of my hands.

[*The condemned from the court's second row are brought in, like a flock of dazed sheep. They are placed standing in a row along the wall.* DANTON *immediately adopts a pose.*]

SANSON. All's ready. We're off.

[*A few of the condemned faint.* SOLDIERS *support them.*]

DANTON. Forward, brothers! We will stand without fear before the tribunal of future generations, to which today I summon the victorious foe! A few years from now my name will shine in luminous letters in the Pantheon of history, while yours—you villain Robespierre—will be imprinted forever in its indestructible black book!

DELACROIX [*fervently, as the others are led out*]. Oh, Danton! What a great actor perishes with you!

Scene 5

398 rue Saint-Honoré. The evening of 16 Germinal. ROBESPIERRE *alone, lying on the bed, on his back. The noise of the passing convoy outside. The voices of* CAMILLE *and* DANTON*: the first of them shouts out of despair, the other roars curses.* ROBES-PIERRE *reacts to neither, nor to the knock on the door that follows. Only after the second knock does he respond, though not at once.*

ROBESPIERRE [*in quite a normal voice*]. Come in.
ELEONORE [*enters and, despite herself, behaves as if in the presence of someone dying. Whispers*]. The evening post, Maxime. Nothing important.
ROBESPIERRE [*unmoved, loudly*]. Thank you.

[ELEONORE *does not dare approach him, or to speak; she waits for a sign, looks around shyly, then leaves the room quickly, on tiptoe. Meanwhile the onlookers have rushed after the convoy; the streets are empty, hence an unnatural silence to the end of the scene.*
     *Knocking again—*SAINT-JUST*'s rhythm.* ROBESPIERRE *again delays his reply.*]

ROBESPIERRE. Come in.

[*He reluctantly lifts himself onto his elbow, shakes his visitor's hand and lies down again.*]

SAINT-JUST. You stay at home in the middle of the day, idly too?! I looked for you everywhere. Still not rested?
ROBESPIERRE. No. Well, what's the news?
SAINT-JUST. A definite victory. No sign of resistance; the crowd is even indifferent. Camille's impassioned cries cause only a murmur.
ROBESPIERRE. Yes. And laughter.

[*lifts himself on a straightened out arm, and looks passively towards the window*]

     I could hear him from here . . . the poor little thing . . .

[*a short pause;* SAINT-JUST *thumps his fingers on the table top.* ROBESPIERRE *folds his pillow in two and lies down again as comfortably as possible*]

SAINT-JUST. Well, the Tribunal and the city Commune deliberated for an hour on the form of transport. Pache was just as restless as when the king was executed.

ROBESPIERRE. My God! You still don't know the Parisian crowd?! Oh, how I envy you! That crowd, which enjoyed the trial as if it were a cockfight, with all their baiting and shouting, do you imagine that they would rise in defense of those who have been *defeated*?!

SAINT-JUST. Wait, Maxime. It was a Parisian crowd too that captured the Bastille, and broke three times into the Tuileries, scratched the floor a bit, yet did not take a single spoon, even as a souvenir; and watched the shameful return of the captured fugitive king—in silence.

[ROBESPIERRE *slowly lifts himself and sits at the edge of his bed.*]

ROBESPIERRE [*very surprised*]. Yes—of course. It's true. [*pause*] How could *I* forget about that!...

SAINT-JUST [*leans over him*]. Listen, Robespierre: pull yourself together. I am not asking what it is that ails you, for, alas, you said it all too clearly a few hours ago. You do realize, don't you, that now you have to assume dictatorship over France?

ROBESPIERRE [*gets up and begins to wander round the room*]. Stop nagging me.

SAINT-JUST [*watching him*]. I will go on nagging until I get you out of that horrid prostration! You are the dictator, man! How did you dare shout at the Committee that the revolution was lost?! After all, you are on this earth to achieve its aims *in spite of everything*! The people have now given you full powers...

ROBESPIERRE [*stops by him, supports himself on his hands against the table*]. Listen, Saint-Just, why do you submit to me? Why don't you think that dictatorial power is due not to me, but to you?

SAINT-JUST. That last question is not bad. My dear friend: dictatorship is not something to be envied. It's not a royal crown, with pomp, comforts, everything that miserable human vanity can long for. Dictatorship is a terrifying position. If it were someone else, I would understand that he was afraid of it. And why do I submit to you? Isn't it obvious, Maxime? You are a genius, and I am not—and our aim is the same. So it's quite natural that I have put my talent at your disposal.

ROBESPIERRE. So you don't consider yourself my equal?

SAINT-JUST. No.

[*During the following speech* ROBESPIERRE *goes to the window, stops there, comes back, then falls onto the chair, his dull gaze fixed on the wall*]

If you've turned soft to such a degree that you are looking for someone on whom to thrust your dignity, forget it, for God's sake. You know yourself that no one but you measures up to the situation. Besides, no one is mature enough for power: the purest revolutionary will grow infantile at once, drunk with his ridiculous personal greatness. You alone will never forget that you are the watchdog of the nation . . .

. . . but I think you're just ill. If so, then—thank God.

ROBESPIERRE [*with a torpid movement leans forward and supports himself on his hands*]. No . . . I am not ill. [*softly*] I've lost my bearings.

SAINT-JUST [*astonished*]. Lost your bearings?!! You have before you a superhuman task, you know precisely what you have to do—and . . .

ROBESPIERRE [*shouts in a whisper*]. My boy, I *don't* know what I am to do! I don't know anything any more . . . literally *nothing* . . .

SAINT-JUST [*after a while*]. Robespierre: you alone have the responsibility for the life and future of twenty-five million people. The Revolution will perish, if you don't save it. Does anyone ask you whether you have confidence in yourself or not? Or whether you *want* to assume power? What you personally think, how you feel—all of this just doesn't come into account. Doubt yourself, torment yourself, tremble—so much the worse for you. But in any event, you *must* win.

ROBESPIERRE [*drops his hands, leans against the back of the chair*]. Child, if only I doubted myself, but knew *what* it was that the universal good demanded . . . I would not shock you with the sight of my desp . . . helplessness.

But I don't know anything any more . . . all that I believe in, all that I live by, has suddenly shattered into pieces. . . . I still can't think how it happened . . . How it *could* have happened. One deadly thought was enough.

SAINT-JUST. I don't understand.

ROBESPIERRE. I tried to regain my equilibrium after this ominous glimpse into the future. I kept saying to myself that although the disaster seemed inevitable, I had to avert it. That—as you put it—this is what I exist for in this world. Suddenly it was as if I heard someone behind me speak, asking one simple question: what seems a defeat to us, leaders of the revolution, would it not in reality be . . . salvation for the people?
. . .

[SAINT-JUST *rises slowly*]

And to this question there is *no* answer . . .

[pause. ROBESPIERRE *catches his breath]*

That's how it began. . . and then blow after blow. I sometimes thought it was the beginning of madness. . . everything I grasped, every thought, every fact melted in my fingers. Nothing remained. . . every point in the program of the revolution, every demand of the Rights of Man—is lying before me, annotated with a question mark. I am drowning.

SAINT-JUST *[after a long while, in a hard tone].* What right have you to tell this to *me?* Have you forgotten that through me you can infect hundreds of thousands?

ROBESPIERRE *[lifts his head].* So your faith, apostle of Freedom, wavers in the first breeze of someone else's doubts?

SAINT-JUST. The human mind has little resistance. And your thoughts always carry mine along. So, keep silent until this. . . this attack passes.

ROBESPIERRE. This attack. . .

[suddenly stands up and stops motionless, one hand leaning against the table]

ROBESPIERRE. Maybe I should. . . maybe for the whole of Europe it would be better if I suddenly. . . step aside. . . if the revolution collap. . .

SAINT-JUST *[spontaneously].* Don't dare think so!

ROBESPIERRE *[turns round impetuously].* What then? Go on groping in the dark?! Though there may be an abyss just round the corner?. . . *[suddenly with a tense calm]* You admit yourself that dictatorship is now a necessity, isn't that so?

SAINT-JUST *[watchfully].* Yes.

ROBESPIERRE. And if so, it means that the people cannot govern themselves—that democracy, the foundation of the civil system, is an illusion!

SAINT-JUST *[calmly].* No, my friend. Things are different in normal conditions, and in a crisis. But this is just a morbid scruple.

[Moving a step he comes to stand just behind his friend. He puts his hands on ROBESPIERRE*'s shoulders; as he speaks, he leans over and comes very close to him, then embraces him with one arm and almost clasps him, sideways]*

What the deuce, man, pull yourself together! For those millions of helpless and defenseless people *you are the only one!!* Set against this task, Robespierre—the abstractions which make you rage—are childish! Yes, indeed—grope in the dark! In the dark, if one cannot do otherwise—as long as one moves *forward,* Robespierre! As long as there is no stagnation, because stagnation means decay!

If our program is wrong, we will change it. To the core. Democracy or autocracy? Maxime, in the end, this *is of no significance*! Even though the ground of doctrine has vanished from under your feet, the people's misery is a *fact*! To the people it's all the same on what theoretical basis you will win them the right to be human. Or what form of government the state will take, as long as all of its citizens will at last be able to *live* in it like human beings! It's no use bothering about attacks of doubt, until we have fulfilled the undoubted needs of the people.

ROBESPIERRE [*in a tight clasp, slowly turns his head round to face his friend*]. The people—what does that mean, Saint-Just?

SAINT-JUST [*lets him go, straightens up*]. What sort of a question is that? The people means eighty-five percent of mankind, oppressed and exploited for the barren aims of selfishness. They are those who, because of poverty and work which is too hard, cannot develop into human beings.

ROBESPIERRE. Yes. And now look at humanity in a longitudinal cross-section: it's a ladder of a thousand steps, leading from big bankers to Negro slaves in San Domingo.

At every one of those steps, Antoine—there stands an oppressor and exploiter of those below him, who is himself oppressed and exploited by those above.

Separate then, if you please, the oppressor from the oppressed.

[*a long pause*]

[*looking at the table top*] What is man? What laws of nature guide the lives of societies? What do people need? Have they really been created for freedom? Or maybe the present cruel conditions. . . are the most appropriate? . . . [*with a sudden, painful smile*] Danton would shout for joy in his pit, if he knew how well he's been avenged! . . .

SAINT-JUST. But this is absurd, man! It was the desire for that freedom and the faith in it which roused the people after ten centuries of passivity! The same desire and the same faith have kept it for over four years in a superhuman strain of heroism!

ROBESPIERRE [*sullen, leaning against the headrest of the bed*]. What of it, child? This desire, this faith—could be an illusion. They may lead to chaos.

SAINT-JUST [*sits down. After a long silence*]. Even if it is so. . . one must go on. Let there be what must be. Even then it is worth dying for that faith, it is worth drawing the ultimate defeat on oneself. . . for there is nothing of more value on earth.

ROBESPIERRE [*looks at him fascinated*]. Worth dying. . . for a lie! A lie the highest value on earth!! . . .

[*His legs give way under him. He sits at the edge of his bed*]

Oh, you have finished me, you know.

SAINT-JUST [*leaves the table, walks aimlessly*]. And you have broken my back. Let us thank each other. The revolution is losing us both.

ROBESPIERRE [*lifts his head as if in a daze*]. But this is not possible... an hour ago...

[*he straightens up with a sudden jolt, frames his face with outstretched hands, knits his brows sharply*]

Maybe it is madness.

SAINT-JUST [*over his shoulder*]. It is not madness, it's despair.

[*He turns round. Speaks nonchalantly, but clearly*]

Shoot yourself.

[*He stops by the window, aimlessly looking at the yard.* ROBESPIERRE *slowly falls onto the bed, lies down.*]

ROBESPIERRE [*all of a sudden very calm and sensible*]. You're right. I am no use to anyone now. [*He then develops this thought trying to comprehend its significance*] That means I am... free... [*pause. Suddenly with a sigh of longing*] For once I will sleep like an animal... Antoine!

SAINT-JUST [*by the window, hoarse*]. What?

ROBESPIERRE. Don't wake me when you go—I'm falling asleep. Goodbye.

SAINT-JUST [*suddenly turns round, suspiciously—then returns to his previous posture*]. Very well.

[*For a moment neither of them moves. Suddenly* SAINT-JUST *starts at seeing something outside. He retreats into the room, looks at his friend asleep, then runs out*]

BARERE'S VOICE [*excited, approaching*]. I don't care, I tell you...

[*He rushes into the room.* ROBESPIERRE, *brutally wakened, lifts himself on his shoulder with a slight hiss of fright. In a second he gives the intruder a deadly look, which totally puts* BARERE *out of countenance.*]

BARERE. Oh... I'm sorry. May I?...

ROBESPIERRE [*motionless, sits on the bed*]. You're asking that question somewhat late...

[SAINT-JUST *comes in with a helpless shrug of his shoulders.*]

BARERE. I am most awfully sorry—but I *must* talk to you...

ROBESPIERRE [*coldly*]. Sit down.

[*They sit opposite each other.* SAINT-JUST *walks to the window.*]

BARERE. Well, we are... [*sees* ROBESPIERRE*'s face at close quarters*] Oh...are you ill?

ROBESPIERRE [*with a chalky smile, so forced that it is like a twitch*]. I? Oh, not at all!

[*He is so distracted that he yawns almost incessantly*]

SAINT-JUST. He hasn't slept for four nights, Barère. While you didn't exactly overwork yourself. At least be quick and leave him in peace.

BARERE. Well, we have a fierce argument going on. And lately we're so... used to your deciding all the important questions—that my colleagues have sent me here to you.

ROBESPIERRE [*biting his lip*]. I am very flattered, but today I will definitely not be able to help you. I haven't been so tired since the Constitutional Assembly days.

BARERE. Hm...that's bad. Let us at least have your opinion!

SAINT-JUST. Don't be so persistent, Barère!

ROBESPIERRE. Couldn't this be postponed till tomorrow?

BARERE. Alas—it doesn't depend on me...

ROBESPIERRE [*with a heavy sigh*]. A la bonne heure. Go on, speak. In any case, Saint-Just can deputize for me, if it's absolutely necessary.

[SAINT-JUST *approaches and sits between them.* ROBESPIERRE *yawns again and hides his face in the hand with which he is supporting his head.*]

BARERE. It concerns that prison conspiracy...

ROBESPIERRE [*raises his head, suddenly revived*]. What...already?!

BARERE. Yes...

ROBESPIERRE. But we don't know anything certain about it yet! It may all be that informer's imagination...

BARERE [*with a gesture*]. What can we do? The Committee of Security threw itself on it like a starved animal. The matter is important so we've joined in the discussion. Now some of us—among them Carnot and myself—are of the opinion that the matter should be treated as lightly as possible, following your view that it was an outburst of despair. And so Lucile Desmoulins, a few bankers, suspect already, a few prisoners, lost causes already for one reason or another, will suffer the penalty, and that's that.

ROBESPIERRE [*very attentively*]. Quite right—if there is at all a reason for them to do so.

BARERE. You see. But Comsur are bent on arranging a veritable doomsday.

[ROBESPIERRE *rises*]

They say that the rebellion has to be nipped in the bud,

[SAINT-JUST *smiles and slowly shakes his head.* ROBESPIERRE, *while listening attentively, adjusts his clothes in front of the mirror*]

that one must make a deterrent and sensational example—they mention dozens of names.

SAINT-JUST [*half to himself*]. In a word, we have antagonized half the population, so let us hasten to antagonize the rest.

ROBESPIERRE [*freshens up his coiffure*]. At what time did you leave them? Were you looking for me long?

[SAINT-JUST *watches him with glowing eyes.*]

BARERE [*turns round with his chair*]. Oh, so you will come?!

ROBESPIERRE. I should hope so . . . When did you leave there?

BARERE. You needn't hurry: they've announced an hour's adjournment. We're resuming at half past eight [*looks at his watch*], that is to say in twenty minutes.

[BARERE *rises, bows and leaves.*]

ROBESPIERRE [*ready*]. I am *most* grateful to you. I'll be on time.

[*Both* gens de la haute main *look at each other as if mutually hypnotized by their appearance. A long pause of perfect immobility.*]

ROBESPIERRE [*at last*]. My—God . . .*

SAINT-JUST [*to test him*]. Stay, have a good rest. I can easily dissuade them myself from that stupid notion.

ROBESPIERRE [*distracted*]. Thank you . . . You know, Antoine, I would be a happy man, if I could believe that it really is just stupidity.

SAINT-JUST [*raises his eyes, with an angelic look*]. Well . . . it is even possible . . .

ROBESPIERRE [*with a sour smile*]. I had hoped that you would at least be surprised . . . [*he begins to walk round*] It's no use deluding ourselves. Even old Vadier is not *so* stupid that he would in good faith try to put out the fire by blowing into it. They *want* to intensify the terror . . . [*he stops*] They want to bring about disaster.

Yes, the revolution is taking a tragic turn. It has ceased to be conven-

---

*English words in the original.

ient to those gentlemen. So they want to break it, at any price. What does the state's welfare matter, if the comfort of its rulers is threatened?! The Republic lacks its most basic foundations. We have lost two years because of those factions; now one literally doesn't know where to begin. The work grows in geometric proportion to the number of days that pass...but they've had enough! They're tired! I will lull you to sleep, my faithful comrades. You're dreaming of a deterrent, sensational example? I will fulfill your wish. In a way that will satisfy you totally... Terror has its good points, after all, gentlemen, colleagues! [*walks again*] Now we must above all put an end to the war. Go North with the whole might of the people. We must break the coalition this summer: enough of this waste of resources and strength! But to achieve that one must control the generals at close quarters. They *like* war... [*sudden turn*] Saint-Just, you will go tomorrow to the Northern front.

SAINT-JUST. Hm...you know...

ROBESPIERRE [*like a steely razor*]. What?...

SAINT-JUST [*with an understanding smile*]. Spare me, you bloody tyrant, I'll go.

ROBESPIERRE [*stands before him, speaks with intensity*]. Our move must be uniform, purposeful, Saint-Just! Against those who seek their own fame instead of the people's victory we shall have terror. But the moral basis of our action is more important than victory itself. There is only one step from a war in defense of national existence to a war of aggression. By taking that step we would annihilate the revolution. If the victory were to bring France to *that*, it would be better to lose the war. Make a note of it. [*walks away; over his shoulder*] And keep an eye on Monsieur Pichegru; I don't want that young man to collect personal laurels.

SAINT-JUST. Then you must see to it that the Committee entrusts that mission to me as from tomorrow. Well...

ROBESPIERRE. However, the Committee must not feel that the idea is mine. [*he is lost in thought; speaks slowly*] To wield dictatorial power, but in such a way that nobody notices!...

[*He realizes the comic aspect of the situation and bursts out laughing; it is a hearty laugh but also full of despair.*]

SAINT-JUST [*enlivened*]. You see, Maxime, that is why I leave you with such reluctance. After all, your present situation cannot last. You will not manage to conceal your functions as an absolute ruler for more than a few days. But the death penalty for even the suggestion of assuming the supreme power is no joke. Just think how your seven hundred tired colleagues, whom you will have pinned down with terror, will seek any pretext to accuse you of usurpation of power. And that surely is a deadly weapon.

ROBESPIERRE. I can't help smiling.* They've blunted that deadly weapon against my person so thoroughly in the last couple of years that it is fit only for a museum of curiosities.

SAINT-JUST. Slander was harmless. From now on it will not be just slander; and the first who dares to hurl the accusation will wipe you out with one movement of his hand.

ROBESPIERRE. He will have to dare first.

SAINT-JUST [impatient]. Don't be rash, Maxime! Listen: leave me here. I will go to work on public opinion. In three weeks, Maxime, you will be able to assume dictatorship officially on the unanimous demand of all Paris. Just consider how much time you would save this way, not to speak of security!

ROBESPIERRE [thoughtful]. I can't, my boy: the front is more important.

SAINT-JUST. I shall not have a moment's peace. If you fall, everything will be lost!

ROBESPIERRE. Then you will tremble for me. You would not believe how sweet it is to know that there is someone who trembles for me and not before me . . . But you will have no reason to do so. Nothing will happen to me. There is a special Providence that watches over tyrants . . . I'll manage somehow. If only I had two years . . . I must transform the government from within, without nominally changing it. The spirit of Danton has demoralized the Convention in a terrible way. It must have discipline restored, as well as its broken contact with the people, and it must be given so much work that there will be no time left for personal squabbles. But the Committee must persevere on high, whether it wants to or not; after all, there must remain something that the people can trust absolutely. The city Commune must be renewed. We have no time now to endure sabotage.

[short pause; jocularly:]

The spiritual unification of France! . . . Dozens of years of hard work are needed before France is thoroughly imbued with revolutionary thought. In the countryside people still don't know what we are about. Most of the disturbances and revolts are only the result of this terrible moral ignorance. Our first, most important aim is to educate people to

*English words in the original.

be people. This is a special task for the Jacobins. But their affiliated clubs are either asleep or do nothing. They must be harnessed to this in earnest...The administration has to be weeded out. One shudders to think what is happening in the provinces. Those people's associations, local communes and revolutionary committees without any sense of direction, without control...France must be flooded with thousands of energetic commissioners, intelligent, morally mature. But there are only a handful of men to whom one could entrust the material and spiritual welfare of even one department. Stupidity in responsible positions causes catastrophic harm everywhere. Emissaries of the Convention prowled round the revolted provinces like the plague: instead of remedying the wrongs and winning over the population, they strengthened its fierce resistance. Lyon, Bordeaux, Nantes have been ravaged...

Oh, to be able to be *just*...to be able to afford this luxury once, and send Fouché with Collot to the scaffold—for Lyon!! I know I can't... but the thought of that mangled city sometimes makes me lose my self-control. Malicious cretins, both of them...and there are many more like them!

So far we have avoided economic disaster. But what we have is not prosperity.

[*He stops by the window. In a changed voice*]

And there is so very little time left...

SAINT-JUST [*struck by these words, turns round quickly. Speaks softly, without emphasis*]. Why? You are still young...

ROBESPIERRE [*again distracted and tired*]. Why? I don't know. But I know that it is so.

SAINT-JUST. But at least you can now work at the right pace. The factions have been liquidated; your path is free.

ROBESPIERRE [*turns round, with a tired smile*]. Well...I suppose you are right. Now I can really move forward...Although, from now on, in place of barricades blocking the road, whole invisible armies are lurking in ditches and behind fences, with thousands of missiles at the ready.

[*He walks back to the middle of the room*]

We have not killed Danton. We have multiplied, disseminated him. His blood has already begun to yield its crop. Like the blood of a mythical hero, it breeds an avenger from its every drop.

[*He leans on the table. His rhetoric is slightly marked with sarcasm:*]

When we fall—you and I, Antoine—quicklime will swallow and consume us, our thought will be blown away like a breath; only our names
will remain as prey for historians. [*lifts himself up*] But Danton cannot be
killed. For Danton is the colossus of life—the first-born son of Nature—
the immortal beast in man.

[*he is more and more excited*]

Until man outgrows this beast in himself, he will time after time rebel
and bleed—in vain. Revolution will not survive to achieve its aim this
time, or the second, or the fifth time. Danton's corruption, Danton's
lie will after a while outweigh the upward momentum...
        Christ...what am I saying!...
SAINT-JUST [*almost with a smile*]. Fortunately I know now that one doesn't
    have to take these prophetic attacks of yours seriously...but your
    nerves are going to pieces, my friend. And in your situation...a mo-
    ment's exhaustion can have disastrous results...

[*perturbed, he rises, speaks with passion*]

Maxime: take a week's rest. Six days only! And *leave* me in Paris!
ROBESPIERRE. Oh, stop it. How many times am I to repeat that it's impos-
    sible...
SAINT-JUST. At any rate, when will you let me come back?
ROBESPIERRE. After the breakthrough has been achieved. But you will then
    go immediately to the provinces. I need you everywhere...Oh, if only
    I could have fifteen of you, Saint-Just! You, who pacified and won over
    rebellious Alsace—without bloodshed! Lack of talented people is at the
    core of all our misfortunes.
SAINT-JUST. Well, we have good generals. You must admit that much.
ROBESPIERRE. Yes, I must. I can only hope that none of them is as good as
    Dumouriez.
SAINT-JUST [*irritated*]. Don't be a maniac, Maxime! Instead of thanking God
    that the country at least has capable defenders from outside threats, you
    . . .
ROBESPIERRE. ...I am afraid of them. And hate them...I *hate* them...
You call me a maniac? But don't you yourself know them? The soul of
someone who is a soldier by calling is not a mature human soul. It is the
half-animal soul of a malicious child. It is a dwarfish mind, horrifyingly
narrow, but pathologically drawn to the one animal function of con-
quering. Like every spiritually deficient being, he recognizes in this
world only himself. Let his country suffer even a decisive defeat, if only

he finds in it a revenge for some trivial affront. Let Europe turn into a heap of rubble, if only *he* gains by it power and glory.

When they doted on Dumouriez, I trembled for the future . . . knowing that as a military genius he had to be an utter villain. Where I want to be wrong, I am always dead right. So now I fear those young ones, Hoche, or Jourdan, like the plague . . .

SAINT-JUST. Oh! Even the most ebullient of these gentlemen wear solid dog-collars on their necks. The government's control is always there.

ROBESPIERRE [*with intensity*]. For as long as there *is* a government, my friend . . . But as soon as corruption finishes me off, all those rotten Dantonist blackguards, those political profiteers, speculators and provocateurs will snatch power . . .

The invigorating impact of the Revolution has generated in the French people an unusual abundance of active energy. Its amount is so considerable that, by its use, the development of the new nation could be achieved in a dozen, instead of hundreds, of years, and attain a hitherto unheard of degree of social perfection.

But—for this to be brought about my successor would have to be a genius. And I shall more likely be succeeded by such people as Tallien, Barras, and Fouché. When that happens, any enterprising little son of Mars will focus this power round *himself.* The invaluable instrument of life will be wasted in the hands of an idiot on destructive orgies of the soldiery; a beastly athlete will squander for his dull enjoyment creative energies the like of which this country will never again be able to produce . . .

France is so loaded with vitality that it could swell up to the Urals—for a few hellish years—if it fell into the clutches of such a brainless plunderer. Haha! What a fulfillment of the dreams of a Universal Republic: Europe devastated as if after an earthquake, trembling with hunger and fear at the feet of a divine Caesar . . . *Such a one* will be made dictator all right; they will even beg him to lead them to their doom . . .

[*he falls onto the chair*]

Instinct! Oh yes, the unerring instinct of the masses, the same that makes insects fly straight into the flame . . .

[*after a while—quickly, softly, almost hysterically*]

Oh, how I am *tormented* by that thought! Everywhere something seems to hang over me. In everything I hear its threat. It's as if something was slowly burning through my skull, ever and again at the same inflamed point... You know, I have moments of outright mad desire: to wipe out, cut down all those military talents in the country. Kill— exterminate—even boys in the cadet school. Let the country have peace just for a few years... at least until the Republic develops from its nucleus... Who after me will protect the defenseless foolish people from the greed of those cannibals?!!

[*he leans back with a spasmodic breaking sigh*]

Ooooh... I must calm down.

[*He is seized by a brief attack of nervous coughing. Having overcome it, he grins and laughs unpleasantly*]

If I went on like that I would soon get a hemorrhage... consumption on top of everything else!

[*he drops his head on his hands; whispers with dismay*]

Great God... how powerless I am...

SAINT-JUST [*calmly*]. You have a fever; you have not slept for four days and nights, so you fall into hysterics. And as for the future, my dear friend— as for that hellish omnipotence of chance—you are powerless, for you are a man. And so, you are wasting your life when you torment yourself with it. Shut yourself in the present; put blinkers on your eyes, like a horse. What happens after you—that you cannot change: in the meantime you mustn't take fright, for you are pulling the state behind you.

ROBESPIERRE [*straightens up slowly*]. This—I cannot—change... [*in a feverish whisper*] And yet I must, by hell! I *must*!!

You are right. I'm making a clown of myself. [*suddenly erupts in a laugh which terrifies* SAINT-JUST] I was about to proclaim the discovery that one could not overcome death!

SAINT-JUST [*knits his brows sharply*]. You... ou... know, it's better for you not to laugh.

ROBESPIERRE [*tense all of a sudden. Dead silence in the room*]. Do you hear?...

SAINT-JUST [*sulking*]. What?

ROBESPIERRE. The crowd is coming back.

SAINT-JUST. Requiescant in pace. Don't raise your left hand, the sleeve has caught something.

ROBESPIERRE [*carefully disentangles the lace and again turns his head to the window*]. One cannot overcome death! You are wrong, Antoine. It is only I who can't. Only I am powerless with regard to the future. The future belongs to the late Danton.

[*he looks at his watch*]

Come on, Antoine. It's time for us to go.

19 ventôse An CXXXVII, 13 h.

Thermidor

CHARACTERS

Jean Nicolas Billaud-Varenne
Jean Marie Collot d'Herbois
Joseph Fouché
Lazare Carnot
Bertrand Barère de Vieuzac

Antoine Louis Saint-Just
Jean Lambert Tallien
Maximilien François Marie Isidore
  de Robespierre
Vilate

This list of characters has been prepared by the translator.

Act I

It is about eight in the evening. July. In the conference hall of the Comité de Salut Public, BILLAUD, COLLOT, *and* VILATE *sit close together by a long table, at its right end. They are leaning over a sheet of paper.* CARNOT *looks absentmindedly ahead; so does* FOUCHE *who, nervous and undecided, walks round the room from time to time. Usually he returns to his favorite chair by the window. It is hard to tell where he will direct his steps next.*

BILLAUD *moves away from his colleagues, sinks into an armchair, and falls into a kind of stupor. He is even more tired than* CARNOT. *His blood and every cell in his body are permeated with fatigue.*

CARNOT *throws but a single glance at the sheet of paper. The satisfaction that results from that glance is like a momentary flash, and is so removed from his mood at the time that it reaches his consciousness only as a tiny pause in the normal trend of his thoughts. He arranges his papers, puts them into a leather briefcase, gives another look round and makes as if to leave.* FOUCHE *watches him discreetly.*

CARNOT. Good night.

[*The two deputies raise their heads, muttering something.*]

FOUCHE [*bars his way*]. If you please. [*hands him a piece of paper*]

CARNOT. Ah . . . [*reluctantly takes the paper, restrains himself from tearing it to bits, folds it*] Thank you *so much.* [*he has to return to the table in order to put the paper neatly into his briefcase*]

FOUCHE. Have you got a fever?

CARNOT. No. Why?

FOUCHE. I only thought . . . all your colleagues have a touch of fever; it's in the air—and then your hands are shaking so.

CARNOT. I've been here continuously since yesterday evening.

FOUCHE. At least you'll be able to sleep it off a bit now. [CARNOT *starts. Their eyes meet.* FOUCHE *is quite innocently amazed, in a most natural way:*] What? . . . No, you've misunderstood me. I didn't mean anything.

CARNOT [*emphatically*]. You mean SOMETHING with every word you utter. You lie in wait for whoever is tired, to open up his thoughts like an oyster, when his resistance is low. *What* do you want to know from me? Cards on the table, please.

213

[BILLAUD *frowns; the two others, roused, are looking at the speakers*]

COLLOT. Will you be quiet, you two?

VILATE. We have enough arguments as it is. Let today be an exception, please!

FOUCHE. You're terribly overworked, Carnot. You can't go on like this. The Republic needs you.

CARNOT [*shrugs his shoulders*]. Quite right: I must take a holiday. Now, when I have the coalition at our frontiers, and in the country. . . [*he clenches his fists, speaks through his teeth*] . . . *in the country*. . .

FOUCHE. Indeed, I do advise you to take a holiday. [CARNOT *looks at him*] If these two are so keen to take your place, why shouldn't they do it?

CARNOT [*quietly, his teeth chattering*]. Go on, quick.

FOUCHE. While reading this letter, I was struck by Saint-Just's politeness. He expressed his opinion of your orders fully and comprehensively, without even *one* insulting word. It's a masterpiece.

CARNOT. The villain has a talent—for writing.

FOUCHE. But so far I know only *his* opinion. Audiatur et altera pars. That other party is you. So what do you think about those orders of yours?

CARNOT. What business is it of yours? What do you understand about these things?

FOUCHE. Of course, I am not a military man. But. . . if lawyers can understand something of it, why not priests too. . .

CARNOT [*after a while*]. Is he behind it? *This* time too?

FOUCHE. No, of course not. I only thought. . . You know how much interest he took in your work. Now he's taken his hands off the wheel. Incidentally: does anyone else in Paris, apart from yourself, know about this particular order?. . .

[*they look into each other's eyes*]

CARNOT [*shivering*]. A colleague discussed this idea with me; earlier, of course. No one must know about the order itself. . . [*his face grows pale*] Treason again with secret documents?

FOUCHE. N-no. Something. . . else. Well, a colleague, you say, *suggested* that idea to you, Carnot. [CARNOT *starts*] Of course, the idea was too clever in its. . . well. . . absurdity. . . to have originated with that colleague. It came from a source, which had caused many a confusion. It came from *another* colleague. And you let yourself be ensnared like an enamored nightingale. And the obliging colleague informed *his* colleague, who, as you know, over there in Belgium is, shall we say, putting your plans into practice. And the colleague of your modest colleague did not leave the matter without an answer; it now lies heavy on your stomach. [*he points to the briefcase*]

The order thought up by your colleague carries your signature. It was a state secret. But the sad situation you find yourself in, and the result of that order, are *no* secret.

You are a courageous man, Carnot, since you still let yourself be seen among us. Someone else would have hidden himself underground long ago.

[CARNOT *listens with his head lowered. His jaws are tightly shut, his clenched fists turn white. A moment's silence—then he suddenly leans back, breathes in some air with a jerk, grabs his briefcase from the table and disappears. The way he slams the door makes the building shake to its foundations.* FOUCHE *does not smile; he withdraws toward his window.* BILLAUD *starts up; he restrains himself from uttering a swear word, but his face becomes twisted in a painful grimace.*]

COLLOT [*has read the piece of paper; laughs*]. Congratulations!

VILATE [*keenly*]. Not bad, eh?... Only one would have to bring it to his attention.

COLLOT [*a momentary glance*]. Do it then.

VILATE. Hm-m. [*rubs his hand against his neck*] Certainly. Quite right. Well? What do you think of it? [*looks across at Fouché*]

COLLOT. Not bad... here and there. That is to say, for a beginner like you. You are a beginner, aren't you?

VILATE. My very first product. A double necessity stood at its cradle. Written with the blood of my heart. Everyone will be able to recognize it on close reading. [*again gives a sidelong glance—then whispers in* COLLOT's *ear*] Ask him...

COLLOT [*turns around*]. Fouché, you are asked to give your opinion.

FOUCHE [*a friendly look*]. As you know, that never pays.

[BILLAUD *unexpectedly shrugs his shoulders, puffs his mouth. They both look at him. He suddenly points to the paper.*]

BILLAUD. *What is that?* [*silence of incomprehension*] That shit rag... *today?*

[FOUCHE, *without letting it be seen, listens in. He sits down in the chair on the right, as if to signify that a performance is about to begin*]

VILATE. Shit is the most effective weapon when fighting demigods.

BILLAUD [*laughs and cheers up a bit*]. O you idiots, you pitiful idiots! [*suddenly very thoughtful*] Yes, time makes us gradually lose our equanimity, isn't that so? Especially since there is nothing sensible about it. One can't keep up the pace at all. This is absolutely indecent. Time has bolted from us like a young colt. Quite a few people have bruised themselves trying to run after it.

VILATE. It's not just anyone who can jump on its back and enjoy the ride.

COLLOT. But everyone can and should hasten to help to bridle it. You agree, I hope?

BILLAUD. No. But try and do it at least! Even though you lack the capacity for *it*.

FOUCHE. Have you had a bad dream, Billaud?

[*silence for a while*]

BILLAUD [*motionless, looks at the leaflet*]. Listen to me, Vilate. Why are you doing it?

VILATE. My inner life is disgusting. Why are you interested in it of all things? As if there were no other curiosities in abundance.

BILLAUD. Your lampoon is simply bad. So bad that one gets the impression that deep down you wanted it to produce the opposite effect. If we seriously hate someone, we do not start by acting in such a clumsy way. To accuse *him* of vice! Of sexual perversions, *him*!

You have brought out his moral rectitude, and quite effectively too. If *that* was your purpose, you can be satisfied.

FOUCHE. Billaud is still wandering up in the Milky Way. He thinks that any calumny will appear to the masses too flagrant to be believed.—But the less probable it is the better. A people's tribune must not parade his too exalted soul before the worthy public, Billaud. You've had five years to find that out.

BILLAUD. Don't waste your words, Fouché. Everything that is in you and on you has inestimable value. [VILATE *laughs*] What a pity the good old days are over, isn't that so, young man? The days when you could live on the most miserable jokes uttered by others, as long as you were able to burst out laughing at their every word. You would have made a useful court jester. It would be hard to find someone more servile. As it is, all that you're left with is informing. A hard way to earn your bread and butter!

COLLOT [*irritated*]. Eh, Billaud, what's the matter with you? Stomach upset? Toothache?

BILLAUD. You all hate him like mongrels beaten with a stick. You're afraid of him. Afraid—that is too weak an expression. You're just part of the Paris mob; he is a somebody.

He is somebody, for the Republic exists only through his will. Yes, he's the one and only. He gives you a free hand, nobly withdraws, allows you to make the first move and lends you a month for the purpose. *Can* one imagine more irony in his contempt?—Such treatment deserves murder.

You rehash some nonsense taken from the ancient Romans and to print it use up the paper meant to print proclamations on. *Those* are your chess moves, your tactics, your revenge! *There!*

[*he crumples the leaflet and throws it out of the window*]

FOUCHE [*starts*]. Aah!

COLLOT. What does this mean?

FOUCHE. Attention everybody. The die is cast.

COLLOT. What are you saying?

FOUCHE. That was an eloquent gesture. I like it when great orators throw their lives into the scale. Billaud has done it in a new, simple, and enchanting way. That paper ball contained something more than life; our destiny was there. I am eagerly awaiting what happens next.

BILLAUD. What do you want exactly?

FOUCHE. To congratulate you. You are either a born actor or a hero. [BILLAUD *shrugs his shoulders.* FOUCHE *unexpectedly changes his tone of voice*] With one movement of your arm you have taken upon yourself a task not everyone could cope with.

[*a long silence*]

BILLAUD. . . . and which you'd rather see on my shoulders so that you can be spared it.

[*a pause*]

VILATE [*with satisfaction*]. Oh yes, he's right, you know. You should undertake this great task.

[*a long pause*]

COLLOT [*whispers, fearfully*]. I don't understand anything. . .

[*a long pause*]

BILLAUD [*in a strange tone of voice*]. No. I won't take it on.

[FOUCHE *laughs meaningfully*]

VILATE. Now do you understand *me?* We can shake hands. Inability to act on both sides. And both sides admit it now.

[*pause*]

COLLOT [*surprised*]. You are under his spell, you are all hypnotized by him.
FOUCHE. And who isn't, Collot? Only the strongest heads have stood up to
him.
VILATE. You mean the *hardest* heads.
FOUCHE [*dryly*]. O, really.
BILLAUD. Yes. Fouché is right. And. . .and I shouldn't refuse. But my own
strength is not enough. Do you realize what has to be done?

It means toppling a man who out of an idea has built a state, and who
by his sheer will is holding this state at the highest level.

When that head falls into the basket, not a single atom will shake in
the cosmos; but that head contains a brain such as God does not create
twice in any century; and when that brain ceases to function. . .

You see, that is what frightens me. My duty is to topple the usurper!

But then it is enough for the first fat Bourbon to cross the frontier,
and it will be as if the Revolution had never happened! Now you know
what the Republic is; you know that no one except him is able to preserve it. I can't do it, Fouché can't do it, no, no one can! You say he is a
dictator? Yes, he rules, because he *can*, because he *must* rule. A genius of
that caliber must rule, whether he wants to or not. And we should raise
altars to him, because he carries the burden of ruling, without usurping
its splendors unlike any king on this earth. Yes, indeed, we could raise
altars to him, instead of thinking how to get rid of him.
VILATE. But the one goes very well with the other.

[FOUCHE *looks at him with interest*]

BILLAUD. The Romans had this superiority over us: they could worship
their heroes without having to destroy them first.

[*Those present, forming an exclusive company, do not have to play the comedy of indignation. Only* VILATE *imitates the gestures of a chorus, wringing his hands in despair*]

BILLAUD. Indeed, the best we could do would be to raise altars.
COLLOT. Oh, my friend, has this not been the case everywhere up to now?
VILATE [*in a voice they have not heard him use*]. The guillotine is an altar too,
Billaud. Perhaps even a holy one. The table at which Jesus on that night
transformed the bread and wine and gave them to his disciples was an
altar too. As an ex-priest I know these things. And so, no scruples
please.

FOUCHE [*after a short pause*]. So this is the point we've reached. Billaud, you completely misunderstood what I said about a task. With your megalomania, it was only to be expected. Leaving that aside, how is it that here, in the very heart of Comsal, I find the same concepts of throne and altar as those held by the earlier owners of this residence?

To the bold villain, who was good enough to put up a throne and place himself on it, you want also, out of sheer gratitude, to raise an altar. Ah, the human soul!... But let us leave this dangerous subject; my harmless joke has gone a little too far beyond its original intention.

COLLOT [*after a while*]. Now you're retreating, and talk about raising altars, but only because for six weeks you've been breathing freely, without feeling his paws around your throat. Raise altars to him! To the... the man whom you, you yourself charged to his face with high treason! Raise altars to the epileptic weakling whom once I almost grabbed by the collar and shook.

BILLAUD. It is not every day that one hears such silly charges. But I will explain things clearly. I hate the man and consider him an usurper. All right. My convictions are beyond discussion. But I am also able to appreciate his mind, his politics. One shudders at the thought of destroying such a precious gift of God.

FOUCHE. Well, that was at least a sincere confession. The thing must be done, but by somebody else. I don't dare do it myself. Really, gentlemen, let's leave it. Let us leave it.

VILATE. By God, Fouché, come to your senses. How are we to "leave it"? It's impossible. Thank God you don't have to meet the Inviolable face to face every day. He is as merciful as the Jewish God and he spares you! You keep your distance from him. You never look him in the eye. One hardly mentions his name. But only try to think of something else! "Where two or three gather, there am I." Even though he sits quietly at home, writing sonnets perhaps, his spell continues to hold you all enthralled.

COLLOT. So what! Every lunatic or hoodlum let loose arouses the same feelings.

BILLAUD. O no. We think about the hoodlum because we're afraid...

ALL [*together*]. And what about him...?!

BILLAUD. About him too we think out of fear. [*vague sniggers which he ignores*] But *this* fear is much more important; it is healthy. [*murmur*] We forget the hoodlum once he has ceased to threaten us. *Him* you will... we will never forget. [*jeering murmur*] We are bound to him with all our life nerves. He is a man of the highest order, a saint—as such people used to be called once. He could have become more than a ruler and a leader; he could have become a father, a patriarch in the eyes of twenty-five million people. Well, he is not that...any more. For he is selfish. That is his Achilles' heel, a sore on the body of a seraph. He is selfish in an exalted sense, but so much the worse. He misuses his strength, his gift for ruling. He loves the masses, but hates man; he mistreats individuals for the good of society. Yes, he has mastered our minds, he is bleeding our brains dry, and in his hands we go to pieces.

He is a mighty creator. His achievements are astounding. The works he has created lack nothing except for the highest perfection: life.

A demigod with the potency of Priapus—and yet sterile.

[VILATE *gives a long laugh, with purposefully accentuated vulgarity*]

COLLOT. I implore you, Billaud, stick to the facts, or—with all due respect—shut your golden mouth. Since Danton went down into hell, we have all been secretly deliberating on how to carry out certain...certain further changes. Now this matter comes out almost in spite of us. For a long time we have been united in a common aim. Today, as you know, a common danger cements this bond even more. For six weeks now we have been living in an unbearable uncertainty, which grows every day; with astonishment we have become aware of the degree of our dependence and—defenselessness. Gradually, one must admit, we have come to the painful impression that we've fallen into a trap. How was it that he dared to leave the Committee to its own devices for six long weeks? Does he have any illusions as regards our feelings? What *can* he have up his sleeve? What is he doing—now, up there in his attic? We used to say at first: a breakdown, he's finished. But he, who in the course of six weeks has brought into being the world's most dangerous police bureau, and who with his sheer silence keeps all France in check, cannot be finished.

BILLAUD [*murmurs*]. Certainly not.

FOUCHE. Ah, you exaggerate, Collot, and how. He simply gave himself a holiday. He is not yet finished, perhaps, but not far from it. The whole mystery is amazingly simple; the answer to it is: consumption. You know how it usually is: for years the disease breeds in secret, the victim hardly feels anything. One fine morning it breaks out openly. From then on a short struggle, whose result is a foregone conclusion. With him it will go even faster, since he has not spared himself. Understandably, he does not want us to see his downfall. He, the Invincible, now weak as a child, physically broken, spiritually exhausted! He remains in hiding; I understand this bashfulness in someone who is rotting alive. Perhaps within a week he will be harmless forever. Within a week.

[*a short silence*]

But, as you know, those who are dying sometimes have very funny ideas. It is a great pity that he still wields that almost unlimited power.

[*tense, though short, silence*]

BILLAUD [*quietly*]. A great pity that you do not keep your. . .imagination under control. Why are you leading us astray? Do you have an inkling of the truth? I don't know. You disgust me, and yet you are a puzzle to me. Do *you* understand him? I doubt it. You are much too sly for that. Among you all, I am the only one who has seen through that man.

VILATE. O, Billaud, then you must tell all. You must!

BILLAUD. That is precisely what I am going to do.

Just look at our Republic, as she is today. It is hell. Only a short time ago the provinces were raging, a cauldron of revolt was boiling over all round Paris. Today everything is silent. Doesn't this deep silence seem strange to you? Does a healthy country lie so still? Has not the Revolution, defending itself in Paris against all France, imposed its will in too radical a manner? Not long ago Europe was storming through all four of our frontiers. Today our army celebrates in Brussels the conquest of Belgium; the coalition is in disarray.

But here, in Paris, the true state of affairs reveals itself. The impulsive Parisian people have entrenched themselves silently behind closed shutters. The government sits isolated, in the midst of a world to which it has become a stranger, surrounded by a depressing void. Deprived of support among the people, demoralized, the government has entangled itself in unsurmountable problems. Contradictory forces clash; nothing runs smoothly any more. For six weeks now not a single step forward has been taken.

The Republic is falling to pieces. Terror is reigning and devouring itself on the imposing pile of rubble which two years ago was still the most beautiful country in Europe. But this pile of rubble is not to be conquered. Beaten armies flee from its frontiers. This pile of rubble sends winged forces out, defends itself more stubbornly than the strongest fortress.

This miracle has its source in us. In the ten of us who, in the midst of this mortally silent, burning city, are the focal point of immense power. The Convention is a corpse, devoured by worms; but Comsal lives—for its own sake, for the Convention and the whole Republic. We keep up appearances. All this is, of course, in vain, and we know it. We wish only to forget, and we hope for nothing. Why then do we still act? Only through political vanity, to hide from the world the utter defeat of our idea? No, these reasons would be too weak, too trivial to produce such a strain. We act because *he* compels us to it. This compulsion keeps up the rotten Republic and forces Europe to pay homage. Because of that compulsion the world does not learn the truth about such an important question as Life or Death. I hope this gives you at least a hazy notion what our esteemed colleague is.

COLLOT. Do you realize, Billaud, that your rhapsody is just a stream of empty words?

BILLAUD. Quite. These facts cannot be expressed in words. But that you, you eight on whom the responsibility rests, are not able to see what is happening around you! That you can't do anything except tremble for dear life all the time! Maybe my point of view is mad; but yours is shameful.

VILATE. Do you care if others share your opinion, or not?

BILLAUD. I care. Now that the Republic no longer exists, I seek for her bright traces in every soul. Everything that came into contact with her had to be clean and sharp, crystal clear. But instead . . .

FOUCHE. You still don't understand, Billaud, that man is not a mineral. Even if we agree about the substance, let it be *a little less clean*. But how many more forms that mineral can have! How much more interesting they are! The year eighty-nine brought with it the regrettable fashion of regarding people as precious stones and treating them accordingly. We now have the results.

Dear friends, man is too intimately related to swine not to come into contact with dung and dirt. You have prepared for him a crystal dwelling of snow and ice. No wonder then if the happy recipient freezes to death overnight.

BILLAUD. Yes . . . Fouché. Thank heaven only a few have been condemned to such a way of seeing and thinking.

VILATE. Do you mean to say he is not right?

BILLAUD. Unfortunately, facts are on his side. A small part of mankind had the courage to try to make man into . . . man. Well, the experiment was not successful. Thousands of crippling years cannot be undone in a few days. Perhaps the excessive effort has had a disastrous effect on the people. Perhaps it would have been better if not all of us leaders were under forty. In any event we have irrevocably lost our freedom.

VILATE. The sooner we drag its corpse from its throne and bury it the better.

FOUCHE. Well then, Billaud—we are going to get ourselves openly a dictator . . .

[VILATE *crosses himself and springs to his feet.* FOUCHE *reassures the astounded* COLLOT *with a gesture and a smile*]

BILLAUD. It's no use provoking me. I've already said we have one, and a very real one at that. He is, however, strong enough to manage without regalia. He is also the only man to keep up the lie of the Republic. The Republic lives only in him, but, as you can see, it lives intensely enough to keep in check all the nations in Europe.

VILATE. Where is this going to take us?

BILLAUD. What is this to us? Have you any idea, any inkling where we are rushing to? While the state externally holds out so brilliantly, and internally is convulsing like an earthworm chopped up into a thousand pieces, *we,* the only remaining group of leaders, are walking down an untrodden road in an unknown direction.

VILATE. In that case, Billaud, I can't understand why you do not consider as proper any means that can bring that man down; why you simply don't look for a chance to, why . . .

FOUCHE. Yes, why? Since you say that even the fattest Bourbon would be better than *such* a Republic. . .

BILLAUD. *When* did I say that? On the contrary, I very much doubt if even the most limited royal power would be better than our Republic, even though it is now dead. Why don't I grab him by the throat? I've told you already: I don't trust myself. He is the only genius that hell has bestowed on us. We've seen him in action: Year Two is his work, never mind how much it costs us to admit it. I see right through his present state, and I tell you: I do not trust myself. I hate him with my heart, but not like all of you; for in you there is only the common hate of the weak who are forced to act. I have hated him only since that moment when our reason for existence collapsed. Since that evening when all of us together, and each of us separately, came to the conclusion deep down that the Revolution had been won in vain. A blow like that leaves its marks. I can hardly understand how we have survived it. We are still thunderstruck. Our souls have begun to sprout strange shoots. A mystic egotism has developed in him, resistance to the void caused by his breakdown. He has fallen into self-deification, he has surrounded his psyche with a mad, God-aping love. . . This is terrible. In me, immeasurable hate has replaced the dried-up life source. This hate is directed against him because he has failed. Because he was not equal to his task. Because human misery clings to him as it does to everyone else. That's the reason, the only reason why, taking delight in the mishaps of others, all of you were able to feast your eyes on my constant clashes with him; that's why I hammered away at his nerves day after day with ever new attacks.

COLLOT. Do you consider him mad?

BILLAUD. Not yet, but perhaps he is going that way. It is already grave when one falls on one's knees before the deity in oneself. And he engages in such worship. He knows only that as the one who carries the spirit of Revolution he cannot fall. He really thinks himself a holy monstrance. He does; not that young enthusiast who out of love for him wants to conquer the world. In order not to allow the profanation, he supports—with all his remaining strength—the form, the dead form, the Republic in name only. And: après moi—le déluge.

FOUCHE. You may be right about his madness. But, Billaud, those who worship themselves seek isolation not on the heights where access is difficult and where their superiority is every day put to the test, but in a quiet wilderness, like hermits. Our esteemed colleague, whose name apparently can only be spoken by high priests, does not worship himself but his creation. That is more dangerous, more human and, at so high a level, more probable. He has invented that Republic of his. He has created it, he is madly in love with it. It seems to him that he cannot even die without it. He knows that the dream is over and that his house of cards has fallen to pieces. He knows it, but he keeps it a secret, deluding himself that no one except him knows about it. You are right when you say that he keeps up appearances.

He knows that life tramples on ruins, melts them down into other, equally shortlived structures. *That* he will not accept, as long as he still lives. Like an alsatian dog watching over the body of his master, he will not allow the earth to take what is hers. The Republic rots and will infect the world, if she is not ripped from him and—as Vilate rightly says— buried in the ground.

That will not be easy, though. His intuitive vigilance is really something extraordinary, and to do anything *against* his will is hardly possible. The situation is critical indeed.

BILLAUD. But you say, and with such certainty, that he is finished.

FOUCHE. Yes, he is. But someone like him will not depart peacefully into the great silence. He will first try to arrange all by himself a wake that people will long remember. I can see it coming: his aim is to blow France up like a powder store. Not the system of government, of course, which is worthless anyway, but the state itself. It sounds very romantic: because his beloved France is not strong enough to be the Republic, she should rather perish than return to the brothel of monarchy. He who has once had an unfaithful lover and suffered on her account can easily put himself in his frame of mind.

VILATE [*dully*]. He has no right to do it!

BILLAUD. A lover paying attention to what is right and what is wrong would be a eunuch.

COLLOT. But he *cannot* do that!

FOUCHE. Can't he indeed!

Just think, gentlemen: why has France not yet fallen to bits? You have said it yourselves: first, because of the unexpectedly favorable war situation; second, because the Comsal exists plus five or six experienced outsiders, not to mention him, the Incorruptible. Should he, this *spiritus movens*, pass on to the other world, there would be a bit of chaos at first, but in the end, the liberated leaders would come into their own and help the country to find a new, more practicable form of government. On the other hand, should it happen that the Lord calls the *entire* Comsal suddenly to heaven, then France would be left without a head. The results can easily be guessed: in the country—the Last Judgment; on the frontiers—first a long pause in hostilities, as no instructions would be forthcoming from Paris, and every general would use the delay to clear a way for himself to the imperial throne. If all goes well, three weeks after the Republic has been guillotined, the shamefully defeated king of Prussia will be able to tell his master of horses to take over this hall as his quarters.

That is his plan. One fine morning he will put in an appearance here, demand the heads of his colleagues in Comsal, get them—and will never come again. Having achieved one's aim, one can commit suicide with satisfaction.

COLLOT. But . . . what are your grounds for thinking that that is his intention? It seems you've gone a little too far . . .

FOUCHE. I know one thing anyway: that in the last few days all the prominent people have been watched by a swarm of spies. Besides, I know that it's because of him that the good Carnot, the brains of the army, fell into a dangerous trap. *He*, whose genius intervened often enough, in the strategic-tactical field, always to good effect, has now in a round-about way prompted poor Carnot with a hellish idea. An instruction thus concocted went out to the Sambre-et-Meuse army and could cost us the entire campaign. That, however, was not the purpose of the intrigue, for the master's beloved young disciple received the news in time, generously revoked the orders as he thought fit, and sent to the Comsal a communication about the whole thing that will probably cost poor Carnot his head.

[*a long silence*]

BILLAUD. What communication? I haven't seen anything like that.

FOUCHE. It arrived early this morning, friend. You two were not here; and those who read it were struck dumb. Carnot has just given me that note to read. Tomorrow you will be able to judge for yourselves.

BILLAUD [*suddenly turns round*]. Why don't you make an outcry? Why don't you stop being a coward just *this once*? Is it indeed so dangerous to assassinate this man? On what is his power really based? Neither on money nor on a party—on nothing in fact! And yet the terrible tension that his rule engenders has become unbearable for *everyone*, for the whole nation! It's difficult to get at the ruler of a healthy state—if he is a genuine ruler—for the very state guards and supports him; but he? He who imposes on a reluctant people, against the spirit of the time and nature, artificial forms of existence? His creation is lifeless! It does not speak for him any more; its creator stands unprotected, defenseless! He holds us, Paris, all France in check—with his gaze. That's how things are. To defend himself, to impose his sinister will, he has nothing, literally *nothing*, except his pair of light green eyes. You tremble, you faint when he throws a glance at you. You, the leaders of France, here in Comsal, would obediently follow his every whim, if my will and my hate did not protect you from him. Have you never noticed how he starts whenever an unexpected courier is announced, whenever an unaccustomed face appears in the doorway? *He* knows very well that his Republic is an illusion, and that the whole might of his despair will not be enough to keep that illusion from disappearing, as soon as people realize this fact publicly. He trembles all the time, for every messenger, every visitor can bring the news; the news that somewhere someone's good sense has awakened to reality. This is all that is needed; in three days twenty-five million people will wake from their hypnotic dream. Just imagine what sort of life he has! At any moment in the day the trumpet can sound to announce the Last Judgment! You go weak in the knees in front of him—but what must his fear be like! Horror stares out of the face that you dare not look at.

VILATE. In a word it's a race: of the opponents the one who is first to break under the pressure of fear will lose.

BILLAUD. A child could topple him. He wouldn't be human, if he were still able to defend himself; he is simply crying for death. Just think: perhaps only one signal would be enough for the whole of Paris to spring at him and tear him to pieces. . .

But you are unable to give that signal. You feel the will of the master. Against your own wish the servant in you bows to him. And he simply *must* rule, whether he wants to or not; nature has created him for the purpose. Such men do not die in battle; no rebellion will succeed against them. That's why all genuine rulers die through assassination; not defeated but surprised from behind.

It should come easy to you. His creation is falling to pieces. Over his head hangs the heaviest curse—that of pointlessness. Nature itself damns him to perdition, since he will not desist from killing. He no longer has any living strength left. Your animal life instinct has all the chances. You only have to realize that you have a patriotic duty to fulfill. Call your comfortable cowardice heroism and put a knife into him somewhere in the dark.

COLLOT. Nonsense! It is you, you who disguise your cowardice in wild hallucinations! You tremble before him in the same way as all the others; but they at least admit it. While out of a miserable, finished man, broken through overwork, you make a Hindu god of evil. This is ridiculous, Billaud. When I listen to you, and see before me that green face of a dead man, those wild, shining eyes, with widened pupils, that half-dimmed expression he sometimes has in the small hours, when his look simply begs for pity, you know what? I could burst out laughing. One can see fear in that look, oh yes; not the fear of a demigod or a titan; but the same fear as ours: fear of annihilation. Besides, he lives in constant terror of a sudden physical breakdown. An epileptic Heracles with consumptive lungs.

VILATE. You are both amusing. You're hurling the same missile back and forth. But, my esteemed gentlemen, the truth is that the Inviolable has become Christ—all the more so because that role was there for the taking. Billaud, as an enlightened man, prefers to talk about a Hindu Shiva. The women in market stalls and ordinary laborers digging ditches keep to the good old Son of God. You toss insults at each other and each wants the other to strike the blow first. But, gentlemen, an individual

cannot do anything against religion. Only a whole people can overcome
it and reject it. Every one of you would rather lose his head than utter
the blasphemy that one could lift a finger against the Inviolable. That's
how things stand.

COLLOT. Indeed. Even though as a result the hell of our uncertainty seems
endless, it must find its end—in the bosom of our beloved widow guillotine. We are all waiting for it, he as well as we, with growing
impatience...

[*a noise outside; they give a start, then freeze in motionless concentration*]

BILLAUD. You grow paler than he does as soon as a mouse rustles.

COLLOT. Yes, damn it, who in this madhouse can keep his nerves intact? It's
a miracle I am not yet a nervous wreck like all the others...

VILATE. The situation is in truth—hm...worrying. To have to feel one's
neck all the time, to find out if it's still there; to have to think about the
Widow all the time. Never plan beyond the next day...

Your God is not quite so defenseless, Billaud. To my mind one is not
so badly protected, when one has put the guillotine between oneself
and one's opponents.

BILLAUD. You are very much afraid of it, are you not? And you know that
forced into the claws of his power you cannot enjoy what your hungry
mob calls life. You are literally torn by the desire to remove him. But he
looks at you constantly, and that is enough to paralyze your brains and
hands. Should he fall asleep even once, then you could enmesh him like
Gulliver in the web of your endless intrigues; but he has no intention of
falling asleep. So you can do nothing else but practice assassination in secret on his shadow, and set up infernal machines on the road along
which he has just passed. But is a genuine attempt going to take place?
Good God! You had your only chance with the Théot affair, but you
had to entrust it to that dithering old man, Vadier, and that learned
poodle, Barère, which guaranteed a masterly fiasco from the outset.
What idiots! While that affair was attracting attention, one could have
set the panicked populace on the man. The harmless sect of female
bigots provided you with a unique opportunity to roar so that all France
could hear you: the man who holds the fate of us all in his hands is
mad.—That would have been something.

And what did you people do with it?

Barère can't take anything seriously. Barère is terrified at his own wild daring whenever he extracts from the Inviolable a contemptuous smile. Barère cannot compromise himself until the victory of his party becomes absolutely certain. And Vadier, ah well! In *his* head the Revolution has turned into a hole-and-corner affair, and its leader into a vicious eunuch like Vadier himself. He approached the man with gossip and thought that the people on the platform would laugh. And then he related amusing little anecdotes in a facetious style. Paris stared and shrugged its shoulders. The matter was thus irrevocably buried. Those few who were in the know were amused, but their laughter falls heavily on *you*. The man in peril did not, of course, say a word: it wasn't worth him pinning down the stupidity so obvious to anyone.

And that was your attack on the tyrant.

COLLOT. It's true. Fouché is right: in this case a collective action is advisable. But I do not believe it is necessary to bring in the masses to do it. The man is clever, experienced, terribly cunning, but some of us can compare with him in that respect.

VILATE [*in a low voice*]. Collot d'Herbois, for example.

COLLOT [*irritated*]. Naturally, I too—as a member of the Comsal. Since *we* are the spiritus movens or, as Billaud says, the only organ in the Republic still intact. As a group, we can dispose of him. According to all the rules of art, what we need is only to become a blind instrument of his will. Let us try—to execute his program on schedule in all its details, like a machine, without any changes, without taking account of the situation at any given moment. Let us overstep the limits drawn by reality, let us cross into the realm of the absurd. He will soon lose control over the evil spirits he has summoned. He will drown in the blood like a fly, for the pressure of the terror will in a few days have unsettled the whole balance of things.

BILLAUD. Yes, terror, the sickly jade of all incompetent fools!

FOUCHE. You know, Collot, you should not forget about his—now confirmed—divine origin. Personally I think that the terror has flowered quite impressively as it is. The number of those executed rises every day, and yet our divine child does not show any symptoms of suffocation.

VILATE. Ah, when a god thirsts for blood . . .

BILLAUD. He does not thirst for blood at all! What are you blabbing about?

VILATE. At any rate he is the best swimmer of us all. Paris is drowning, France is drowning, but he sits calmly with his trusted friends and ponders on ways of further ennobling mankind.

BILLAUD. To tell the truth, Collot, your idea is worthy of someone like Vadier: to carry his program to the absurd! But we are doing nothing else. He lost control over his evil spirits long ago, and this suits him, because in spite of us, he wants to blow up the whole business. The state rolls thundering downward like a blasted rock, and you want to speed up that fall and do that criminal Caesar the best service on earth!

You want him to suffocate in blood. Easier said than done. I thought about that too until I realized the truth about our situation. I too clung to the thought of the terror as a cursed last refuge. I wanted to rouse in the masses their instinct for self-preservation and direct it against their master. I managed to get control of the Committee for Public Safety and pushed the bill of 22nd Prairial through. A fatal, stupid mistake on my part. I let the terror rage unharnessed. Now I supply the good Fouquier with his daily load of summonses, and would like to punch myself in the nose whenever I think about this heroic deed, that is to say some forty-five times in a day. When I think about our actions in the last few weeks, I get the shivers. It has come to the point where I curse you with my every breath, but I am not a whit better than you. We have done all we could to bring him to his destruction, and what's the use of it all?

[*short silence*]

VILATE [*in a strange voice*]. Billaud—I don't understand. What did you mean by speaking of the terror and the Prairial bill?
FOUCHE. That's enough, children. I *know* that as far as cutting off heads is concerned, we are the next in line. I can't be wrong. His destruction alone is the condition for others to remain alive. Thank God the Inviolable has certain principles and needs a pretext to "deliver you to the people," as the formula goes. The fact is that he will do it without any fuss, unlike on the 2nd of June. He has long since given up any constraints. *On the day he reappears in the Convention*, just *one* word—from you or from him—will be enough for the Sections to demand our heads. Just think of the Girondists!
VILATE. You believe he will come back?
COLLOT. Then we're finished!
FOUCHE. And one more thing. You know the exorbitant demands the people have learned to make of their representatives. At any moment you can be called to account. I ask you now: which of you is in the position to give a detailed account of his private affairs without discomfort?
COLLOT. For God's sake, will you finally tell us what . . .

[*Suddenly a tense silence, as someone is approaching from outside. In the hall a humming, as if it were a swarm of mosquitoes: it is blood pulsating in four human organisms. That someone outside hesitates, evidently listening; the tension mounts with every moment.* VILATE *begins to hold his breath, his mouth wide open.* BILLAUD *again assumes his agonized expression.* COLLOT *turns ash gray.* FOUCHE, *perhaps worst affected—because among this company of nervous wrecks he is the most nervous—sits with a face of stone, an expression of absolute, ominous blankness. He gives the impression of being asleep with his eyes open. He is not pale, but the blood which he holds in his veins with the effort of a fakir seems solidified under the skin.*

In the midst of this silence which seems like an eternity the door opens and BARERE *appears, surprised at the deathly silence. On seeing him* COLLOT *and* VILATE *erupt in liberating laughter. Even* FOUCHE *and* BILLAUD *smile.* BARERE *joins them gladly; laughter does him good, it overwhelms him.*]

BARERE. Oh brothers, how grateful I am to you for your sheepish looks! For six weeks I have not experienced anything of the kind. It does me good. [*he bows again*] Collot, you're looking quite well with your Ammon's face; but you, Fouché, looked, well, indescribable. Simply indescribable.

FOUCHE [*politely and with dignity*]. I am glad to have cheered you up.

COLLOT. Now listen, Barère. It is easy for you to laugh so shamelessly. You know we are used to something worse. But in your place I would behave . . . less impudently.

BARERE [*it is his turn to become gray in the face*]. What's happened?

COLLOT [*fixes him with his stare, obviously making fun of him*]. On principle we do not call anything by its name, whether persons or things. He who feels guilty, let him consult his conscience. Providence will do the rest— at Sanson's behest.

BARERE [*now he is the only one without a smile*]. Then tell me what . . .

COLLOT [*emphatically*]. There are among us certain gentlemen who disregard public opinion. There is great misery. Every heart that beats for the fatherland has long ago offered his culottes up on the altar of freedom. But those gentlemen will not do it, and shamelessly parade their princely splendor before the people.

BARERE. Does the Prairial law extend to good taste as well?

COLLOT. Not yet, for the time being, but it does to public outrage. That has been the case for a long time with notorious counterrevolutionary activities. And you, my friend, arouse public outrage with your every breath.

BARERE. And so?! . . .

COLLOT. And so, I strongly urge you to take care. Your record with the highest authority is not good.

BARERE. How do you know this? Tell me!

FOUCHE. First, you must understand the situation. You boast of your newly acquired riches before the most sensitive audience there is: the Paris proletariat. But, between ourselves, my friend, your audience, apart from their lust for beauty, have other needs too, and demand that all these needs be seriously taken into account. They are not so dumb as to expect their representatives to give them concrete help. They expect, however, that one should act as if one was trying to do so, and that one should justify one's inability to help. The people exist in order to be useful for our purposes; for this they want to be treated seriously and with compassion—a just demand. And so woe to him who bruises their vanity! And you, my friend, have constantly irritated the people during the last four years.

COLLOT. Not only the people! You have also antagonized all the prominent people in government circles. Just look around you: you are surrounded by enemies.

FOUCHE. Have you never thought how much at certain moments one needs the support of one's followers?

BARERE. Followers... for what?

FOUCHE. For what? [*silence*] To defend the Republic.

BARERE [*feverishly*]. Stop this nonsense! What's happened? Am I attacked? [*silence*] Go on, tell me, dammit!!!

FOUCHE. Sit down, Barère. And curb your just indignation. An insidious plot has been hatched against you.

[BARERE *trembles from indignation*]

VILATE [*amidst general silence*]. Barère, haven't you by chance heard about an alleged proscription list, circulating among the voting mob of the "Marsh," I beg your pardon: the Center. They say it comes from the tyrant's most secret breast pocket from where a young patriot stole it, risking his life. So now everyone can read for himself when he is going to mount the steps to put his head through the little hole...

BARERE [*turns and stares at him;* FOUCHE, *smiling, reassures the others*]. And...

VILATE [*lowers his eyes*]. Well, we have just heard that this list...is your work...

BARERE [*half starts—and freezes, flabbergasted. A long silence*]. From whom...

VILATE [*as above*]. From whom? From—him.

[*One can hear* BARERE'*s heavy breathing, full of intense torment, until* VILATE, *as red as a turkey, bursts out laughing. The three others join him.* BARERE *is speechless from astonishment*]

COLLOT. Yes, he who laughs last. . .

BARERE [*beside himself, but already infected by them*]. What impudence! And I nearly got a stroke! [*laughs with the others*]

FOUCHE. It's uncanny how well we amuse ourselves. . .

[*a sudden, total silence*]

BARERE [*strained*]. Really, Fouché, that is not kind of you at all. With the terrible things we are now going through every day, the nervous tensions and the constant danger we are in, you grudge us those few moments of innocent relaxation, a few minutes of relief for the weary heart.

FOUCHE. I envy you your strong nerves. My nerves gave up today after the exertions of my work.

BARERE. Today?

FOUCHE. Don't you find that this particular day has been unbearable? There is no more air to breathe in the entire city and, as far as I am concerned, I have the feeling that I am constantly under observation. It is unpleasant.

COLLOT [*laughs*]. That's nothing new! His spies follow each of us. . .

FOUCHE. Yes. Doesn't it get on your nerves?

COLLOT. A little. In any case, in the last ten days I haven't slept at home once.

BARERE. Neither have I. And the spies. . .well, it felt a bit strange at first. But I soon realized how very tangible my shadows were. I'm used to them by now.

But guess who I have just met.

COLLOT. Please, what do we care about your love affairs?

BARERE [*laughs*]. Ah, you've missed the point! Unfortunately it wasn't a woman.

FOUCHE [*towards the window*]. That doesn't tell us anything. . .

VILATE. An army supplier? A banker? A broker?

BARERE. Someone quite different.

BILLAUD. Can one still find something *different* in Paris?

FOUCHE [*meows ingratiatingly*]. Surely not. . .Saint-Just?

[*sensation*]

VILATE. But he's away!

COLLOT. He's not in town!

BARERE [*agitated*]. By God!. . . Saint-Just and his theories are raging on the Northern front, thanks and glory to Heaven for that. Indeed, all we need now is to have that dangerous beast among us.

No, gentlemen. I had the honor to accompany the Supreme Person himself.

FOUCHE. Aah! Tell us then.

BILLAUD. Why does he roam around the city, and so late at night?

COLLOT. What? Is he already venturing out? So visibly?

BARERE. I should like to see someone venturing out invisibly. Your guesses are quite right. The meeting with him crowned my "working" day, which was full of the most awful bad luck. I was just leaving the Palais-Royal. . .

VILATE [*with compassion*]. You had bad luck there too?

[*all laugh*]

BARERE. No, I haven't yet sunk that low. And I must say that no tarts can equal those in Paris. Even so, my relations with them leave me quite indifferent. I don't know why.

COLLOT. Hm. You need new sensations. Love must not be one-sided. And with the highest example before your eyes. . .

BILLAUD [*as if he did not believe his ears*]. What are you talking about?

BARERE [*smiling*]. Ah, you're jealous? Waste of time, Billaud. *You* will never find favor in his eyes. Just look at yourself in the mirror. Not in vain has nature created the one and only—Saint-Just. . .

BILLAUD [*almost terrified*]. God, how sordid you all are. . .

BARERE [*laughs, not unfriendly*]. Why so? It is exactly this quirk in his taste that points to a divine origin. Just think of Achilles. . .

FOUCHE. But now tell us what happened.

BARERE. Not much to tell. We bumped into each other on a street corner. He missed me by an inch: I was lucky, for he was rushing along with the speed and impact of a bullet. He apologized, recognized and greeted me.

COLLOT. He. . . greeted you. . . first?

BARERE. Yes.

BILLAUD. A courtesy worthy of a king. What did you talk about?

BARERE. What a question! What could we talk about, having met by chance; united and divided in so many vital matters as we are? About the weather, theater, and fashion.

BILLAUD. You did not have enough guts to surprise him with important, and for that reason unexpected, questions? You won't have another chance to gain insight into the situation.

BARERE. *You* try to surprise him. And then I don't feel like breaking my head, which I am bound to lose anyhow. I very easily get a migraine when I have *him* as a partner for diplomatic discourse. I only asked him before we parted how he was feeling now. He hates that subject, so he curtly denied that there was anything wrong with him. He said he was fine, had not been ill, and that he had given himself some breathing space not to get rid of fatigue, but rather to prevent it.

FOUCHE. This is arrogance in princely style. Only the greatest can be *so* impudent. It becomes him, though, doesn't it?

BARERE. What do you mean?

FOUCHE. I would like to ruffle your calm. For, finally and unambiguously, he gave you to understand the following: "I left you alone for a while to find out how far you would go astray. Now I have you all in my hands and do not have to pretend any more."

COLLOT. There is something in that...

BARERE. What hellish designs are you imputing to him?

FOUCHE. What a question! In the situation in which we have, with God's help, gotten embroiled, he can have only one design. You have been struck blind and cannot see where you're going...

VILATE. Were you not tempted, Barère, to murder him when he jeered at you?

BARERE. Not at all. And he did not jeer at me. And you, my friends, will not succeed in rousing a lust for murder in me. Not a chance.

COLLOT. Barère is like you, Billaud: he'd much rather wait for destruction than strain himself for action.

BARERE. You're quite right, if you have in mind a treacherous stab in the back. Besides, there would be no point. The man looks burnt out from an inner fever already.

BILLAUD. He is destined for death and he himself feels that his end is close at hand. What a life his must be: balancing on a rope over an abyss!

COLLOT. But in any case you may be sure that your end is closer than his.

BARERE. Well, let it be, why not? Death has lost its sting since the guillotine has been overused. It is difficult today to make anyone even a little afraid of death.

FOUCHE. Yes, we had the chance to find that out only a little while ago. But that's why, children, come to your senses! Leave this madman in power just for a few more days, and everything will really be over.

First, he will make sure that we all disappear from the face of the earth; then he will follow our example with a light and happy heart. And then the dance will begin. The Dantonists will establish the rule of whores. The lovers of great courtesans, having put themselves in the highest places, will offer themselves and their power for sale, without any scruples. All the kinglets of Europe will hasten to the auction. And the Revolution will end when the surviving republicans give themselves and the ruins of the state to whoever pays the most; the price will be moderate as the goods are shop-soiled. [BILLAUD *cannot restrain himself from uttering a groan*] He knows it; this is precisely what he wants. Total destruction...

But now think: should you rouse yourselves to action, it would be enough for you to raise your fingers, and he will fall. For Billaud is right: he is quite alone and unarmed. And when we get rid of that nightmare, the golden age will come, metaphorically, of course. Think only about this one phrase: *it will be possible to live.*

COLLOT. Possible to live...indeed, to be able to sleep at home, not to have to be on the lookout all the time...

BARERE. To walk the streets without a trembling heart, without starting at every little sound one hears...

COLLOT. To be able to think what one wants to; shout out one's thoughts. Not to stifle one's hate, or rage, as one stifles pain by gnashing one's teeth...

VILATE. All that is nothing; the main thing is—to be what one wants to!

FOUCHE. But you must hurry, for who knows if even tomorrow he...

BARERE. Fouché, you are beginning to convince me. But...I find it hard to believe in the necessity of a coup, for after all that man knows what he is doing; he can rule, he was born to it...

With such magnificent gifts the man would have to be intent on some impossible lunacy and jeopardize everything! It is really very sad, you know, that the greatest talents as a rule have the most dangerous ideas...

BILLAUD. Talents! You are measuring him by your own meter-rule. You simply do not have the capacity to recognize a genius. How do you think you can find out what he intends to do, if you cannot rise to the level of his thoughts?

BARERE. Yes, I agree he must be eliminated—but without him everything will fall apart, and much more surely than under his, like it or not, masterly leadership.

FOUCHE. Who would have thought that Barère had such a sensitive conscience? Do put it at rest, though. It's only our miserable free republic that will fall apart; a republic for whose artificial propping-up France is now paying a bitter price. And in order to call into being a normal constitutional state we have *talent* enough, very well trained too, so don't let's fear for our beloved fatherland.

BARERE. It is really strange. God knows I do not like the man. I have even tried to stir the . . . the Center against him with the help of a forged proscription list. Like you I belong to the hunted beasts, and I do not feel at all comfortable in my skin. And yet I would rather have my head cut off than join your offensive. At least as long as it is conducted with the weapons of monsieur Vilate.

VILATE. May I ask why?

BARERE. You journalists are as dangerous as scorpions. I cannot overcome my disgust for vermin. [VILATE *grows pale and starts to his feet*] All right, keep calm, don't get angry. We must stick together and be united, so that all our heads may fall together at one stroke. Among members of the same faction there is no need to take offense at every little disagreement. And so I can safely say, Vilate: you bring our faction shame.

VILATE [*in a stifled voice*]. What? . . .

BARERE. . . . I beg your pardon, our clique. You are making us look ridiculous.

COLLOT. It is just like you, to reject the only effective weapon—for reasons of good taste.

BILLAUD. Effective! I like that. This miserable dishwater from an old hag's sink is to be an effective weapon?! This is absolute garbage, which can at most evoke pity, not even ridicule.

His contempt for us must be something simply painful in its hopelessness. And then you wonder that he wants to eradicate such riffraff, so they'll be forgotten forever . . .

BARERE. Why then did you help to remove Camille, if you have such a poor opinion of journalism?

BILLAUD. You pretend to have the tiny brain of a woman. Camille's sarcasm, sharp as steel, was a force to be reckoned with. His slander was like a poisoned arrow. That was an enemy to beware of!

BARERE. Ah, then your principles, as far as the pen is concerned, are not unswerving?

BILLAUD. Certainly not, as long as it reaches its aim. You, Barère, have no idea about the nature of fighting. All practical experience is strange to you. You mistake labels for substance. The name, the empty sound of it, is decisive for you. The name creates your relation to things. A mind like yours cannot encompass anything; it is, as it were, stripped of common sense. For your corrupt nerves life and death seem an idyll. You do not feel the fear of death, for your life has no value at all. That honorable man who, when encountering the enemy, declined to fire the first shot to prove his good manners, was your kind. Such a deed should be called mass murder. His immaculate manners cost France half an army, and nearly cost us the victory as well. That person should have been hanged, in spite of his being a nobleman. A ruler like the one we have at present would certainly not have hesitated to do so.

When one fights for something, one must put one's personal honor and one's human feelings in one's pocket. I despise Vilate's hack writing because it is worthless. On the contrary Camille's silliest, commonest personal attack meant in my view as much as a death sentence.

COLLOT. It's true. If our powerful ruler does not drown in blood, he certainly won't do so in Vilate's dirty ink.

FOUCHE. One more thing: Vilate is not rich. How are you going to know from whom he receives his pay tomorrow?

[*silent surprise*]

VILATE [*undisturbed*]. God, why are you all so interested in my way of making a living? Corruption is human; it is the healthiest thing in France today, since everything else that was human has been wiped out. It is corruption that allows a wholesome return to earthly reality, and will help the state be saved. I firmly believe in it, since corruption assures social balance.

BILLAUD [*has listened with growing attention*]. That is so. [*He sinks into his chair, seems broken and pale as a corpse all of a sudden. Those present look at him with concern. He then raises his head and says the following as if something obvious*] But it should not be so.

BARERE. What's happened, Billaud?

COLLOT. What's the matter with you? . . .

BILLAUD [*softly, tired*]. What's the matter with me? Did none of you hear the witty aphorism to which that scribbler has just treated us? Or perhaps you did? And you're asking what's the matter with me, when I have to admit he is right?

But no. France will not be saved in *such* a manner. Her ship should rather go down, with all her crew. Even that magnificent tyrant has not been able to shake this soulless nation out of its "wholesome balance." You are so indolent, rotten through and through, that even the invigorating flood of the Revolution could not bring you to life. You have manners instead of morals, elegance instead of passion, corruption and lust for gold instead of instinct for self-preservation!

But now I will join forces with him; against your rotten gang—and against nature. I will help him to keep his great, dead Republic upright on her feet, in spite of the laws of this world and in spite of you. I will shake both Committees and renew the Committee of Safety, which has been rotting for a long time now. And then, both Committees, filled with his spirit, will deal with your "human nature." The opposition will crumble when I no longer protect them from him with my person. And we will put a definite end in France to the "wholesome connection with earthly reality." The state will doubtless fall because of its use of too drastic measures; but it will at least be spared our attempts at saving it.

VILATE [*serious*]. These flights of fancy are easy, Billaud. Drastic measures are wonderful in theory. But we have also the regions below, the "Plain," the "Marsh," where they are carried out. I am a jury man, so I know what *that* aspect of the situation looks like. Billaud, the present state of tension cannot last any longer. Its intensification simply does not bear thinking about. Ultimately, it is we, the Revolutionary Tribunal, who put the ideas of the terror into practice; and we ourselves cannot bear it any longer. There are rotten elements among us too, though fewer in number than elsewhere. The rest of us are losing our strength and are near to madness. Take Fouquier-Tinville, our chief instrument. As prosecutor, he was an unblemished official—incorruptible, indefatigable, unerring in his professional judgment. But what has happened to the man since the Prairial law was passed?! He gets attacks of fury, shouts at the accused, condemns them without a hearing, then laughs and weeps like an old maid, drinks himself blind, gets hallucinations, loses his mind. We are not faring any better. Our sittings drag on into eternity; but how can a day be long enough to interrogate and sentence forty people? Stunned by the horror of that nonsense, we fall asleep. We cannot judge, and yet we must pronounce sentence. Sooner or later everyone will realize that he is committing mass murder. You complain of corruption, Billaud?! What have you to say about *that* corruption which has corroded the very organ of justice, since on orders from above, it must violate the innate laws of mankind?

We envy our "victims." If there were among them only emigrés, food profiteers and counterfeiters! But we well know that there are innocent people: servants, dairy women, tottering old men! Accused on the basis of a wrongly overheard word, a silly grimace. They just sit terrified in the court house, say yes, no, or nothing—and are taken away to their deaths. Thirty people a day, gentlemen.

We no longer have the courage to bear such horrible guilt. A year ago we would have sentenced even our own mothers, for the stake was freedom. Today we commit murder and feel disgust for our impunity. Hundreds go to their deaths, because a lawyer wants an imperial throne. The entire, terrible responsibility falls on us; and we have nothing more left, no love, no faith, to resist this pressure.

You call me a swine because I concoct lampoons against him. I ask to be paid because poverty has dragged me into the mud. Otherwise I'd do it for free. I don't believe that any of you people, who live on theories, hate him as much as I do. You're right that I can't tear myself away from him. I think about him when I'm awake, and when I'm asleep—I dream of him. I worshipped him, I literally prayed to him. I'm afraid I still haven't rid myself of him. His integrity makes me mad. Though I try hard to find something ugly in him, I can only find what I invent. I wanted to give him a fright—after all, his sickly nervousness is well known. So I wrote him—yes, anonymously, you'll be overjoyed to know—a childish love letter with death threats set out in detail. I know for certain he is not familiar with my handwriting. So next day I was dumbfounded when I met him and he turned to me with particular interest, smiling forbearingly, without a trace of resentment. That smile could only mean an answer to my letter; even chance witnesses had to interpret it so. So I went and composed the thing that is lying before you now. To all the disgusting things I could think of, I added the sort of business swindles the Dantonists used to commit. That is worth at least fifty livres.

So you see, I balance my deeds against each other: first I commit murder, then I revile myself on account of the man for whom I commit murder. In this way I silence my conscience which is now quite limp from fear.

BARERE. "For whom I murder"—that expression speaks volumes.

BILLAUD. I must butt in here. It's not the man who you have in mind that is guilty. You're wasting your precious lyricism in vain. The Prairial law holocausts are *our* work, my dear young man. It was my invention, yes, mine, in order to turn the apathy of the people into rage. It was the most stupid blunder of my life. For it was I who tore the Prairial law—his creation—out of his hands, and I realized too late, alas, how valuable it was. It was a truly magic weapon—unfailing and dangerous, like Satan's instrument, and costly to use. In his hands that still-unique remedy could have saved the Republic; in my hands it became warped at once.

I gave it up, of course; but the others—my followers—threw themselves onto that instrument, finding pleasure in the fact that they could put this half broken mechanism into motion. To be able to cut thirty heads daily without any effort at all fills them with a special feeling of power which one does not give up easily. [COLLOT *has grown deadly pale*] I am not trying to excuse myself, but I really didn't know *what* I robbed him of. A struggle is a struggle, but his Republic was also the essence of *my* life; and yet I, I *myself*...

It is understandable that he now lives only for revenge, that he imperceptibly sets the machine in such a way that, at a given moment, it must explode at a touch. I still hesitate: whether it is worth saving from utter ruin—this rotten state, the land of sun-kings and salons?

VILATE [*astounded*]. Billaud—Billaud—is this really true?

BILLAUD. Ask my colleagues. *He* would not have made you mass murderers. With the help of the Prairial law, he would have purified France. He would have restored to society its blood circulation. *He* would not entertain himself with the idiotic slaughter of little girls, gibbering old men, harmless squires, simply because they use the prefix "de" before their names.

FOUCHE. The thing is to forestall him and put an end to this game. A conversion is not enough, because now he will not let you come to your senses and escape self-destruction.

COLLOT. But what can one charge him with? The Terror? No.—The press? No. Corruption? No. What then?

FOUCHE. His dictatorship.

[*absolute silence*]

BARERE. The Gironde tried to ride *that* horse. From the very beginning.

VILATE. And it got them a long way: to the grave.

FOUCHE. The Gironde was the Gironde. But we must, on this particular count, set up the right charge, which will strike France right between the eyes, so that the sluggish beast rears.

[*a short silence*]

BILLAUD. All right. She rears, throws him and tramples him to death. But what then, Fouché?

It is all the same to me on what grounds you desire his fall; but I cannot remain neutral and must at least be certain that his fall will profit society!

FOUCHE [*shrugs his shoulders*]. Your scruples are tiring in the long run. I at any rate consider it an advantage, if the nation escapes anarchy, foreign invasion and economic disaster, whose effects cannot be foreseen.

BILLAUD. Will the nation escape anarchy when it devours the only ruler who is equal to the situation . . .

FOUCHE [*with convincing force*]. He is *not* the only one. And the situation will shape itself differently, calling for talents of a different kind.

COLLOT. We are all determined, Billaud. The coup is a necessity, as we have realized for months.

FOUCHE. Consider this: on the one side a disturbed country, whose natural development has been violently brought to a halt. A state with an astounding capacity for expansion, threatened with a defeat brought about artificially, at the point when its army has surpassed all hopes by its unexpected achievements. Millions of people, who are breaking down today under the constant pressure of lurking death, and tomorrow will be exposed to all the horrors of economic crisis. And on the other side, one man, whom his personal despair pushes in the direction of the most senseless of all crimes; a man who has taken up a fight against God and nature and who, without any pity, will carry out anything which his feverish brain prompts him to do.

BARERE. One can admire Nero, but is there anyone who would want to help him start a fire for artistic effect?

BILLAUD [*tired*]. No, surely, that wouldn't do. All right, all right, I'll go along with you. I'll help you to strike the mortal blow against him. And it is all my fault—o, damn, damn that Prairial day!

VILATE [*uneasy*]. But, gentlemen, there must be a terrible mistake somewhere. You cannot seriously believe that he . . . Fouché, I regarded your arguments about the dictator's intentions as a game with words, an elegant, effective parable. And now I realize that . . .

Just consider: how *can* a man love an idea as one loves a woman? It is an altogether different feeling, much stronger maybe, but to talk about jealousy! To kill the republic so that no one else can possess her! . . . [*suddenly bursts out with loud laughter*] Wake up, by God! A man with such a shrewd mind, so prophetic in his mastering of reality! That he should . . . [*He breaks off in mid-sentence, surprised at the seriousness of their looks. A long, tiring moment passes; suddenly he goes wild, points his finger at* FOUCHE] He is deceiving you! He shamelessly leads you by the nose with any old kindergarten story! He does not even take the trouble to substantiate his damned lies! And you fall for such utter nonsense! Like servant girls! Such utter nonsense!!!

FOUCHE. Young man, stick to your instructions. You've been paid to listen in on our conversation. Your outburst will not bring you a sou, and may be dangerous. . .

VILATE [*staggering*]. Wh. . .hat? . . .

[BARERE *jumps to his feet; so does* COLLOT; BILLAUD *remains in his chair and with an attentive stare transfixes the young man who, as if struck by a blow, moves to the edge of the table and breathes heavily*]

COLLOT [*shakes him*]. Go on—out. Before I kill you.

VILATE. Oooo-o-o . . . [*he throws his head down on the table and erupts in violent sobbing*]

BARERE. God, that's all we needed!

BILLAUD [*thoughtful, to* FOUCHE]. How do you know this?

FOUCHE [*shrugs his shoulders*]. What do I have five well-developed senses for?

BILLAUD. So, you're lying. You have mortally offended him. I know that kind of weeping. It can't be misinterpreted. [*shouts*] Quiet!

VILATE [*masters his fear*]. Ah. . .th. . .thank you.

BARERE. What are we going to do with him?

BILLAUD. He's only a boy. There is nothing to be afraid of.

FOUCHE. We cannot kill him, or throw him out, unless we first tear out his tongue. We must bind him to us, for good or ill.

VILATE. Do as you will. You can send me to the guillotine; that would be simplest.

BARERE. So that you could denounce us from the tumbril on your way there. No, Vilate, we have had tales enough.

VILATE [*wipes his tears*]. That's true, I would be capable of it. O what an incorrigible ass I am! I would like to know why I blubbered so.

BILLAUD. Because you are an amusing brat who would like to be taken for a black character. And as soon as someone pretends to have discovered your game, you get into spasms and cry for the guillotine, as you cannot survive such an insult. I'd like to know how many people had a hand in your education.

VILATE. You're right, unfortunately. But you can't deny that I am a villain. Since my school days I've felt an awful fear of certain words, for instance the word: spying. Even so, a man who is as familiar with hunger as I am will stop at nothing that can somehow bring in money. For someone like me it is an honorable thing to be a spy, provided, of course, one doesn't do anything for free. Believe me: even as an innocent five-year-old, I only cried when caught red-handed.

COLLOT. You are very crafty, but now listen carefully: if you speak one word of what you have heard here, you are finished. It won't cost me much to crush a worm like you.

VILATE. You don't have to tell *me* that. Nobody knows better than I how futile such an action would be. And yet, I am honest in my poverty, and would not think of avoiding the risk of death, if for my tale I could get a good supper. I fear nothing on this earth as much as an empty pocket. For two hundred louis I would drag the devil out of hell by his tail.

BARERE. Your demands are not exorbitant. You can rest assured. I am not a miser, and I'm certainly better off than . . . your previous employer.

VILATE [*laughs*]. O God! So you believe in what I have just said!

FOUCHE. You will write on our behalf. You are not altogether without talent.

VILATE [*passionately*]. From now on—never that. Never more! [*silence—he laughs, though somewhat helplessly*] Of course. With the greatest pleasure! But all the profit must go into my pocket, and then I must get my thirty pieces of silver from you each time, plus a sizable percentage.

COLLOT. You mustn't be quite so shameless, young man, if you don't mind.

FOUCHE. But why? He is right: we cannot expect him to sell his master just for a slice of bread and butter.

VILATE. Besides, I must re-educate myself, Billaud. Give me a lesson in lampoon-writing.

BILLAUD [*quietly, thoughtful*]. You must attack him as a great statesman, not as a shopkeeper. Try to follow the great line of his thinking. That will be sufficient to disturb the quiet sleep of all citizens at night. You must trumpet out loud about his dictatorship, impute to him the most bloody intentions, prophesy bloody upheavals in the near future. Alarm all faint-hearted people with the specter of the agrarian law! Heap all the hideous atrocities committed in France onto his head! In every issue of your paper sound the requiem for liberty! Don't spare the most glaring melodrama, but no more of your dismal obscenities!

VILATE [*with shining eyes*]. Marvelous! Now you'll see how I'll bring him to his knees! . . . Ten louis per column, gentlemen.

COLLOT [*indignant*]. What?!

BARERE. All right. But not a sou more. And no advances.

VILATE. Oh dear . . . Well, perhaps they won't be needed.

BILLAUD. And now, gentlemen, we have to agree finally on a plan. If we are to strike, we must do it decisively.

COLLOT. It is a mistake on our part to be debating here. Four pairs of ears outside can overhear our words.

FOUCHE. You should have thought of that before.

VILATE. Besides, you know that at any time of day we can be surprised by the warrants for our arrest. Here you are simply delivering yourselves into his hands. Or maybe you regard this temple of freedom as providing asylum for law-givers? Those who are privileged cannot escape the law anywhere.

BARERE. Then would you please be so kind as to name a place where five party leaders could hide on even one occasion? There is no such place, my boy. And so, it is all the same if the arrest warrant finds us here or in a brothel, except that the latter place would be more picturesque, for posterity that is. He lies in wait, up there in his attic, and watches all the nooks and crannies of the city.

COLLOT. He must have a legion of informers in his pay.

VILATE. He has a well-provided civil list for the purpose. I wonder where he gets them?

BILLAUD. That is his secret, like so many others, and the secret of his awesome police department downstairs, which has just sent out a night patrol. I don't know for certain, but I almost believe that those young men work for nothing, or rather—for a single glance from him . . .

VILATE. That is what I call popularity!

BARERE. I call it practicing seduction rather. He is so plain, and yet the atmosphere around him is loaded with eroticism. His very presence, not even at close quarters—goes to the boys' heads, takes their breath away. They move as he beckons; his gestures are calculated to that purpose. In those immature beings there grows a tension, an explosive force, whose impact they do not realize themselves. Most of them would gladly die for him, or because of him.

COLLOT. It's the same with women. That impotent weakling!

FOUCHE. Weakling! Does your cheek still hurt, Collot?

[*To the surprise of the uninitiated,* BILLAUD, *then* BARERE *erupt in uncontrollable laughter*]

BILLAUD [*calm now*]. We are not immune to his influence either. The thing is that in our case the force of attraction has turned into repugnance; but even that is not without reservations. [*gives* BARERE *a passing glance*]

One more proof that he is an exceptional man, with a magnetic, attracting force. You can call it erotic; but in reality the matter reaches far
more deeply. Let's leave it at that, and get out of here. He could appear
here in person.

[BARERE *and* COLLOT *rise from their seats*]

FOUCHE. We must still wait. For Tallien and Barras, who has promised me
shelter for the night. I too am reluctant to stay the night where I can
easily be found. I think Barras is taking care of Tallien meanwhile.
VILATE. Does Tallien now hide in the daytime too?
FOUCHE. I wish to God he did. He's gone altogether mad with fever, and I
am afraid that he might do something very stupid. So I begged Barras to
keep him away from the Convention.
BARERE. What does he want then?
FOUCHE. His mistress is in prison and would like to get out. For that purpose she has asked him twice already to topple the government—but he
forgot to do it each time! So she wrote him a letter and said she would
gladly die, and that she regretted only one thing: that she had loved
such a wretched coward.
BILLAUD [*somewhat bitter*]. Well, she plays right into our hands...
VILATE [*nervously*]. Attention!...

[*they listen, all perturbed except Billaud*]

TALLIEN [*enters, relaxed, his eyes shining from fever, his cheeks flushed*]. Good
evening. The conspirators all here?
FOUCHE. What have you done with Barras?
TALLIEN. He's *still* not here? Then we must wait. That's bad!
FOUCHE. You're right, the place is not safe...
TALLIEN [*stands leaning against the table*]. There is none safer.
BILLAUD. When do you attack?
TALLIEN [*turns round quickly*]. What do you mean by that?
BILLAUD. What do I mean?!...Only what...is...self-explanatory, Tallien.
BARERE [*conciliatory manner*]. You looked so menacing—and we had the im-
pression...
TALLIEN. Keep it to yourselves then.

[*Silence.* TALLIEN *lightly touches the floor with the tip of his foot*]

FOUCHE. This place is deaf; you can safely say what's on your mind.
TALLIEN [*sharply*]. I don't want to.

[*silence again*]

FOUCHE. This is bad. You'll be very sorry, Tallien, for you can't succeed alone. [TALLIEN *looks at him over his shoulder, shrugs and remains silent*] Have you been to the Convention today?

TALLIEN [*after a while, weakly*]. No. . .I don't think so.

VILATE. You don't *think* so?

TALLIEN. My memory is quite confused—because of the fever.

BARERE. A welcome condition—under the circumstances.

[*They smile secretly;* TALLIEN *cowers, hurt, pale with rage, but only for a few seconds*]

FOUCHE. To tell the truth, life is only an unpleasant dream; so why should one try to remember?

VILATE. In the next world, perhaps. But on this side of the river Lethe there is only harsh reality.

BILLAUD. And so, Tallien—when do you strike?

TALLIEN [*turns round, impatient*]. What do you really want of me? I am sick, it's true, but I haven't yet lost my senses. Do you rejoice at the idea that I will become a laughing stock for your entertainment? I have no intention of attacking on my own, like a madman. That would lead me to being lynched on the nearest lamppost and nothing else.

FOUCHE [*seriously*]. But it can't be, Tallien. You *must* do something.

TALLIEN [*losing his temper*]. Good God! Leave me in peace at least, since no one wants to help me.

COLLOT, FOUCHE, BARERE. Is that so certain? Why do you think so?

[*silence*]

TALLIEN [*changed*]. What I have in mind is concrete help, esteemed gentlemen! I have considered the situation comprehensively, I know it with precision. We would have to move en masse. But even that will be unbelievably hard. We have done all we could already to tear that villain from the hearts of simple folk. All to no avail. The masses will not budge from him. I don't understand it. And even in the government the ''Marsh'' is so intimidated that we must give up hopes of their collaboration.

BARERE. Agreed. Yes, the Marsh! You know my proscription list, Tallien? I observed the impression it made. The idiots see their names written there clearly. Each of them without exception falls for it, but just rolls his eyes—and waits for the police to come and fetch him.

FOUCHE. I am afraid, Barère, that it is you who have really fallen for it. Who knows if the authentic, unwritten list does not far surpass yours in the number of names...

For I repeat: he will begin by removing us from power. That is certain. Why else would he leave us for so long in charge of state affairs, in the face of our confirmed, and now proved, incompetence?

TALLIEN. Heaven alone knows what villainous moves have been devised and decided during his absence!

BARERE [*shrugs his shoulders*]. Above all else the man is ill from overwork.

BILLAUD. No doubt. However, you have known him long enough to realize how he conserves his strength. It is almost as if fatigue cannot touch him. He is a machine, but also something more reliable, more durable. You know well that he must have had very serious reasons for his sudden withdrawal. He does not lift a finger while we here cry out of anger and helplessness, and in our fear devour one another. He did not leave this room forever, or for very long. No.

BARERE. Strange that he is not even afraid of this fear of ours.

BILLAUD. He leaves us means which carry no risk for him. [*looks sideways at* TALLIEN] He brings the matter to its limits, and will lay it bare as soon as it is not necessary for him to carry it any further. Anarchy, mass executions, the inner decay in the Convention, a mythical fear into which we have plunged, and nerve-racking tension—these are his instruments. Only a man of great caliber can handle such instruments, through which any nation can fall to pieces. He is preparing a real explosion, and you want to counter his thunder with weak half-measures.

COLLOT. And we talk, talk, talk...

TALLIEN. It seems that you want to use me as weapon, maybe because I am the youngest among you and could summon up the most energy. Unfortunately, I can still think.

An open declaration of war would be a mistake. He has behind him the people, the soldiery, the clubs, the city commune, the suburbs, the elected assemblies, the police department, the press, the demoralized Convention, *and* twenty thousand Jacobin branches, through which he rules France as no king has done before him. On the other side, we have the remnants of what he destroyed in his victorious march: shaking freaks, ex-noblemen, ex-Girondists, ex-moderates—and the terrorized world of finance, with its proverbial knightly virtues. What chances then?

BILLAUD. You have forgotten the two Committees, the nerve centers of the Revolution. They belong to me, not to him.

TALLIEN. Even if that were so! Besides, what have you achieved during this all-important pause when he was not leading you by the nose?

Public opinion must be rid of his influence. It is the only way that offers some hope. We need people, yes, people! We must speak, and a great deal too! Propaganda! Stories with clues! Counteraction at each and every point! An army of agents, soap-box orators, clowns, and loudmouths—we need all these, Collot! Until at least half of Paris is liberated from the power of his suggestion and turned against him, one can hardly talk about toppling him.

BILLAUD. The dictator has a trusted friend in you, Tallien. You can count on his full gratitude, for you are giving him what he needs most: time.

TALLIEN. Don't you see that any attempt to resist in our situation would be senseless suicide?!

FOUCHE. An army of agents and clowns would indeed help us a great deal...

TALLIEN [*laughs*]. Ah yes! I understand at last what you want of me. Unfortunately, I must disappoint you; I value myself too highly to resort to murder.

BARERE [*dully*]. It figures. The lady was right...

TALLIEN [*almost threateningly*]. What do you mean?...

BARERE [*as above*]. I always heard how she valued your wisdom, your perspicacity...your talents as an orator...your caution...

TALLIEN [*out of breath, loses self-control*]. More plainly, if you please...

COLLOT. Please, pull yourself together, Tallien. We *want* to do something.

BARERE. Eight tumbrils went by today...

COLLOT. It won't be long before your lady friend goes by, Tallien. The prosecutor need not wait for the half of Paris that is against her to be converted.

TALLIEN [*pulls himself together, masters his uncertainty*]. Yes, her! I'll get her out! [*the others smile, except* BILLAUD, *who remains aloof and thumps his fingers on the table top*] I should like to know what a representative of the people is really good for if his influence is not worth the life of one woman. If I can't manage it by myself, I'll demand that a relevant decree be issued. She will be set free, I shan't have any trouble with that
. . .

FOUCHE. Don't be a child, Tallien. Even that young outsider is smiling out of pity over the quite unbelievable comedy you're playing.

BARERE. Friend, the Conciergerie is like death. Many roads lead to it, but none leads back to the world. Even death sometimes allows its victims to escape—that is called lethargy. But there is no lethargy in the Conciergerie. And the death to which she leads people is always genuine...

The tribunal works now with an inhuman speed. The day after tomorrow you can hire a window in front of the scaffold barrier. At least
she will not be quite alone when they are binding her to the wooden
plank . . .

VILATE. It's so moving when a pair of lovers take leave of each other on the
first step of the ladder . . .

TALLIEN [*wild*]. Why are you blabbing about this?

VILATE. To rouse the man in you, if there is one at all.

TALLIEN [*laughs*]. The man in me! And what do you want of him, eh? What
should I do? Stand on my head? Stab the duumvirs? If I do, shall I stop
even for a quarter of an hour the Revolutionary Tribunal, that crazy automaton pushed to the point of madness?

The Tuileries, together with their hell let loose can sink into the earth,
which may God grant! Yes, even the Highest one can go to hell; and all
Paris can turn to stone from fear. But whatever may happen, the Revolutionary Tribunal will remain unmoved; the Revolutionary Tribunal
will not for one second stop issuing death sentences. The Revolutionary
Tribunal will continue its activities inexorably, as long as one suspect is
left breathing in France . . .

Let the tribunal pulverize Theresa too. She has stolen my life from
me; it will only be justice if the same now happens to her. She has
caused me enough anguish, quite enough—and I've had enough of her
love which degrades a man to an instrument of lust. First she made me
loathe my existence, when I could not call even the smallest thing my
own. Now she expects me to go and topple the government, scatter the
Convention, raze the Revolutionary Tribunal to the ground, for the
sole reason of saving her from the effects of her idiotic recklessness. Did
I ask her to follow me to Paris? But such was her whim. And I am the
one who is to carry her to the "happy ending" over the corpses of the
mighty, over the ruins of nations. If I do not succeed, then my spirit
should not wish to survive her calamity. After all, she had blessed me
with her favors! But I do not intend to go mad just to show my good
manners. Let her hate me as much as she desires.

BARERE. Unfortunately, that's not it. She does not hate you; she despises
you. And that's something more unpleasant.

TALLIEN [*red with shame*]. The devil she does; I am not interested! As if I did
not despise *her* with all my heart.

BARERE. That is something different. A man must despise a woman, otherwise he will not have pleasure with her but children. A woman must
tremble before his brute force, shudder as before a ravisher; she must

feel dependent on him like a domestic pet on the whim of its master, never knowing in advance when he will fondle her, or when he will beat her; and why he caresses her, or why he torments her. That is not respect, of course, but fear of God. Without it things don't work. You must always play the part; be an unpredictable beast, following your instincts, always ready for a jealous rage. You must also be jealous of death, and save her for that reason, not because you need her! A glimmer of fear, or a momentary hesitation—and all is lost. A tart will forgive her pimp even cowardice; but then a tart is a creature that fights spontaneously for its existence, like a hare, or a wild cat. Not so a great lady: she is a luxury, a performing animal, trained for certain tricks and bereft of all that is human. She will never forgive, if a man forgets himself and shows himself in his true light.

TALLIEN [*listening attentively*]. Yes, you are right. Now, when everything has been made clear to me, I can even rejoice that she too like so many others must sacrifice her head, offended and full of airs though she may be.

BARERE [*surprised at first*]. Well, I'll be damned! . . .

[BARERE *bursts out laughing*]

BILLAUD. The Inviolable must really be a sly wizard, if at the very sound of his name every heroic heart sinks to the lowest depths. . .

Get together, plot, spend your nights in the catacombs. As soon as he has had enough of your fidgeting, he only needs to utter three sentences at the Convention. Not even that. Against the Dantonists he did not deign to speak at all. A quarter of an hour later you'll be under lock and key—and after three days at the latest—in a mass grave. Up to that moment he displays a smiling forbearance for the eruptions of your terrified hate, for the curses you utter with chattering teeth and send flying about his ears.

Avoid migraines, Barère, they are a nuisance. Posterity will value highly your manly calm in the midst of storms. And you, Tallien, topple the usurper, but do it very slowly and cautiously so that we don't lose any advantage. The day after tomorrow you'll be able to accompany the lady of your heart.

If we do not stake everything right now, France will not only be lost, but in a short time—as soon as that hapless genius disappears—will also be put to shame. To all of you, of course, it makes no difference; but just think of your own salvation, resurrection after your own taste, ample satisfaction for all your torments—and all this for the price of one effort, yes—one! We need nothing more to destroy that lonely might; to

crush that unparalleled courage and ardent will with sheer material superiority. There is just hypnosis and nothing else besides—no backing,
no point of resistance, nothing—only one man and one pair of eyes,
against nature and time!

TALLIEN. But do you believe that the terror will then cease?

BILLAUD. Hard to say. The chaos which will then prevail is beyond imagination. No, the terror will not ease up at once, because it is too convenient. But money, and the influence of the right people, will regain
their importance. And you are rich, Tallien; so is your lady friend.

TALLIEN [*with youthful verve*]. Have you already got a plan? [*silence*] I'll do all
I can! I'll even stab him to death, if it can't be done any other way.

[BILLAUD *erupts in laughter*]

COLLOT. Well, we must wait for him to reappear. In the meantime get to
work on the Convention . . .

BARERE. Are violent measures really necessary? Maybe it would be enough
to hold him up to ridicule. He will then go back to Arras and hide in the
darkest corner of his house. Forever.

VILATE. Many have tried that. Paris had good amusement—at their cost.

COLLOT. He is in fact almost immune to attack. Fouché himself admits that
the man has only one weak point, and they have so often tried to get
him there . . .

FOUCHE. Gentlemen, do you know what day it is?

[*a short pause*]

VILATE. The Seventh of Thermidor. Why? . . .

[COLLOT *starts from his seat;* BARERE *sinks in his chair and slowly counts the days;*
TALLIEN *claws at the table and utters a stifled cry of terror;* BILLAUD, *baffled at first,*
remembers and nods his head; VILATE *looks in astonishment at everyone in turn*]

BILLAUD. Yes, it's the deadline. That much is clear.

BARERE. Tomorrow, good God!

VILATE. What's happened? What about tomorrow?

COLLOT. Is he back already?

FOUCHE. Who?

COLLOT, BARERE. Saint-Just . . .

BILLAUD. Probably—or he'll arrive in a few hours.

VILATE [*astounded*]. Saint-Just! . . .

COLLOT. Then we are lost. We're not ready at all.

BARERE. Maybe the report will be deferred. We haven't heard a word about
it . . .

BILLAUD. Of course not. But Saint-Just will never miss a deadline.

BARERE. Then we are lost. The Convention, taken by surprise, will not dream of resistance, but will decree its own death sentence with servile applause.

TALLIEN [*animated*]. No, my friends. Tonight the criminal will be put to death. My silly little Theresa will not fall victim to that power-crazy man.

VILATE. What is to happen tomorrow?

FOUCHE. Saint-Just's report, announced six weeks ago. And your innocent little Theresa will be free, Tallien, without your having to become an executioner of heroes on her account.

VILATE [*to himself*]. An executioner of heroes. . .

FOUCHE. Besides, we can manage without the Convention.

BARERE. I wonder how?

FOUCHE. That is to say without its active participation. We intend to *use* the Convention as a mass. Preparations on our part are superfluous. We don't need them any more. The duumvirs can hardly muster ten steadfast friends among the seven hundred.

BARERE. So it's the question of dictatorship after all? Fouché, it's a waste of your time.

BILLAUD. Not quite. I am beginning to make things out. If one wants to get at somebody's throat, one must have a *real* basis for the attack. Pretexts are always bound to fail. Imaginary crimes weaken the attack and only harm the attackers. In which case *only* this remains: the real tyranny, known to all. But one must know how to make use of it; nobody has succeeded in this up to now.

COLLOT. Yes, you're right. Since Louvet everyone has carped at trifles, unimportant symptoms, words taken out of context. . .

VILATE. Everyone resented what hurt his vanity, and *only* that. Naturally the masses remained indifferent to it all.

FOUCHE. He can *hardly* withstand a well-organized attack against his despotic tendencies. But Paris is a woman, and he is her master. The city, driven to extremes, is capable of making him an emperor, obliterating the Revolution, sacrificing herself and us, in order to save him. Don't let's forget: our era is ruled by impulses. It makes no sense today to appeal to the common sense of the masses. Let us appeal to their passions, rouse their instincts, and *then*—success is certain.

BARERE. It means propaganda!

TALLIEN. It means days, weeks of delays, tactics, hair-splitting, while the terror goes on raging as before! Fearful, confusing conspiracies, chatter with thousands of contradictory meanings—and nowhere will there be

one brave heart! Diplomacy, where a dagger is needed! No, I will not retreat for a second time. I'll trust to my hunting knife and destroy the
monster; but you...!

[*he wants to go out*]

FOUCHE. Eh, wait a moment. *Your* dagger will not stop the Revolutionary
Tribunal, you know. With his physical destruction you will assure him
immortality.

TALLIEN [*shocked*]. No... [*again inflamed*] How can I believe you! *You!*
When my girl cries to me for help! What other man would be capable of
tormenting that child, threatening that little black-haired head with
death, who but that monster could resist the appeal of those two eyes?
Does one conspire a plot against a gorilla, who robs someone of his
child, of his beloved? Indeed, you do that sinister beast too much hon-
or. He is not worthy of my dagger's blow, but Theresa must not wait in
prison until I haul him up on the gallows.

[*he runs towards the door*]

FOUCHE. Get him! [VILATE *and* COLLOT *grip the raging* TALLIEN *by both arms*]
Now listen! There is only one way: suddenly to get at him in the Convention. With lightning speed. From all sides at once. We'll let him
come forward to reveal his intentions. We'll wait till the apprehension
caused by his speech turns into fear and the chattering of teeth. Tallien's
murderous leap will then follow. In your outburst the silent terror of all
those present must explode. Your rage is genuine, so it will be a fatal
weapon. It will stun him for quite a few seconds, and then *we* will master the situation. He will not regain the upper hand any more. One after the other, we'll leap onto the platform and shout out his crimes.
The blows must create a hellish racket, the Marsh and the galleries will
fall into a rage. We won't let him utter a word, or call for help. We won't
let anyone have the time to come to their senses. No speeches—only a
roar. We must evoke a state of ecstasy: an ecstasy of fear and hate and
lust for death. It is imperative to have a simple, deadly indictment decreed in half an hour. He will be taken to the Conciergerie before he has
had a chance to utter two words. The two others will go with him. A
couple of hours later, in the afternoon—a hearing, and then, in the evening... [*he tightens his cravat meaningfully round his neck*] he must get the
axe between the disks of his neck before Paris recovers and realizes what
has really happened.

[*A deep silence. Those present are surprised and awestruck.*]

BARERE [*almost begging*]. Listen...it's not really proper...

COLLOT. But will it be proper when we are all thrown into the lime pit?

VILATE. For the last couple of days they've been digging a new one out at Monceau. It's as big as the Champ de Mars.

[TALLIEN, *who is able to think only of Theresa, utters a high-pitched groan*]

COLLOT [*thoughtful*]. For us...

BILLAUD. Yes, indeed. They will throw us in there, that is certain. Because, my dear Fouché, the bloody head of a leader whom the people worship is not the right kind of gift to win the favors of those same people. Or have you found a way to dispense with those favors for *today*?

FOUCHE. Not yet for today, I think. But, my friend: that man has already become a stranger to the masses. They are now satiated, have no passion for him any more [BILLAUD *laughs*] and no other ideals beyond bourgeois order. The masses do not love him any more. He simply hypnotizes them and keeps them in passive obedience. From there to hate is but one step. It won't cost us much to bring that hate into the open, if only his suggestive eyes are no longer in the way of *our* efforts to influence opinion. The moment people are satiated, and because of that become cowards, they lose all sense of reality. Words become more important than deeds, and it is words that are worshipped or condemned. In ninety-two freedom was something intangible that people desired and fought for. Today it is a word with two clearly accented syllables, in whose honor one can make feasts, or indulge in indignation. Dictatorship, gentlemen, is also a beautiful word; it creates the delights of hate and unbounded cruelty. Believe me: the mob will...never give up these two sources of pleasure, even though the object thrown to them might be their own idol.

VILATE. And not even one in a hundred knows what dictatorship is.

FOUCHE. Why ever not? Every child knows what it is, the stupidest kitchen maid knows what it is. Dictatorship means for them the possibility of brutish behavior and the maltreatment of one by all the others. A dictator or tyrant is he who is taken in the tumbril to his death and is maltreated on the way. Are these not clear definitions? You may rest assured, gentlemen: the cutoff head of a hero is not the right gift for the masses. But his living, suffering body, with hands tied, thrown defenseless to their greed by the sentence of the nation—in the course of a two-hour-long journey and at the moment of impressive death—that is a gift for which one can receive from the masses the name of father of the nation.

BILLAUD [*shaken*]. Yes—but the madness must pass, the beast in man has a short life. Just think: in the afternoon they will tear him to pieces, but in the evening they will realize whom they have torn. What then?

FOUCHE. Then, my friend, we shall again talk of dictatorship. That magic formula is more powerful than you think. Even when his nerves, which writhed in pain before, are rotting in his grave, the name will remain, still to be abused. The memory of the man will remain, his appeal to posterity. All this can be jeered at. For as long as he remains as a shadow, to delight the beast in us, anyone without exception will be ready to serve as an overzealous Brutus for that shadow.

BILLAUD [*sighs*]. One can almost understand why there are counter-revolutionaries...

VILATE [*shaking*]. Tallien...Tallien... [*the latter very slowly turns in his direction*] Tallien, kill him!...

[*a commotion*]

FOUCHE. Don't let Tallien out of your sight. The people would never forgive us the death of their hero, if we dared to deprive them of a couple of hours' amusement. Only they have the right to enjoy the death throes of those who have devoted themselves to their service.

[VILATE *weeps*]

BARERE [*trembling*]. Oh, stop it...stop it, or else... [*he stifles a sob and saves himself at the last moment with an outburst of hearty laughter*] My God, what nervous wrecks we all are!

FOUCHE. Yes. I see the deadline as being the day after tomorrow. He will refer to Saint-Just in his speech, that is clear. We will not start our attack before the Marsh gets scared. I am going now. Perhaps one of those two will come here. If so, he should not find me.

[*all except* BILLAUD *start to their feet*]

Do not leave Tallien to himself, even for a minute!

TALLIEN [*animated at last*]. Have no fear. I have no wish to make it easier for the monster to die. [VILATE *sobs;* TALLIEN *turns to him, trembling from rage*] Save your tears for the hour when we bury the dog.

[FOUCHE *departs*]

BARERE. For God's sake, let us go! What if he should decide to have us arrested before any others?

COLLOT [*collects his papers*]. Most probable. Then things would be much easier for him at the Convention.

BILLAUD. Impossible. He won't undertake anything without the agreement of the Committee. Even less so now, when he could in fact do so.

VILATE [*calm now*]. I must say, I envy you. You all against him alone. You will see the Inviolable tottering and falling, you will have to resist his look. Why am I not a deputy?

BILLAUD. Shut up, Vilate. I'm getting sick.

BARERE. And now the big question: in what form is man best suited to serve as a laxative: en masse, as Fouché puts it, or. . . as an individual? [*he nods slightly in* VILATE's *direction*]

VILATE [*all look at him*]. You don't anger me. Among people with the same purpose, one must not resent anything in anyone. And, after all, we are such people.

COLLOT [*with melancholy*]. Ha, ha! Not bad.

BARERE. Hush.

[*deadly silence*]

VILATE. Ah! The arrest warrant! For me too!

[COLLOT *gives him an angry look*]

BARERE. Brothers, we must now behave like men. . .

BILLAUD [*without fear, loud*]. Nobody's coming. . .

COLLOT. And yet. . .

BARERE [*loud*]. No one. He's right.

TALLIEN [*breathes with relief*]. God be praised. My life has great value today.

BILLAUD. Indeed. Oh, if only you were a little older!

BARERE. Then he wouldn't be crazy. And that is what is most valuable in him.

[*Fast, quiet footsteps. Two seconds of absolute silence*]

ACT II

SAINT-JUST *enters slowly, without a sound.*
Thunderbolt.
He closes the door carefully—does everything with mathematical precision—turns round and walks toward the table. Those present gradually recover their composure.

VILATE [*throws a glance in the direction where earlier his penwork had lain; speaks very softly*]. Bon appetit.

[BILLAUD *stiffly nods his head to the entering* SAINT-JUST, *then looks at him carefully.* BARERE *walks a couple of steps toward him.* COLLOT *and* TALLIEN *stand rooted to the ground.* VILATE, *a little behind them, puts on a friendly smile. For fear of making a clumsy remark nobody says anything.*

SAINT-JUST *returns the silent greeting with a slight bow, his face white and indifferent. Over his left arm he carries an overcoat. He puts it on the first chair he chances upon, and himself sits in the chairman's armchair.*

He is unusually handsome, with fascinating, but deeply repellent, overly perfect good looks. Just now his overwhelming fatigue dims the excessive brilliance of his person. Because of that he seems more accessible and—for some—almost likable. On this particular day he has experienced some great shocks, and he knows that even greater ones are still awaiting him. Yet there is absolute calm in his soul. His eyelids blink and droop against his will. Deep down in his dark consciousness his inner self is haggling with the gods: "One hour of sleep—and I'll give years of my future life for it." But the gods laugh: "Years? Years?! Do you think the capital of your strength is inexhaustible? You have bought something very expensive for your years."

In the midst of his enemies, surrounded on all sides by the fire of hate, he is too proud to shake off his sleepiness. The awareness of who is around him manifests itself at most as a pleasant, promising pricking in the tips of his fingers.

He stands out from the others in every detail of his attire. Black riding clothes, dusty now, but one can see that he had put them on in the morning fresh and pressed; high riding boots, covered with mud, on his nonchalantly crossed legs; overlong black hair, not powdered today; deep, cloudy black eyes; black beard growing on the delicate face of an archangel; forehead provocatively white, as are the hands (carefully protected against dust during the day by a pair of gloves), the only restless thing about him. These hands (manly, but too thin, sharply tapered) tap on the ta-

ble, run this way and that along its edge, lean against the hard boards, his nails catching splinters. When on occasion he realizes it, he abruptly stops the shuffling and moving of his hands.

No one can get an idea of what he is up to when he withdraws into himself, as he is doing now. He is not one of those banal people whom one cannot categorize as geniuses or madmen, saints or criminals. The impression one has of his personality corresponds clearly to all points on the scale of human psyche, and not just to the two extremes. He could equally well be (in his present state of passivity, of course) a carefree student, a genius, or a lunatic. And, instead of a saint or criminal, he could be taken for the overrefined offspring of a noble family, somewhat underdeveloped spiritually and morally. Or even for a philanderer with a soft heart. Anyone who had never heard him speak could smilingly regard him as a dreamer—and experience a healthy reaction to the uncanny impression produced by his passive presence. One thing, however, seems improbable: that he should be healthy. And yet, he is.

Almost everyone willingly gives way to him. It would be resented if he were to take a seat in a modest chair, instead of in the only stately armchair.]

SAINT-JUST [*to* BARERE, *who has greeted him*]. Good evening, citizen. Has Robespierre been here yet?

[COLLOT *starts,* TALLIEN *has to sit down,* BARERE *blinks his eyes and feels for the back of a chair, unable to speak*]

BILLAUD [*only now addresses* SAINT-JUST *directly*]. Good evening, Saint-Just. No, Robespierre has not been here for four weeks. As you well know.

SAINT-JUST [*who did not know, gives him a questioning look, but controls his surprise and lets his head sink in his hands*]. Oh, why not?

BARERE. He is ill . . .

COLLOT. Doesn't enjoy our company any more . . .

BILLAUD. Indeed. He complains about us . . . [*stops*]

SAINT-JUST [*out of good manners, motions denial*]. What about? . . .

BILLAUD. That we're ousting him.

SAINT-JUST. Yes. Let's drop it. You, who have the unparalleled honor of being the Republic's leaders and guardians, *you* are paralyzing the government with your childish grudges. Orgies of wounded pride where unremitting, hard work is needed, work till you're ready to drop, work with absolute discipline . . .

And if he takes amiss that Vadier [*a passing glance at* BARERE] with his senile prating puts both Committees and the Convention to ridicule, well, I am not surprised.

TALLIEN. You know, Saint-Just, you could stop playing the schoolmaster. Do you imagine that we do not know who you intend by "we"—as opposed to "you"—and what that means? Do you think that only your almighty friend can feel hurt?

[COLLOT *tugs him hard by the sleeve; meanwhile* BARERE *pulls* BILLAUD *back a little and whispers to him*]

BARERE. We must try to get out of here, as soon as possible. They've arranged to meet here; certainly not without some purpose. And then the two of them will cross-examine us, and him over there. [*points to* VILATE] Nothing good can come of it.

BILLAUD [*thoughtfully*]. Or in the end it might be for the best— [BARERE *loses patience*] All right, let's get out of here—but how? [TALLIEN *starts*] For God's sake, go to Tallien and shut him up. What a moron!

BARERE [*walks a few steps and divides both groups*]. You look exhausted, Saint-Just. Ah yes, I congratulate you on behalf of everybody for Charleroi. The victory has made a great impression in Paris.

SAINT-JUST [*has not noticed* TALLIEN's *outburst, and does not look up now; almost harshly*]. Thanks.

BARERE. You may rest assured we did not forget you at the Convention when the news was celebrated...

SAINT-JUST [*suddenly, without moving a muscle in his face, raises his fanatically piercing eyes*]. The news about victory! What do you care about the victor's name? Are the French interested in *who* has captured a fortress for them?

BARERE. Robespierre seems to share your view. On that day he even came to the Convention.

SAINT-JUST. And poured a bucket of cold water on the cheap incense brands of your idiotic hero worship, for which he deserves special thanks. On history's behalf.

[*a short pause*]

BARERE. Take it as you will. But I am very glad that this is how you look at it.

[COLLOT *has an idea, connected with the words just uttered, and the idea obviously electrifies him; he goes on thinking about it while following the speeches*]

SAINT-JUST [*a bit faintly again, but watchfully*]. What did he say?

BARERE. ...Nothing. That was exactly what was so strange, even unexpected. It was easy to explain, in fact: as we know, he was ill just then. The heat was unbearable, and, of course, speaking is an exhausting business. He must have felt he would not do justice to the hard task. But for me his concentrated attention was highly flattering. For it fell to me to give the account of the victory and capture of Charleroi. Well, I have a different opinion than yours about gratitude, duty, and personal merits. So I did not curb my sincere admiration. Your friend fixed me with his gaze and observed me continuously, but his face was a mask without any expression. He only bit his lips, which stood out like a red wound, the only sign of hidden emotion to appear on that stonelike face.

SAINT-JUST. That's a detailed account, if ever there was one. Good God, what's so important about all that?

BARERE [*with a marked smile of astonishment*]. Don't be a child, Saint-Just! In a word: all through that time Maximilien gave us no inkling of *his* attitude. With good will one could regard his silence as approval. But when the session was over, and half of the Jacobins from the upper benches gathered round him, he turned to me—I was standing quite near—and with a friendly-biting smile advised me not to praise victories with so much syrup. Because syrup, apart from its many other deficiencies, is also deceptive.

[SAINT-JUST*'s severe countenance brightens up for a second with a knowing smile.* BARERE *notices it and becomes afraid, more than he realizes himself*]

COLLOT [*from a distance*]. Do you consider this so unimportant too, Saint-Just?

SAINT-JUST [*again quite matter-of-fact*]. Oh no. Not at all.

BARERE [*butts in suddenly*]. I wonder how Paris is going to appear to you now. It has changed a bit—in that time . . .

VILATE. Robespierre has disappeared—only seemingly, to prove his omnipresence. He has achieved his aim totally. His name is written in letters of flame on the sky, he has become the nation's deity.

BILLAUD [*unexpectedly*]. He behaves accordingly too . . . [*goes on, in answer to* SAINT-JUST*'s inevitably demanding look*] Yes, like God, like Alexander. Men of his caliber lived in antiquity and we, of course, are following in its footsteps. Such behavior is in the blood of those very rare imperious natures.

SAINT-JUST. And you, Billaud, quite the opposite, have in your blood the nature of a serf. It must be for this reason that you are so insatiable as a revolutionary. You find it easy to brand as moderates those who keep their five senses in check. But to express your negative opinion, as a free citizen, unambiguously and honestly—that far, after three years of bloody madness, you have not yet come.

TALLIEN [*erupts again*]. What impudence! To express oneself freely! And it's

Saint-Just who demands *that!* Saint-Just, who drowns every, absolutely every independent thought—in the blood of the lunatic who would dare in *your* free Republic to demand freedom of thought! One must beware of expressing one's opinion even of the weather, until one knows for certain that HE approves it! Do you want someone to say "it's raining today," if Robespierre has decreed sunshine for that particular day? For smaller things heads have been cut off! To speak out freely, unambiguously and honestly! Well, there you are. Are you happy now?

[COLLOT, *white with fear and rage, crushes his arm, but is pushed away.* BARERE *tries to stop him, then gives up, smiling*]

BILLAUD [*has listened with a somber expression, and now shouts*]. Shut your trap, you stupid ass!

VILATE [*in a quiet moment after this bomb*]. You are giving our lord reasons to frown, Tallien. Restrain your tirade.

[TALLIEN *turns his face to them, swollen with rage, gives everybody a look, and prepares to go on with his tirade against his patiently dozing victim. He is much taller than* SAINT-JUST, *a thin giant facing a fine-boned shapely figure*]

TALLIEN. And this is allowed! This is tolerated! There must be good reasons . . .

BILLAUD [*emerges near him, small and silent, strong as a bull; catches the raging* TALLIEN *at the height of his chest, and pushes him back*]. That's enough, finished!

TALLIEN [*resists vigorously at first, then quiets down like* BILLAUD]. Damn . . . [*softly, trembling slightly*] Billaud, let me speak. Let me speak, Billaud . . . otherwise . . . I'll do something stupid.

[BILLAUD, *who has understood, lets him go.* TALLIEN *refers to his previous words, as if there has been no interruption.* SAINT-JUST *is half-dozing, but listens with growing attention to the flow of this cascade of images and words*]

You two are being tolerated. Paris is cowering, gray from fear and exhaustion. Three quarters of the population are sick of starvation, but no one utters a peep, there are no riots among the unending lines in front of the half-empty shops. People wait on empty stomachs in the scorching heat for a slice of straw bread, they wait and don't even break a window at the baker's.

It wasn't as bad in the tyrant's time, on October the fifth. The women were not *so hungry*, and yet they went and stormed the royal palace and dragged the imprisoned despot back with them to Paris. Nothing happened to a single one. No Royal Highness had the thought of greeting the starving women with cannon or riding them down with a cavalry charge.

Today, if just one section in an unarmed crowd tried to *beg* for bread, the free Republic would not let the sovereign people go without an answer. Out of a thousand people, perhaps five would be able afterwards to talk about that answer.

So nobody asks for anything. Nobody needs anything. Everybody is happy, according to regulations.

VILATE. Is hunger worse today than two years ago?

TALLIEN. Yes, it is worse. Much worse. In ninety-two we were fighting for freedom. In ninety-two one had to save the fatherland. Therefore people gave up bread altogether, ate plaster, and thrived on it. People were defending *their* land, argued fervently about *their* cause at the meetings, controlled their representatives at the Convention, shouted when the heads of *their* enemies were falling off. Today not many are interested in us at the Convention. Young men swindle their way out of conscription while at the scaffold barrier only the dregs of the people gather out of boredom to look at the stupid death show, repeated daily in an idiotic manner. They do not applaud any more, Saint-Just! The revolutionary fervor is burnt out completely. The deputies care only for their own profit. The government is alien to the people, as if it were English, not French. The Republic is just a word—and a great misfortune. The French people already have the feeling that they have sacrificed their lives, and those of their children, in vain; that they are starving in vain, and have fallen into unprecedented poverty in vain. After all, they are dropping dead in the streets! This city, once the liveliest on earth, now seems dead. People believe they are breathing the smell of carrion. The boundless sacrifices were for nothing. For nothing? *You two* do not believe this. You are now about to gather the whole harvest. The people are tolerating it. But for how long? You do not think about it, you imperious natures.

SAINT-JUST [*without raising his eyes, matter-of-fact*]. Thoughts are not written on foreheads. What *we* think, *you* cannot know. [*short pause; he breathes in and turns his head a little*] And your panorama is incomplete. It has to be balanced against quite a different view: the Palais-Royal, the brothels and the brand-new residences of the innumerable revolutionary Croesuses. To encourage the starving patriots: Look, brothers, we made it. I assure you, Tallien: we think about this too.

[*The silence after these words becomes embarrassing.* COLLOT *then comes to the conclusion that it is time for him to come forward with his idea. After a few advance bows left and right, he begins to speak in a studiously measured voice, without lifting his eyes*]

COLLOT. Gentlemen, things are going too far. Our game is becoming distasteful. [*All listen attentively, trying to guess the roles assigned to them. The speaker addresses his opponent directly*] Saint-Just, don't you realize that you've been led up the garden path?

SAINT-JUST. I must admit I wasn't paying much attention.

[BARERE *smiles to himself*]

COLLOT. Oh yes, you were. But you didn't know that your cool superiority was an object of amusement, yes, amusement. That your blind faith in the permanence of certain...connections...was observed with a keen, malicious joy. That your nonchalant, insulting self-confidence was a source of delight...

[*the total lack of response to his pronouncement begins to irritate* COLLOT, *but he too is able to control his emotions*]

BARERE [*has received a sign from* COLLOT *and pretends to be concerned*]. Shut up, Collot! Are you mad?

COLLOT. No. I am not afraid of persecution, I despise the vengefulness of certain gentlemen. I will unmask them, even if I have to pay for it with my head; for there are things one would not wish to happen even to an enemy. I cannot be silent.

[TALLIEN *lifts his eyes, whose expression changes from astonishment to downright dismay*]

SAINT-JUST. Ah yes, and well I know it.

[*He suppresses a yawn, a real one resulting from the exhausting tension.* COLLOT *has achieved his aim; his young opponent imagines that the worst may be on its way. Maybe Robespierre has been toppled—such a thing may happen overnight. Perhaps he is dead—there has been no news from him for three days. It is self-control that is the most difficult. Terrified, he anticipates the blow—he is afraid lest he turn pale.* BARERE *has noticed* TALLIEN's *fatal naïveté; he steps between him and* SAINT-JUST *and delicately steps on* TALLIEN's *toes. Wordlessly he signifies to* TALLIEN *the need to alter his facial expression, at the same time whispering to him in a calculated tone of voice.*]

BARERE. Well, he'll see the light at last. But even so, it won't help him much. [SAINT-JUST *regrets that his heart is not encased in steel bands—for safety's sake.* BARERE *completes his speech to* TALLIEN] I'd rather go home and to bed. Come with me. I must eat something first, and for that I need company.

BILLAUD [*bored and somewhat disgusted*]. I'll be glad to come too, if you invite me. Will you, or won't you? How about you, Collot? Aren't you coming too?

COLLOT. In a moment.

[*After a few seconds* COLLOT *addresses his victim with double impact.* BILLAUD *and* BARERE *are standing at the back, near the door, listening attentively.* TALLIEN *is now standing under* BARERE*'s close protection, held fast by the arm—for lack of a rope— and looks downwards with a troubled expression.* VILATE *is comfortably seated in* FOUCHE*'s chair, with the pale smile of a city urchin on his cynical youthful lips.*]

COLLOT. Better not rely on anybody, Saint-Just. Mistrust is a bourgeois virtue which has flowered richly among us. It really is a splendid example of a virtue. And those who are absent always come off worst.

VILATE [*approaches with a bow*]. May I offer the highly esteemed oracle my faithful services as an interpreter? Without me the state of things is never complete. Only two francs a line... I mean: a sentence. Officially certified presence of mind and witty, though belated, repartee. Many years' practice in Charenton. Numerous letters of recommendation...

COLLOT [*deep and demonic*]. All in vain, young man. None of your tricks will dissuade me from fulfilling my human duty. So let go. [*to* SAINT-JUST *again*] Once upon a time, in the dark past, there lived two men, who differed in height but were considered equal. No doubt you're thinking: the smaller one fared better. No, Saint-Just, you are wrong. The smaller one lived in constant expectation of the moment when the truth would come out. And he, the smaller one, attached immense importance to being considered great, the greatest. Do you know what he did?

SAINT-JUST. Nothing, I suppose. For he must have known that he really *was* the greatest. Otherwise he would not be regarded as such. The public *does* have eyes.

COLLOT. Yes, that's how *you* would think. I knew it. No, my friend. The smaller one did not rest until he had shortened the great one by a considerable, and in a sense decisive, part of his person.

That happened centuries ago. But the method was considered expedient. For—the great one was not the only one that was great. Besides, there is a phenomenon called growing up.

You are young, Saint-Just. You have taken Charleroi. You are growing—growing.

[*An immense fear suddenly restores* SAINT-JUST'*s composure: what is the purpose of this chaotic chattering, if not to put his watchfulness to sleep, to persuade him to accept another's view, or even to pressure him into it? He decides to listen to a few more remarks and then to cut the arguments short.*]

SAINT-JUST [*friendly*]. Why are you straining yourself so, Collot? If you have absolutely nothing new to say, we can remain silent. I won't hold it against you.

COLLOT [*softly*]. Oh no. You would be glad, even thankful, if I wished to remain silent. [*in a shrill whisper*] For you are trembling before the truth you can see coming—you have known it for a long time...

[COLLOT'*s masterly play disguises the awful farce inherent in his words. The listeners are fascinated.* SAINT-JUST, *torn by contradictory suppositions, controls himself with difficulty. He expects every possible disaster; otherwise these villains would not dare to deceive him.*]

SAINT-JUST. Billaud, maybe you can tell me what game that ham actor is playing? Is he ill—or just drunk?

BILLAUD [*icily*]. I don't know. I care little about the spiritual state of my colleagues.

COLLOT [*still in a shrill whisper*]. Why did you have to say that, Saint-Just? Why do you pretend to be so confident, in spite of the doubts in your heart? Listen, I hesitated, the way you look would arouse compassion even in a tiger; I was ready to spare you the truth. I suppose death would only be half as bitter for you. But you don't want any consideration, so I will do my duty, and you will live—if you still have enough strength left.

[*pause*]

Robespierre has denounced you.

[BILLAUD, *the most intelligent of them, frowns. He considers the intrigue childish.* TALLIEN *and* BARERE *are interested,* VILATE *even fascinated. But* SAINT-JUST *feels immensely relieved. Only after a time does he realize the doubtful import of the news: he does not believe it entirely, but has to allow it a degree of probability. Even so he manages to preserve an absolutely unmoved expression*]

COLLOT. Now you understand why they wanted to observe you once more in the full glare of your cocksure insolence, your unbounded arrogance? With what malicious joy they listened to your ceremonious "we"? Your lack of understanding of your situation was sheer delight. But Billaud and I are above a desire for petty vengefulness. Of course, I am not warning you out of sentiment. I consider you a valuable force, which should be preserved for the good of the Republic.

SAINT-JUST [*to* BILLAUD, *though not directly*]. Has the decree been issued? Are you authorized to arrest me? [*he regards Billaud's silence as affirmation and gets up*] Then we can go.

COLLOT [*somewhat put out*]. Don't let yourself be ruled by impulses, man! Suicide on the spot, because a friend has betrayed you! Come on, sit down!

SAINT-JUST. I am not thinking of suicide. I only want to obey the law and give an accounting before the judges. You know as well as I do that I have nothing to fear.

BARERE. Sit down. There is no question of a decree yet. You little know Robespierre, as he is today, if you are thinking about an open indictment. He exudes poison with irritating slowness. His charges are elusive and far-flung. It's not a sword but a net.

[SAINT-JUST *is deeply lost in thought*]

COLLOT. Listen. After Charleroi he spoke at the Jacobin Club—that's where he began, so the effect was more deadly. He said: the generals are more and more the subjects of a personality cult. This is regrettable, but human. But now to the Sambre-et-Meuse army a commissioner has been sent who exceeds the limits of his powers, removes the responsible commanders, and captures one fortress after another. Instead of immediately recalling him, Paris gives him a place of pride on the altar of its idols.

As I see it, the Republic has reached in two years the position occupied by the Roman empire at the height of its decline: the era of caesars appointed by the army.

SAINT-JUST [*wan smile*]. Ah yes, I see it now. The usual story.

COLLOT [*having misunderstood him*]. Exactly. He always knew how to destroy people with equal amounts of malice and precision. As far as you're concerned, he wants to deprive you gradually of your popularity, and then to overthrow you. If I were in your place, I would either immediately call him to account—but then I could at best only save my head—or I would let him be, and emulate him. For it is sweet to see a traitor raging like a madman in a trap he has set for someone else—

VILATE [*agitated, mysteriously*]. Perhaps it is sweeter to rage oneself in that trap, perhaps it is the pinnacle of pleasure to mount the steps toward shameful, painful death, if that death is a present from. . .from a friend.

SAINT-JUST [*looks at him closely, assesses correctly his clammy look*]. Could you tell me, colleagues, how that individual got into your company?

BARERE [*softly, ahead*]. Egality raises her sickle. . .

SAINT-JUST. Egality, esteemed sir? What has she to do with it? Have you made it your task to turn the principles of our morality upside down? Since when do they oblige you to let morally defective street urchins be present in the most exclusive venues of government deliberations?

For this reason I am sorry for you, Collot. It was an irresponsible recklessness on your part not to prevent the idiotic intrusion of this creature. His smile alone has revealed to me the whole abyss of untruth. Perhaps it would even pay to dig farther. More care, friends, more care in *so* dangerous a game.

[*he turns away, head in his hands*]

VILATE [*his hands shake*]. Auuu. . . [*Suddenly his face lights up with violent hate. He smiles a long time with half-closed eyes, looking at Saint-Just. Very softly:*] Just you wait, Gaveston.

[*Those who are near the door start and grow pale.* BARERE *listens attentively, then makes frantic signs*]

COLLOT [*pale with rage, looks round for his overcoat*]. I regret my naive sympathy for you. After all, I knew the childish stubbornness of your infatuation. You will now tell him everything and believe what he tells you. You will help him to dig our graves—and yours too. For if my head falls, my dear young man, you should ask to be given Extreme Unction as soon as possible. That is my last advice. Adieu.

[*He darts about and finds the others frozen, in tragic readiness. One can hear soft footsteps—the sound turns the four men into stone statues, and at the same time brings* SAINT-JUST *back to life.*

ROBESPIERRE *enters, not so effectively as* SAINT-JUST, *but strikingly because of his evident naturalness. It is as if he were coming back to the study which he had left an hour ago. He remains standing, somewhat disappointed that those present do not seem to consider his entry something as natural as he does. Dead silence all round. Almost in spite of themselves, those waiting form a lane through which he must now pass.*

Like his friend, he is at the same time attractive and repellent, but in a different way. Stiff and fragile when standing still, catlike in his soundless suppleness when moving, he gives the impression of an uncanny lightness. It is the lightness of a cat, or a dried-up mummy, depending on the situation. His posture, his gestures— economical to the highest degree and mathematically precise—are strikingly controlled, like a dancer's, and clearly thought out; not the slightest reflex is spontaneous. His body slender, immaculately symmetrical, his limbs thin, too thin to impress. His face without expression, shiningly pale, yet with an unhealthy tinge. His outlines, almost perfectly beautiful, are out of harmony with their artificial lack of expression. His light green eyes have aggressive pupils. His mouth, without cruelty, is firmly delineated in a neutral horizontal line. His lips, wonderfully drawn, mark clearly his nervous delicacy and near-abnormal sensitivity; the corners of his mouth show an obstinate, sharp, cold ruthlessness. Unusually thick hair, whose light red complexion only slightly shows through the powder. In rare moments he blushes, without betraying his emotions; a blood wave suddenly overruns his face, inflaming it for a few seconds, then disappears at once without a trace.

In order to negotiate the lane, he remains standing and greets those present in turn with a handshake; he ostentatiously takes the glove off his right hand for the purpose. He takes VILATE'*s hand last, grips it hard, and gives the young man an unusually long look, friendly but expressionless.*]

ROBESPIERRE. So you are deputizing for me, Sempronius? Isn't the responsibility somewhat too great, for a debut?

VILATE [*ill at ease*]. Insofar as . . .

ROBESPIERRE. Since only members have access to the premises of a confidential government committee. Otherwise suspicion can arise that spies are being admitted.

[*While* ROBESPIERRE *calmly approaches* SAINT-JUST, *who observes him intently from his chair,* BILLAUD *forcibly prevents another eruption from* TALLIEN. *The whole thing is played out in silence, very quickly and with exaggerated gestures—all behind the back of* ROBESPIERRE, *who does not take part.* COLLOT *suddenly finds his hands too heavy; he does not know what to do with them.*]

VILATE [*softly, his eyes turned upwards to heaven*]. God almighty, I *am* getting my just dues today . . .

[BARERE *smiles, holding* TALLIEN *fast. The latter, blue with rage, exchanges glances with* BILLAUD, *who silently threatens him and is gripping his other hand*]

ROBESPIERRE [*in front of both*]. Am I in your way?

SAINT-JUST [*emphatically*]. Not in mine.

[SAINT-JUST *does not extend a hand to his friend, but looks at him stiffly, with almost impolite pertinacity*]

ROBESPIERRE [*returns his glance with slight surprise, smiles almost imperceptibly, a little mockingly*]. Good evening, Saint-Just. Perhaps you still recognize me?

SAINT-JUST [*motionless*]. I . . . don't know.

ROBESPIERRE [*brings himself a chair*]. Something wrong?

SAINT-JUST. Nothing wrong out there, on the frontier.

[*The others stop by the door.* COLLOT *is all ears.* ROBESPIERRE, *who observes them out of the corner of his eye, sits down in an effeminately nonchalant manner*]

ROBESPIERRE. Am I black in the face? [*reviews his attire*] Have I put my clothes on backward? [SAINT-JUST *shakes his head*] Are you not quite well? No wonder. This hellish heat dries out the brain. I tried to stick it out at the Jacobins for an hour, and I couldn't. After three quarters of an hour my disciplined will failed me. In the entire room there was, perhaps, one cubic meter of genuine air; that was supposed to be enough for listeners and speakers. The voices sounded as if they were coming from the sixteenth century. Such days could prove fatal for public morality. The communal sense dies out, a man hates his neighbor. And, what is much worse, one feels one's democratic principles totter under the onslaught of the rebellious senses. I myself had to flee to save my soul, because I caught myself longing for the public of eighty-nine, those laced, coiffured, perfumed people, when our Club tried to rival the opera . . . [*turns round and shows an admirable row of teeth in a smile full of sweetness*] My dear friends, would you mind shutting the door? Saint-Just is so susceptible to draughts.

[*they hasten to the exit*]

BILLAUD [*turns round in the doorway*]. Why shouldn't Saint-Just tell us all right away what he has to say?

ROBESPIERRE. Certainly, that would be the simplest thing to do, and that's why I arranged to meet him here. But for this purpose we would have to be members only, and ask the outsiders to leave. I cannot request anything so impolite.

BILLAUD [*tersely*]. Good-bye.

ROBESPIERRE. Adieu.

[*He turns to see the door closing, and sees* BILLAUD *unexpectedly hesitating, then stopping in his tracks.* BILLAUD *is quite pale; they look intently at each other.*]

BILLAUD [*hoarse*]. Robespierre...

ROBESPIERRE [*surprised, almost unsure*]. Yes?...

BILLAUD [*crosses the room with a few quick steps; it can be seen that he is trembling*]. I did not want to offend you, Robespierre. [*He extends his hand, which* ROBESPIERRE *takes after a moment's hesitation, surprised but not unwilling*] Good-bye.

ROBESPIERRE [*encouragingly*]. You wanted to say something.

BILLAUD [*looks toward the window and makes a tired gesture of resignation*]. Nothing important. But it has occurred to me that tomorrow it will be exactly a year since you joined the Committee. In twelve months you have forced the state to go through developments that would normally take half a century. You've succeeded. [*after a pause*] But now, do you have the courage to take upon yourself the burden of the *second* year? If this first year has not devoured you completely, what's happened to the implacable law of balance in nature? Aren't you at the end of your strength?

ROBESPIERRE. No. And even if I were, I have not yet completed my task.

BILLAUD [*almost affectionately*]. How do you know that?

ROBESPIERRE [*smiling*]. Because I am still alive. Which of us can hope to accomplish his task before he dies?

[*pause*]

BILLAUD [*shakes his hand firmly with both his hands*]. Adieu.

ROBESPIERRE [*casually*]. Good-bye.

[BILLAUD *looks round quickly at that word, but then turns once more to the door and goes out.*

ROBESPIERRE *feels stricken. Gray in the face, he leans forward, twists his hands convulsively, leans his hand on the straightened tips of his fingers. Suddenly he gets up, walks to the window and remains there for a while. His vacant eyes stare at the horizon, his teeth bite his lower lip, his hands are so tightly clenched that his wrists turn white like chalk, and the way they are twisted expresses something like imploringness.* SAINT-JUST *does not take his eyes off him. Only later, when* ROBESPIERRE *moves aside, clearly on purpose so as not to be observed all the time, does he take pity and stop looking.*]

SAINT-JUST [*for whom this lasts too long, speaks without turning*]. Hallo, Robespierre!

ROBESPIERRE [*controls himself at last and returns*]. I am sorry.

SAINT-JUST [*looks at him insistently*]. Why did you ask me to come here, of all places?

ROBESPIERRE. Wait. [*looks at the door*] Be so good as to see first if we are alone here.

SAINT-JUST [*gets up reluctantly*]. You're crazy with your persecution mania . . .

[SAINT-JUST *rips the door open;* VILATE *leaps back so abruptly that he must grip the wall. From there, at* SAINT-JUST*'s silent behest, he enters the room, his head raised high*]

Forgive me, Robespierre. Your intuition is amazing.

ROBESPIERRE [*looks at the young man with melancholy amusement*]. A poor little rat—in the lion's den . . .

VILATE [*with sudden violence*]. Yes . . . oh yes! The parallel goes further! [ROBESPIERRE *adopts a negative attitude.* VILATE *mobilizes his whole emotional strength in order not to let himself be rejected*] Robespierre, allow me to speak! You don't know why I am here.

ROBESPIERRE [*sweetly*]. You have forgotten your lampoon, no doubt?

VILATE [*sobs, half from fright, half from despair. He has grown very pale. After a while he clears his throat and speaks, with a voice stifled by rage*]. My memory is not that bad. I have hidden it well.

ROBESPIERRE. Then your handkerchief, your watch, your buttonhole flower? My God, say something. I want to help you get out of this mess.

VILATE [*still softer*]. You've no reason to be so pleased with yourself. I did not forget anything; I was listening.

ROBESPIERRE. But, child, we know that. It's not the truth we are concerned with, but a pretext. You've lost your chance. Pity, you know. Why put your own head on the block?

VILATE [*looks at him*]. Why do you make a villain out of me?

ROBESPIERRE. I . . . always I. Soon I shall be held responsible for every love tragedy in France.

VILATE. Yes, you. I have thrown my soul at your feet—it's an offensive gesture, but can a rat offend a lion? You could have taken it up from the ground with your white hands; dirty though it is, it's still a living human soul . . .

But when I made a nuisance of myself with my childish attack, you ridiculed me—in front of many people—and you know well how to make someone ridiculous . . .

Today, when by pure chance I was sitting here with your colleagues, without thinking what this place was, you called me a spy. That I have never yet been; but your word is an order, or a spell. I became a spy right away . . . [*he laughs and shouts*] Yes, at once, doubly so, doubly so!

So now I wanted to overhear your conversation with Saint-Just so that I could sell it to your enemies. I assure you, there is no lack of buyers for such goods. Yes, you can laugh at me, if you like. I'll never, never detach myself from you. So if you are keen on retaining power, you must take the trouble to have me arrested.

ROBESPIERRE. To do that I would have to call someone. And there would be more bother later. I am too tired from the heat. But you are a noble, chivalrous spy, who can help me much and harm me little. At worst, your very existence will bear witness to my magnanimity. Go in peace and go on sinning as much as you like.

VILATE [*bows and goes out; on the way he turns back once more*]. Frankly, no man should make a rat mad, Robespierre; for *every man* could find himself one day lying on the floor, bound or wounded. And then...

ROBESPIERRE [*to* SAINT-JUST *who is approaching* VILATE *threateningly*]. Let him run.

SAINT-JUST [*in the doorway*]. If you're caught once again, you will be put in the pillory.

VILATE [*bows back*]. Oh never fear—I'll not be so stupid twice in a row. [*goes out*]

SAINT-JUST [*sits down, with satisfaction*]. I have lost to you again.

ROBESPIERRE [*a bit embarrassed, imperceptibly avoids the other's glance; not looking*]. He was not eavesdropping.

SAINT-JUST. ...What then?...

ROBESPIERRE [*softly, but quite naturally*]. Wanted to warn me.

SAINT-JUST. What of?

ROBESPIERRE. I don't know.

SAINT-JUST [*losing his composure*]. And you didn't let him speak out! So this ...

ROBESPIERRE. Any clue relating to a public matter I would have accepted eagerly and with gratitude. But I felt it concerned only my personal safety. And how could I personally be indebted for anything to such a creature? I was very sorry, but it was impossible.

SAINT-JUST [*very worried*]. It was a terrible mistake. God knows what it could be...

ROBESPIERRE [*yawns discreetly*]. An attempted coup, or an ordinary plot. We shall see in the next few days. In any case... [*suddenly freezes in a solemn pose, deathly pale, with ever-widening pupils*]

SAINT-JUST [*very frightened*]. What's the matter?

ROBESPIERRE [*springs to his feet*]. Billaud! Billaud's strange behavior!

[*he begins to walk quickly round the room*]

SAINT-JUST. Well...?

ROBESPIERRE [*turns his burning eyes towards him for the first time*]. This matter could be serious. Perhaps they have decided to do something, *after all!* God be praised, if that is so!

SAINT-JUST [*abruptly*]. Then speak now the way you should! [*a pause;* ROBESPIERRE *is astounded,* SAINT-JUST *himself somewhat embarrassed*] You needn't beat about the bush, Maxime. I get the picture, since you remain silent now.

ROBESPIERRE [*not understanding*]. ... Yes? ...

SAINT-JUST [*motionless*]. Are...we...still comrades in arms? [*as* ROBESPIERRE, *half-conscious, does not reply at once, he whispers*] Don't lie!!!

ROBESPIERRE [*sits down*]. As far as I am concerned—that goes without saying. What is the matter?

SAINT-JUST [*only half in control*]. *Have* you denounced me? *Have* you turned them against me?

ROBESPIERRE [*amused*]. Ah, Collot?!

SAINT-JUST. How do you know about that?

ROBESPIERRE. Wasn't he standing over you very visibly just when I came in? Wasn't he in the middle of a rousing improvisation, that stageworthy Iago? And his eyes, when you glanced at me! He looked at you with the eyes of a master poisoner waiting for the effect of his potion. [*glances at* SAINT-JUST] And it has worked, indeed. [*he lowers his eyes for a moment; has no reply to give to* SAINT-JUST *'s tormented entreaty emerging from the depths of his suspicions*] Collot is cunning and obviously gave you some childish story to swallow...For only an altogether stupid suspicion will not be eradicated. Faith in the unbelievable is almost incurable.

SAINT-JUST [*with difficulty*]. Unfortunately philosophy cannot help me.

ROBESPIERRE [*looks at him*]. No one can help you, Saint-Just. A probable accusation I could easily refute. Faced with ridiculous, pure nonsense, I am powerless. He must have told you that I had denounced you behind your back. That for no reason at all I had renounced my only ally, harmed him, turned him into a relentless enemy. I, who can only with difficulty bear my loneliness...

One must have something more than just intelligence to hit like *that.* I would never have thought Collot capable of such a stroke of genius. His hate must be reaching its zenith, if he derives such ideas from it... [*after a pause*] Yes. All this points in the same direction. [*looks at* SAINT-JUST *again*] Politically we are bound together, Saint-Just—until the end. Never mind how you stand with me personally. For I see that something is being cooked up against us both.

SAINT-JUST [*wringing his hands*]. Maxime, you couldn't have done it! Prove it
to me!

ROBESPIERRE [*very sadly*]. It can't be done.

SAINT-JUST [*sinks dispirited*]. So that's how it is. [*his pupils are wide with terror;
very softly*] You . . . [*pause*]

First I thought I had been slandered. It would then have been your
duty to denounce me. But in that case you would not have concealed
anything, and I could have explained things right away.

But it wasn't slander. It was a secret, monstrous checkmate. I never
really knew you. It may be that your genius is tainted with madness.
Perhaps you are secretly given to hidden vice. [ROBESPIERRE *shudders*]
God, at least control yourself!

Your action was, perhaps, the result of idiotic vileness, born of a simple lust for evil—what do I know about you . . .

ROBESPIERRE [*beside himself*]. Confound it, man! Have you lost your senses?
It is a lie, you idiot, a lie! A damned, stupid lie, and you fell for it!!!

SAINT-JUST [*exhausted, sinks into his chair*]. God be praised . . .

[*A long deep silence. He looks ahead with an expression of true happiness.* ROBES-
PIERRE, *who, for the first time in his life, has tainted his lips with a swear word, is
still shuddering with rage. Suddenly* SAINT-JUST *tilts his head back and laughs—
softly and calmly, with a laughter delicate, damp as if through tears, bright as daylight*]

Why can't you for *once* in your life be simple, you the great statesman!
Simple as a child, as a woman . . . Your intellect has played us both a dirty
trick. It needed a monstrous intelligence to keep calm at *such* an
accusation—and to master the situation right away. Any other person
would lose his self-control after such a blow; he might be sublime, but
helpless. I was watching for you to retreat, speechless. In that way you
would have proved to me that you were innocent, without uttering a
word. My nerves shouted for you to try and defend yourself with mud-
dled words, without finding the right ones; for you to repeat one weak
excuse ten times over; for you to lose all your superiority like a trapped
mouse in its blind frenzy, and behave the way that an investigating mag-
istrate expects the accused to behave. But you didn't bat an eyelid! You
initiated philosophical deliberations! You explained with regret that my
suspicions were irrefutable! . . . mmm [*he shudders*] Well, now the sun is
shining again. In the end you did lose your composure. [*he rises and
stretches himself*] What a uniquely splendid evening!

ROBESPIERRE [*smiles calmly*]. Now I seem to myself infinitely stupid. Infinitely. A truly refreshing feeling.

SAINT-JUST. I would like to dance. [*leans against the back of his friend's chair*] I don't think you would. What would you like to do?

ROBESPIERRE [*leans his head so far back that it comes to rest on* SAINT-JUST*'s crossed hands, and their eyes meet*]. I can't say it. I would be ashamed.

SAINT-JUST. That's nothing. I wasn't ashamed. I know, for that matter: you would like to sleep.

ROBESPIERRE. Yes and no. I would like to die now.

SAINT-JUST. O, what bad taste!

ROBESPIERRE. Mmm—and yet that *is* what I think. Ridiculous, how much courage there is in wishing for things which are in bad taste.

SAINT-JUST. Yes, because everything that is sublime is only looking for a means of escape in that notion.

ROBESPIERRE. I warn you, soon you will seem very silly to yourself.

SAINT-JUST. No.

ROBESPIERRE. Why—no? I am speaking from experience.

SAINT-JUST. Yes. You have been thinking and still are thinking of yourself. But I am thinking—about you too. And so I have no interest in myself. I am too occupied with trying to find you again.

ROBESPIERRE. Are you succeeding?

SAINT-JUST. I don't know yet. The face must be captured anew line by line. No expression must escape, not the smallest shade must disguise itself. It is an arduous, intense work; until one knows for certain: yes, it is he, not a stranger.

ROBESPIERRE. That certainty comes with the first glance.

SAINT-JUST. One can't trust it. How often is the face that one sees but a badly fitting mask after a terrible transformation! For the body changes so slowly... [ROBESPIERRE *lowers his head*] But...! You musn't interrupt me, Maxime...

ROBESPIERRE [*touches the nape of his neck*]. *You* try to get through ten minutes with a broken neck! Try! And then, you know, childishness is dangerous. There is something uncanny about this business. It is as if one discovered venomous teeth in a paper snake, or a hangman's rope in a young girl's sewing case, or an unusual, hair-raising meaning in the dialogue of a drawing-room comedy. It is much safer to hide behind a wall of thick-skinned superiority and pride.

SAINT-JUST. Why are you so insincere, so evasive?

ROBESPIERRE [*disconcerted, does not answer at once; after a while*]. Have I changed?

SAINT-JUST. Very much so. Your tendency to run away is odd and quite new. Your grim sense of humor moves slowly toward hysteria. And in the too widely opening pupils of your eyes, one can see deep down a tiny nucleus of panic being born, the panic of a man at bay.

ROBESPIERRE. Hm... Have I aged?

SAINT-JUST. No. But you have got seared. Through hate, I suppose.

ROBESPIERRE [*smiling*]. I suppose... [*after a while, dreamily, enjoying it*] I have recently been reading at bedtime the memoirs of an English traveler. He tells of an oriental magician, who put a curse on his enemy. There it is written that he stood motionless in his garden at sunrise and cursed the name of his hated opponent for a whole hour until the eyes turned white in his face and the foam from his mouth dripped to the earth.

I dared not go on reading another line. I was so shocked that I became dizzy. Never has any representation of an erotic nature, or its recollection, so shaken me to the marrow of my bones. My body became weak all over. I don't think I shall ever forget that night.

I soon fell asleep and in my sleep must have cursed God's name from the rostrum until my eyes turned white in my face. Eight times I tried to wrench myself away and, breathing heavily, bring myself awake. But eight times I fell back into the abyss and gurgled unthinkable phrases with numb lips, against my paralyzed will, without my brain taking part; each word sent shivers down my spine and pangs of pain down both my sides, right to the fingertips. [*pause*]

I had chosen that book, as it seemed to me a good soporific. And in all other respects that's what it actually was.

[*pause*]

SAINT-JUST [*pulls something on the table this way and that*]. I cannot follow you to those regions. To hate, with soul *and* body...

ROBESPIERRE. Such things begin only when hate detaches itself fully from individuals and directs itself against... the whole. Then the body cries out, and the innocent nerves curl up. Hate against individual people is idyllic, something refreshing. The *other* kind burns right through a man.

[*pause*]

SAINT-JUST. Tell me, is it true that you have withdrawn because of constant attacks in the Committee?

ROBESPIERRE [*astounded*]. For God's sake, Saint-Just, who do you take me for?

SAINT-JUST [*very softly*]. It is very strange how we have pulled away in different directions.

ROBESPIERRE. I wouldn't say that. I am surprised at your uncertainty, because my attitude to you has not changed at all. Whatever may have happened, it is *you* who have moved away from me.

SAINT-JUST. An estrangement is always mutual, by its very nature.

ROBESPIERRE. You are right, but don't let's split hairs. My disappearance is connected with a matter round which my life now turns. It was a war stratagem and a subterfuge. The result surpassed... far surpasses all my expectations... [*with difficulty, forcing himself*] perhaps too far... [*bracing himself*] The sun covered its face when my absence was announced in the Convention. A most profound silence emanated from my empty seat; a shiver went through the hall at the very sight of the arm on my chair. The feverish activity which then ensued in the resulting chaos, betrayed a panic, concealed only with the utmost difficulty. Billaud sulked and swore, Fouché smiled to himself. Phrases about my inevitable breakdown were learned by heart and thrown into any conversation, whether public or private, to raise people's spirits. Tomorrow he will be on his death bed, they were saying already. Oh what joy, if only one *could* believe it for sure!

SAINT-JUST. You have embarked on a terribly dangerous game.

ROBESPIERRE. Indeed, yes. But it was necessary. Frankly, that necessity suits me fine. For I had reached the point where private people think of calling the priest. Every step demanded wonders of acrobatics from me, nerves of steel; and I had an unpleasant tendency to pay for every public appearance with a hemorrhage. Hardly a day passed without my going into a faint. All this I could bear. What was really bad was that with every encounter, with the smallest bite of a Marsh mosquito, I was beside myself. They trembled, not without pleasure, when the first onslaught of rage came over me, an alarm bell of the storm, whose cost I had to pay. For the terror of a raging Orlando is unreal and has that doubtful likeness to the aesthetic experience which moves a spectator in the theatre. In the Committee at least we all stood on stage, and so things happened that were beyond description. The prestige of my dangerous unfathomable calm began to disappear. And I cannot do without it. Through my sudden disappearance I regained it.

SAINT-JUST. But have you really recovered your strength?

ROBESPIERRE. Of course. [*he smiles in a kind of grimace, but without bitterness*] I have never loved life so much as during those six weeks. Every minute was a delight.

SAINT-JUST. Why do you sneer?

ROBESPIERRE. I don't—it's nature. Nature sneers eagerly and with subtle humor. For instance, when one wishes most to take the world in one's arms, set it on fire, or smash it to pieces, when the blood pressure is pounding in one's head, when one is knocked out for a week. Or when those suffering from consumption—I am not talking about myself—feel a wild urge to breed children en masse, poor things incapable of living from the outset. All proofs of joyous humor. . .

SAINT-JUST [*leans forward to look him closer in the eyes*]. What are you really thinking about, Maxime?

ROBESPIERRE [*momentarily switches from deep thoughtfulness to an insincere jocularity*]. I waste my thought on fantasies remote from this world—but deep down I am worried by one question only: how are you going to receive the news I am bringing you?

SAINT-JUST [*unpleasantly surprised*]. What is it? It's the first time that you have doubts. . .

ROBESPIERRE. Indeed. But today you are far from me, my son; it's a bad sign. What's going to happen if you don't understand me any more? Fear, common fear is gripping me. Perhaps even that you will find impossible to understand.

SAINT-JUST. But yes, all the more so because my nerves too have a share in that feeling. . . [*he rises all of a sudden and catches Robespierre's outstretched arms as with a pair of tongs*] Maxime—what is happening to you?. . .

ROBESPIERRE [*suddenly quite apathetic—speaks softly and fast*]. I am burning out, decomposing physically. An awesome and mysterious phenomenon. Neither pain nor recognized illness lessens my awareness of the unnatural state I am in. A raging fever consumes my tissues, without a moment's respite. My health interests me precious little, as long as I know I am in control of the nerve centers. But now I've lost control. I am a little drunk—slightly, warmly dizzy, which seems harmless, even pleasant; it is frightening only when I see myself in the mirror. . .

[*silence;* SAINT-JUST *will not let go* ROBESPIERRE's *arm*]

My capacity for thinking is affected, you know!. . . [*silence*] Things have gone so far that—I am not sure of myself any more. I have doubts. . . My intuition, once infallible, is now failing; impaired through my dizziness, it may see reality in a false light. Not even for a minute does the fever recede! Not for a minute am I my normal self! Not to be able to trust my own senses—can you imagine what a torment that is? I can be wrong. . .

[*A long pause. He breathes in deeply—takes a grip on himself*]

Still the same nonsense. Boring self-torment of a feverish man. Chasing
one's own tail. I know with certainty that a mistake is out of the question. Facts hard as a rock, crying for vengeance. No other choice, time is
short—and I let my nerves bind my hands. Let's put an end to it. Now
you, my dear friend, tell me a little about what the indivisible Republic
looks like in the year II at the northern frontier.

SAINT-JUST [*somewhat calmed, sits down again*]. There at any rate it is bursting
with health.

ROBESPIERRE [*with a strange expression*]. Not, perhaps, a little—well...
apoplectic?

[*an empty pause*]

SAINT-JUST [*insecure within; a painful suspicion rising again*]. And now, will you
tell me why you wanted to meet me here, in a public place?

ROBESPIERRE. It's very simple. Were you to come to me directly from your
trip, tomorrow all the newspapers would sound the alarm on account of
the secret conference of the duumvirs. Am I the only one to have spies?
If I meet you here, the pretext disappears. And whether it was difficult
for me to keep away our common friends, you could judge for yourself.
Satisfied?

SAINT-JUST. Yes. What did you have in mind when you spoke of the apoplectic Republic?

ROBESPIERRE. I am not a doctor, so the choice of expression was probably
wrong. I call apoplectic an organism in which excessive expansion of the
blood is no longer matched by the strength and elasticity of the blood
vessels. Too narrow and fragile, they allow the blood to flow only with
difficulty, they expand for as long as they can, until finally...

SAINT-JUST [*after some sharp reflection*]. You are right again, of course.

ROBESPIERRE [*slowly*]. I am right again, of course.

[*The last words, almost inaudible, are spoken with a normal accent. His head,
leaning deeply forward, is supported by his right hand, while the left taps on the arm
of the chair. His leg hangs over the chair, and he beats time with his foot.*]

SAINT-JUST [*almost hostile*]. Well then? What now?

ROBESPIERRE [*raises his lead-gray, quite changed face and lies shamelessly*]. I nearly
fell asleep. [*hysterical, but controlled*] Oh that damned boredom, always to
know everything in advance—always—every time! And to think I let
doubt consume me alive! I don't believe my eyes any more! Good God!

[*he laughs with difficulty and apathy*]

SAINT-JUST. This time you're not in good health, old man . . .

ROBESPIERRE. Not only me, and that's the whole tragedy . . . But let's get down to facts, at least. To avoid all that's not essential, I'll tell you first what I, as a modest civilian, know about your military exploits. Then you can explain the details to me.

SAINT-JUST [*with difficulty hides his distraction*]. I am sorry. But: is this an interrogation, or not?

ROBESPIERRE [*somewhat sharp*]. No. Since when do we talk to each other using the cowardly symbols of diplomatic speech? An interrogation I would have begun right away as such. Now listen and correct me.

While the army of the North, commanded by Pichegru, cut off Austria from England in the North-West, and isolated York, the newly-formed Sambre-et-Meuse army under Jourdan moved on its irresistible victorious march across Belgium. You, as the great standard-bearer of France, brought her luck and more than that: your iron ruthlessness, your will to victory. First to fall was the fortress of Ypres. From that day the coalition was in retreat, providing only weak points of resistance, all of which fell under your ever-stronger blows. Charleroi fell on the eighth Messidor—the army had you to thank for that. After Fleurus the road to Brussels stood open for you and your army. You reached Brussels on the twenty-second Messidor. There you joined forces with the army of the North. Without effort you occupied all other points. The enemy was irrevocably beaten, and left the territory—partly across the Channel, partly across the Rhine. The Netherlands were ours.

In part at least you tore out the poisoned teeth of Carnot's vile idiocy: he wanted, for propaganda reasons, to send Pichegru to Holland with all of his force, and with fifteen thousand of your men. Even so, the order could not be completely ignored, and that is why Pichegru, who at that time was close to destroying York, as well as Coburg and Clairfayt, was suddenly thrown off his line of action. But this did not have bad consequences, as you reacted in time.

SAINT-JUST. It was so, indeed. I should like to know from whom that infamous decision originated. Do you have an inkling?

ROBESPIERRE. From Carnot. Or maybe he had forgotten to sign it.

SAINT-JUST. Carnot is the collective name of many generals and even more numerous statesmen. I am curious to know who stood by his side this time as his muse.

ROBESPIERRE [*stops and goes through the papers in his briefcase which is lying on the table*]. Hm. The suggestion came by a roundabout route.

SAINT-JUST [*softly*]. Damn, *who* was it then?
ROBESPIERRE [*likewise, throws him a sidelong glance*]. It was I.

[*deadly silence*]

SAINT-JUST [*staggers*]. Don't play jokes . . . It's not true!
ROBESPIERRE [*firmly*]. Yes, my friend.

[*He gives up playing with the papers, stands leaning against the table, leaning forward slightly, concentrated, icily calm, but his pulse beats rapidly*]

SAINT-JUST [*his head thrown against the back of the chair, his hands stretched out helplessly, breathes heavily, shouts*]. If that is so . . . then you are [*hardly audible*] mad . . .
ROBESPIERRE. I think not. I wanted to help you to a shattering defeat.
SAINT-JUST [*after a breathtaking silence, speaks softly and fast, his eyes glued to* ROBESPIERRE]. You are mad—mad—great God! To bring about my defeat after laboriously breaking the resistance of the enemy's superior forces, which moved back inch by inch; after a weeklong battle which reduced three provinces to ashes; after bloodletting on a scale that, without victory, would have meant death! It only needed our defeat at Fleurus for the split coalition to joint their forces in a flash, and appear together before our tired troops. *We* would then be fleeing before them, and behind us there would move a wall of fire, a rain of sulphur over downtrodden Flanders, over our North, hardly yet returned to normality after the outrages of the Royalists. Just think, between Lille and Paris there are no Thermophylae, no Valmy, where in the last hour of need one can bar the enemy's way with one's body . . . And so . . .
ROBESPIERRE. *That is* what I wanted to bring about! A sudden unexpected invasion, a panicky destruction of our armed force.
SAINT-JUST [*a hollow voice*]. And then . . .
ROBESPIERRE. *Then*—la liberté ou la mort.
SAINT-JUST [*after a short, tense silence—pale and impetuous*]. Explain yourself.
ROBESPIERRE [*concentrated*]. Now I know the reason for our estrangement. I was prepared for this change in you. You are too sensitive for a statesman, particularly a revolutionary one. You are not fully possessed by the idea. It is always the spur of the moment that can get the upper hand, as far as you are concerned. Your principles are deflected by the vast riches of your experience. Just now you have seen war in its full element, the war of a people against a monarchy, which uses mercenary and trained human flesh. It was natural for you to be thrilled. Unfortunately, your thrill went so far that it changed you. Your way of thinking is different; you have put new concepts into old words.

SAINT-JUST [*forced*]. Fascinating, as always . . . but *why* are you evading the issue again?

ROBESPIERRE. Not any more. I had to draw your attention to the fact that today you would be able to understand me only with difficulty.

[*Silence. He is lost in thought and stands still; makes his decision and begins to speak, obviously constrained*]

My boy, in the nearest future I will send some laws to the devil. I will stake on a single card . . . more than just one campaign. In this I counted on you with the usual certainty, but now I have some doubt. For I must destroy you, if you try to hinder me. I would very much prefer to avoid that necessity. Then choose: am I to talk, or would you rather not know?

SAINT-JUST [*suddenly revives in joyous astonishment*]. But you have already revealed yourself . . . !

ROBESPIERRE [*lowers his head; matter-of-fact*]. True. [*a long pause; he looks up carefully at his friend*] To leave you, to give you up . . . [*a short pause*] No. I do not leave you any choice; share my secret.

[*he sits down again*]

SAINT-JUST [*lowers his head with relief, almost with admiration*]. What a tyrant you are! I already feel how my will is surrendering to yours. That's how it happens with all of us.

ROBESPIERRE. Us? . . . who is "us"?

SAINT-JUST [*slightly surprised*]. Right—I mean myself and the rest of your subjects or helpers . . .

ROBESPIERRE. No, my son. Us—means you and I; exclusively and unreservedly. And so it will remain. In spite of everything.

SAINT-JUST [*completely disarmed, trembling with happiness, though not quite aware of it, and smiling for the same reason; with half-closed eyelids*]. Now I shall soon be at home again . . .

ROBESPIERRE [*with a touch of melancholy*]. We shall soon see about that. [*pause*] In the name of God, forwards! Hear then why I so longed for defeat. War as such is unavoidable. In ninety-two we had no choice. The Revolution had to prove its vitality. Defensive is healthy, but offensive is poison. Counterbalanced by nothing, the heroic defensive war of the past turned into attack and territorial gains. What a shame! We, the first and only nation in Europe which aims to satisfy the needs of its people, we of all others grab the land and property of our neighbors, and crush underfoot what we can't gobble up . . .

SAINT-JUST. You forget that we were to propagate the Revolution. How else is it to expand? How could it even gain respect for itself? Divine grace on earth is always spread with fire and sword.

ROBESPIERRE. How true that is—and how perverse! You can't seriously believe that our glorious army could be the bearer of an idea *today*. The only gift carried by them to neighboring countries is syphilis. Death and destruction do not count, they are only barter wares.

SAINT-JUST. The army does not carry an idea, but clears the way for it. Move your viewpoint ahead ten years, and you will be speechless.

ROBESPIERRE [*almost with a groan*]. Ten years! Not to take into account ten years of Egyptian plagues, for in ten years an idea will, perhaps, grow out of this rotten chaos as a lonely flower.

I, my friend, hold on fast to the living hour; hold on desperately. My stand point is in the present, damned uncomfortable though it is. I don't let myself overlook the war they worship. I would even treat that sad nastiness with manly indifference, if it did not carry the germs of corruption to the smallest rootlets of society. A nation that wages war without being *compelled* to becomes poisoned to the very tips of its fingers. Just look what this war has done to the French.

Have you never considered what a monstrosity a regular army is? Our volunteers of ninety-two, who treated their rifles like spades, were sublime: men in the full sense of the word, defenders of *their* property, *their* wives, so fired by enthusiasm that, for a few ecstatic hours, they turned into heroes. Of course, the beast lay in wait for the heroes, often took the upper hand. There were panic murders, atrocities, but that only amounts to restoring the balance in nature, as Billaud says. But even the beast is better than—the soldier.

Those who remained after Valmy, who survived the danger and, deserted by the spirit of freedom, took a liking to war—sank so low that we prefer the beast to them. There is not a trace of humanity in those professional soldiers. The Prussian automaton has his soul beaten out of him so effectively that he loses his sense of self and most of his human instincts, and he doesn't even feel the fear of death. *We* want to emulate that model. The motley hordes of heroic defenders have turned into an army hard as steel—but still today not yet past saving, not yet quite lost . . .

SAINT-JUST. I don't understand how a part of the people can be lost just because they have learned *some* discipline, some organization . . .

ROBESPIERRE. Discipline is necessary in critical moments, but must not become the substance of anybody's life. Compared with that, physical castration is but a trifle. Military economy does not organize, but disorganizes. And the army is not people any more; it is separated from society. Renouncing his humanity, a man in the army loses all bonds with nature. He is now deprived of the wholesome power of the earth, which binds and nourishes him. The soldier has no God, except his general; no family, no property, no fatherland. His soul is discipline; his holy duty—carrying out orders. It is good if he *loves* war because he can indulge in amorous adventures and moral laxity.

It is no pleasure to see the steady degradation of those one hundred and fourteen thousand men, who were once the select part of a powerful people! An effective means of educating Europe for freedom...

[ceases to speak, exhausted, without faith in the future; notices that SAINT-JUST *has grown pale up to his eyes]*

It's painful for you too? Gets you down?

SAINT-JUST *[after a long pause]*. Curse your eyes, as the English saying goes.

ROBESPIERRE. Yes, sometimes one would be willing to follow the unfortunate Oedipus.

Within the country the same destructive process is taking place. The citizen finds the war atmosphere to his taste and revels in it; he is even more disgusting than the mercenary soldier, since his pleasure is derived from pure imagination, it goes round and round in a vacuum. His emotions, removed from reality, feed on empty dreams and breed nightmarish visions. And here breaks the umbilical cord that binds man to earth. Phantoms appear in the place of concrete objects. Class feeling is replaced by an abstraction: nationality. The natural hatred of the exploited for his exploiter makes room for the pointless elemental hatred of a Frenchman for an Englishman. Communal feeling takes the form of a perverse idolatry of the French army. Truly, what a splendid organization!

A war waged for profit isolates people from each other, and from the earth, makes them prey to empty prejudices and groundless animosities. In a vacant trance, deprived of spirit, these unhappy lonely people, are enveloped by the thick fog of lies, breathe them in in the place of air, drink them like poison. Can you imagine how this process runs? Nothing in the surrounding reality can resist this destructive influence. Mass madness destroys the meaning of concepts, while leaving the words untouched. All around there grows unchecked and rank a hellish weed; its name is deceitful propaganda. Compare the meaning of the word "patriot" in eighty-nine and now. Then it meant a freedom fighter; today it means a cutthroat.

SAINT-JUST [*desperately*]. I swear that you're exaggerating. You have hit the mark, but you're inflating the facts out of all proportion. That is just as bad as being wrong.

ROBESPIERRE [*smiles vitriolically*]. I shall follow your advice and move my viewpoint ahead one year only. I gladly admit that things are not quite that bad *yet*.

Let us now review the political aspects of this enviable state of affairs. While the small pigs turn round and round in a delirium, without realizing what helps to keep them together, the big swine have so enriched themselves on innumerable calamities that they now strain their fat brains by thinking how to use their oceans of money. Soon even they will realize that in their coffers they have locked the greatest power on earth.

In that soil are the roots of the nineteenth century. The seeds have sprouted already. And the God of that future century is born too: it is called Capital.

Our Republic is its Bethlehem. All according to tradition: a regular stable, cattle enough, soon a crowd of kings and shepherds will turn up, and fall on their knees in this dirt. Only the star is missing. No light anywhere.

This. . . THIS is the fruit of four generations' hell. It was *for this* that man had to remind himself of his humanity, destroy the old order, demand life for himself. From *this* a state was born in birth pangs from which the earth shook. . .

SAINT-JUST. Stop it, Maxime. I can't keep up with you any more.

ROBESPIERRE. Stop it? Because of a laughable personal setback you *demand* that I should leap out of my skin. And that I should keep calm when dealing with matters because of which my skull is splitting. How can I pretend to be superior to all that, when I see man being robbed of his spirit, his right to exist? Capital! The monster lies pink in its cradle, while preparing to cheat the Revolution out of all her achievements. In a hundred years it will change the face of the world, transform man and his intellect into a well-oiled machine; with murderous vitality it will devour the whole universe, and—choke. Capital!

SAINT-JUST [*weakly*]. For God's sake, hold on to reality. I am slowly losing my mind.

ROBESPIERRE. So am I. [*He rises, approaches the window, rubs his hand against his temple. He speaks in a totally changed voice and pitch, contemplatively*] A heavenly night. This stillness opens endless perspectives of shimmering, quivering joy. This darkness conceals a living force. The raging fever breathes therein more easily. Life is a lost paradise. Why can't one be simple and enjoy it. . .

Not even simple,: but a being free from the knowledge of good and evil. . .

[ROBESPIERRE *looks through the window with hungry eyes, which express pain and desire; he takes two steps and stops by the open half of the window, leaning out slightly*]

SAINT-JUST [*looks at him all the time*]. Don't forget, Maxime, that you have no wings. This is the second floor.

ROBESPIERRE [*turns round, smiling*]. Thank you for the warning. But I really had no intention of looking for my primeval fatherland in that way. [*he sits down*] I am still a gentleman, in spite of two years at the Convention, and I always leave a room by the door. Listen to me a bit longer.

Very soon Capital will do wonders. As soon as there is the organized power of money, it will decide the fate of nations. The Dantonists are to be thanked—indeed, no one can deny them that glory—for the brilliant idea that one must buy at one stroke the whole body of the government, instead of bribing its individual members in a petty manner. Once one has taken possession of the government this way, then to provide it with a name, principles, and a program will be child's play.

SAINT-JUST. You're right. Danton's gang tried it, and they were taken where they deserved. Why this absolute fiasco, my friend? I recognize the potential power of gold, but to buy a government one would need to have more billions than exist on earth.

ROBESPIERRE. Governments are not so expensive. You overestimate people, as usual. And those billions do exist, though they are not yet minted. Wait, my friend, till science provides the technique magically to turn force and matter, up to the last atom—into money, not even gold. Then there will be enough billions! For governments there will be a separate market, with experts and all the paraphernalia.

Just look at our own government. *They*, my son, are ripe for the hammer, but also for the ax, if the devil hears my implorations. The Convention, openly reactionary under the guise of their revolutionary slogans, care only for running up the bidding to the highest possible price. After the auction, glorious and victorious France will be arranged anew by her buyer according to his taste. Probably the private goldmine will be left her pompous name Res Publica, in the style of a street whore, but no more than that. Should Capital be ready for a new baptism, the world will see a new kingdom under the scepter of Orleans, or

York. Perhaps caesarism will be in fashion again. The French Empire—
that would not sound bad. There are as many possibilities as there are
lined pockets, and even more names.

[*he rises, puts his hands behind his head, looks for a while at the ceiling; puts his
arms down again and leans against the table*]

Capital quivers with impatience, the government restrains itself with
difficulty; but they dare not annul the Revolution openly, like an invalid contract; they do not dare do that, because I still live.

And I shall live as long as hate burns in me. As long as a force, which is
never given to jest, is driving my heart forward and will not let me sleep.
My mind turns facts into dynamite. My will is a burning furnace. I am a
man possessed. An element acts through me; but maybe an element directed by human spirit is not enough to kill the rising beast. It is enough
anyway to inflict some wounds on his belly; and that is *something*. I want
to preserve for man his humanity, his right to his own life, which he has
finally won for himself. I want to safeguard him from the nineteenth
century. I want to wake him from his drunken sleep and compel him to
keep awake and defend his freedom against thieves, like a vicious watchdog. I want to supply the new deity with more martyrs than hell can
contain. Let the thought of their amassed millions in gold enable them
to rise above the fear of death when their necks are being shaved for the
guillotine. Let the five-figure numbers turn their bloody death into a
feast. There are hours when I bitterly regret that death has been made
so light for criminals. Each of these modern martyrs has fully deserved
to be tortured like Damiens.

[*he stoops and leans his elbows against the table, as if he were breaking down under
his own weight; softly*]

I want to root out the first generation of those infernal swine, and
then to train men to bite through the throat of every new emerging
beast at once. And if time, if nature itself stands on their side, then I
shall want to destroy them in spite of time and in spite of nature.

[*A seemingly endless pause for rest after the effort. A while later he returns to his
seat and examines his friend's expression.*]

Do you follow me?

SAINT-JUST [*breathes deeply*]. The main drift, yes. [*pause*] Your dynamite will
tear you to pieces. You are already burning in the blast furnace of your
spirit. *You* alone. You cannot inflict wounds on nature's belly.

ROBESPIERRE [*takes up his restless wandering again*]. You romantic boy poet. Nature. Even a hundred-franc note means serious danger for it.

SAINT-JUST. Nature has time. You grudge yourself the hours to sleep. What is it to *her* if, for the price of your life, you snatch away ten years from her? For you cannot delay longer the logical development of earthly matters, even if you destroy one whole generation. You must be aware of this, surely?

[ROBESPIERRE *leans so inertly against the window sill that* SAINT-JUST *springs to his feet but is reassured by his friend with one look*]

Please do not go into a faint. I would be in awful trouble.

ROBESPIERRE. I will do my best, but I cannot promise you that for certain.

SAINT-JUST. In that case I will simply leave you lying here. I don't know how to deal with people whom no sensible word can reach...

[*He looks round and is terrified; for* ROBESPIERRE *looks through him, as it were, with the unnatural concentration of an impending loss of consciousness.* SAINT-JUST *rises and approaches him with disbelief*]

And yet it seems you're going to... [*he is simply frightened*] Robespierre, are you giddy...or...have I offended you somehow...?

ROBESPIERRE [*very slowly lowers his eyes, without the slightest movement*]. Don't worry. [*more softly, matter-of-fact*] You have—hit the mark. My Achilles' heel. With all the ruthlessness of youth. I have to fight this charge every few hours. It lies in wait for me everywhere, it never changes, always refuted—it stands unrefuted. It is a demon and a neuralgia, incurable, terribly painful and—I guarantee it—harmless. But I never thought that this charge would be uttered by *your* lips.

The answer, for that matter, is just as simple as the Satanic idea itself: after ten years' delay, the natural development of things *must* take an altogether different course from that originally foreseen. Nature is eternal, but that is her only advantage. She has no mind and no will. Man can master her in her eternity.

SAINT-JUST [*puts on a tired smile*]. You have parried the blow, but how dully and convulsively. You have been hit, you, brilliant swordsman, you are mortally pierced. You cannot return the blow; your opponent has no heart. [*long pause*] But you *have* deviated from your course. Through the nineteenth century right into eternity. And I still don't know what your abuse of Carnot's innocence really means.

ROBESPIERRE. What...you still don't understand?!

SAINT-JUST. I can guess, but I would like to have it confirmed.

ROBESPIERRE. I wanted to break the poisoned spell of victories. I wanted to bring about the invasion of Europe's coalition through our frontiers. A sudden, terrible danger could still rouse the man in the soldier and save him—while he can still remember his threatened property and children. Likewise, in the citizens the thin web of lies would break. With the thunderous alarm of the bells, no falsehood could stand intact, and hard, bright, healthy reality would return. An end would be put to the cheap dream sensations, to the cult of demigod heroes, to the glory of our arms, to the whole empty madness of patriotic obscenities! The endangered existence, the endangered family, the endangered roof over their heads, and the endangered cow in the shed! A danger, a resounding danger, imminent, closer with every passing hour! A people, try to understand, an entire *people*, would have to rise and exert all its energies. While escape, or passivity would mean certain annihilation! A people in the glory of its highest might, where before some stark raving madmen had roamed free, and machines of imitation iron had clattered. That people would have to flock round the government, be at one with it, throb with the same blood stream. Can you imagine the power such a government would have? Can you visualize the mutual growth in strength, the mutual purification of body and spirit? The parasites would fall off like a bad dream. The army would be a live weapon in the hand of a good swordsman. All of Europe's automatons put together could not break that weapon. Such a unity of the people means magic invincibility.

A crushing defeat was the only sure means to bring the Republic, now dying of blood poisoning, to health and resurrection.

SAINT-JUST. Mmm . . . I am not so *sure* of that. Just think what would happen next: a sudden reversal of luck; the Northern frontier crossed. Paris, in fact effeminate and demoralized, finds out the truth. The inevitable result would be panic.

ROBESPIERRE [*quietly*]. I would put down the panic in six hours.

SAINT-JUST [*springs to his feet with wide open eyes*]. You think you could do that . . . ?

ROBESPIERRE [*even more quietly*]. No. I am certain.

[*a long pause*]

SAINT-JUST [*still astounded*]. And what if you were assassinated . . .

ROBESPIERRE. Impossible. In such circumstances the people have their instinct, and the leader grows to the proportions of a giant. I would be untouchable. I would beat them so that blood gushes, and they would not even try to evade the blows.

SAINT-JUST [*almost with divine worship*]. It is possible. . . But even if you were God, one stab of a knife from the hand of the most miserable English spy would bring you down.

ROBESPIERRE. Yes, *that* is the danger. I am not quite sure if you are yet up to taking over my legacy; if not, then indeed. . .

SAINT-JUST. Then indeed—a total disaster. Then indeed the end, the irrevocable end of the Revolution and the Republic, if not of France's independence.

This is what you wanted to expose the Republic to, at the time when she had finally, finally defeated her worst enemies and began to pick the fruit. . . !

ROBESPIERRE. Somewhat rotten fruit. . .

SAINT-JUST [*with growing vehemence*]. You alone see rot where others admire abundance and richness. How can you follow your personal inclinations, against the opinion of all the others?

ROBESPIERRE. The suburbs share my view since they show an ominous lack of interest. That is enough for me. But even without that testimony I would not hesitate.

SAINT-JUST [*tries to regain his composure*]. You exaggerate in painting everything black. After all, those are all suppositions, remote leaps of a bold chain of thought. Thank God, between the thought and its realization there lies an abyss, over which one succeeds only seldom in throwing a small part of one's plans.

ROBESPIERRE. You know well that there is no abyss, as far as I am concerned. *I* at any rate am no dreamer. Of course, I too regard reality as an abyss, a gehenna, but I stand in the center of it.

SAINT-JUST [*after a pause, with awesome admiration*]. True, you were already setting out to put that devilish idea into effect. The catastrophe would indeed have happened, neatly and dead on time—because you had already embarked on the shortest, surest road, chosen with cold calculation and leading to a calamity. . .

[*silence quivering in the air*]

ROBESPIERRE [*closes his eyes; uses every second of the pause to rest; after a while, sleepily*]. Stop being surprised, or we shall not move much farther. . .

SAINT-JUST [*leaps to his feet*]. Mad you are not—your eyes can *see*, in spite of fever. . . [*he takes a few shaky paces and suddenly stops; in an accusing tone*]

Robespierre, just look what irresponsible risks you take. Your—your plan with the disastrous order was a stroke of genius; its result was assured, the execution correct, except for one move; and that one move caused the whole scheme to come to nought. It was *I* who stood, uninitiated, between Carnot and the generals. I saw the error, took upon myself the responsibility for exceeding my powers, and put the fuse out. Your masterly scheme misfired; and all that was lacking was that one move!

The outcome of the final act will decide the fate of France. It depends, however, on two things: first, your ability to prevent panic and to take the reins of government alone; second, on your life . . .

[The manuscript breaks off at this point; it is quite possible that Przybyszewska did not complete the play. When *Thermidor* was first performed in Wrocław in 1971, as directed by Jerzy Krasowski, the actor playing Saint-Just—after his last speech—addressed the audience, saying that four days later Robespierre was guillotined.]

Bibliography

Works by Stanisława Przybyszewska

Dramaty. Edited and introduced by Roman Taborski with an afterword by Jerzy Krasowski. Gdańsk: Wydawnictwo Morskie, 1975.

Listy. 3 vols. Edited and introduced by Tomasz Lewandowski. Gdańsk: Wydawnictwo Morskie, 1978-85.

Works about Stanisława Przybyszewska

Helsztyński, Stanisław. *Przybyszewski*. Warsaw: Ludowa Spółdzielnia Wydawnicza, 1973.

Janion, Maria et al. "Stanisława Przybyszewska." In *Osoby,* 97-186. Edited by Maria Janion and Stanisław Rosiek. Gdańsk: Wydawnictwo Morskie, 1984.

Kolińska, Krystyna. *Stachu, jego kobiety, jego dzieci.* Cracow: Wydawnictwo Literackie, 1978.

Kosicka, Jadwiga, and Gerould, Daniel. *A Life of Solitude. Stanislawa Przybyszewska: A Biographical Study with Selected Letters.* Evanston: Northwestern University Press, 1989.

Lewandowski, Tomasz. *Dramat Intelektu: Biografia literacka Stunisławy Przybyszewskiej.* Gdańsk: Wydawnictwo Morskie, 1982.

Rogacki, Henryk Izydor. *Żywot Przybyszewskiego.* Warsaw: Państwowy Instytut Wydawniczy, 1987.

Works about *Thermidor* and *The Danton Case* in the theatre

Greń, Zygmunt. *Czwarta Ściana.* Cracow: Wydawnictwo Literackie, 1972.

Grodzicki, August. *Polish Theatre Directors.* Warsaw: Interpress, 1979.

Karpiński, Maciej. *Andrzej Wajda—teatr.* Warsaw: Wydawnictwa Artystyczne i Filmowe, 1980.

293

Kłossowicz, Jan. *Mgliste Sezony.* Warsaw: Wydawnictwa Artystyczne i Filmowe, 1981.

Koenig, Jerzy. *Rekolekcje Teatralne.* Warsaw: Krajowa Agencja Wydawnicza, 1979.

Plays about the French Revolution

1789	*Paris in an Uproar, or The Destruction of the Bastille*	Astley's Amphitheatre, London (military spectacle)
1789	*The Triumph of Liberty, or The Destruction of the Bastille*	The Royal Circus, London (military spectacle)
1793	*The Demolition of the Bastille, or Liberty Triumphant*	William H. Prigmore (American)
1794	*The Fall of Robespierre*	Samuel Taylor Coleridge and Robert Southey
1794	*The Fall of the French Monarchy, or Louis XVI*	John Bartholomew
1828	*The Death of Louis XVI*	Armand Renée Duchatellier
1829	*The Death of the Girondins*	Armand Renée Duchatellier
1830	*Robespierre, or 9 Thermidor*	Auguste Anicet-Bourgeois and Francis Cornu
1830	*The Taking of the Bastille*	Ferdinand Laloue, Henri Villemot, and Theodore Nezel
1831	*9 Thermidor, or the Death of Robespierre*	Henri Bonias
1835	*Danton's Death*	Georg Büchner
1840	*Robespierre, or Two Days of the Revolution*	William Bayle Bernard
1845	*Maximilien Robespierre*	Rudolf von Gottschal
1847	*The French Revolution*	Fabrice Labrousse and J. Mallian
1848	*The Gironde and the Mountain*	Marc Leprévost
1849	*Maximilien Robespierre*	Wolfgang Robert Griepenkerl (Swiss)
1850	*Charlotte Corday*	François Ponsard
1851	*The Girondins*	Wolfgang Robert Griepenkerl
1859	*The Dead Heart*	Watts Phillips
1866	*The Country in Danger*	The Goncourt Brothers
1870	*Danton*	Otto Franz Gensichen
1870	*Danton and Robespierre*	Robert Hamerling (Austrian)
1871	*9 Thermidor, or The Death of Robespierre*	Gaston Crémieux

1878	*The Revolution; from Mirabeau to the Fall of Robespierre*	Ottevaere-Larcher, comte d'Everghem
1880	*Danton*	Max Bewer
1887	*Théroigne*	Ferdinand Dugué
1887	*Paul Kavaur*	Steele MacKaye
1888	*Robespierre or the Dramas of the Revolution*	Louis Combet
1888	*World Tribunal*	Karl Bleibtreu
1890	*Robespierre*	Juan Maya (Mexican)
1891	*Thermidor*	Victorien Sardou
1897	*Robespierre*	Domenico Oliva (Italian)
1898	*The Wolves*	Romain Rolland
1898	*Liberty*	Maurice Pottecher
1899	*The Green Cockatoo*	Arthur Schnitzler
1899	*Robespierre*	Victorien Sardou
1899	*The Only Way* (based on Dickens, *A Tale of Two Cities*)	Freeman Wills
1900	*Danton*	Romain Rolland
1901	*Robespierre*	Nikolai Lomakin (Russian)
1901	*Du Barry*	David Belasco
1902	*The Fourteenth of July*	Romain Rolland
1902	*Théroigne de Méricourt*	Paul Hervieu
1909	*Revolutionary Trilogy: Early Unpleasantness, Figaro, The Defeated*	Jaroslav Viktor Dyk (Czech)
1909	*The French Revolution*	Arthur Bernède and Henri Cain
1912	*Beauty and the Jacobin*	Booth Tarkington
1913	*Christmas Night under the Terror*	Henri Cain and Maurice Bernhardt
1918	*Danton's Death* (adaptation of Büchner's play)	Aleksei Tolstoi
1918	*The Death of Robespierre*	Nikolai Adrianovich Kuznetsov
1919	*Danton*	Maria Evgen'evna Levberg
1919	*The Carmagnole* (based on Hervieu, *Théroigne de Méricourt*)	Georgii Ivanovich Chulkov
1920	*Marat*	Anton Amnuel'
1920	*The Day of Marat's Death*	Andrei Globa

1922	*Scenes from the French Revolution*	Ernst Toller
1922	*The Gods Are Athirst* (based on Anatole France's novel)	Pierre Chaine
1925	*Citizen Darnay* (based on Dickens, *A Tale of Two Cities*)	L. F. Makar'ev
1925	*Thermidor*	Stanisława Przybyszewska
1925	*The Game of Love and Death*	Romain Rolland
1926	*Madame Roland*	Giovacchino Forzano
1927	*The Conspiracy of Equals*	Mikhail Yulievich Levidov
1928	*93*	Stanisława Przybyszewska
1929	*The Danton Case*	Stanisława Przybyszewska
1929	*Danton*	Giovacchino Forzano
1929	*Danton*	Alessandro de Stefani
1929	*The Red March*	Karol Hubert Rostworowski
1931	*Robespierre*	F.F. Raskol'nikov
1931	*Danton's Blood*	Saint-Georges de Bouhélier
1931	*Danton*	Camil Petrescu (Rumanian)
1936	*Charlotte Corday*	Fritz von Unruh
1937	*Robespierre*	Rudolf Värnlund (Swedish)
1938	*Madame Capet*	Marcelle Maurette
1939	*Robespierre*	Romain Rolland
1948	*Thermidor*	Claude Vermorel
1948	*The Public Prosecutor*	Fritz Hochwälder
1949	*Dialogue of the Carmelites*	Georges Bernanos
1951	*Charlotte Corday*	Bernard Zimmer
1955	*The Jacobins*	Frederico Zardi
1955	*The Widow Capet*	Lion Feuchtwanger
1956	*Poor Bitos*	Jean Anouilh
1956	*The Empty Chair*	Peter Ustinov
1958	*The Animals of Count Cagliostro*	Andrzej Bursa (Polish)
1964	*Marat/Sade*	Peter Weiss
1970	*Revolutionary Tetralogy: Mirabeau, Marat, Andre Chenier, Robespierre*	Ivan Mrak (Croatian)
1970	*1789: The French Revolution, Year One*	Le Théâtre du Soleil, Ariane Mnouchkine
1972	*1793: The Revolutionary City is of this World*	Le Théâtre du Soleil, Ariane Mnouchkine

1972	*The Hiding Place*	Géza Páskándi (Hungarian)
1976	*The Jacobin Drapers*	André Benedetto
1978	*Maximilien Robespierre*	Bernard Chatreux and Jean Jourdheuil
1979	*Danton and Robespierre*	Robert Hossein
1979	*The Task*	Heiner Müller
1983	*Gracchus Babeuf*	Dominique Houdart
1986	*Thermidor*	Michel Deutsch
1988	*The Trial of Louis XVI*	Romain Cocheril
1988	*The Circus Celebrates the French Revolution*	Alexis Gruss
1988	*Liberty or Death* (revision of *Danton and Robespierre*)	Robert Hossein
1988	*Thermidor—Terminus, or the Death of Robespierre*	André Benedetto (Théâtre du Soleil)
1988	*The Second Year of Liberty*	Alexander Buravsky
1989	*Sweet Liberty*	Jeff Clarke
1989	*Germinal Year III*	Claire Etcherelli
1989	*Olympe and the Executioner*	Wendy Kesselman